European Capital Markets with a Single Currency

ABOUT ECMI

The European Capital Markets Institute (ECMI) was founded in 1993 as an independent non-profit organization aiming to serve as a central forum for practitioners and academics. The principal objective of the Institute is to initiate projects, programmes, and conferences related to the functioning and growth of the European capital markets and to the development of cross-border trading and investment. ECMI currently comprises some 140 member institutions from more than 20 European countries.

ECMI's registered office is located in Pza. de la Lealtad 1, 28014 Madrid (Spain), Tel. 34 91 5891191, Fax: 34 91 5312290, E-mail: ecmi@tsai.es, Homepage: www.ecmi.es.

ABOUT THE SPONSORS

Banco Central Hispano (BCH) is the parent bank of a large financial and industrial group (Grupo Central Hispano) which performs banking and financial activities both in Spain and abroad. Through its network of 2,572 branches, the largest in Spain, BCH offers all kinds of saving and investment products, loans, fund management, pension fund management, and stockbroker–dealer and international services. BCH is present in 28 countries (branches, subsidiaries, and associate banks and/or representative offices). The Bank has forged strategic alliances with major European banks of a similar size: Commerzbank, Banco Comercial Portugués (BCP) with which BCH has cross-shareholding agreements, as well as with other European banks for some specialized services: Société Générale and Credito Italiano.

The International Securities Market Association (ISMA) is the self-regulatory industry body and trade association for the international securities market. Its primary role as a self-regulator is to oversee the fast-changing marketplace through the issuing of rules and recommendations relating to trading and settlement practices in this market. Established in 1969, ISMA currently comprises some 750 member organizations from 51 countries and has a proven track-record in representing their best interests. ISMA's 24-hour real-time cross-border trade confirmation, risk management, and regulatory reporting system—TRAX—is tailored to accept every type of equity and fixed-income security. ISMA also provides the market with authoritative financial data and maintains a commitment to enhancing standards within the marketplace through education, training, and research programmes throughout its member regions.

The Société des Bourses Françaises (SBF–Bourse de Paris) organizes, operates, and promotes France's regulated securities markets—Paris Bourse for equities and fixed-income securities, the Nouveau Marché for growth stocks, and MATIF and MONEP for financial derivatives. A private commercial company, the SBF Group is responsible for the management, control, security, and development of the markets, open to companies of all sizes in every sector of activity, and derivatives markets, which offer a constantly expanding range of futures and options contracts. In addition to disseminating price quotations, the SBF group works with issuers, intermediaries, finance industry professionals, and private investors in France and abroad to develop and promote each market.

European Capital Markets with a Single Currency

EDITED BY

JEAN DERMINE AND PIERRE HILLION

A Report of the European Capital Markets Institute

OXFORD
UNIVERSITY PRESS

OXFORD

UNIVERSITY PRESS

Great Clarendon Street, Oxford OX2 6DP

Oxford University Press is a department of the University of Oxford.
It furthers the University's objective of excellence in research, scholarship,
and education by publishing worldwide in

Oxford   New York

Athens Auckland Bangkok Bogotá Buenos Aires Calcutta
Cape Town Chennai Dar es Salaam Delhi Florence Hong Kong Istanbul
Karachi Kuala Lumpur Madrid Melbourne Mexico City Mumbai
Nairobi Paris São Paulo Singapore Taipei Tokyo Toronto Warsaw

with associated companies in Berlin Ibadan

Oxford is a registered trade mark of Oxford University Press
in the UK and in certain other countries

Published in the United States
by Oxford University Press Inc., New York

© European Capital Markets Institute 1999

The moral rights of the author have been asserted

Database right Oxford University Press (maker)

First published 1999

British Library Cataloguing in Publication Data

Data available

Library of Congress Cataloging in Publication Data

Data available

ISBN 0–19–829539–1

3 5 7 9 10 8 6 4 2

Typeset in Minion and Rotis
by BookMan Services
Printed in Great Britain
on acid-free paper by
Biddles Ltd., Guildford and King's Lynn

To Isabelle
Nicolas, Martin, Suzanne, Alexandre, Augustin and Juliette

To Anne
Aude and Camille

Executive Summary

One of the greatest events in financial history will occur in 1999: the birth of the euro and the emergence of a unified European capital market. Although a large series of papers and conferences has been concerned with the timing and sequencing of the introduction of the new currency and with an estimate of the costs that would be incurred, few published studies have attempted to evaluate the medium-term impact of a single currency on European capital markets. One single question is being addressed in this book: Once the euro is in place, what is likely to change in European capital markets? This can be broken down into other, more specific questions. How is the structure of the bond, equity and derivative markets going to be affected? Are these markets going to be fully integrated? Is the disappearance of exchange rate uncertainty going to affect risk premia on the equity and corporate debt markets? Is the euro going to compete with the US dollar and does this matter? Is the introduction of the euro likely to change the sources of competitive advantage of financial institutions? What are going to be the key factors for success in the financial industry? The European Capital Markets Institute commissioned a report to address these issues. Drawn from various countries and fields of research—banking, economics and finance—the contributors analyse the structural effects of the introduction of the euro on European capital markets.

The book is divided into four major parts. The first analyses the macro-monetary economic environment under the euro, including its international role; the second part analyses the impact of the euro on the bond market—public and corporate—and the derivative industry. The third part analyses the impact of the single currency on equity markets. Finally, the fourth part analyses the impact of the euro on the competitive dynamics of the fund management and investment banking industries.

In the first chapter, Dermine presents an overview of the various channels through which the euro will affect capital markets. A complete analysis of these effects follows in the subsequent nine chapters. A main argument is that national currency was a main source of competitive advantage in the bond, equity and foreign exchange markets. This arose because of a well-documented 'home bias' preference for asset allocation and a local expertise in monetary policy. The changeover to the euro will erase this significant source of competitive advantage raising the question of the significance of economies of scale and size in an integrated euro market. Moreover, Dermine points out that the inability of individual countries to devalue their currencies could change the nature of credit risk; this calls for a larger degree of international diversification

In the second chapter, Gros and Lannoo provide a detailed description of the monetary institutions that will prevail. They point out that European capital markets will not be perfectly integrated because domestic central banks will have incentives to retain national responsibilities and idiosyncrasies to protect local employment. Moreover, being concerned that a particular country could free-ride the system in running a large public deficit, they recommend strict limits on individual banks' holdings of public debt.

In the third chapter, Wyplosz develops an analysis of the economics of international reserve currencies. He observes a virtuous cycle where reserve status brings liquidity which reinforces further the international reserve status. Although some requirements are met by the euro—low inflation, deregulated markets and political stability—he mentions the need for an external shock to launch an international currency—such as the Second World War in the case of the US dollar—and wonders whether the creation of the euro in 1999 will be the trigger that will create the international reserve status. Moreover, Wyplosz points out that a bipolar international monetary system could become more turbulent. Some form of international cooperation will be necessary to shape the future of a stable international monetary system.

In the fourth chapter, Nielsen analyses the likely determinants of credit spreads on national government bonds. In principle, devaluation spreads will be replaced in part by credit spreads as countries cannot rely any more on printing money and inflation to reduce the real value of their debts. The budgetary discipline imposed by EMU, if successful, will limit the default risk and default premia on government bonds. Nielsen points out that a tool often used to build credibility will not be available any more to individual countries: the issue of debt denominated in foreign currency to convince international markets that the risk of a devaluation was small. Under EMU, foreign currency denominated debt will not be a 'credibility' tool for a particular country since that country will not control its exchange rate. This implies that individual countries will have incentives to issue more nominal euro-denominated debt and less indexed debt or non-euro-denominated debt than is socially optimal. This argument points to a need for a mechanism to coordinate the public debt management of member countries.

In the fifth chapter, Delianedis and Santa-Clara present innovative work on the international corporate bond markets. In the first part, they report the realized credit risk premia on bonds with different credit risk and/or currency denomination. Next, they attempt to evaluate the various determinants of the corporate bond credit risk spreads. Their conclusion is that it is very unlikely that the disappearance of exchange rate risk in the European Union will alter fundamentally the risk premium on corporate bonds.

In the sixth chapter, Steinherr analyses the dynamics of competition in the derivative industry. For stock options, EMU produces significant, but only indirect effects. A unified capital market will put pressure on the existing configuration of stock—and hence options—markets. Index products will evolve from national to sectoral indexes. The main direct effect of EMU will be on money, bond and interest rate derivative markets, as a single currency implies a single money market. Steinherr observes that the success of screen-based trading has changed competition and that the convergence of the derivative markets to one exchange is questionable. Electronic exchanges make cooperation particularly easy, so that an alliance among Continental electronic exchanges could assure the continuing activity of the participants.

In the seventh chapter, De Santis, Gerard and Hillion are concerned with the pricing of foreign exchange risk in international equity markets. Their empirical methodology presents estimates on the foreign exchange risk premia. These premia are negative for the US dollar, and slightly positive for the European currencies. Given the size of these premia, they do not believe that the eradication of foreign exchange risk will change significantly the risk premia on equity markets.

In the eighth chapter, Biais reviews the microstructure of equity markets under EMU. One of his observations is that the race is very much open, as Continental European stock exchanges have gained back a large part of the market share lost to London. In this competition very much driven by technology, Biais raises the need for a European regulation to enforce transparency and priority rules, so as to create the appropriate incentives for stock market traders to offer liquidity. Biais recommends lifting regulatory constraints on investment in foreign assets to facilitate an efficient allocation of capital in Europe.

In the ninth chapter, Walter presents an innovative study of the competitive dynamics in the global fund management industry and the impact of the euro. Walter forecasts rapid growth in a very competitive market. The increased correlation brought by EMU will increase the need for portfolio management skills applied to diversification outside the EMU region. The development of a deeper pan-European capital market spurred by the rapid development of the institutional asset management industry will fundamentally alter the European market for corporate control. Finally, it will pose a challenge for the management of universal banks in structuring and motivating their organizations and in managing the conflicts of interests and professional conduct problems that can arise in asset management.

In the tenth chapter, Smith presents both a historical perspective on the international investment banking industry and his own analysis of the factors for success in that industry. From a review of the birth of the Euromarket, the deregulation of the capital markets in New York and London, and the creation of the European single market, Smith reminds the reader that the creation of the euro is just an additional step in the process of complete deregulation and globalization. To succeed, European firms seeking to remain important wholesale players will need to undertake further major management reforms to bring about streamlined organization and decision-making systems that are highly flexible, risk-oriented, less hierarchical and adaptive. European banks must cope with these important developments while at the same time realizing that, despite the creation of the euro, the future opportunities may not be contained in the European Union, but in Asia, Eastern Europe, Latin America and the United States.

As the study is completed, it is a pleasure to acknowledge the support of the European Capital Markets Institute for this great opportunity. We are also grateful to the INSEAD Centre for International Financial Services and to the Salomon Center at New York University for the organization of a conference. We hope that readers will share our curiosity in these historic developments.

Jean Dermine and Pierre Hillion

Fontainebleau, February 1998

Contents

Part I. The Macroeconomics of EMU

Part II. The Fixed-Income Markets

Part III. The Equity Markets

Part IV. Strategic Industry Implications

Contributors

Bruno Biais, Université de Toulouse

Gordon Delianedis, UCLA

Giorgio De Santis, University of Southern California

Jean Dermine, INSEAD

Bruno Gerard, University of Southern California

Daniel Gros, Centre for European Policy Studies

Pierre Hillion, INSEAD

Karel Lannoo, Centre for European Policy Studies

Lars Tyge Nielsen, INSEAD

Pedro Santa-Clara, UCLA

Alfred Steinherr, European Investment Bank

Charles Wyplosz, Graduate Institute of International Studies

Ingo Walter, New York University

Roy C. Smith, New York University

1
European Capital Markets: Does the Euro Matter?

Introduction

The Maastricht Treaty on European Union provides for the introduction of a single currency by 1 January 1999 at the latest. Although a large series of papers and conferences has been concerned with the timing and sequencing of the introduction of the new currency and with an estimate of the costs that would be incurred, few published studies have attempted to evaluate the medium-term impact of a single currency on European capital markets. The purpose of the introductory chapter is to identify the various ways through which a single currency could alter fundamentally and permanently the European capital markets. The focus will be entirely on the medium- and long-term impact. One question is being addressed: Once a single currency is in place, what is likely to change in European capital markets? To address this issue, references to a wide economic literature will be made, ranging from the theory of market microstructure to international monetary economics. The chapters which follow discuss in great depth the various channels identified in this introductory chapter.

The analysis will attempt to show how, besides an obvious fall in revenue from intra-European currencies trading, a single European currency could change fundamentally and permanently the sources of competitive advantage of financial institutions. Indeed, an analysis of the structure of the financial industry raises the question of the importance of a currency factor. For instance, the markets for pension funds and mutual funds management or the Euro-francs and Euro-guilder bond markets are quite fragmented, with domestic institutions capturing a very large market share. Although this fragmentation is explained in part by regulations and history, it could

The author acknowledges the help of Mr Davydoff (SBF, Paris), Mr Delcommune and Mr Petit (Petrofina, Belgium) and Mr Karsenti (EIB, Luxembourg), and financial support from the European Capital Markets Institute.

reflect the importance of a national currency factor. Another example is the leading role of American institutions in the dollar-denominated Eurobond market. Will the emergence of a new world currency competing with the US dollar help the competitiveness of European banks? The purpose of this chapter is to show how the introduction of a common currency is likely to change the sources of competitive advantage in various markets such as those of government bonds and their fast-growing appendices the interest rate derivative markets, of corporate bonds and equities, of foreign exchange and of fund management.

The chapter is structured as follows. The first two sections review briefly the origin of European Monetary Union (EMU) and the current issues surrounding the introduction of a single currency. The core of the chapter is in Sections 3–6. Section 3 presents the impact of a single currency on European capital markets. The government bond markets, the corporate bond and equity markets, the fund management industry, the Euro-deposit markets and the market for foreign exchange are successively analysed. Section 4 assesses the prospect for the euro as an international currency and evaluates the likely benefits for European banks. Section 5 evaluates the impact of a single currency on credit risk and makes an argument for an increased international diversification of credit risk in asset portfolios. Section 6 questions the need for the creation of pan-European banks. Finally, Section 7 concludes the chapter and summarizes the effects that a common currency could have on European capital markets.

1. The Origin of EMU, a Reminder

In 1985, the European Commission published the *White Paper on the Completion of the Internal Market*, which provides for the free circulation of persons, goods and capital in the European Union. In 1989, the Committee for the Study of Economic and Monetary Union recommended in the *Delors Report* a three-phase transition spread over ten years. Its conclusions were incorporated in the February 1992 Maastricht Treaty on European Union. Stage I, which ran from 1 July 1990 to 31 December 1993, provided for the freedom of capital flows and the coordination of national monetary policies. Stage II started in July 1994 with the creation of the European Monetary Institute. One of its missions was to prepare the monetary institutions and the European System of Central Banks. Finally, Stage III will lead to European Monetary Unification. Article 109j of the Treaty is quite specific on the date of 1 January 1999. According to the Treaty, at the latest in December 1996, the Council of Heads of State and Government by qualified majority will decide if a majority of states qualify, will decide to start Phase III, and if it is the case will fix the starting date (at the latest 1 January 1999). If no decision has been taken by the end of 1997, the starting date will be 1 January 1999. Before 1 July 1998, the Council will decide which countries will join EMU.[1] Recently, it has been announced that the nomination of countries will take place in May 1998.

The potential economic benefits and costs of EMU were discussed in the European Commission's study *One Market, One Money* (Emerson, 1990, 1992). The report cited four major benefits arising from the introduction of a single currency: a reduction in transaction costs, a reduction in risk, increased competition, and the emergence of an international currency competing with the US dollar. The first benefit is the obvious reduction of transaction costs linked to a reduced need to exchange European currencies. With intra-European trade representing 61 per cent of the international trade of the European Union, the savings were estimated in the Emerson study at ECU 13.1–19 billion,[2] representing 0.3 to 0.4 per cent of European Gross Domestic Product. This reduction of transaction costs comes at the expense of financial institutions providing foreign exchange services; it would represent around 5 per cent of banks' value-added.[3] The second benefit attributed to EMU is a reduction of foreign exchange risk and of substantial changes in relative prices. The reduction of transaction costs and foreign exchange risk will presumably facilitate the realization of the single market programme, allowing firms to choose their appropriate size and optimal location, and facilitating restructuring, investment and economic growth. The third identified benefit is derived from the use of a single denomination measure, which will make price comparison easier, increasing competition and consumers' welfare. Finally, the fourth benefit of EMU is the creation of a world currency competing with the US dollar and the assumed (but unidentified) benefits of an international currency status.

One potential cost of EMU was mentioned by several economists. It is the sacrifice of national monetary autonomy and of the possibility of controlling interest rates or adjusting exchange rates to restore competitiveness. In their reviews of EMU, Eichengreen (1993) and Currie (1997) expressed doubts that the four benefits alone can outweigh the cost linked to the loss of monetary autonomy. In their views, EMU can be argued to be a major benefit only if a single currency is a necessary concomitant of the single market programme, the benefits of which are likely to be substantial. Resistance to the creation of the single market would be reduced if the single currency could prevent 'beggar thy neighbour'-type competitive devaluations. EMU is therefore the cement of the single market, which by integrating previously fragmented markets will allow firms to realize gains in productivity and competitiveness.

For reference, Table 1.1 documents the relative economic importance of the European Union of fifteen countries (EU15) in the world at the end of 1995. The EU15 population amounted in 1995 to 372 million (vs. 263 million in the USA and 125

[1] The single European currency will replace national currencies in those countries meeting the macroeconomic convergence criteria (see the complete discussion by Gros and Lannoo in Ch. 2). The United Kingdom and Denmark have kept their option to join open. Sweden has announced that it will not be part of the first wave.

[2] Although the single currency will be named the *euro*, we shall follow the current practice of keeping the ECU as the unit of account throughout the chapter.

[3] Gross revenue before provisions and operating expenses.

Table 1.1. Macroeconomic statistics, end of 1995

	Population (m.)	GDP (ECU bn.)	Imports (ECU bn.)		Exports (ECU bn.)		ECU rate
			Total	From EU15	Total	To EU15	
Austria	8.5	172.2	51.9	37.6	45.7	29.9	13.66
Belgium[a]	10.0	197.9	122.3	92.6	134	101.3	40.1
Denmark	5.2	135.6	33.72	23.66	37.9	24.57	7.45
Finland	5.11	94	23.5	13.6	32.2	13.6	5.81
France	58.0	1,168	222.9	142.6	225.1	145	6.56
Germany	81.6	1,778	353.8	193.5	405.9	231.7	1.946
Greece	10.46	87.16	20.77	11.6	8.8	5.35	303.85
Ireland	3.58	51.8	25.8	14.5	34.9	25.2	1.342[b]
Italy	57.2	857.4	165.5	100.1	187.6	106.7	1,914
Luxembourg[a]	0.39	14.4	—	—	—	—	40.1
Netherlands	15.45	292.6	111.8	66.4	127	96.2	2.17
Portugal	9.9	70.8	26.8	19.9	18.6	15.06	194.3
Spain	39.2	531.5	91.6	59.9	73.1	52.9	131.28
Sweden	8.83	201.1	49.2	34	61.8	36.2	8.13
UK	58.3	949.4	207.7	113	190.1	108.6	1.356[b]
EU15	372	6,602	1,507	923	1,583	992	
USA	263.03	5,789	593.4	105.3	465.3	98.6	1.253
Japan	125.2	3,371	268.1	39.0	353.4	56.2	142.6
Switzerland	6.9	216.1	63.8	50.9	65	40.5	1.687
World			3,333		3,368		

[a] The external trade of Luxembourg is included in the export and import figures for Belgium.
[b] ECU per £.

Sources: *International Financial Statistics* (IMF), OECD.

million in Japan), Gross Domestic Product to ECU 6,602 billion (vs. ECU 5,789 billion for the USA and ECU 3,371 billion for Japan), and the exports to non EU-countries to ECU 591 billion (vs. total exports of ECU 465 billion for the USA and ECU 353 billion for Japan).

Table 1.2 documents the relative importance of capital markets in Europe. In 1996, the capitalized stock market to GDP ratio stood at 54 per cent in Europe, compared to 116 per cent in the United States and 71 per cent in Japan. Within Europe, this ratio varies greatly, with on one side the United Kingdom at 146 per cent and on the other side Austria at 15 per cent. The same ratio for the bond markets, dominated by public debt, stands at 91 per cent in Europe, compared to 156 per cent in the United States and 115 per cent in Japan. Within Europe, there is a wide difference, with Denmark at 172 per cent and Ireland at 46 per cent. European capital markets are expected to grow because of changes in demographics, the creation of pension funds, and the privatization of large state-owned companies.

Table 1.3 documents the rapid increase expected in the Elderly Dependency Ratio, that is the number of retired people as a percentage of the working population. For

Table 1.2. Capital markets, 1996

	Stock market capitalization		Private bonds market		Public bonds market	
	ECU bn.	% Of GDP	ECU bn.	% Of GDP	ECU bn.	% Of GDP
Austria	25.7	14.9	57	33.1	59.8	34.7
Belgium	95.8	48.4	106	53.6	225	113.7
Denmark	57.3	42.3	140	103.2	94	69.3
Finland	49.4	52.6	30	31.9	42.8	45.5
France	472	37.4	457	36.2	565	44.8
Germany	531.6	29.9	825	46.4	684	38.5
Greece	19	21.8	0.1	0	78.5	90.1
Ireland	27.7	53.5	1.3	2.5	22.3	43.1
Italy	207	24.1	320	37.3	1,019	119
Luxembourg	26	180.6	8.8	61	0.8	5.6
Netherlands	302.4	103.3	52.8	18.1	164	56
Portugal	19.7	27.8	14.3	20.2	35.8	50.6
Spain	195	36.7	35.6	6.7	228	42.9
Sweden	194	96.5	130	64.6	120	59.7
UK	1,383	145.7	172	18.1	346	36.4
EU15	3,606	54.6	2,350	35.6	3,685	55.8
USA	6,750	116.6	3,453	59.6	5,559	96
Japan	2,397	71.1	1,160	34.4	2,721	80.7
Switzerland	322	149	126	58.3	48.6	22.5

Sources: Federation of European Stock Exchange, International Federation of Stock Exchange, BIS.

instance, this ratio is expected to increase in Italy from 30 per cent in 1990 to 45 per cent in the year 2020. The very rapid change expected in demographics has raised the need for funded pension schemes, and substantial increases are expected in institutionalized savings, pension funds and life insurance policies. If cross-country comparison is a guide, one can expect a major increase in this type of saving. Indeed, as Table 1.4 documents, in 1995 pension assets represented 92 per cent of Gross Domestic Product in the Netherlands compared to only 3 per cent in Italy.[4]

The anticipated change in demographics has two major implications. The first one is that the financial resources raised traditionally by banks under the form of deposits will have to be replaced by life insurance reserves and/or pension funds. The successful move by banks into life insurance is a testimony of the need to access a growing market. The second implication is that pension funds are sophisticated investors likely to invest domestically and internationally in the capital (bond/equity) markets. As is documented in Table 1.4, the degree of international diversification of pension funds varies significantly, with 27 per cent of assets invested in international securities in the United Kingdom and 4 per cent in France. One can therefore anticipate an enormous growth in the size of capital markets in Europe and in cross-border trading.

[4] Cross-country comparisons are an imperfect guide to the future because tax differentials can have an important effect on the relative size of pension funds.

Table 1.3. Elderly dependency ratio (%)[a]

	1990	2020
Austria	24	33
Belgium	31	43
Denmark	33	45
Finland	27	48
France	30	43
Germany	29	40
Ireland	28	38
Italy	30	45
Netherlands	26	40
Portugal	29	37
Spain	30	38
Sweden	38	48
UK	34	40
USA	27	36
Japan	24	55

[a] Number of persons aged 65 and over as a percentage of the number of persons aged 25–64.

Source: Poortvliet and Laine, 1994 (author's calculation).

Table 1.4. Assets of pension funds, 1995

	Stock of assets		Holdings in domestic equities (%)	Total domestic holdings (%)
	ECU bn	% Of GDP		
Austria	1.6	1	2	78
Belgium	7.98	4	17	63
Denmark	24.7	18	21	92
Finland	13.57	14	9	n.a.
France	39.1	3	6	96
Germany	101.4	6	6	94
Greece	2.4	3	10	97
Ireland	20.8	4	23	61
Italy	23.1	3	3	95
Luxembourg	n.a.		20	82
Netherlands	268.2	92	11	77
Portugal	6.4	9	9	94
Spain	14.4	3	4	97
Sweden	56.7	28	19	89
UK	646.5	68	55	73

n.a. = not available.

Source: Merrill Lynch (1997).

2. Issues with the Introduction of a Single Currency

Since early 1994, there has been a series of papers and conferences on the way to replace national currencies by a European one and on the implementation costs.[5] The practical issues mentioned in those studies refer to changes in computer programs, accounting and payment systems (including ATM/POS, coins/notes), and the legal issues linked to the status of financial contracts denominated in national currencies with maturity overlapping the date of introduction of the single currency. The total costs incurred through the introduction of a single currency have been estimated by the Banking Federation of the European Union (1995) at ECU 8–10 billion, the equivalent of 2 per cent of banks' operating expenses, repeated over three or four years. The estimates for single banks vary widely, with figures ranging from ECU 100–150 million for large banks (Association for the Monetary Union of Europe, 1994) to an estimate of ECU 6 million for a Belgian bank (Swings, 1994). Estimates of the costs of the change-over for securities firms appear much lower, from a high of ECU 8 million to a low of ECU 110,000 (Scobie, 1997). These studies have referred to the very practical problem caused by fractionalization, as the conversion from national rounded prices into euro prices is unlikely to be equally rounded. Levitt (1994) puts it nicely: 'Management of exchange rates is not normally undertaken to facilitate mental arithmetic.' Not only the public will need to adapt to decimals, but, apparently, computers as well. An expert from Euroclear is quoted as saying, 'It should not be taken for granted that all bond-related securities systems can accommodate decimal figures for nominal amounts' (Dinne, 1995).[6] Besides references to arbitrage opportunities, these studies on the practical aspects of the introduction of a single currency have referred to the historical experiences of the United Kingdom and Germany. The Decimal Currency Board in Great Britain planned the decimalization over a six-year period from 1966 to 1971 (Bishop, 1994; Levitt, 1994). But German Monetary Unification took place in a much shorter period. From the proposal for monetary union in February 1990, via the treaty signed on 18 May 1990, to the effective change of currency in the first week of July 1990, it took five months (Schröder, 1994).

A large part of the discussion has centred on the sequencing of events and whether there would be a big bang in which all denomination, payment systems and means of exchange would be converted into euros in a very short period, or whether there would be a dual-currency process in which the euro and national currencies would coexist. In May 1995, the European Commission, building on the results of the Maas Committee's report, published a consultative Green Paper (European Commission, 1995) which sketches the framework. It proposed a 'mounting wave' approach with three phases spread over four years. In November 1995, the European Monetary Institute presented

---

[5] Association for the Monetary Union of Europe (1994), ECU Banking Association (1994), Levitt (1994), Maas (1995), Banking Federation of the European Union (1995), and European Commission (1995).

[6] For instance, the French Treasury has announced that the redenomination of bonds will be rounded to the nearest euro (with a cash payment to compensate the loss of the decimal part).

a proposal for *The Changeover to the Single Currency* (1995a). The plan was endorsed by the EU heads of state and government at the Madrid Summit held in December 1995.

Period 1: The launch of EMU. In early May 1998, the decision to launch EMU was taken by a qualified majority and the participating countries were nominated. The heads of state and government made their decision on the basis of the recommendation of the Council of Ministers, taking due account of the reports submitted by the European Commission and the EMI (European Monetary Institute, 1995b).[7]

Period 2: 1 January 1999. The exchange rates of the participating countries will be irrevocably fixed. To create a significant volume of transactions in euros, monetary policy, including foreign exchange interventions with third countries' currencies, bank reserves management and open market polices, will be run in euros. New government debt will be issued in euros. And the wholesale interbank market for real value transfers operating through TARGET will be run in euros. This phase will last a maximum of three years, ending with Period 3 in 2002. Conversion facilities will translate amounts from European into national monetary units and vice versa, at the irrevocably fixed conversion rates. In principle, these facilities will be set up in financial institutions. However, for those institutions which have not been able to equip themselves with the necessary conversion facilities, the national central banks could provide such facilities.

Once the single currency is created, the collection of national central banks will be replaced by a new structure: the European System of Central Banks (ESCB).

The European System of Central Banks comprises a European Central Bank (ECB) located in Frankfurt and the national central banks (NCB) of each country participating in the euro. The Governing Council of the ESCB will formulate monetary policy. It is made up of the governors of each central bank participating in the euro and of the members of the Executive Board of the European Central Bank (four to six persons). The Executive Board of the European Central Bank will implement monetary policy, giving the necessary instructions to the national central banks.

The final choice of the conversion rates and the timing of its announcement have attracted a lot of attention recently. Not only must the timing be right to avoid disturbances in capital markets; it must come early enough to facilitate the operational changeover to the euro.[8] At the September 1997 meeting in Mondorf (Luxembourg), the EU finance ministers agreed that bilateral conversion rates would be announced in May 1998. The bilateral rates that were adopted are the central rates of the European Exchange Rate Mechanism.

Period 3. By 1 January 2002 at the latest, European banknotes and coins will be intro-

---

[7] According to the German Ratification Act on the Maastricht Treaty, the vote of the Federal Chancellor in the European Council was subject to the approval of the upper and lower chambers of the German parliament (Bundestag and Bundesrat) as regards the strict examination of the convergence criteria. This was confirmed explicitly by the Federal Constitutional Court (Deutsche Bank, 1995).

[8] The choice of conversion rates is discussed by Gros and Lannoo in Ch. 2.

duced, and a dual currency system involving the euro and national currencies will be run. Six months later (1 July 2002 at the latest), national banknotes and coins will no longer be legal tender and the euro will become the sole currency.

It appears clearly from the work on the introduction of a single currency that there is no technical impediment to its introduction in 1999, and that the costs are bearable. The legal validity of financial contracts extending beyond 1999 has been questioned. Norton Rose (1996) concludes that EU legislation will create legal certainty in all fifteen members of the European Union. However, there is still an uncertainty to be tested eventually in court in third countries, such as the United States, where a party could call for the termination of a contract as a result of the legal theory of frustration. However, legal experts point out that the rules of international public law state that each state is entitled to sovereignty over its own currency and that the sovereign rights of a state are entitled to recognition by all other states.

Although there is much reference to 1 January 1999 or to 2002 as the relevant dates, it will become clear from the following analysis that it is May 1998 and the decision to fix irrevocably exchange rates that will generate most of the impact of the single currency.

3. European Money and Capital Markets with a Single Currency

The impact of the single currency on capital markets is systematically reviewed in this section. We shall analyse successively the government bond market, the corporate bond and equity markets, institutional fund management, the Euro-deposit market and the market for foreign exchange.

3.1. The government bond market

The first observation is that the arrival of a common currency will create the need for a single risk-free interest rate yield curve matching interest rates to maturities to act as an anchor for the pricing of securities. A unique characteristic of the single European market is the absence of a federal debt, the price of which could help to derive a yield curve. It will be left to market forces to choose the national government bonds that will qualify as risk-free bonds. The country ratings provided in Table 1.5 show that six out of the fifteen countries have today an AAA status,[9] with an additional three with an Aa1 status (Belgium, Denmark, Finland). Together in 1995, these six AAA countries represented 53 per cent of outstanding European public debt. Notice the particular place of the Aa3-rated Italy, whose public debt amounts to 28 per cent of total European debt.

A first and very likely rapid impact of the creation of a European risk-free yield curve will be the consolidation of the fast-growing derivative industry. Indeed, as very few instruments are needed to ride a yield curve in a particular market, the single currency

---

[9] Austria, France, Germany, Luxembourg, the Netherlands and the United Kingdom.

Jean Dermine

Table 1.5. Country ratings

	Moody's		Standard & Poor	
	Foreign	Domestic	Foreign	Domestic
Austria	Aaa	n.r.	AAA	AAA
France	Aaa	Aaa	AAA	AAA
Germany	Aaa	Aaa	AAA	AAA
Luxembourg	Aaa	n.r.	AAA	AAA
Netherlands	Aaa	Aaa	AAA	AAA
UK	Aaa	Aaa	AAA	AAA
Belgium	Aa1	Aa1	AA+	AAA
Denmark	Aa1	Aa1	AA+	AAA
Finland	Aa1	Aaa	AA	AAA
Greece	Baa1	A2	BBB–	n.r.
Ireland	Aa1	Aaa	AA	AAA
Italy	Aa3	Aa3	AA	AAA
Portugal	Aa3	Aa2	AA–	AAA
Spain	Aa2	Aa2	AA	AAA
Sweden	Aa3	n.r.	AA+	AAA

n.r. = not rated.

Source: McCauley and White (1997).

implies that there will be a need for only a few euro-based interest rate instruments. Table 1.6 shows that the number of interest rate future contracts traded in Europe in 1996 reached 238 million, ahead of the 221 million contracts traded in the USA. The European interest rate derivative market is fragmented, with LIFFE having a market share of 55 per cent, compared to 21 per cent for MATIF and 15 per cent for DTB. If the American case is a guide, there is little doubt that the nineteen European interest rate future contracts will be replaced by a few (three or four) euro-rate contracts. Indeed, we do not observe in the United States the creation of contracts competing with those already established. Moreover, since the economics of clearing-houses is based on netting of positions and pooling of counterparty risks, it will be efficient to link the exchanges and clearing-houses to facilitate the accounting, netting and clearing mechanisms.[10]

A second observation about the government bond market in Europe is that, in many countries, it is very much a fragmented market, with domestic players capturing a large market share. This raises the question of the sources of competitive advantage for local institutions. The economics of underwriting of securities and secondary trading typically refers to four potential sources of comparative advantage in securities markets:

- long-term historical access to customers;
- credit risk evaluation expertise;

[10] A complete discussion of European interest rate derivatives is developed by Steinherr in Ch. 6. A discussion of the economics of credit spreads on government bonds is available in Ch. 4 by Nielsen.

Table 1.6. Interest rate futures

Instrument	Exchange	1996 volume (Jan.–Nov.) No. of contracts traded ('000)
Belgian Bond	Belfox	375
90-day Bibor	Belfox	142
Portuguese Bond	BDP	150
German Bund	DTB	16,497
German Bobl	DTB	18,269
German Bund	Liffe	39,802
German Euromark	Liffe	36,231
Danish Bond	Futop	308
Long Gilt	Liffe	15,408
Sterling	Liffe	15,794
Euro-Swiss	Liffe	3,299
Italian Bond	Liffe	12,604
Eurolira	Liffe	6,937
10 Ys Italian	MIF	2,240
10 Ys French	Matif	35,322
Pibor	Matif	14,133
ECU Bond	Matif	550
10 Ys Pesetta	Meff RF	18,536
MIBOR	Meff RF	1,275
Total EU		237,872
Swiss Bond	Soffex	913
Total USA	CBOT and CME	220,603
Total Japan	TIFFE and TSE	41,786

Source: *Futures and Option World*, February 1997, EFSE.

- national currency denomination, which facilitates the placement power with access to local investors, the understanding of national monetary policy, and the understanding of trade (demand/supply) flow patterns; and
- financial sophistication in the design of structured products.

As concerns the underwriting of government risk-free bonds, Feldman and Stephenson (1988), a Federal Reserve study (1991), and Fox (1992) show that the dominance of local players is the result of three main factors. The first is historical, with local players having privileged access to public issues. The second is domestic currency denomination, which facilitates the access to a large home investor base, providing a significant advantage not only in placing, but also in understanding the demand/supply order flows. Finally, expertise in the domestic monetary environment provides essential information to operate on the secondary bond market.[11] Will these sources of competitive advantage survive with a single currency?

Since domestic currency denomination, the main source of competitive advantage

---

[11] The second factor, credit risk evaluation, is less applicable in the case of European government bonds.

identified for local banks in the literature, will disappear, it is quite likely that we shall observe the emergence of a truly integrated European bond market.[12] If access to information on the supply/demand order flows seems essential for secondary trading, then very likely operations at the Europe-wide level will become a necessity.

3.2. The corporate bond and equity markets

As is the case for government bonds, a key issue here concerns the sources of competitive advantage of local institutions in corporate bond and equity underwriting and secondary trading. As explained earlier, customer relationships, assessment of credit risk, currency denomination and financial sophistication[13] are critical sources of competitive advantage. The Eurobond market presents an interesting case. A study by the Federal Reserve Bank of New York (1991) reported a strong correlation for non-dollar issues between the nationality of investors and that of the lead bank manager. This is confirmed in a study by McCauley and White (1997). Table 1.7 shows that the lead managers in the Eurobond markets in French francs, Dutch guilders and German marks were invariably local institutions. The domestic currency denomination facilitating the access to a home investor base was a key source of competitive advantage for placement and also for secondary trading. Moreover, an understanding of local monetary policy gives a competitive advantage in understanding price movements. On the dollar-denominated issue, the Federal Reserve study reports a strong correlation between the nationality of the issuer and that of the bookrunner. This is explained by the relative importance of customer relationships and a better assessment of credit risk, which seem to dominate the currency and home-investor factors in the case of a widely accepted currency.

The overall Eurobond league documents in Table 1.8 the leading role of American securities firms. This is explained not only by large issues by American companies and their expertise developed in their home corporate securities markets, but also by the important advantage linked to the dollar denomination of many bonds. Indeed, an understanding of US order flows and US monetary policy provides a decisive advantage in secondary trading as it helps to predict price movements.

A single currency in Europe will change fundamentally the competitive structure of the corporate bond and equity markets, since one key source of competitive advantage, namely home currency, will disappear.[14] Indeed, savers will diversify their portfolios across European markets, the exchange rate risk being eradicated. Moreover, a single currency will suppress the secondary trading advantage for domestic banks derived from a better understanding of order flows and monetary policy in the domestic

---

[12] Complete integration will require further work to harmonize market practices (European Commission, 1997; Federation of European Stock Exchanges, 1997; London Investment Banking Association, 1997).

[13] An example from France is the successful role of Bankers Trust in the privatization of Rhone Poulenc with the design of synthetic options to protect the value of employees' shares.

[14] This will be even more the case if effective Chinese walls between departments prevent the use of the home-based clientele to place underwritten issues.

Table 1.7. Currency and home-country relationship in the choice of the bond bookrunner, 1996[a]

German bookrunners Borrower	Currency		*French bookrunners* Borrower	Currency	
	Mark	Other		French francs	Other
German	44	16	French	86	10
Other	37	2	Other	75	2
All	39	4	All	77	2

UK bookrunners Borrower	Currency		*Dutch bookrunners* Borrower	Currency	
	Pound	Other		Guilder	Other
UK	40	21	Dutch	83	26
Other	48	3	Other	85	2
All	44	4	All	84	2

US bookrunners Borrower	Currency		*Japanese bookrunners* Borrower	Currency	
	Dollar	Other		Yen	Other
USA	86	46	Japanese	75	46
Other	54	13	Other	87	6
All	64	16	All	84	8

[a] Percentage market share won by bookrunners of indicated nationality.

Source: McCauley and White (1997).

Table 1.8. Eurobond league, 1996

Manager	1996 ECU bn.	Market share (%)
Merrill Lynch	41.3	7.66
Morgan Stanley	29.6	5.48
SBC Warburg	29.1	5.39
Goldman Sachs	27.2	5.05
JP Morgan	27.0	4.99
CSFB/Crédit Suisse	22.6	4.17
Deutsche Morgan Grenfell	22.4	4.14
Lehman Bros	21.6	4.01
Nomura Securities	19.9	3.68
UBS	19.7	3.65

Source: Capital Data Bondware.

country. Therefore, the two main sources of comparative advantage remaining for local players will be historical customer relationships and the understanding of credit risk through a better knowledge of the accounting, legal and fiscal (not to mention language) environment. In our view, whenever the credit risk embedded in corporate securities can be assessed better by domestic banks, it is likely that these players will control underwriting and secondary trading. However, two factors call for the necessity of an international coverage. The first is that the credit risk of a particular firm is going to be subject to the competitive dynamics of the international industry in which that firm operates. For instance, Swedish expertise is not sufficient to deal with the Volvo car manufacturer. What matters is international expertise in the car industry. A second factor could alter the corporate underwriting business. If manufacturing firms consolidate across Europe and centralize their finance departments in the country of the parent, the portfolio of domestic client firms would have to be reviewed.

As concerns competition in the corporate bond and equity markets in third, non-EU countries, an expansion of the role of the euro as an international currency[15] will reinforce the position of European banks. That is because, very much as is the case today for American firms with dollar-denominated bonds, European banks will enjoy a competitive advantage in the euro-denominated securities market.

Finally, since the activities of underwriting of securities and secondary trading have been identified as somewhat complementary (Brealey and Kaplanis, 1994), one will have to see whether the trading of domestic securities could migrate to a European exchange located in another country, *de facto* modifying the competitive advantage of domestic players.

As concerns the competition between securities exchanges, several authors[16] refer to the network externality of a stock market. A market, like any communication network, is subject to network externalities. The demand for immediacy (liquidity) is more readily satisfied the more traders there are in the market, because the probability of executing an order increases with the number of traders. As a result, a market has a natural monopoly that benefits from being the first mover. London has often been referred to as the candidate for a European securities market given its size or turnover in foreign equities. A study by the Bank of England[17] reported that 587 overseas securities were quoted on SEAQ International, and that in 1992 more than 20 per cent of the overall turnover in those shares took place on SEAQI.[18] However, recent studies by Benos and Crouhy (1996) and Pagano (1997) report that Continental bourses have recovered most of the trade from London, thanks to a low-cost automated auction system. For instance, trading of French shares in London declined from 25–30 per cent

---

[15] The role of euro as an international currency is analysed in Section 5 of this chapter, and in Ch. 3 by Wyplosz.

[16] e.g. Stoll (1990), Amihud and Mendelson (1991), Scott-Quinn (1992), and Hawawini and Schill (1992). See the complete discussion of the microstructure of equity markets by Biais in Ch. 8.

[17] *Bank of England Quarterly Bulletin*, March 1993.

[18] Several authors (e.g. Jacquillat and Gresse, 1995; Pagano, 1997) have questioned the significance of these trade statistics in a dealer-type market.

Table 1.9. Market shares of Paris SBF members, 1996

Ranking (anonymous)	Transactions: (purchases + sales)/2 (ECU m.)	Market share: (purchases + sales)/2 (%)
1	11,664	6.8
2	10,972	6.4
3	9,493	5.5
4	9,147	5.3
5	8,182	4.8
6	8,071	4.7
7	7,740	4.5
8	7,184	4.2
9	7,150	4.2
10	6,212	3.6

Source: SBF, Paris.

in 1990–93 to 5–15 per cent in 1995. In the case of a smaller stock exchange, Brussels, and of a large company with multiple listings, 71 per cent of trading in shares of Petrofina S.A. in the first quarter of 1997 took place in Brussels, vs. 27 per cent in London and 2 per cent in Paris.

Furthermore, centralization into one market is likely to be defeated by new information technologies that will allow the bypassing of floor-based trading. With information technology that disseminates information rapidly and the fact that European exchanges are moving to some form of screen-based trading, the location of an exchange will matter less and less for secondary trading. These authors anticipate a web of interlinked exchanges with efficient transmission of information and centralized clearing and settlement systems.[19] The important implication in the context of this study is that secondary trading can be initiated from any place by the banks developing an expertise in domestic securities. If the developments of the last seven years put into question the emergence of a single dominant stock exchange, the issue of the size of member firms in a particular market can be raised. Data for France in Table 1.9 show a fairly low level of concentration, with the five largest firms capturing 29 per cent of the order flows in 1996.

To conclude this analysis of the impact of a single currency on the corporate bond and equity markets, it seems that two forces will play a role. Customer relationships and an understanding of credit risk will remain two sources of strength for domestic firms. But international industry expertise is likely to dominate pure local expertise in the case of large customers. As was the case for government bonds, the issue of size and international coverage is central. By way of an indication, it is symptomatic to observe from Table 1.10 that the five largest underwriters in the investment grade US market control 62 per cent of the market in the USA.

[19] For a discussion of the problem of clearance and settlements systems in Europe, see Giddy *et al.* (1995) and Steil (1996).

Table 1.10. Top ten bookrunners of investment grade in the USA, 1996

Manager	1996 ECU bn.	Market share (%)
Merrill Lynch	79	18.3
Salomon Brothers	54	12.5
Goldman Sachs	46.9	10.8
JP Morgan	45	10.4
Lehman Bros	43.7	10.1
Morgan Stanley	40.8	9.4
CSFB	29	6.7
Bear Stearns	29	3.1
Smith Barney	12.8	3.0
NationsBank	12.3	2.8

Source: Securities Data Co.

3.3. Fund management

An important segment of capital markets business is the fund management industry, pensions funds or mutual funds. Tables 1.11 and 1.12 document the structure of the European mutual funds industry. Notice the relative importance of money market funds in some countries, such as France (45 per cent of total assets), while equity funds dominate in others countries, such as the United Kingdom (88 per cent of total assets). Moreover, Table 1.12 confirms the existence of the 'home-country' bias; that is, equity funds are mostly invested in domestic equities. Market share data for France and the United Kingdom provided in Tables 1.13 and 1.14 confirm the existence of fragmented markets entirely controlled by local players. All top ten players are domestic firms (even if some of them in the United Kingdom, such as PDFM or Morgan Grenfell, were purchased by Continental European banks). In view of this extreme fragmentation, especially in comparison with other segments of the capital markets, one wonders about the impact of the single currency on the fund management industry. In this case too, an understanding of the main sources of competitive advantage needs to be developed.[20] These concern the retail distribution network, the home-currency preference, and the existence of economies of scale.

The first source of competitive advantage in the retail segment is the control of the distribution network by local banks (Kay *et al.*, 1994). Domestic control of distribution is even protected under the current European legislative framework, which gives to each national authority the right to regulate the marketing of funds into its territory. Obviously the advantage derived from the control of the distribution network applies to retail investors only, as it will not be a barrier to entry in the institutional market. A second source of competitive advantage is the customer preference for home-currency assets, often imposed by regulation. A single currency will of course eliminate this

---

[20] See the complete discussion by Walter in Ch. 9.

Table 1.11. The European mutual funds industry, 1996

	Assets (ECU bn.)	Relative share of equity funds (%)	Relative share of money market funds (%)
Austria	32	5.7	0
Belgium	22	34.1	9.7
Denmark	8	46.7	0
Finland	2	31.5	40.6
France	426	10.9	45.3
Germany	110	26.7	16
Greece	13	2	59.3
Ireland	6	37.1	2.3
Italy	104	16.7	36.4
Luxembourg	272	17.8	27.4
Netherlands	54	53.8	10.1
Portugal	13	5.5	32.6
Spain	114	2.8	50.8
Sweden	28	74.6	0
UK	159	88.4	0.5
Total EU	1,363		
Switzerland	38.4	62	0

Source: FEFSI, April 1997.

Table 1.12. The European mutual funds industry, 1996 (%)

	Equity funds (100 %)			Bond funds (100 %)		
	Domestic	European	International	Domestic	European	International
Austria	7	—	93	72	—	28
Belgium	49	20	31	58	19	23
Denmark	20	—	80	74	—	26
Finland	78	—	22	100	—	—
France	64	—	36	87	—	13
Germany	62	12	26	53	—	47
Greece	95	—	5	97	—	3
Ireland	25	—	75	100	—	—
Italy	57	8	34	92	—	8
Luxembourg	—	—	—	—	—	—
Netherlands	16	—	84	33	—	67
Portugal	76	—	24	99	—	1
Spain	96	—	4	98	—	2
Sweden	77	—	23	99	—	1
UK	59	10	31	78	—	22
Switzerland	17	—	83	1	—	99

Source: FEFSI, 1997.

Table 1.13. Mutual funds (OPCVM) managers in France, December 1996

	ECU bn.	Market share (%)
Société Générale	31.3	7.4
Crédit Agricole	25.1	5.9
Crédit Lyonnais	24.1	5.7
BNP	23.96	5.68
CDC-Trésor	18.5	4.4
La Poste	16.3	3.9
CIC-Banque	14	3.3
Caisses d'Epargne	12.9	3.1
Banques Populaires	12.3	2.9
Paribas	8.2	1.95

Source: EuroPerformance, AFG-ASSFI.

Table 1.14. UK league of fund managers

	Total assets under management	
	ECU bn.	Market share (%)
Prudential	123.4	9.6
Schroder	119.3	9.3
MAM	116.6	9.1
Morgan Grenfell	93.6	7.3
Commercial Union	92.2	7.2
Fleming	78.6	6.1
Invesco	78.6	6.1
PDFM	77.3	6
Gartmore	69.2	5.4
Standard Union	65	5

Note: Excludes the assets managed by Wells Fargo Nikko, the US fund management arm of Barclays.

factor and reinforce the need for Europe-wide portfolios.[21] A large part of these will be provided by index-tracking investment funds. The existence and relevance of economies of scale for mutual funds is still a debated issue. One of the very few studies on the subject demonstrates in the case of France the absence of economies of scale for funds larger than ECU 450 million (Dermine and Röller, 1993). A third source of success is excellence in research-based management. It would seem that domestic expertise in the assessment of risk will still be a source of competitive advantage for local institutions supplying regional funds. But international industry expertise will be needed for those supplying specialized sectoral funds.

---

[21] Jorion (1994), Kay *et al.* (1994), Solnik *et al.* (1996) and Baxter and Jermann (1997). See the discussions in Chs. 7 and 8 by De Santis *et al.* and Biais.

_ A single currency will eliminate the obstacle to international diversification. One will very likely observe low-cost European index-tracking funds competing with smaller research-based funds (regional and sectoral). On the retail distribution side, domestic banks will keep their competitive advantage in those countries in which the branch network remains a significant channel of distribution.

3.4. The Euro-deposit market and cross-border payments

An extremely efficient Euro-deposit market was created thirty years ago to circumvent various forms of domestic regulations.[22] Table 1.15 documents the success of some countries, such as Luxembourg and the United Kingdom, in attracting the deposits of foreign non-bank investors. The size and location of the Euromarket[23] is directly related to the relative size of the Net Regulatory Burden imposed by national rules (Levich, 1993). An important issue yet to be clarified by the European Monetary Institute concerns the size, the coverage and the eventual remuneration of the reserve requirement in the future. Indeed, foreign deposits are not subject currently to reserve requirements in most countries. More important, but unrelated to the single currency,

Table 1.15. External position of banks in individual reporting countries (ECU bn.)[a]

	December 1991	September 1996
Austria	6.6	9.7
Belgium	36.2	65.2
Denmark	2.9	7.76
Finland	1.7	0.5
France	40.7	56.8
Germany	52.3	146
Ireland	5.2	16.3
Italy	10.4	12.8
Luxembourg	100	142.3
Netherlands	40	51
Spain	26	36.4
Sweden	11.9	7.76
UK	281	322
Switzerland	194	211.9
Japan	13.6	17.6
USA	68.2	85.3
Cayman	142.7	153.5

[a] All currencies *vis-à-vis* the non-bank sector.

Source: BIS, *International Banking and Financial Developments*, February 1997.

---

[22] Aliber (1976) or Dufey and Giddy (1994).
[23] The arrival of the euro calls for a rapid redenomination of this market.

will be the fiscal treatment of the income earned on these assets in the future (Dermine, 1995, 1997).

Another dimension of Euro-banking is the cross-border payment system and the current role of correspondent banks. The current situation is that international payments are made through the accounts of banks in foreign countries and through the various national clearing systems. The European Monetary Institute (1995c) has provided some indications on the future European payment system. In essence, it favours a decentralized nationally based system complemented by TARGET,[24] a linkage between the various national real-time gross settlement systems. Only the payments related to monetary policy will have to pass through TARGET. Other payments will have a choice between the direct route, the traditional correspondent banking system and competing private systems such as the former ECU Clearing System put forward by the ECU Banking Association (1996). If the role of correspondent banking is likely to be altered, it seems that this movement would happen independently of the existence of a single currency for the sole reason of reducing settlement and payment risks.

3.5. Foreign exchange markets

A first observation is that not only intra-European foreign exchange transactions will disappear, but also the competitive advantage of a particular bank in its home currency *vis-à-vis* third country currencies. As an example, a Belgian bank operating in New York will not be any more the Belgian franc specialist, but will compete with other European banks for euro business. As is the case for the government bond markets, for which an understanding of the supply/demand order flows is important to assess the direction of price movements, we are likely to observe a consolidation of the commodity-type low-cost spot foreign exchange business. This conjecture is consistent with the analysis by Tschoegl (1996) of the sources of competitive advantage in the currency market, namely size and the international status of the home currency. Differentiated products based on quality of service or innovations such as options will be another source of competitive advantage.

The conclusion that emerges from the above analysis of European capital markets is that there will be quite significant changes in some specific segments of the industry. We forecast a rapid consolidation of the commodity-type businesses: government bonds, interest rate derivatives, and spot currency trading. We believe that, if domestic expertise in the accounting, legal and fiscal environment gives some competitive advantage to domestic players in the corporate bond and equity markets, an understanding of the international dynamics of an industry will be necessary. On the fund management side, Europe-wide index-tracking funds will compete with specialized funds. Finally, the rules of monetary and fiscal policies still have to be known to assess the impact of a single currency on the size and location of the Euro-deposit markets.

---

[24] TARGET is the acronym for Trans-European Automated Real-Time Gross Settlement Express Transfer system.

4. The Euro as an International Currency

One of the asserted benefits of EMU is that the single currency will become a challenger to the US dollar as the dominant international currency used for units of account, store of value and means of payment (Emerson, 1990; Alogoskoufis and Portes, 1991, 1992; European Commission, 1995). But one has to realize that in contrast to a national currency, which is imposed as sole tender by national legislation, the role of an international currency is fixed by demand and supply on world capital markets. Our objective in this section is twofold. First, we document the relative importance of the US dollar as an international currency and evaluate the chance of the euro to compete with the dollar.[25] Secondly, we assess the benefits of the international currency status of the euro for European banks.

As is the case for any domestic currency, the role of an international currency is threefold. It serves as:

- a unit of account for measuring and comparing market values;
- a store of value in which assets or liabilities are denominated; and
- a mean of exchange for the settlement of financial contracts.

Unit of account. Besides the fact that several commodities, such as gold and oil, are denominated in US dollars, one observes the central role of the dollar in the currency market. This is of course the result of an efficient market which by directing demand and supply to a few (dollar-related) contracts creates maximum liquidity in the market. With only $(n-1)$ independent currencies, this is the traditional problem of replacing a constellation of $n(n-1)/2$ pairs of cross-rates by only $(n-1)$ independent exchange rates. If the single currency will of course eliminate intra-EU currencies trading, it is doubtful that the pivotal role of the dollar in the foreign exchange market will disappear.

Store of value. Whether one looks at the 41.4 per cent share of dollar-denominated international bonds (Table 1.16) or the 46.7 per cent share of cross-border bank claims (Table 1.17), one draws the conclusion that the relative importance of the American currency vastly exceeds the relative share of the United States in world exports (14 per cent). But even if the international role of the dollar is very strong, one can notice a continuous erosion of the dollar's position. For instance, the share of the dollar in foreign exchange reserves fell from 84.5 per cent in 1973 to 56.4 per cent in 1995, while the share of the DM rose from 6.7 per cent to 13.7 per cent.

Mean of exchange. The share of the dollar as a mean of exchange in international trade has been documented by Emerson (1990). For instance, 17 per cent of Belgian imports are denominated in dollars, while imports from the United States amount to 5.3 per cent of total Belgian imports.

---

[25] Wyplosz, Ch. 3, provides a complete discussion of the international role of the euro.

Table 1.16. International bonds outstanding, 30 June 1996

Currency	ECU bn.	%
USD	262	41.4
Yen	77	12.1
DM	94	14.8
£	45	7
FF	46	7
Swiss franc	23	4
Italian lira	22	3
Dutch guilder	19	3
ECU	3.5	0.6

Source: *Financial Times*, 30 June 1996.

Table 1.17. Currency composition of banks' cross-border claims, 1996 (%)[a]

Currency	1994	1996
DM	14.3	14.9
FF	2.6	3.1
Swiss franc	4.6	4.8
£	2.4	2.4
ECU	4.3	3.6
Yen	4	4.3
US$	52	46.7
Total outstanding (ECU bn.)	1,018	1,083

[a] Foreign currencies to all sectors.

Source: BIS, *International Banking and Financial Markets Development*, 1996.

Whether one looks at the role of the dollar as a unit of account, a store of value or a mean of payment, it is still today by far the primary international currency. Will the euro be able to compete and at what speed? To assess the euro's chance of accelerating the relative decline in the dollar, it is instructive to look at history and the relative fall of sterling and rise of the dollar in the international payment system.

In 1914, on the eve of the First World War, the City of London was indisputably the world's leading international financial centre, with the pound sterling the major international currency. According to economic historians,[26] the weakness of the pound started with the First World War. The war of 1914–18 saw the emergence of large bond financing in the USA. This was coupled with the events of 1931—the insolvency of the Creditanstalt in Vienna and the inconvertibility of the pound. The developments of the

---

[26] Dehem (1972), Kindleberger (1984), McKinnon (1993) or Roberts (1994).

Second World War succeeded in increasing even more the stature of the dollar, which was confirmed in its international role by the 1944 Bretton Woods agreement.[27] One can conclude that the rapid rise of the dollar over a thirty-year period was very much helped by the two world wars, and that despite the abandonment of convertibility into gold in 1971 and significant volatility, the dollar still maintains its leading role as an international currency. Based on the last two decades, which have seen a progressive erosion of the dollar and a slow rise of the Deutsche Mark, in view of the relative economic size of Europe, and building on the potential for growth in the eastern part of Europe, one can extrapolate and forecast that the euro will replace the D-Mark and be a strong competitor to the dollar. But in the author's opinion, any forecast on the relative importance of the US dollar and the euro in the future is premature.

What are the implications for banks of having the euro as an international currency? Three benefits can be identified. The first one is that an increased volume of euro-denominated assets or liabilities will ease the foreign exchange risk management of equity. Indeed, a large proportion of bank assets will be denominated in the same currency as the equity base, easing the control of asset growth and capital management. Secondly, access to a central bank discount window will make the liquidity management of euro-based liabilities potentially easier. Finally, if third countries issue assets denominated in euros or use the European currency as a vehicle, European banks will be well positioned for secondary trading for the reasons mentioned earlier.

5. EMU and Loan Credit Risk

Many of the channels which have been identified concern the money and capital markets. Last but not least in this evaluation of the impacts of the single currency is the potential impact on loan credit risk. There are reasons to believe that the nature of credit risk could change under a single currency. The argument is based on the theory of Optimum Currency Areas and on the objective of price stability inscribed in the Treaty on European Union.

There is an old debate on the economic rationale leading a group of countries to adopt a common currency (the theory of the Optimum Currency Areas[28]). This debate has been revived by the proposal to introduce a single currency in Europe (Emerson, 1990; Eichengreen, 1994; von Hagen and Neumann, 1994). The story is the following. The more that countries are subject to asymmetric economic shocks, the more they appreciate monetary autonomy to cancel the shock. Indeed, with symmetric shocks there would be a consensus among the members of a currency union on economic policy, but with asymmetric shocks the policy run from the centre may not be adequate for all the

---

[27] According to McKinnon (1993), a key factor increasing the role of the dollar was the European Payments Union established in September 1950 for clearing payments multilaterally, using the US dollar as the unit of account and as the mean of payment.

[28] Mundell (1961), McKinnon (1963).

members of the union.[29] The loss of monetary autonomy is often regarded as the major cost of European Monetary Union. Recent economic developments have strengthened the argument. The 1994 *Annual Report* of the Bank for International Settlements shows that the 1993 exports of the countries whose currencies depreciated (Finland, Ireland, Italy, Portugal, Spain, Sweden and the United Kingdom) were able to overcome very sluggish demand conditions in Europe and take advantage of rapidly expanding export markets in North America and Southeast Asia. Their export volumes combined rose by 7.5 per cent while the exports from the group of stable currencies (Germany, Austria, Belgium, Denmark, France, the Netherlands and Switzerland) stagnated.

How could the introduction of a single currency affect credit risk? If a bank concentrates its business in its home country, and if that country is subject to asymmetric shocks, it is quite possible that monetary policy will not be able to soften the shock. For instance, one can wonder whether the rapid recovery enjoyed by British banks in 1994 was not helped partly by the devaluation, which reduced somewhat a bad debt problem. An indirect and interesting corollary of the Optimum Currency Area theory is that for banks operating in a single currency area, the need to diversify their loan portfolios increases the more their home country is likely to be subject to asymmetric (uncorrelated) shocks. This can be achieved through international diversification or the use of credit derivatives.

A second effect of EMU is that the Statute of the European Central Bank will prevent inflationary policies. *Ceteris paribus*, this could increase the potential for losses resulting from default, as one will no longer be able to count on a predictable positive drift for the value of collateral assets.[30] The inability of a country to devalue and the very strict anti-inflationary policy of the ECB imply that, whenever a need to restore competitiveness arises in a particular region, the only tool available will be a *reduction of nominal wage and prices*. This will change fundamentally the nature of credit risk, as firms and individuals will not be able to rely any more on the nominal growth of their revenue to reduce the real value of their debt. This new world calls for innovative techniques to handle potential deflations.[31]

6. Pan–European Banks

In Europe, the last ten years have seen a very large number of domestic mergers. Table 1.18 partially documents this series. These are often defensive mergers that allowed a substantial reduction in the number of branches or staff. Few international mergers

---

[29] This theory assumes essentially rigid prices and a relatively immobile workforce. Tentative empirical work by von Hagen and Neumann (1994) suggests that Austria, Benelux, France and Germany do form a homogeneous zone, but that Denmark, Italy and the United Kingdom are subject to asymmetric economic shocks.

[30] Although an argument can be made that non-inflationary policies would reduce the amplitude of business cycles.

[31] A tool could be the creation of securities indexed on regional prices.

Table 1.18. Domestic mergers in Europe[a]

	Date	Merger
Belgium	1992	CGER–AG (Fortis)
	1995	Fortis–SNCI
	1995	KB–Bank van Roeselaere
	1997	BACOB–Paribas Belgium
		CERA–Indosuez Belgium
	1998	KB–CERA
Denmark	1990	Den Danske Bank
		Unibank (Privatbanken, Sparekassen, Andelsbanken)
Finland	1995	KOP–Union Bank of Finland
France	1996	Crédit Agricole–Indosuez
Germany	1997	Bayerische Vereinsbank–Hypo-Bank
Italy	1992	Banca di Roma (Banco di Roma, Cassa di Risparmio
		di Roma, Banco di Santo Spirito)
		IMI–Cariplo
		San Paolo–Crediop
	1995	Credito Romagnolo (Rolo)–Credit Italiano
	1997	Ambroveneto–Cariplo
Netherlands	1990	ABN–AMRO
	1991	NMB–PostBank–ING
Portugal	1995	BCP–BPA
Spain	1988	BBV (Banco de Vizcaya–Banco de Bilbao)
	1989	Caja de Barcelona–La Caixa
	1992	Banco Central–Banco Hispano
	1994	Santander–Banesto
Sweden	1993	Nordbanken–Gota Bank
Switzerland	1993	CS–Volksbank
UK	1995	Lloyds–C&G–TSB

[a] Not complete, for illustration only.

have taken place yet, although a wave could be on its way.[32] As Table 1.19 documents, international mergers essentially involved the purchase of merchant banks in London, such as the acquisition of Barings by ING, or Morgan Grenfell by Deutsche Bank.

The key issue is whether the arrival of the euro will precipitate the creation of pan-European banks. The analysis developed in this chapter has shown that size and international coverage will likely be very important in some specific segments of the industry, such as bonds and equities markets, fund management and foreign exchange. This seems to indicate a need for size and international coverage for those firms wanting to be successful in those markets. But for other activities, such as retail banking, local expertise could allow the survival of local firms. This will be particularly valid as long as the branch network allows banks to capture a clientele. Whenever consumers

[32] Significant cross-border mergers include Dexia, a merger between the Belgian Crédit Communal and the French Crédit Local, Fortis, a merger between the Dutch AMEV/Mees Pierson and the Belgian AG/CGER/SNCI, the Scandinavian merger between the Merita Bank of Finland and Nordbankern of Sweden, and the purchase of the Belgian Banque Bruxelles-Lambert by the Dutch ING.

Table 1.19. International mergers in Europe[a]

Buyer	Target
Deutsche Bank	Morgan Grenfell
ING Bank	Barings
Swiss Bank Corp	Warburg, O'Connor, Brinson, Dillon Read
Dresdner	Kleinwort Benson
ABN–AMRO	Hoare Govett
UNIBANK	ABB Aos
FORTIS	Mees Pearson
Merrill Lynch	Smith New Court (UK)
	FG (Spain)
Crédit Suisse	BZW (equity part)

[a] Not complete, for illustration only.

start to trade financial services over the telephone or Internet, then the importance of the branch network will disappear and, very likely, a large size will also be required to establish a strong national or European brandname. As cross-border restructuring becomes necessary, a second issue will arise. Should this international restructuring occur along specific lines of business, such as fund management, corporate and investment banking, or should it take the form of a large diversified international universal bank?[33]

7. Conclusions

The objective of this chapter has been to identify the various ways through which a single currency would alter the sources of competitive advantage of European financial firms. Our analysis has identified various markets which will be significantly affected. Besides the obvious fall in revenue from intra-European currencies trading, the analysis has led to nine main conclusions.

1. The structure of national *government bond markets* and their fast-expanding appendices, the interest rate derivative markets, will change fundamentally. The fragmented national markets will be replaced by a European consolidated market. This is due to the fact that two main sources of competitive advantage for domestic banks which have been identified in the literature, namely access to home-base investors and expertise in national monetary policy, will vanish. Moreover, many of the national interest rate derivative instruments which have been created in recent years will disappear, being replaced by a few euro-based instruments.

2. An analysis of the *corporate bond and equity markets* suggests significant but less fundamental changes. In these currently fragmented markets, three main sources of competitive advantage are client relationships, assessment of credit risk, and currency

[33] See the complete discussions on strategic positioning by Walter and Smith in Chs. 9 and 10.

denomination, which may facilitate placing to home investors and secondary trading through a better understanding of the macro-monetary policy. With a single currency, the benefits derived from a national currency will disappear. The two remaining sources of competitive advantage for domestic players will be historical client relationships and assessment of the credit risk of domestic firms. The currently observed correlation between the nationality of the issuer and the nationality of the underwriter will remain strong whenever these two sources of competitive advantage are at work. But international sectoral coverage will also be a necessity.

3. The fast-growing, currently fragmented *institutional fund management* industry will change permanently. Index-tracking funds will operate at the European level, competing with funds built on research-based expertise in specific industries or countries.

4. The *Euro-deposit and the cross-border payment systems* will be affected by the introduction of a single currency. Since the location of the Euro-deposit market is affected by the relative size of the net regulatory and fiscal burden, one waits to find out the tools of European monetary policy, and in particular the level and coverage of the reserve requirement, as well as the fiscal rules that will apply.

5. The role of euro as an *international currency* has often been mentioned as a major benefit of European Monetary Union. Based on the history of the last thirty years, with the growing share of the D-Mark, one can anticipate that the creation of a euro managed by an independent European central bank will accelerate the competition to the US dollar. But, as economic history shows, this process is likely to take many years. An international role for the euro will facilitate the underwriting and secondary trading of bonds and equities issued in third countries.

6. *Currency trading* between the euro and other currencies will be altered fundamentally. Indeed, very much as is the case with government bonds, the arrival of a common currency will erase the source of national comparative advantage. Very likely there will be a consolidation of foreign exchange activities to benefit from scale economies.

7. Another impact of the single currency concerns *credit risk.* The creation of a single currency will change the nature of domestic credit risk, as domestic recessions might not be softened by flexible national monetary policies. This should encourage further the diversification of credit risk through international lending or credit derivatives. Financial innovations will be required to deal with potential regional deflations.

8. The creation of *pan-European banks* could be necessary to achieve size and international coverage.

9. Finally, a fundamental impact of the euro is that it will make *irreversible* the creation of the single market. A more predictable environment will facilitate the exploitation of economies of scale and the optimal location of processing units.

The objective of the 1992 single market programme was to reinforce the efficiency and competitiveness of European firms. As concerns banking, it is a clear conclusion not only that the introduction of a single currency will make the creation of a single market irreversible, but that it will, besides the obvious fall in revenue from intra-European currencies trading, alter fundamentally the nature of several businesses. This will be particularly the case in the money and capital markets. If this challenge is met successfully by European banks, there is little doubt that it will reinforce the competitiveness of those operating in the capital markets of third countries, such as United States and the rapidly expanding Asian and Latin American countries.

References

Aliber, R. (1976), *The International Money Game*, New York: Basic Books.

Alogoskoufis, G. (1994), 'The ECU, the International Monetary System and the Management of Exchange Rates', in L. Bekemans and L. Tsoukalis (eds.), *Europe and Global Economic Interdependence*, Bruges: European Interuniversity Press.

Alogoskoufis, G. and R. Portes (1991), 'International Costs and Benefits from EMU', in *The Economics of EMU*, European Economy.

Alogoskoufis, G. and R. Portes (1992), 'European Monetary Union and International Currencies in a Tripolar World', in M. Canzoneri, V. Grilli, and P. Masson (eds.), *Establishing a Central Bank: Issues in Europe and Lessons from the US*, Cambridge: Cambridge University Press.

Amihud, Y. and H. Mendelson (1991), 'How (not) to Integrate the European Capital Markets', in A. Giovannini and C. Mayer (eds.), *European Financial Integration*, Cambridge: Cambridge University Press.

Association Belge des Banques (1994), 'Les Banques et l'Union Monétaire Européenne', *Aspects et Documents*, 160.

Association for the Monetary Union of Europe (AMUE) (1994), 'Preparing the Transition to the Single Currency'.

Banking Federation of the European Union (1995), 'Survey on the Introduction of the Single Currency: A First Contribution on the Practical Aspects', Brussels.

Baxter, M. and U. Jermann (1997), 'The International Diversification Puzzle Is Worse than You Think', *American Economic Review*, 87(1): 170–80.

Begg, D., F. Giavazzi, J. von Hagen and C. Wyplosz (1997), *EMU, Getting the End-Game Right*, London: CEPR.

Benos, A. and M. Crouhy (1996), 'Changes in the Structure and Dynamics of European Securities Markets', *Financial Analysts Journal*, May/June, 37–50.

Bishop, G. (1994), 'Lessons from the Decimalisation in the UK', EBA Study.

Brealey, R. and E. Kaplanis (1994), 'The Growth and Structure of International Banking', London: City Research Project.

Currie, D. (1997), *The Pros and Cons of EMU*, London: Economic Intelligence Unit.

Davis, P. (1995), *Pension Funds: Retirement Income, Security and Capital Markets, an International Perspective*, Oxford: Clarendon Press.

Dehem, R. (1972), *De l'Etalon sterling à l'etalon-dollar*, Paris: Calmann-Lévy.

Dermine, J. (1995), 'International Trade in Banking', in American Enterprise Institute (ed.), *International Competition in Financial Services: Should National Regulatory Systems Be Harmonized?*, Washington, DC: American Enterprise Institute.

Dermine, J. (1997), 'Eurobanking, a New World', Laureate of the 1997 EIB Prize. *EIB Papers*, vol. 2.

Dermine, J. and L. H. Röller (1993), 'Economies of Scale and Scope in French Mutual Funds', *Journal of Financial Intermediation*, 2: 83–93.

Deutsche Bank (1995), 'A Stable Currency for Europe', Special Report, Frankfurt (November).

Dinne, M. (1995), 'Path of Conversion', *The Banker*, March.

Dufey, G. and I. Giddy (1994), *The International Money Market*, 2nd edn., Englewood Cliffs, NJ: Prentice Hall.

ECU Banking Association (EBA) (1994), 'The Impact of EMU on Banks' Activities', June.

ECU Banking Association (EBA) (1996), 'From ECU to Euro: The EBA's Future Business Potential', December.

Eichengreen, B. (1993), 'European Monetary Unification', *Journal of Economic Literature*, 31: 1321–57.

Eichengreen, B. (1994), *International Monetary Arrangements for the 21st Century*, Washington, DC: The Brookings Institutions.

Emerson, M. (1990), 'One Market, One Money', *European Economy*, 44 (October).

Emerson M. (1992), *One Market, One Money*, Oxford: Oxford University Press.

European Commission (1995), 'Green Paper on the Practical Arrangements for the Introduction of the Single Currency', COM (95) 333 final, Brussels.

European Commission (1997), 'The Impact of the Introduction of the Euro on Capital Markets', COM (97) 337 final, Brussels.

European Monetary Institute (1995*a*), 'The Changeover to the Single Currency', Frankfurt (November).

European Monetary Institute (1995b), 'Progress towards Convergence', Frankfurt (November).

European Monetary Institute (1995c), 'Report to the Council of the European Monetary Institute on the Target System', Frankfurt (May).

European Monetary Institute (1997), 'EU Securities Settlement Systems', Frankfurt (February).

Federal Reserve Bank of New York (1991), 'International Competitiveness of US Financial Firms', Staff Study, New York.

Federation of European Stock Exchanges (1997), 'The Transition to the Euro', Brussels (May).

Feldman, L. and J. Stephenson (1988), 'Stay Small or Get Huge—Lessons from Securities Trading', *Harvard Business Review*, May/June: 116–23.

Fox, M. (1992), 'Aspects of Barriers to International Integrated Securities Markets', *Journal of International Securities Markets*, 6 (Autumn): 209–17.

Giddy, I., A. Saunders and I. Walter (1995), 'Barriers to European Financial Integration, Clearance and Settlement of Equities', INSEAD Working Paper 95/87.

Hawawini, G. and M. Schill (1992), 'Current State and Prospects of Equity Trading in the European Community', *Journal of International Securities Markets*, 6 (Winter): 325–40.

Jacquillat, B. and C. Gresse (1995), 'The Diversion of Order Flow on French Shares from the CAC Market to the SEAQ International: An Exercise in Transaction Accounting', Working Paper, Université Paris Dauphine.

Jorion, P. (1994), 'Mean/Variance Analysis of Currency Overlays', *Financial Analysts Journal*, 50 (May/June): 48–56.

Kay, J., R. Laslett and N. Duffy (1994), *The Competitive Advantage of the Fund Management Industry in the City of London*, London: The City Research Project.

Kindleberger, C. (1984), *A Financial History of Western Europe*, London: Allen & Unwin.

Levich, R. (1993), 'The Euromarkets after 1992', in J. Dermine (ed.), *European Banking in the 1990s*, 2nd edn., Oxford: Basil Blackwell.

Levitt, M. (1994), 'Introducing a Single Currency', paper read at the European Finance Convention, Frankfurt (29 November).

London Investment Banking Association (1997), 'LIBA Progress Report on the Transition to the Euro Capital Markets', London.

McCauley, R. and W. R. White (1997), 'The Euro and European Financial Markets', BIS Working Paper 41 (May), 1–57.

McKinnon, R. (1963), 'Optimum Currency Areas', *American Economic Review*, 53(4): 717–25.

McKinnon, R. (1993), 'The Rules of the Game: International Money in Historical Perspective', *Journal of Economic Literature*, 31(1): 1–44.

Maas, C. (1995), 'Progress Report on the Preparation of the Changeover to the Single European Currency', Brussels: European Commission (10 May).

Merrill Lynch (1997), 'Influence of the Euro on European Financial Markets and Market Participants', Merrill Lynch Global Securities Research and Economics Group.

Mundell, R. A. (1961), 'A Theory of Optimum Currency Areas', *American Economic Review*, 51: 657–65.

Norton Rose (1996), 'A Legal Analysis of the Impact of EMU on Financial Obligations', London.

Pagano, M. (1997), 'The Changing Microstructure of European Equity Markets', in G. Ferrarini (ed.), *The European Securities Markets: Implementing the Investment Services Directive and Beyond*, Dordrecht: Kluwer Law International.

Poortvliet, W. and T. P. Laine (1994), 'A Global Trend: Privatization and Reform of Social Security Pension Plans', *Geneva Papers on Risk and Insurance*, 19: 257–86.

Roberts, R. (1994) (ed.), *Global Financial Centers: London, New York, Tokyo*, London: Edward Elgar.

Schröder, H. (1994), 'EMU, What Lessons Can Be Drawn from German Monetary Union', EBA Study (May).

Scobie H. M. (1997), *The Cost and Timescale for the Switchover to the European Single Currency for International Securities Markets*, Zurich: ISMA.

Scott-Quinn, B. (1992), 'Networks and the Changing Structure of the European Securities Industry', *Journal of International Securities Markets*, Autumn: 11–18.

Scott-Quinn, B. and J. Walmsley (1993), *Towards a Single European Securities Markets*, Zurich: ISMA.

Scott-Quinn, B. and J. Walmsley (1997), *The Repo Market in Euro: Making It Work*, Zurich: ISMA.

Solnik, B., C. Boucrelle and Y. Le Fur (1996), 'International Market Correlation and Volatility', *Financial Analyst Journal*, 52 (September/October): 17–34.

Steil, B. (1996), 'The European Equity Markets, a Report of the European Capital Markets Institute', London: Royal Institute of International Affairs.

Stoll, H. (1990), 'Principles of Trading Market Structure', mimeo, Vanderbilt University, 1–42.

Swings, A. (1994), 'Europe's Passage to a Single Currency—A Kredietbank View', in *The Single Currency, an Immense Challenge for the Banks*, Paris: EFMA.

Tschoegl, A. (1996), 'Country and Firm Sources of International Competitiveness: The Case of the Foreign Exchange Market', The Wharton School (September).

von Hagen, J. and M. Neumann (1994), 'Real Exchange Rates within and between Currency Areas: How far away Is EMU', *Review of Economics and Statistics*, 76(2): 236–44.

Part I

The Macroeconomics of EMU

2
EMU, Monetary Policy and Capital Markets

DANIEL GROS AND KAREL LANNOO

1. Introduction

The introduction of the euro will lead to common monetary policy for the participating countries. This will have profound consequences for capital markets as well. This chapter provides therefore a general description of the environment in which monetary policy of the euro area will be conducted. The Treaty obligations together with the Stability Pact for fiscal policy will produce an environment conducive to sustained low inflation and interest rates.

The details of the instruments that will be used by the European Central Bank (ECB) have not yet been decided, because it was not possible to reach a consensus on these detailed technical issues within the European Monetary Institute (EMI). The final decisions will thus be made only by the ECB once it is established, which will happen immediately after the final decision to start EMU has been taken by the Council. However, what is known today is already sufficient to discern two broad tendencies: first, it will take some time before a really unified European capital market emerges, and, secondly, the ECB will be an 'incomplete' central bank. We will come back to these two points at the end after a detailed description of the framework for monetary policy under EMU.

This chapter is organized as follows: we start in Section 2 with a description of the remaining steps that have to be taken to make EMU happen, namely the decision on the convergence criteria and the fixing of the conversion rates. Section 3 describes the framework for the common monetary policy, including the structure of the E(S)CB, its likely monetary policy instruments and targets. Section 4 then discusses other central banking tasks that are not related directly to monetary policy. Section 5 concludes with some reflections on the implications for capital markets.

2. The Remaining Steps towards EMU

The final go-ahead by the European Council came in May 1998 at a special meeting of all the fifteen heads of state and government. At that meeting, the European Council

---

Box 2.1. Establishing the ECB

The timing for the establishment of the ECB is determined in Article 109l, which says:

1. Immediately after the decision on the date for the beginning of the third stage has been taken in accordance with Article 109j(3), or, as the case may be, immediately after 1 July 1998:

   – the Council shall adopt the provisions referred to in Article 106(6);
   – the governments of the member states without a derogation shall appoint, in accordance with the procedure set out in Article 50 of the Statute of the ESCB, the President, the Vice-President and the other members of the Executive Board of the ECB. If there are members with a derogation, the number of members of the Executive Board may be smaller than provided for in Article 11.1 of the Statute of the ESCB, but in no circumstances shall it be less than four.

   As soon as the Executive Board is appointed, the ESCB and the ECB shall be established and shall prepare for their full operation as described in this Treaty and the Statute of the ESCB. The full exercise of their powers shall start from the first day of the third Stage.

2. As soon as the ECB is established, it shall, if necessary, take over the tasks of the EMI. The EMI shall go into liquidation upon the establishment of the ECB; the modalities of liquidation are laid down in the Statute of the EMI.

The reference to Article 109j(3) refers to the possibility that the European Council sets a different date for the start of EMU before the end of 1997. The Council referred to in the first indent is Ecofin.

---

decided that the third stage of EMU should start as foreseen by the Treaty on 1 January 1999.

The ECB was created by the giving of the go-ahead for EMU by the European Council. It will thus start to function in accordance with Article 109l of the Treaty as of 1 July 1998, in the sense that it can take all the decisions concerning the practical implementation of the common monetary policy that are still outstanding as discussed below (the EMI, created in January 1994 to prepare EMU, is automatically liquidated upon the establishment of the ECB). The common monetary policy will, of course, be implemented only after the formal start of Stage Three; that is, after the irrevocable fixing of exchange rates.

2.1. The convergence criteria

The Treaty established with some considerable emphasis the need for a high degree of economic convergence as a precondition for the entry of each member state into EMU (see Box 2.2). The decision on the passage to the third stage was based on the four main criteria:

1. an inflation rate at most 1.5 per cent above that of the three best performers;

Box 2.2. The convergence criteria

The Treaty lists in Article 109j four criteria for evaluating convergence. It is worth citing them completely:

(1) the achievement of a high degree of price stability; this will be apparent from a rate of inflation which is close to that of, at most, the three best performing Member states in terms of price stability;

(2) the sustainability of the government financial position; this will be apparent from having achieved a government budgetary position without a deficit that is excessive as determined in accordance with Article 104c(6);

(3) the observance of the normal fluctuation margins provided for by the exchange rate mechanism of the European Monetary System, for a least two years, without devaluing against the currency of any other Member state;

(4) the durability of convergence achieved by the Member state and of its participation in the exchange-rate mechanism of the European Monetary System being reflected in the long-term interest rate levels.

The four criteria mentioned in this paragraph and the relevant periods over which they are to be respected are developed further in a Protocol annexed to this Treaty.

The separate Protocol clarifies that the first criterion implies that a member state must have reached a rate of inflation, measured by consumer prices, over a period of one year before the examination of at most 1.5 percentage points above the average[a] of the three best national performances. The fourth criterion implies the same condition, but for long-term interest rates, with a slightly larger margin of 2 percentage points.

[a] The formulation in Art. 109j is not unequivocal in this respect, but a subsequent Protocol clarified that the average is indeed the benchmark.

---

2. long-term interest rates at most 2.0 per cent above those of the three best performers in terms of inflation;
3. Exchange Rate Mechanism (ERM) membership without serious fluctuations over the preceding two years; and
4. exemption from the excessive deficit procedure because the general government deficit is below 3 per cent of GDP and the debt to GDP ratio is below 60 per cent or declining at a satisfactory rate.

An additional criterion that is often overlooked is the independence of the central bank. How did member countries measure up on these criteria? Table 2.1 gives an overview of what was expected for 1997 as of November. Two aspects are thus already clear now: first, even among the 'willing' not all countries will be able to participate in the move to the third stage; secondly, the fiscal criteria will be the key hurdle to be overcome for most countries. Most countries are forecast to have a deficit of 3 per cent but many also have a debt ratio above 60 per cent. Moreover, as of mid-1997 it was far from certain that the 3 per cent of GDP deficit target could be fully reached.

Table 2.1. Compliance with criteria for EMU membership as of late 1997

	Inflation[a]	Interest rate[b]	Excessive deficit[c]	ERM membership	Independent central bank
(a) *Effective candidates*					
Belgium	OK	OK	NO (2.7)	OK	OK
Germany	OK	OK	NO (3.0)	OK	OK
Spain	OK	OK	NO (3.0)	OK	OK
France	OK	OK	NO (3.0)	OK	OK
Italy	OK	OK	NO (3.2)	OK	OK
Austria	OK	OK	NO (3.0)	OK	OK
Portugal	OK	OK	NO (3.0)	OK	OK
Finland	OK	OK	OK (1.9)	OK	OK
Ireland	OK	OK	OK (1)	OK	OK
Luxembourg	OK	OK	OK (−1.1)	OK	OK
Netherlands	OK	OK	OK (2.3)	OK	OK
(b) *Non-candidates*					
Denmark	OK	OK	OK (−0.3)	OK	OK
UK	OK	OK	NO (2.9)	NO	OK (NO)[d]
Sweden	OK	OK	NO (2.6)	NO	OK
Greece	NO	NO	NO (4.9)	NO	OK

[a] At most 1.5% above the average of the three best performers.

[b] At most 2% above the average of the three best performers in terms of inflation.

[c] Existence of an excessive deficit: the entry 'NO' means that Ecofin has found the country to have an excessive deficit in the sense of Article 104c; in parentheses is the deficit forecast for 1997 as of May.

[d] Under proposals of the new Blair Government, the Bank of England has become independent to set interest rates while the inflation target is set by the government.

Source: European Commission.

Our evaluation concentrates on the eleven member countries that had shown the political will to participate in EMU. The four 'definite outs' are the UK and Denmark (which are most likely to use their opt-outs), Sweden (which will disqualify itself by not participating in the ERM) and Greece (which, apart from also not being in the ERM, is by common consent too far from meeting any of the convergence criteria to have a chance to participate in EMU by 1999).

Table 2.1 presents a schematic score card. Panel (a) presents the data for the eleven effective candidate countries whereas panel (b) deals with the non-candidates.

The three criteria that pose no problem of interpretation and that will not constitute a hurdle for a decision by the European Council to start EMU on 1 January 1999 are:

1. The criterion concerning price stability (an average inflation rate of at most 1.5 per cent above that of the three best performers) is most likely to be fulfilled by all willing candidates.

2. The criterion concerning interest rates (a long-term interest rate at most 200 basis points above that of the three best performers in terms of inflation) is now fulfilled by all effective candidates (and is likely to be fulfilled also by early 1998).

3. The criterion concerning exchange rate stability (membership in the ERM within 'normal' bands of fluctuations) is now understood to be fulfilled by all countries that were members of the ERM as of end-1996.[1] This includes all member countries with the political will to participate in the first group of EMU.

Independence of the national central bank is implicitly also a criterion, but it is easy to fulfil, provided the country has the political will to enact the necessary legislation.

But there remains one big hurdle: the fiscal criteria. The fact that even by 1997, five years after the ratification of the Treaty, the fiscal criteria still constitute the main hurdle is a powerful reminder that fiscal policy is dictated by domestic political considerations and that it adjusts only very slowly.

All one can say is that the tension between criteria and the deadline that the Treaty contains did put the Council 'between a rock and a hard place'. In particular Germany was put in a delicate position as it has always emphasized that the fiscal criteria needed to be interpreted strictly while its own deficit might well end up slightly above 3 per cent of GDP and its debt to GDP ratio is slightly above 60 per cent and rising (albeit slowly). We would argue that it does not really matter whether the deficit in a given year is 2.99 or 3.1 per cent of GDP. Even a deficit of 3.5 per cent of GDP would not endanger the stability of the euro as long as the sustainability of public finances is assured in the long run.

Could one not argue that even a slight relaxation of the 3 per cent deficit limit would be a signal to financial markets that the euro will be a weak currency, so that long-term interest rates increase? This seems far-fetched: financial markets will base their evaluation of the future stability of the euro mainly on their view of how monetary policy is likely to be set over the long run. Whether the fiscal deficit in some countries was slightly above or below 3 per cent of GDP in 1997 will soon begin to look irrelevant to an assessment of the qualities of the euro.

At any rate, it is likely that the decision in 1998 was, at least partially, forward-looking. The outcome for 1997 was only one element. The decisive argument should be whether future deficits will remain clearly below the reference value under normal economic conditions and without any need for additional drastic measures. Factors such as the trend in financing requirements for the social security system and the structure of tax revenues should thus play an important role. If this were the case, France and Germany would certainly be found to have sustainable fiscal positions provided they continue to reform their social security systems as planned. We therefore see no reason to delay EMU even if one or both have temporarily a deficit slightly in excess of 3 per cent of GDP in 1997. The same could probably be said for a number of other countries as well. But this approach would also imply that a country that plans to reach 3 per cent for 1997, but would not be able to keep the deficit below this level unless it makes serious additional efforts should not join. Moreover, if the debt to

---

[1] When the Treaty was signed, the normal bands were understood to be ±2.25%. In August 1993, the official fluctuation limits were raised to ±15%, but it is generally understood that any currency that were to move in the wide bands would not qualify.

GDP ratio is not declining rapidly, as is the case for Italy, a country might not qualify easily.[2]

Because of the political significance of a common currency, it would be desirable for this final step to be taken at the latest in 2002 by as many member states as possible. But there is little the EU can do to help countries join more quickly. The speed at which the 'willing, but temporarily unable' can join the euro area depends mainly on the domestic political choices these countries are able to make to bring their public finances in order.

2.2. Setting conversion rates

The other main unresolved issue concerning the transition is the setting of the conversion rates. Conversion rates between each national currency and the euro, which will be 'irrevocable', will be set by the Council at the start of the third stage. On what basis should these rates be set? The key to any discussion about the final conversion rates must be the provision in the Treaty that their determination 'shall by itself not modify the external value of the ECU' (Art. 109l(4)). This provision was taken from a regulation that concerned revisions of the ECU basket. It will be shown below that the wording is not really clear in the context of the start of EMU. One interpretation could be that the provision means that the conversion rates have to be equal to the official rate of the ECU as a currency on the last day of business of 1998. The term 'external' in this article refers to the rate of the ECU basket in its totality against any currency.[3] It has, however, given rise to different interpretations, which have sewn much confusion.[4] A strict interpretation could be that the fixing of the conversion rates should not affect the value of the ECU/euro in terms of any currency.

It was often argued in 1996–7, by market participants and officials of the European Monetary Institute, that the conversion rates should be based on average rates of market exchange rates over a given period. This is meant to avoid situations in which a conversion rate is influenced by last-minute speculation and volatility. This suggestion is difficult to implement, however, not only on legal but also on practical grounds.

The legal issue mentioned above can probably not be settled definitively until after either the European Court of Justice or the European Council makes an explicit decision. But if a strict interpretation of 'no change in the external value' cannot be ruled out, any difference between conversion and market rates would be open to legal challenge. This situation should be avoided.

Also, from a practical point of view, a more relaxed interpretation of Article 109l(4) would be difficult. Any discrepancy between the market rates and the conversion rates

---

[2] See Gros (1996) for a concrete proposal on how to judge whether a country makes sufficient progress under this criterion.

[3] A 1978 European Council Resolution on the establishment of the EMS says that revisions of the value of the ECU will not modify the external value of the ECU. It means that weight revisions in the basket (the internal values) will not affect the exchange rate of the ECU (the external value) on the day of the change.

[4] See e.g. Arrowsmith (1996).

would imply large losses for some (and correspondingly gains for others). These losses could be very large indeed. The ratio of nominal assets held by the public to GDP is close to 1 in most member states. If there were only a 1 per cent difference between the conversion rates and the market rates, this would imply losses for holders of assets in one currency potentially equivalent to 1 per cent of GDP—potentially ECU 15 billion for Germany alone.

It is difficult to imagine that the heads of state will be able to agree unanimously on such a move. It would also be difficult to reconcile with the repeated assurances that EMU is not a currency reform and that no one will lose out. Moreover, while a 1 per cent discrepancy between market and conversion rates would lead to large capital gains and losses it would not be sufficient to confer a perceptible competitive advantage or a significant boost to exports. To obtain an economically relevant adjustment through different conversion rates, the adjustment would have to be at least 5 per cent. A capital levy of this order of magnitude would never be acceptable.

Many argue (e.g. Begg *et al.*, 1997) that it is sufficient to announce the conversion rates in advance. Even if a certain set of numbers has been determined and announced to the public in advance, however, there may still be problems. Such an announcement can never command 100 per cent credibility. There will always be interested parties who will complain that a particular currency is undervalued or overvalued. This creates the possibility of two equilibria:

1. Market exchange rates move towards the pre-announced values so that the Council can easily confirm its earlier decision.
2. Market exchange rates do *not* move towards the pre-announced values so that the Council faces a difficult decision at the end of 1998. Either it confirms its earlier decision and incurs the risk of legal action and the political reaction of groups that lose out, or it reverses its earlier decision and adopts a new set of conversion rates. The market will anticipate this uncertainty and price it into interest rates and exchange rates.

The second equilibrium does not have to materialize, but it is difficult to rule it out a priori. If these two equilibria are possible, the last days of 1998 could be characterized by some turbulence as the markets manifest their doubts about the steadfastness of the Council.[5]

The stark contrast between announcing (a rule for) conversion rates beforehand and accepting market rates of the last day (and doing nothing) does not exist in reality. What is certain, however, is that a simple announcement by the European Council that it would use a certain set of bilateral rates (or a certain method) to fix the conversion rates into euros as of the start of Stage Three would not be sufficient *alone*. Such an

[5] What if everything goes wrong and there are wild fluctuations in market rates (±10% for the FRF–DEM rate)? Such a development is only possible if EMU is abandoned. In this case, there will also not be any problem with conversion rates. As long as the preparations for EMU proceed more or less as planned, there is no reason for speculative attacks on the FRF–DEM rate because there is absolutely no indication that this rate is misaligned.

announcement would be of little value in the absence of any simultaneous agreement between the participating central banks to defend these rates.

The key point is whether the participating central banks will insist until the end on the 'indivisibility' of monetary policy that has prevented any real cooperation so far or whether they are willing to anticipate *de facto* EMU by half a year. Gros and Lannoo (1996) propose that the Council, in agreement with the participating central banks (and, of course, the EMI/ECB), should declare that a certain grid of bilateral rates[6] represented in its view equilibrium rates that would constitute an appropriate basis for the conversion rates to be fixed on the first day of Stage Three. In order to give potential speculators less of a fixed target it would be useful to have a small band of fluctuations around the rates that have been declared to be the basis for the conversion rates, but this is not crucial. The most important part of the package would be an agreement among the participating central banks that they would defend these rates. The national central banks should stand ready to intervene with increasing amounts because the 'indivisibility' argument should become more and more untenable as EMU approaches. On the last working day of 1998 national central banks should be willing to intervene with unlimited amounts since at that point the distribution of national money supplies becomes really irrelevant for price stability.

The key for a stable pre-EMU period is thus the willingness of national central banks (and in particular of the Bundesbank) to effectively anticipate EMU. Speculative attacks will become highly unlikely if the national central banks that will participate in EMU a few months later agree among themselves to intervene with unlimited amounts.

In what market should the intervention take place? In general central banks prefer to intervene in the spot market but in this special case one could argue that an exception should be made. In this case one could argue that intervention should take place in the *forward* foreign exchange markets, namely on contracts maturing on the last working day of 1998. Once the decision on what countries will participate in EMU has been taken the criterion regarding exchange rate stability becomes inoperative. National central banks will then be perceived to be less concerned about the spot exchange rate during the run-up to December 1998. Moreover, the only important rates should be the conversion rates which will hold forever and they have to be based only on the market rates of the last day of 1998. Hence national central banks should aim directly at this target. Intervening only in the forward market would give national central banks the choice to let either interest rates or the cash exchange rate take the strain if there really are speculative attacks.

It is often argued that some countries will be tempted to engineer a last-minute depreciation of their currency to given them a better competitive starting position. For

---

[6] Using current market rates is, of course, based on the view that the current grid of exchange rates (which in turn is close to the central rates of the ERM, except for the Irish pound) is economically acceptable in the sense that there is no clear sign that any currency is misaligned (with the possible exception of the DEM, which looks a bit overvalued by many indicators). This view also implies that the market should not see a need for exchange rate changes—a view that is compatible with the very small interest rate differentials in the core EMS.

anybody familiar with the working of the EU, and the Council in particular, this sounds far-fetched. Even if some (parts of some) governments had such (secret) dreams they would have difficulties in implementing them since national central banks are independent. What central banker would actually take any concrete action to weaken his own currency? Loose talk about the desirability of a weaker national currency might of course come from politicians (former ones and from the opposition). But it is not likely that such talk will be taken seriously by financial markets.

This leaves the issue of self-fulfilling speculative attacks under which financial markets push the central bank into such high interest rates that it has no choice but to give in and conduct an expansionary policy. However, the potential for this type of attack must be much lower in 1998 than in the past. First, speculators have learnt by experience that attacks on exchange rates that were close to their equilibrium (i.e. the ones inside the core) did not work in the past. Secondly, and more importantly, national central banks under attack would have to endure higher interest rates for just a short while, at most until the end of 1998. Their willingness to resist should thus be much stronger than in the past. As financial markets know this they must rate the possibility of an attack succeeding rather low.

A worst-case scenario might be instructive: assume that markets assign a 10 per cent probability that France (or Spain or any other confirmed participant) will suddenly engineer a devaluation to enter EMU with a FF–DM rate 10 per cent below the rate prevailing during early 1998. In this case the interest rate differential on six-month instruments required to keep the exchange rate constant would be 2 per cent by June of that year. This should be bearable. The differential would rise over time and reach infinity the last second before trading stops if financial markets do not change their evaluation of the intentions of the country that has been suspected of the intention to devalue. By October the interest rate differential on three-month instruments would be 4 per cent, but this would not last long. Enterprises might want to wait with their investments until the uncertainty is removed, but again the impact cannot be too severe since there is a definite end to the waiting period.

Large forward market interventions should make it even less likely that markets hold expectations of the type outlined above. If the central bank that has been attacked has a large amount of forward contracts outstanding, markets know that it will have to weigh the immediate losses on these contracts against the supposed long-term gain for the country of entering EMU with a better competitive position.

It should be clear that it will not be possible to fix the conversion rates of the national currencies into the euro before the start of the third stage. At that date all ECU-denominated assets have to be converted into euros, since the ECU also contains some non-EMU currencies whose exchange rates can in no case be fixed and are likely to fluctuate quite strongly during the transition period.

3. The Environment for the Common Monetary Policy

3.1. The governing bodies of the ESCB: centre vs. national central banks

The ESCB will consist of a central institution, the European Central Bank (ECB), and the national central banks of EU member states that have joined the final stage (Art. 1). The ECB (located in Frankfurt) will have two governing bodies: the Executive Board and the Governing Council.[7] The Executive Board will have *up to* six members: a President, a Vice-President and up to four other members (Art. 11). The Board members will be nominated by the European Council for a maximum period of eight years, not renewable, after the Ecofin Council has given its opinion, and after consultations with the European Parliament and the Governing Council of the ECB. (If Italy and the UK do not participate from the start it is possible that initially only four Board members will be nominated.)

The Governing Council (Art. 10) will comprise the (up to) six members constituting the Executive Board and the governors of the participating national central banks (Art. 10, see also Art. 109l of the Treaty, cited in Box 2.3). The terms of office of the latter shall be no less than five years (Art. 14.2). All members of Council will have one vote (Art. 10.2).[8] This last provision is very important. Acceptance of the one-man-one-vote principle must be seen as an important concession by Germany (and to a smaller extent by other large member states). It was obtained in return for the explicit mandate to preserve price stability and the high degree of independence for the ESCB as discussed below. Together with assured long periods of tenure, and the role of the ECB Governing Council in nominations for the Executive Board, the voting rule should ensure that this decisive policy-making body develops a high degree of cohesiveness and collegiality. Weighted voting could have fostered the thinking that governors were primarily representing national interests and not equal members of a collegiate body charged with formulating a common policy for Europe.

The Governing Council is vested with the main overall authority: 'The Governing Council shall formulate the monetary policy of the Community including, as appropriate, decisions relating to intermediate monetary objectives, key interest rates and the supply of reserves in the system, and shall establish the necessary guidelines for their implementation' (Art. 12.1). But as policy could hardly be set in sufficient detail by a Council likely to meet only on a monthly basis this paragraph continues with 'The Executive Board shall implement monetary policy . . .'. Moreover, the Executive Board

---

[7] Central bank governors from EU countries which have not entered the third stage of EMU will not take part in the joint decisions in the Governing Council of the ECB, as foreseen by Art. 109k of the Treaty, which states that, in the case of some member states having been given a derogation in the final stage of EMU, the voting rights for the representatives of the central bank governors concerned on the ECB Council will be suspended. The 'out' governors will have a seat on the ECB *General* Council, which has, however, no influence on monetary policy.

[8] This principle does not apply to voting on financial matters (distribution of profits and loss), for which a special key, based on objective criteria, will be set and revised every five or ten years (Art. 28).

Box 2.3. The legal framework

The legal framework for the practical steps to the single currency is limited to one paragraph in a Treaty article: Art. 109l(4) of the Treaty says that the Council shall

> at the starting date of the third stage ... adopt the conversion rates at which their currencies will be irrevocably fixed and at which irrevocably fixed rate the ECU shall be substituted for these currencies, and the ECU will become a currency in its own right. This measure shall by itself not modify the external value of the ECU. The Council shall act with the unanimity of the member states without a derogation, on a proposal from the Commission and after consulting the European Central Bank.

It furthermore says that

> the Council shall ... take the other measures necessary for the rapid introduction of the ECU as the single currency.

The Madrid Council (December 1995) agreed that 'the specific name Euro will be used instead of the generic term ECU' as 'the agreed and definite interpretation of the relevant Treaty provisions'. The name of the common currency was thus changed from ECU to euro. The Council also adopted a detailed changeover scenario for the introduction of the euro:

1. The decision on the participating member states will be taken as soon as possible in 1998, and the European Central Bank (ECB) will be created at that time to allow preparations to be completed and full operation to start on 1 January 1999.
2. As from 1 January 1999, the exchange rates among the currencies of the participating member states and the euro will be fixed. The single monetary policy will be defined and implemented by the European System of Central Banks (ESCB) in euros (Stage 3A). The ESCB will intervene in the euro on the foreign exchange markets and will encourage its use on these markets. Participating member states will issue new tradable debt in euros.
3. No later than three years after the start of EMU, the euro will be introduced for retail transactions through a big bang (Stage 3B). At most six months later, the euro will become the sole legal tender.

Two Council regulations (a legal instrument directly applicable in the member states) provide for the legal framework for the euro. The first is based on Art. 235 of the Treaty (to be adopted unanimously by all member states) and was adopted in June 1997. It regards the name of the currency, the rules of rounding, the equivalence 1 ECU = 1 euro, the use of decimals and the continuity of contracts. The regulation confirms that the ECU basket will cease to exist at the start of EMU and that the ECU will be substituted by the euro at the rate of one to one in contracts which refer to the official ECU basket.

The second regulation, based on Art. 109l(4), will be adopted by the Council immediately after the decision on the participating EMU members has been taken. It confirms that the currency of the participating member states is the euro as from 1 January 1999 onwards. The currency unit shall be 1 euro, which shall be divided into 100 cents. This regulation furthermore settles some transitional issues regarding the irrevocability of the conversion rates and the changeover of public debt. Its Art. 6 determines:

> (1) The euro shall be divided into the national currency units according to the conversion rates. ... Subject to the provisions of this regulation the monetary law of the participating Member states shall continue to apply.
> (2) Where in a legal instrument reference is made to a national currency unit, this reference shall be as valid as if reference were made to the euro unit.

implements policy 'including by giving the necessary instructions to national central banks' (Art. 12.1). This formulation leaves no doubt as to the hierarchical nature of the system.

In reality, however, important practical issues concerning the division of responsibilities for implementing policies between the ECB and the participating national central banks have been left open, since the Statutes stipulate that[9] 'To the extent deemed possible and appropriate and without prejudice to the provisions of this Article [i.e. the capacity to give instructions], the ECB shall have recourse to the national central banks to carry out operations which form part of the tasks of the ESCB' (Art. 12.1).

A further element that highlights the uneasy balance between the centre and the participating national central banks is that the ECB Board members will have only (up to) six votes out of a total number of votes in the Governing Council of, initially, between fourteen (if only eight member states qualify for EMU, but still six Board members are nominated) and twenty-one if all member states join. That latter number will rise further as EU membership widens. This minority position resembles that of the Bundesbank Board (Direktorium) prior to 1992 with (up to) seven members and a Council (Rat) with a total (maximum) of eighteen members given that there were eleven presidents of *Landeszentralbanken*. However, in Germany all significant monetary policy operations are centralized in Frankfurt, which makes up for any perception of weakness at the centre. Moreover, even in Germany a need was felt to redress the balance when five new *Länder* joined. The sixteen members representing *Länder* were reduced to nine so that currently the balance is eight to nine (for a total of seventeen).

In the United States, the Federal Open Market Committee (FOMC), which meets every five to six weeks, has functions analogous to those envisaged for the ECB Governing Council in setting monetary objectives and in formulating guidelines for the main policy instrument, open market operations, to be undertaken through the Federal Reserve Bank of New York. The FOMC meetings are attended by the seven members of the Board of Governors, nominated by the President of the United States, subject to confirmation by the US Senate, and the twelve Presidents of the regional Federal Reserve Banks. Out of the latter only five have the right to vote at any one meeting, so the majority lies with the Board—provided they agree, obviously. The central position of the Board is further underlined by the attribution to it alone of two important policy instruments: discount rate changes and variations in reserve requirements. The Board of Governors accordingly has a dominant influence both on decisions and on implementation of policy.

---

[9] Some central banks had aimed for more decentralization than this wording suggests and an alternative proposal was for the ECB Executive Board to delegate to national central banks 'to the *full* extent possible'. Why was this formulation not adopted and why did the drafters of the Statute in the end opt for a more centralized mode of operation? They were concerned about the potential weakness of the central institution and its Executive Board, the members of which will be in a minority in the Council, and the implications for the efficiency of operations. The experience of monetary policy execution in the two large federal countries— the United States and Germany—whose central banking legislation has in a number of respects inspired the Statute is relevant in this context.

A first comparison of the ESCB with either of the two main federal models—the Deutsche Bundesbank and the Federal Reserve System—in their present form must arrive at the conclusion that the ECB Executive Board is likely to have a relatively weaker position with respect to both decision-making and policy implementation than both its German and US counterparts. The Board will be squeezed from one side by the Governing Council, the repository of all major policy-making authority, and from the other side by the participating national central banks, anxious to preserve as many operational tasks as possible, partly to retain influence for themselves, partly to defend the perceived interests of their employees. The national governors will argue, on the basis of the principle of subsidiarity, that they can implement policy at least as efficiently as a new and inexperienced operational centre at the ECB under the daily management of the Board.

The ambition to decentralize policy implementation 'to the full extent possible' will have an impact on capital markets because it implies that many of the idiosyncrasies that characterize at present local capital (and especially money) markets will tend to be preserved. Incentives to retain operations in the national financial centres, arising from the desire (1) to protect the employment of specialized staff in the central banks and (2) to extend favours to the private financial institutions in a particular country, would remain.

1. Regarding staff, EU15 central banks together currently employ over 60,000.[10] Total employment in the Federal Reserve System which performs similar tasks, including supervisory and reporting functions, to those to be assigned to the ECB and the national central banks in a future EMU, is less than half this number. Some European central banks operate in a highly decentralized way; both the Bundesbank and Banque de France have more than 200 branches or suboffices. While private financial institutions undergo rapid restructuring, and mergers are common regardless of the size of the partners, central banks appear to modify their operations much more slowly. Decentralization within countries has, as for local and regional public administrations, encountered resistance to change, particularly to the extent that employment is at stake. Table 2.2 shows that the number of central bank staff per million inhabitants ranges from 294 for Belgium to 83 for Spain, with an EU15 average of 160, against 82 for the USA and 50 for Japan.

National central banks are difficult to compare. Differences in geography, financial structure and historically inherited tasks can explain some of the striking differences in staffing. For example, some undertake extensive printing activities beyond those related to the note issue; others—of which the largest, the Banque de France, with about 17,000 employees, is the prime example—are heavily involved in the production of economic statistics, the analysis of company financial statements, etc. Some of these additional activities might be only marginally affected by the move to a single currency and the evolution of the ESCB. Yet the centralization of monetary authority provides

---

[10] The total wage and salary bill may be close to ECU 3–4 billion. Running Europe's monetary systems is a relatively labour-intensive industry.

Table 2.2. Employment in EU national central banks, 1996

	Staff	Population (m.)	Staff per m. population
Austria	1,194	8.0	149
Belgium	2,980	10.1	294
Denmark	560	5.2	107
Finland	883	5.1	173
France	16,917	58.0	292
Germany	17,632	81.6	216
Greece	2,964	10.4	284
Ireland	583	3.6	163
Italy	9,307	57.2	163
Luxembourg	100	0.4	246
Netherlands	1,611	15.4	104
Portugal	1,757	9.9	177
Spain	3,269	39.2	83
Sweden	826	8.8	94
UK	4,170	58.3	72
Total EU 15	64,753	403.5	160
USA	23,727	290.7	82
Japan	6,300	125.0	50

Sources: Eurostat; *The Morgan Stanley Central Bank Directory 1996*, pp. xvii–xviii.

an occasion for the governing bodies of the national central banks to look critically at their own use of resources and to break the inertia of their past practices. The ECB itself should avoid a repetition of the national experience of many of its participants of excessive decentralization of technical, labour-intensive functions, such as the distribution of means of payments and rediscount operations with localized collateral. Differences in this respect will also give regional financial markets a 'national' flavour.

2. *De facto* banks will be able to obtain funds from the ESCB, mainly from the central bank of their own country of origin (because that is where most of their capital is). This is analogous to access to US Federal Reserve credit only through the regional Reserve bank in one's own district.

To the extent that the timing of additions to or withdrawals from bank reserves is left to the discretion of the individual national central banks, risks of favouritism extended by the latter would arise, even if they had no financial consequences for the central bank concerned.

One could easily imagine that a national central bank anticipating a rise in interest rates in the area as a whole would advance the execution of a liquidity injection, for example through a one-month purchase/resale transaction with its commercial banks, hence effectively providing the latter cheaper credit than banks in other participating countries. This would be a further element that would give local money markets a 'national' character. Clarification of these potentially important operational issues will not come until the implementation of the final stage approaches and the ECB has been set up in 1998 and after some experience of harmonizing the methods of coordinating domestic money market operations on a voluntary basis has been gained.[11]

3.2. Pooling of foreign exchange reserves

Even before the euro has replaced national currencies, the dollar and other third currencies will be quoted and traded effectively against only the euro. Decisions on the location of foreign exchange market interventions will actually represent a delicate issue. Should the ECB develop its own contacts with foreign exchange markets or should it go via the national central banks? If it chooses the latter how should intervention be 'distributed' across different financial centres and what if foreign exchange trading concentrates? These questions have yet to receive an answer. The EMI (1997: 26, point 5.3) says only that 'The selection of counterparts for foreign exchange intervention operations will follow a uniform approach irrespective of the chosen organisational set-up for the ESCB's external operations. Such a policy shall not entail a substantial departure from existing market standards and it will be derived by harmonising NCBs' current best practices.'

The importance of foreign exchange intervention in the common monetary policy will also be affected by the size of the foreign exchange reserves of the ECB. A priori one might have thought that the full and definitive transfer of ownership of all international reserve assets, excluding holdings of EMS currencies and ECUs, from the national level to the ECB would have been a logical step to take to mark the irrevocable nature of the final stage.[12]

The ESCB Statute (Art. 30) only says that national central banks are to endow the ECB initially with non-EU currency reserves up to ECU 50 billion. The key for contributions will be based on that for capital subscriptions, viz. weights determined equally by the national shares in EU population and GDP (Art. 29.1).

Is this sum sufficient? One might as well take as an example the USA, which has the same size as the likely euro area. In this case, the ECU 50 billion foreseen by the Treaty

---

[11] According to reports in the financial press in 1997 there has been increasing support in the EMI Council for decentralizing operations to the maximum extent possible, despite the initial rejection of this notion. Many European central banks, including the Banque de France—an initial supporter of centralization—and the Bundesbank, seem to be attracted by the model of the US Federal Reserve System, where the Federal Reserve Board does not itself engage in either money market or foreign exchange operations, but delegates these activities to the New York Fed. In EMU one would even go further, because operations could there be conducted by any participating central bank. Such a system seems unnecessarily cumbersome and would require elaborate information and monitoring procedures on the part of the ECB.

[12] A country which had transferred all means of defending its exchange rate to the ECB would clearly be seen as a credible member of EMU. This is at the same time an explanation of why such a step is not contemplated; member states are not prepared to face the implications or to negotiate dissolution provisions in case one or more member states subsequently want to leave. The Bank of England objected to the transfer of ownership of reserves to the ESCB and considered an agreement to put a predetermined amount of reserves at joint disposal as sufficient. A further complication in the UK—and some other cases—is that the central bank does not own international reserves assets, but would have to have ownership transferred to it from the government prior to participation in pooling.

Table 2.3. ECB shares and potential foreign exchange pooling

	% Share in ECB	Contribution/ call-up (ECU bn.)	Actual reserves (ECU bn.)	'Surplus' (ECU bn.)
Belgium	2.8	1.4	12.3	10.9
Denmark	1.7	0.8	10.7	9.9
Germany	22.5	11.3	60.5	49.2
Greece	2.0	1.0	13.8	12.8
Spain	8.8	4.4	44.6	40.2
France	17.0	8.5	18.5	10.0
Ireland	0.8	0.4	6.2	5.8
Italy	15.8	7.9	35.2	27.3
Luxembourg	0.1	0.1	0.0	−0.1
Netherlands	4.2	2.1	19.2	17.1
Austria	2.3	1.2	17.1	15.9
Portugal	1.8	0.9	12.3	11.4
Finland	1.7	0.8	5.0	4.2
Sweden	2.9	1.5	14.5	13.0
UK	15.3	7.7	29.6	21.9
Total	100.0	50.0	299.4	249.4

Notes: data for end-1996, but November 96 for Austria. Totals might not add up to 100% because of rounding.

Source: own calculations based on EMI *Annual Report 1996* and IMF, *International Financial Statistics*, April 1997.

appear generous, since they would be considerably more than what is held today by the USA. Even a pro rata reduction for the non-participation of the UK and some smaller countries (about 20 per cent) would still leave the ECB with about the same amount as the two US foreign exchange authorities combined, namely about ECU 40 billion.[13]

Table 2.3 gives the official percentage shares of member countries in the EMI, which will correspond closely to those in the ECB. They are based on the average of GDP and population weights, both of which are unlikely to change significantly in the short run.

Financial markets will be affected by the way in which member countries dispose of the more than ECU 200 billion in these excess reserves (mainly in dollars). Article 31.2 states that operations in such assets 'shall be subject to approval by the ECB in order to ensure consistency with the exchange rate and monetary policies of the Community'. This may be a sufficiently clear guideline to avoid outright challenges to the authority of the new monetary institution. However, the greater visibility of the 'excess' reserves at the time of partial pooling into the ECB may make additional initiatives necessary. It should be made clear that these reserve assets are henceforth to be regarded as long-term investments in the currencies concerned rather than as an 'overhang', the disposal of which poses threats of instability and of downward pressure on the dollar.

---

[13] There are two monetary authorities in the USA that hold foreign exchange reserves: the Federal Reserve and the US Treasury Exchange Stabilization Fund. As of end-1996 both held about 20 billion dollars worth of mainly DM and yen (and some Mexican pesos!).

In the previous subsection we discussed briefly recent support for the idea of decentralizing operations to the individual national central banks. If that process is extended to foreign exchange operations as now seems likely, the distinction between the reserves of up to ECU 50 billion which are pooled and the rest, which we have reviewed in the present subsection, will lose some of its significance in the eyes of market participants. All of the gold and dollar reserves will still be held by the individual central banks, though the degree of usability for interventions will depend on whether the reserves are earmarked as legally belonging to the ECB or not. This will not enhance the credibility of the external policy of the euro area. Given the large differences in reserve holdings, this is another potential reason why 'national' markets (even for foreign exchange) might be slightly differentiated.

3.3. Supervision and other central banking tasks

With respect to those tasks not strictly related to monetary policy, the problem is how to reconcile the efficiency of operations and the ambition to decentralize. Article 3 of the Statute mentions as the final task of the ESCB that it should 'contribute to the smooth conduct of policies pursued by the competent authorities relating to the prudential supervision of credit institutions and the stability of the financial system'. National central banks start with a clear comparative advantage over the ECB and its Board with respect to familiarity with the financial institutions in their territory, particularly to the extent that they already exercise supervisory functions nationally. Not all do, however—in half of the EU member states, supervisory authority is vested in a separate government agency and not in the central bank—and there is disagreement between, say, the UK and German authorities as to the desirable degree of responsibility for financial stability to be exercised by a central bank mandated to pursue a monetary policy oriented towards low inflation. A potential conflict between the execution of these two tasks exists if a central bank is seen to be generous in its efforts to prevent financial instability by injecting additional liquidity. Yet all potential participants exercise some lender-of-last-resort function and that could hardly be performed in a fully centralized way. Nor is that the case in existing Federal systems such as in the United States. Some discretion within pre-specified limits would have to be left with the individual participating central banks. The issue is discussed in fuller detail in Section 4 in the context of the discussion on the ECB rule.

3.4. The incomplete monetary union, 1999–2002

Between 1999 and 2002, only a core of operations has to be carried out in euros. The private sector will be free to change to the euro for all other operations at any time during the three-year period: the basic principle is 'no compulsion, no prohibition' in the use of the euro. The euro will not be available in physical form, but a Council regulation will provide for the legally enforceable equivalence between the euro and the participating national currency units.

This official reference scenario had to be based on the premise that before the euro becomes the sole legal tender, the authorities cannot force the private sector to use it instead of national currency. The critical mass has therefore to be created only from transactions that involve the official institutions. The private sector will have to be convinced on purely economic grounds. And that might be difficult, because the use of a currency involves external economic effects which are similar to the network economies in telecommunications: the marginal cost of using a particular currency depends on how much it is used. A widely used currency usually has lower transactions costs.

If everyone in the private retail sector is using only national currencies, it will not be in the interest of any single private operator to switch to the euro. If the euro is already widely used, however, it might be in the interest of many private operators to start using it too. Hence, there are two possible equilibria for Stage 3A: (1) the euro is used only where mandated, or (2) the euro is used widely even where not mandated. Under the second equilibrium, transactions cost might be lower, but the private sector would not go to this equilibrium on its own because no individual operator would have an interest to take the first step.

A key determinant for a fast take-off is thus the initial size of the market in euros. At present, there are only three areas where the euro will be used with some certainty: monetary policy operations, public debt and interbank operations. The use of the euro in a fourth area, that of non-bank deposits, is much less certain, since the greatest share is held by households. The three latter issues are discussed below, while the first is discussed in Section 3.5.

3.4.1. *Public debt*

Under the official changeover scenario, only *new tradable* debt has to be issued in euros, implying that it might take some time to generate liquidity in euro-denominated debt. It is, however, becoming more and more likely that a substantial proportion of the existing stock of national debt will be converted into euros. The French Treasury already indicated in early 1996 that all its outstanding debt would be converted into euros from the start, which would immediately create a deep euro market with prod-ucts of different maturities. The Belgian government indicated in its changeover plan that the linear bonds (OLOs or dematerialized bonds), which amount to 65 per cent of the total Belgian debt, will be transformed into euros. State notes, which are generally held by households, might still be issued in BEF during the transition, 'owing to the fact that they are intended specifically for individuals'.[14] Also the Austrian, Dutch, Finnish and Italian governments have given assurances in this direction. The German govern-ment is also thinking about changing the bunds, but federal government debt only amounts to about half of the total German debt and the debt of the *Länder* and *Ge-meinden* (the other half) is usually in a non-tradable form.

The main reason for redenominating outstanding debt is to guarantee the irrevoc-

---

[14] Belgian Ministry of Finance, *National Changeover Plan*, August 1996.

ability of the changeover to the single currency. If governments offer to convert their public debt into euros, all wholesale markets will change as well. The single largest holders of government debt in the EU are households, but this does not imply that they will come directly into contact with the euro. Their government debt is often held indirectly via unit trusts and other savings instruments. In the countries where banks are big holders of government debt, over 50 per cent of the asset side of their balance sheet will be in euros, whereas the liabilities side would predominantly remain in national currency (deposits) in the transition period, unless banks convince their clients to use the euro for savings deposits.

Conversion of outstanding debt securities is not so easy to achieve, however. It depends on many elements, the most obvious being the liquidity of the paper, the holders, the currency denomination and the physical nature of government debt. Dematerialized bonds can be converted more easily than paper bonds. Conversion of debt physically held by households will be more difficult than conversion of that held by institutional investors, which is kept by professional custodians. Conversion will also apply only to debt held in currencies of the EMU member states. There are finally some tax considerations, which cannot be neglected. Households might consider an official conversion a form of wealth control, which governments might like to use for other purposes as well.

Redenomination also poses a number of technical problems, such as trading of odd denominations, cash repayments for renominalizations, risks of mismatches, etc. Because of this host of legal, tax and practical problems, redenomination will be limited to public bonds. The case of redenominating for private issuers is much less strong, since the costs do not outweigh the benefits.

The conversion of public debt also represents an element of the competition for the position of leading financial centre in EMU and the contest to become the euro-bond benchmark issuer. Although the total volume of German public debt is much higher, French government paper is almost totally dematerialized, which should make it much easier to convert it at once into euros than German public debt. Furthermore, French government bonds cover the maturity spectrum more evenly than the German bunds, and thus provide sufficient liquidity in all segments of the market. Hence French debt might be a more suitable benchmark.

If the outstanding stock of tradable debt is not converted, financial markets will have difficulties in keeping the link between the cash market and futures and/or options on public debt, as these forward-looking financial instruments have to be based on the new euro debt.

3.4.2. *Interbank operations*

In the most likely EMU candidate countries, interbank operations constitute about 33 per cent (or 28 per cent excluding Luxembourg) of the overall balance sheet of the banking system. It is likely that most of these will be converted into euros because the wholesale interbank market is closely linked to the execution of monetary policy. Moreover, interbank operations will have to be redenominated in euros to be

Table 2.4. Size of interbank deposits in selected
EU countries, 1994

	ECU bn.	% Of balance sheet
Belgium	162.6	32.9
Denmark	24.3	21.6
France	936.8	39.0
Germany	644.3	21.3
Italy	86.4	6.7
Luxembourg	267.6	60.1
Netherlands	121.6	18.3
Spain	110.1	15.8
Austria	108.7	29.0
UK	146.1	15.7
Total	2,608.5	26.0

Source: OECD (1996).

Table 2.5. Sectoral distribution of monetary aggregates in France and Germany, 1995
(in national currency)

	Germany		France	
	DEM bn.	% Shares	FRF bn.	% Shares
M3	2,007.4		5,478.5	
Minus savings deposits	−750.3		−2,215.5	
M2	1,257.1		3,263.0	
Minus time deposits	−441.0		−1,446.0	
of which:				
Corporate sector	110.7	25.1	3.4	0.2
Households	285.8	64.7	1,442.4	99.8
Public sector	45.1	10.2	0.2	0.0
M1	816.1		1,817.0	
Minus demand deposits	−578.6		−1,561.1	
of which:				
Corporate sector	196.6	33.9	433.4	27.8
Households	352.0	60.7	948.0	60.7
Public sector	31.3	5.4	179.7	11.5
Cash	237.5		255.9	
Shares in M3				
Cash	11.8		4.7	
M1	40.7		33.2	
M2	62.6		59.6	

Sources: Banque de France and Deutsche Bundesbank.

processed by the TARGET payment system. The total of interbank deposits for Austria, the Benelux countries, France and Germany amounted to ECU 2,241 billion in 1994, or 57 per cent of the GDP of these countries (see Table 2.4).

This implies that from early 1999 onwards bank deposits in euros of over 2.2 trillion will already exist. This is again a stock, but interbank deposits are traded frequently; hence this will be a very active and liquid market segment in euros.

3.4.3. *Non-bank deposits*

About 75 per cent of non-bank deposits (i.e. the money supply) originates in the household sector, which is likely to be guided by different considerations than the corporate sector in its choice of currency. Table 2.5 shows the proportion of the different monetary aggregates held by households, the corporate sector and the public sector in Germany and France. It is apparent that almost all long-term deposits are held by households, and that the share of the corporate sector is higher for short-term deposits. One has to keep in mind that a large fraction of the demand deposits of the corporate sector are likely to arise from their dealings with households.

A significant fraction of non-bank deposits will thus be converted into euros only if households start to use them more. Households are likely to continue using the national currency, but might through their holdings of government and other securities become familiar with the euro as a financial instrument.

3.5. Monetary strategy and instruments

The overriding goal of the common monetary policy is price stability. This goal has been enshrined in the Treaty in very clear terms (see Box 2.4), which is a remarkable political agreement. The wording is less ambiguous than that of the Bundesbank Act of 1957, which defines the main responsibility of the German central bank to be 'the safeguarding of the value of the currency' (Art. 3), while 'the [Bundes]bank should support the economic policy of the government, but can not be subjected to instructions by the

---

Box 2.4. Price stability as the primary objective

Article 2 of the ESCB Statute states:

> In accordance with Article 105(1) of this Treaty, the primary objective of the ESCB shall be to maintain price stability. Without prejudice to the objective of price stability, it shall support the general economic policies in the Community with a view to contributing to the achievement of the objectives of the Community as laid down in Article 2 of this Treaty. The ESCB shall act in accordance with the principle of an open market economy with free competition, favouring an efficient allocation of resources, and in compliance with the principles set out in Article 3a of this Treaty.

This formulation is repeated in Art. 3a of the Maastricht Treaty.

latter' (Art. 12). This leaves more room for interpretation than the ESCB Statute. Other central banks in the Community, particularly those with statutes dating back to the 1930s or 1940s, when the ambition to integrate monetary policy fully into government decision-making was at a peak, operate under legal mandates that are far less clear with respect to the ordering of macroeconomic objectives and more open to the imposition of the preferences of the government at any point in time.

It would be a mistake to attach exclusive importance to legal texts in predicting the future performance of the ESCB. Some national central banks with no special emphasis on price stability in their statutory obligations and little formal independence of their political authorities have nevertheless over an extended period proved able to pursue policies—e.g. through participation in the EMS—which implied these characteristics. Yet it is significant that governments—and not just central banks—in the EU are prepared to subscribe to a clear and permanent, almost lexicographic ordering of their preferences with respect to the objectives of their joint monetary policy. Given the unanimity of central bankers on this point and the absence of any identifiable inflationary pressures it is thus likely that the ECB will in fact be willing and able to pursue its assigned task. The choice of monetary policy targets and instruments has to be seen in this perspective as well, since they constitute the only means by which the ECB can reach its aim of price stability.

3.5.1. *Strategy*

As regards monetary strategy, the EMI Council has opted for a combination of an inflation target for the longer-term framework and a monetary aggregate target. Three other possibilities were rejected: interest rate pegging (because of well-known theoretical objections to the stabilizing properties of such a system), exchange rate targeting (because the Treaty gives little emphasis to this objective, which is appropriate given that the euro area will be relatively closed) and nominal income targeting (*inter alia* because it would also not relate directly to the goal of price stability). The dismissal of this third option is arguably a bit summary, but the two alternatives retained probably suffice to give the ECB the appropriate guidance.

Given the primary role of price stability in the Treaty's assignment of tasks to the ESCB, it is unavoidable that this objective will have to figure as an essential objective. The EMI (1997) adds the important element that there should be a quantified definition of this ultimate objective so as to facilitate the accountability of the joint monetary policy.

However, an inflation objective is not enough: the time-lags between monetary policy actions and their impact on inflation are simply too long to offer sufficient guidance for setting policy on a weekly basis. A first requirement for this strategy to work is for the ECB to develop and make publicly known its inflation forecast one to two years ahead and to contrast it with the quantitative objective. Any discrepancy will constitute the background to the use of the monetary instruments.

Countries which have experience with inflation targeting, notably the United Kingdom within Europe, have found it useful to develop intermediate objectives which can help to assess the risks to price stability. At the insistence of the Bundesbank, which has had favourable experience with monetary aggregates and especially over the past decade with broad money (M3), the latter seems likely to be given the role of prime indicator of future inflation and hence of a useful intermediate objective once it has been demonstrated that its useful qualities carry over into the EMU period. The beginning of Stage Three of EMU is clearly equivalent to a major monetary reform, which makes it uncertain whether the stability in the relationship of broad money to nominal income which has been found in the aggregate for the likely EMU participants (see *inter alia* Monticelli and Papi, 1996) will persist beyond 1999. Most observers believe that the relationship between past and future prices as well as the relationship between prices and the business cycle should not be much affected by the introduction of the euro. Hence the initial emphasis is likely to gravitate towards the inflation-targeting mode. This implies that the indicator to be used for short-run policy changes is likely to be some price index for the euro area. Although the CPI (consumer price index) will probably be the most-used index, other indexes (wholesale prices, wages) are also likely to be used.

The degree to which money demand will no longer be predictable for the first few years of EMU is difficult to gauge. Some observers (e.g. von Hagen, 1997) have argued that the introduction of the euro should leave the money demand for transactions purposes unaffected whereas the demand for precautionary purposes (including savings deposits) might become more unstable as the evolution of interest and inflation rates becomes more uncertain. However, as shown above, most money is held by households, which might not notice EMU until 2002. The transactions pattern of households is indeed likely to be unaffected by the introduction of the euro. But one could argue that for firms the opposite is true: their transactions and payments pattern might be strongly affected as international transactions play a much more important role for the corporate sector. One would expect that the economies of scale in treasury that come with the single currency should lead to a significant reduction in the transactions demand by the corporate sector. Since the corporate sector holds about 30 per cent of all transactions money this impact on the overall narrow monetary aggregate M1 might be limited. The demand for cash, which is presumably used mainly by households, should be completely unaffected until 2002. For savings deposits, again held almost exclusively by households, it is difficult to predict what will happen. Why should the irrevocable fixing of exchange rates lead households to change their propensity to hold this type of asset rather than, say, money market accounts or bonds? The continuous evolution of technology and financial markets will of course have an impact on the demand for savings deposits, but these developments are independent of EMU.

All in all it appears to us that the argument that EMU will make money demand unpredictable and that monetary targets will therefore become useless has been exaggerated. Households hold most of the money stock, whether narrow or wide, and their demand is unlikely to affected by the introduction of the euro, at least until 2002. Moreover, the research by Monticelli and Papi (1996) already referred to above suggests that the aggregate demand for money of the EMU area should be more stable than national money demands (including the German one, which until 1999 constitutes the anchor for the rest of Europe). The main argument for an explicit inflation target might be that the European public, which is not used to the implicit inflation target contained in the Bundesbank's monetary target, might expect one. It is therefore likely that the ECB will have to announce an explicit inflation target and add immediately that its main tool to reach it is a controlled expansion of the euro money supply. Some 'fudging' will be unavoidable to make the mixture between inflation and monetary targets work for the first few years after 1999.

3.5.2. *Monetary instruments*

Only some broad principles regarding the monetary instruments to be used by the ECB were anticipated in the EMI report 'The Single Monetary Policy in Stage Three—Specification of the Operational Framework', and many questions were left unanswered. The EMI envisages prime reliance on open market operations supplemented by two standing facilities offered by the ESCB.

Four instruments will be at the disposal of the ECB for open market operations:

1. main refinancing operations (regular liquidity-providing reserve transactions with a weekly frequency and a maturity of two weeks);
2. longer-term refinancing operations (liquidity-providing reserve transactions with a monthly frequency and a maturity of three months, intended to cater for a limited part of the global refinancing volume);
3. fine-tuning operations (adapted to the prevailing circumstances and to the specific objectives of managing the liquidity situation in the market or of steering interest rates); and
4. structural operations (intended to affect the structural position of the banking system *vis-à-vis* the ECB).

As part of the standing facilities, the ECB will be able to provide (in the case of the marginal lending facility) and to absorb (in the case of the deposit facility) overnight liquidity. These instruments broadly reflect widely used practices in a number of EU countries as shown in Table 2.6. The details of the facilities to be used by the ECB have not been settled yet. The EMI report lists only some rather uncontroversial and conventional broad requirements that have to be satisfied by banks to be counterparts and for the eligible assets.

The main controversial point is the potential use of minimum reserve requirements on bank deposits in order to stabilize interest rates and assist in the control of monetary aggregates. Some countries, notably the United Kingdom, and the European Banking Federation have strongly contested that there will be a need for such an instrument. Given that even the Bundesbank, the most outspoken proponent of reserve requirements, has reduced the rates it applies in Germany drastically over recent years, a likely outcome is that reserve requirements, the use of which has to be finally authorized by the Ecofin Council according to Article 19 of the ESCB Statute, will be retained as an instrument, but that they will be sparingly used and that reserves will be remunerated

Table 2.6. Central bank instruments

	Standby facilities	Open market operations	Reserve requirement
Austria	B	Repo, Swap; W	non-interest-bearing
Belgium	B, P, D	O, Repo, Swap; M	none
Denmark	D	O, Repo, Swap; M	none
Germany	B, P, D	O, Repo, Swap; M	non-interest-bearing, A
Greece	B, P	O, Repo, Swap; W	interest-bearing, NA
Spain		Repo, Swap; M	non-interest-bearing, A
France	P	O, Repo; M	non-interest-bearing, A
Ireland	D, P	O, Repo, Swap; M	interest-bearing, NA
Italy	B, P	O, Repo, Swap; M	interest-bearing, A
Netherlands	B	O, Repo, Swap; M	interest-bearing NA
Portugal	B, P	Repo; M	non-interest-bearing, A
Sweden	D, P	O, Repo; M	none
Finland	D, P	O, Repo, Swap; W	non-interest-bearing, NA
UK	P	O, Repo; M	none

Key: B: subsidized loan facility, D: deposit facility, P: short-term facility for bridging peaks in liquidity demand, O: outright transactions, Repo: repurchase agreements with domestic credit institutions, Swap: swap operations in foreign currency, W: one or several operations per week, M: multiple operations daily, A: with averaging provision, NA: without averaging provision.

Source: von Hagen (1997: 95).

at near-market interest rates. This implies that the ECB will not need to be in the market on a daily basis.

On the whole the prospective strategy and the instruments of the single monetary policy appear less than revolutionary relative to current national practices. The ESCB does appear to start off with a solid background in these respects. The final decision on these issues will have to be taken by the Board of the ECB, who can then decide with a simple majority of the EMU members whereas the EMI must have the consent of all fifteen EU member countries. Given that the UK will not be among the initial EMU members the likely outcome is that the instruments finally adopted will be a mixture between what is currently used in France and Germany.

3.6. The macroeconomic environment for monetary policy

Monetary policy can keep inflation low even if there are inflationary pressures, but in a hostile environment the price of low inflation can be high, since high interest rates to combat inflationary pressures generated by high wage increases or an expansionary fiscal policy could lead to high unemployment. How likely is it that the macro-economic environment will make it difficult for the ECB to maintain price stability? The high level of unemployment in most member countries makes it unlikely that high wage demands will become a danger for price stability. But what about fiscal policy? One key reason why the drafters of the Treaty feared that fiscal policy could put monetary policy under pressure is that in countries with a high public debt the central bank is under constant pressure to keep interest rates low, even if this leads to dangers for price stability.

Public debt also has a special position in banking regulation. At present, public debt is assumed to be risk-free for the purposes of prudential regulation. This implies for the banking system that the prudential rules that limit the amount of credits a bank can give in relation to its own capital give public debt a zero-risk weighting. This should change with EMU because national governments lose the option to print the money they might need to service this debt. Hence under EMU the debt of national governments should be treated in the same way as private debt; that is, it should not be considered risk-free, but as having a modest risk rating (see Box 2.5).

We recommend that, under EMU, banking regulators should apply a higher risk weighting for government debt of a country which is in an excessive deficit and apply the exposure rules to a bank's holdings of public debt. This would have profound implications for the banking system in some member countries and would force governments throughout the EU to rely much less on bank financing, as explained in Box 2.5. The long-term benefit would be to insulate the financial system of the EMU area from funding difficulties member states might experience. The main practical objection to this measure is that E(M)U governments might then have to face a higher cost of funds than non-EU governments from the OECD area, whose public debt has a zero-risk weighting under prudential rules. The additional cost would be minimal, in the basis points order of magnitude, and it would apply only to bank debt, but it is the main reason why finance ministries have so far refused to consider this approach.

However, even if these precautions are taken it remains likely that for some time to come the public debt will be held mainly by domestic savers and the domestic banking system. This implies that a funding crisis for the national government could endanger the stability of the domestic financial system. This could then induce the governor of the national central bank concerned to vote against interest rate increases that might be necessary to combat inflation in the Union as a whole. Other members of the ECB Board might also be tempted to follow a soft line because of the threat of contagion effects on the financial system in other EMU countries.[15]

The enforcement mechanism foreseen in the Treaty thus depends mainly on peer pressure. Until now, no member state has openly defied the legal and judicial system of the Community (for example, by refusing to implement a directive). This might be the reason why the Treaty does not contemplate the possibility that a member country would not heed the requests for fiscal adjustment addressed to it.

The fiscal criteria, however, are different from the rest of the business of the EU, since fiscal policy remains fully under national control—even under EMU. This was the deeper reason why the normal enforcement procedures of the Treaty are not applied in

---

[15] The evidence reported in Grilli *et al.* (1991), which shows that an independent central bank can produce, on average, lower inflation even in the context of lax fiscal behaviour, does not prove the contrary since their result only indicates that an independent central bank can mitigate, not eliminate the inflationary impact of excessive fiscal deficits.

Box 2.5. Prudential rules and public debt under EMU: recognizing the risk of public debt

It has been proposed (see e.g. Bishop (1990)) that once the third stage of EMU starts the prudential rules for the banking system should be changed to take into account the increased riskiness of public debt that comes once the ECB takes over monetary policy. The argument is that once the third stage has started national governments lose the power to print the money they need to service their own public debt.

There are two regulations regarding the prudential rules for banks that might be changed in this context:

1. *The Solvency Ratio Directive (SRD) (Council directive 89/647/EEC)*. What would be the implications for the balance sheet of the banking sector if national public debt were to be treated as regional government debt with a risk weight of 20 per cent? The core of the SRD is that banks must hold own funds corresponding to at least 8 per cent of their risk-weighted assets (the Cooke ratio of the Basle Group of 10). The various risk categories are 0 per cent for government debt (of OECD countries), 20 per cent for certain regional governments, 50 per cent for mortgage-backed loans and 100 per cent for commercial loans.

A question one can ask is whether increasing the risk weighting on public debt to 20 per cent would lead to unreasonably large needs for additional capital. This does not seem to be the case as the following simple calculations suggest. The SRD rule can be written as:

$$\text{Capital} / \text{Assets} \geq 0.08. \tag{1}$$

If public debt enters 'assets' with a weight of 0.2 this relationship can be rewritten as:

$$\text{Capital} \geq \text{public debt (held by banks)} \times 0.08 \times 0.2. \tag{2}$$

If one divides both sides by GDP this boils down to the following requirements for additional bank capital:

$$\text{Capital} / \text{GDP} \geq \text{debt} / \text{GDP} \times 0.016. \tag{3}$$

This implies that even if banks held public debt worth 100 per cent of GDP (with a risk weight of 20 per cent) they would need to hold only 1.6 per cent of GDP in reserves against these assets. Given that banks have reserves equivalent to at least 6 per cent of GDP, on average, in most member countries and about 10 per cent of GDP in some, this requirement does not seem to be very onerous. In most member countries the actual capital ratio of most banks exceeds by a comfortable margin the 8 per cent limit imposed by the SRD. Hence most banking systems should be able to absorb without great difficulties a hypothetical risk rating of public debt.

2. *Large exposure rules (Council directive 92/121/EEC)*. The Large Exposure Directive says that a bank cannot lend more than 25 per cent of its own funds (defined as in the SRD) to a single client. This rule would be extremely constraining if it were to be applied to public debt. Starting with the rule of thumb that the capital of banks amounts to 6–10 per cent of GDP this rule would imply that the *total amount of public debt* held by banks would have to be below 1.5–2.5 per cent of GDP, a very small fraction of the entire stock of public debt of member countries.

In the case of Belgium enormous portfolio adjustments would be needed since at present almost BEF 5,000 billion, about one half of the entire stock of debt, is held by Belgian banks. By comparison the own funds of the Belgian banks amount only to BEF 601 billion, which would allow them to hold only BEF 150 billion in public debt if the large exposure rule were applied to the Belgian government.

The discussion has assumed so far that all or most national public debt is held domestically. This is the case at present for most member countries. However, even if it were to change considerably it would not affect the conclusions for the large countries. Italy, for example, accounts for about 15 per cent of the combined GDP of the EU; with a debt to GDP ratio of about 120 per cent the Italian public debt still accounts for about 18 per cent of the GDP of the entire EU. For the entire EU the ratio of capital of banks to GDP is about 8 per cent. This implies that if all EU banks held Italian public debt up to the limit, they could hold the equivalent of 2 per cent of the GDP of the EU in Italian public debt; about one tenth of the total, which is equivalent to 18 per cent of EU GDP as calculated above. Only a small proportion of the public debt of the larger EU countries could thus be held by EMU banks if the large exposure limit had to be observed.

this area. This, in turn, implies that the effectiveness of the excessive deficit procedure will depend on the sanctions that underpin it (and the goodwill of member countries).

Another drawback of the excessive deficit procedure as specified in Article 104c is that enforcement is discretionary (sanctions *may* be imposed), requiring a decision supported by a qualified majority by Ecofin for each specific step. This body has not even been able to impose IMF-type conditionality towards Greece in the context of large support programmes. It would thus be better if the sanctions were not only more concretely specified, but also subject to more formal decision procedures. Ideally, some action or decision would be triggered automatically once a certain threshold had been passed.[16]

Recognition of these weaknesses led to the proposal by the German Ministry of Finance for a 'Pact for Stability'. The essence of that proposal was later approved by the European Council in Dublin (December 1996) under the name 'Pact for Stability and Growth'. This Pact contains some secondary EC legislation that will speed up different steps in the excessive deficit procedure, listed in Box 2.6. But its core is an intergovernmental agreement which pre-commits voting behaviour in future Ecofin meetings. In essence member states have agreed that they will normally vote for sanctions once a country has a deficit in excess of 3 per cent (subject to one condition, see Box 2.6). Moreover, the sanctions (i.e. the size of the deposits and fines) have been specified in advance.

The implication of this Pact is that deviations from the 3 per cent deficit ceiling will clearly become expensive. For example, a country that ran a deficit of 5 per cent for more than two years would have to pay a fine (or more precisely, forfeit deposits) equivalent to 0.4 per cent of GDP for each following year. For most countries such a sum would be substantially larger than the *net* contribution to the normal EU budget.

---

[16] An excessive deficit procedure that does not 'punish' the offending state, but helps it to get its fiscal accounts under control would, of course, be even better. But this seems difficult to achieve.

Box 2.6. The Stability Pact

The 'Pact for Stability (and Growth)' agreed at the Dublin Council (December 1996) and approved at the Amsterdam Council (June 1997) consists of a resolution of the European Council and two Council regulations, which (1) set out the framework for multilateral surveillance of budgetary positions and coordination of economic policies, and (2) detail the excessive deficit procedure in EMU and the applicable sanctions in case of non-respect. In essence, it consists of the following:

1. The reference value of a 3 per cent deficit would constitute an absolute ceiling, except if the country concerned experiences an exceptional fall in GDP of over 2 per cent.
2. If a country is found (during the semi-annual evaluation performed by the Commission) to have a deficit in excess of 3 per cent of GDP, it would have to make a non-interest-bearing deposit equivalent to 0.2 per cent of GDP plus 0.1 per cent for each percentage point of the excess deficit. The variable part applies only for deficits up to 6 per cent of GDP; the total is thus capped at 0.5 per cent of GDP.
3. The deposit will be returned as soon as the deficit goes below 3 per cent; if the excess deficit persists for over two years, the deposit becomes a fine.

The European Council has, however, retained discretion to decide whether a fall of between 0.75 per cent and 2 per cent of GDP could also be considered as exceptional.

The Pact does not imply or require a change in the Treaty. It also contains a package of secondary legislation to set deadlines for the various steps of the excessive deficit procedure contained in Article 104c. Given the number of steps that have to be taken before sanctions can be imposed and the number of institutions that contribute to the fiscal decision, it appears that in practice there will be a delay of nearly a year before a legally binding decision on sanctions can be taken by Ecofin.

Another part of the Pact is declaratory and has therefore been neglected in public discussions. In this part the governments affirm their intention to actually aim at proximate balance under normal cyclical conditions. It remains to be seen whether this goal will be pursued vigorously given that it is not backed up by any sanction.

Payments of this size would certainly have a large political impact since they would require a substantial increase in taxes and/or reduction in expenditure, unless they were financed by issuing more debt.

However, the Stability Pact does not solve the fundamental problem that for the sanctions to be imposed a decision has to be taken by Ecofin. The Ministers of Finance might in the future (as in the past) find many reasons to be lenient on their colleagues. It is difficult to judge how sanctions will be applied by Ecofin in the future. Some governments might find valid reasons in the future not to vote for sanctions after all, fearing that they might be the next victim. A recent game-theoretic analysis of the Stability Pact that takes this problem into account (Gantner, 1997) comes up, however, with the result that the Pact will work as long as governments have a sufficiently long horizon and as long as there is at least some probability that Ecofin will be strict in applying its provisions. Moreover, most EU governments have invested so much political capital in the Stability Pact that it is unthinkable that they could flout it during the next few years. Finally there is also the Damoclean Sword of the judgement of the Federal Constitutional Court in Germany which ruled that Germany would be justified in leaving EMU if it did not preserve price stability.

The strongest reason to expect that the Stability Pact will be honoured after all is that fiscal rectitude brings long-term gains. This is a point of view that is often overlooked in the academic debate on EMU, but it was important in the US debate about the costs of fiscal deficits when the series of substantial federal deficits started during the early 1980s (although these deficits were almost always below 3 per cent of GDP and the US federal debt has not yet exceeded the 60 per cent Maastricht norm).

The central point in this line of argument is that given an unchanged external current account balance an increase in public sector savings must be mirrored one to one in an increase in investment. This in turn would increase growth. Empirical studies indicate, as a rule of thumb, that an increase in the investment rate (investment/GDP) of 1 percentage point leads to an increase in growth of between 0.2 and 0.3 percentage points. This implies that a reduction in the deficit of 3–5 percentage points of GDP, sustained over several years, could increase growth by about 1 percentage point if it crowds in an equivalent amount of investment expenditure. Given that medium-term growth rates for the EU are usually assumed to be around 2.5–3 per cent per annum this implies that a sustained fiscal adjustment could increase the growth potential of the EU considerably. In the illustrative example used here the increase in growth, say from 2.5 to 3.5 per cent per annum means an increase in the growth rate of 40 per cent!

One has to take into account that growth will decelerate after a while even if the higher investment rate is sustained indefinitely, because eventually decreasing returns to scale set in. This is taken into account in the 1994 Report to the US President, where it is estimated that a 1 per cent increase in the investment rate that is maintained indefinitely will eventually raise real income by about 3.75 per cent.

A number of member countries would have to reduce their deficits by between 3 and 5 percentage points of GDP in order to satisfy the Maastricht criteria if one uses the long-term average as the starting point. The corresponding increase in the investment rate should thus increase income eventually by more than 10 per cent, possibly up to 15 per cent. Increases in output are not equivalent to increases in welfare, but even if one concentrates on purely welfare-theoretic considerations Romer (1988) shows that even the relatively small US deficits could have very large social costs.

To the extent that increased national savings in the EU are not invested domestically (i.e. to the extent that the current account does change) output produced at home will not grow faster, but investment in the rest of the world also yields a return. Moreover, from the perspective of a greying EU population it seems entirely appropriate that the EU exports capital in order to finance at least part of its consumption at retirement with the returns from these investments.

More evidence of the costs of fiscal laxity is provided by simulations undertaken by the staff of the IMF using its macroeconomic model (IMF, 1995). These simulations illustrate that a lower public debt level tends to lead to lower interest rates and hence higher investment. The simulations ask what would happen if all the industrialized countries were to reduce their debt to GDP ratio by 20 percentage points. The outcome, according to the IMF's model, would be, in the long run, a drop in real interest rates of one full percentage point, which would stimulate investment to such an extent that the capital stock would increase by about 10 per cent and world output and consumption would go up by about 3 per cent. Simulations reported in IMF (1996) then show what might happen if some countries were to undertake such a policy. All industrialized countries together constitute essentially a closed economy, but in this case one can take into account the fact that if only one country reduces public dissavings the current account will be affected. The IMF did not simulate a 'Maastricht-inspired' reduction in the public debt of EU member countries from 80 to 60 per cent of GDP. But the simulations it provides for the USA (which is of similar size to the EU) suggest that the impact would still be substantial: real GDP would increase by less (only 0.6 per cent) but consumption could still increase over 2 per cent because of the accumulation of external assets through the current account.

Another recent study comes to similar results. Orr *et al.* (1995) report that a reduction in government deficits of 1 per cent should lead to a fall in the real interest of between one-sixth and two-sixths percentage points, depending on the reaction of the current account. This implies that a sustained reduction in fiscal deficits of 3 per cent of GDP (which would go beyond the minimum required by the Maastricht criteria) could lower real interest rates by between one-half and one full percentage point. The same study also finds that lower and more predictable inflation rates also contribute to lower real interest rates. This is a further reason to expect low interest rates under EMU.

Once the long-term gains from lower deficits become available (which should be the case within a few years) governments will find it much easier than at present to keep their fiscal house in order. Lower deficits, coupled with higher growth, should also lead to a virtuous circle in which the debt ratios fall, which in turn lowers the pressure on interest rates and makes it easier for governments to keep fiscal balance. If fiscal deficits are reduced to about 1 per cent as agreed upon under the Stability Pact debt ratios would start to fall quickly. Assuming a growth rate of nominal GDP of 5 per cent (the average for Germany over the last twenty-five years) a deficit of 1 per cent would cause the average EU debt to GDP ratio, which now stands at 70 per cent, to fall by about 2.5 percentage points each year. In four years it could thus be 10 percentage points lower. With an average interest rate on public debt of 8 per cent this would yield savings of 0.8 per cent of GDP (each year). While this might appear small if compared to overall public expenditure of close to 50 per cent of GDP in many member states it would be important in giving governments some room for manoeuvre. As the events of 1997 have shown it can sometimes be extremely difficult to achieve even a very small improvement in the budget.

All in all we would thus conclude that the general environment under EMU will be conducive to an era of low interest and inflation rates.

4. The ECB, a Full Central Bank?

The essence of central banking has often been described as consisting of a trilogy of activities and responsibilities. That trilogy refers to the control of inflation through monetary policy, the safeguarding of the stability of the banking and financial system through prudential policies, and ensuring the efficiency and integrity of payment systems. It is argued that it is difficult to disentangle a part of the trilogy without loosening the global objectives of a central bank to maintain overall economic and financial stability. If one of the three functions is not working properly, it will contaminate the others and undermine the objectives of the central bank.

Within the euro area, this trilogy of central banking functions will not be managed by the ECB alone. The division of central bank responsibilities was adapted to the specific requirements of the European integration process, where powers are handed over to a higher authority only if they cannot be sufficiently achieved by the member states, and can therefore be better exercised by the Community. Hence, the ECB was granted exclusive competences in the areas of monetary policy, but its functions in payment systems and prudential supervision are limited, or exercised in cooperation with the participating national central banks. In payment systems, the ECB and the national central banks will collaborate to create an efficient and sound system, which is based on an interlinking of national real-time gross settlement (RTGS) systems in the TARGET system (Art. 22). In prudential supervision, the ECB's role is limited to giving advice to the EU Council of Ministers and the Commission on draft Community legislation relating to the prudential supervision of credit institutions and the stability of the financial system (Art. 25).

Some observers have characterized the ECB as being only a monetary policy rule, a limitation which could stifle the development of liquid and securitized financial markets (Folkerts-Landau and Garber, 1992). Liquid securitized financial markets need to be supported by a central bank with broad functions, they argue. The ECB will not intervene actively in financial markets, but stand on the sidelines. The draft ECB monetary policy instruments provide for only weekly refinancing operations and likely supporting instruments for its monetary policy, such as reserve requirements, limit short-term funding in the banking system. This can be observed in Germany, where the existence of reserve requirements provoked the flight of the DEM repo marker to the UK. The ECB might also resist calls for liquidity support to troublesome banks and let unsound banks fail, increasing the risk of systemic shocks. Finally, the real-time gross settlement system TARGET will limit market liquidity and absorb funds to prevent gridlocks.

We will in this section analyse the pros and cons of separating and combining monetary and supervisory functions, examine how this issue was approached in the EU context and put it in the perspective of recent trends in banking supervision. A second part discusses the role of the ECB in payment systems.

4.1. Prudential issues

Monetary policy and banking supervisory functions are separated in one half of the Community countries and combined in the other half (see Table 2.7). Generally speaking, the arguments in favour of combining both functions is the central bank's objective of ensuring the stability of the financial system and preventing contagious systemic crises. The observation of bank supervisory and regulatory functions by the central bank should contribute to a better control of overall financial stability. Through its participation in bank rescues, the central bank is better involved in supervision as well, it is argued. This raises at the same time the argument against combining both functions. A conflict of interest might arise in the observance of both functions: injection of additional liquidity into the financial system might endanger price stability and increase moral hazard.

The fact that both regimes are equally represented in the EU shows that there are no definitive arguments for either model. According to Goodhart and Schoenmaker

Table 2.7. Monetary and bank supervisory functions in EU countries

	Regime	Monetary agency	Supervisory agency
Austria	S	National Bank of Austria (CB)	(Federal) Ministry of Finance (MF)
Belgium	S	National Bank of Belgium (CB)	Banking and Finance Commission
Denmark	S	Danmarks Nationalbank (CB)	Finance Inspectorate (MI)[a]
Finland	S	Bank of Finland (CB)	Bank Inspectorate (MF)/Bank of Finland (CB)
France	C	Banque de France (CB)	Banque de France (CB)/ Commission Bancaire[b]
Germany	S	Deutsche Bundesbank (CB)	Federal Banking Supervisory Office/Deutsche Bundesbank[c]
Greece	C	Bank of Greece (CB)	Bank of Greece (CB)
Ireland	C	Central Bank of Ireland (CB)	Central Bank of Ireland (CB)
Italy	C	Banca d'Italia (CB)	Banca d'Italia (CB)
Luxembourg	C	Luxembourg Monetary Institute (CB)	Luxembourg Monetary Institute (CB)
Netherlands	C	De Nederlandsche Bank (CB)	De Nederlandsche Bank (CB)
Portugal	C	Banco de Portugal (CB)	Banco de Portugal (CB)
Spain	C	Banco de Espana (CB)	Banco de Espana (CB)
Sweden	S	Sveriges Riksbank (CB)	Swedish Financial Supervisory Authority
UK	S	Bank of England (CB)	Securities and Investment Board[d]
Switzerland	S	Swiss National Bank (CB)	Federal Banking Commission
USA	S/C	Federal Reserve Board (CB)	Office of the Comptroller of the Currency (CB)/Federal Reserve Board (CB)/state governments/ Federal Deposit Insurance Corporation[e]

Key: C = Combined, S = Separated, CB = Central Bank, MF = Ministry of Finance, MI = Ministry of Industry.   (*cont.*)

Table 2.7. (cont.)

---

^a The Danish national bank is the granter of liquidity support, while the Inspectorate is responsible for the supervision of banks. The Inspectorate has no formal link with the Nationalbank, although there is in practice cooperation between the two on any issues.

^b The Banking Commission (Commission Bancaire) is a composite body chaired by the Governor of the Banque de France, with representatives from the Treasury. The Banking Commission supervises compliance with the prudential regulations. The inspections and on-site examinations are carried out by the Banque de France on behalf of the Banking Commission.

^c The Federal Banking Supervisory Office (Bundesaufsichtsamt für das Kreditwesen) is entrusted with the supervision of banks. It is responsible for sovereign acts, such as licensing and issuing regulations, whereas the Bundesbank is involved in current supervision by collecting and processing bank prudential returns. The Banking Act provides for cooperation between the Supervisory board and the Bundesbank (i.e. the two bodies communicate information to each other, and the Supervisory Office has to consult the Bundesbank on new regulations).

^d Under proposals of the Blair Government, the banking supervisory responsibilities will be taken away from the Bank of England and put into an extended Securities and Investment Board, which will supervise the whole financial sector.

^e The Office of the Comptroller of the Currency, an agency within the US Treasury Department, supervises national banks and federally licensed branches of foreign banks. The Federal Reserve Board and the state governments supervise state-chartered banks which are members of the Federal Reserve System. State-chartered non-member banks are supervised by the state governments. The Federal Reserve Board has the authority to supervise all bank holding companies and their subsidiaries. In addition, the autonomous Federal Deposit Insurance Corporation has some supervisory responsibilities.

Source: adapted from Goodhart and Schoenmaker (1995: 558).

(1995), the question of the appropriate design has to be seen more against the particular financial or banking structure of each country rather than as being capable of resolution as an abstract generality. Moreover, there is a general trend of retreat in central banks from supervisory functions, which was exemplified recently by the breakaway of the supervisory functions from the Bank of England and the establishment of a 'Super-SIB' (Securities and Investment Board). This new regulatory authority will bring all financial sector supervision under one roof.

Several reasons can be advanced for this trend. First, banking is becoming an increasingly complex business and less clearly defined. Leading banks are active in several jurisdictions as providers of a whole series of financial services. Linked to this are new developments in financial supervision, which increasingly emphasizes the role of self-regulation. Finally, there is increasing acceptance that the government, not the central bank, should take responsibility for ultimate financial support. Supervision could thus be better organized in a body more directly under political control.

In the Amendment to the Basle Capital Accord to Incorporate Market Risk, reached by the Basle Group of 10 in 1995, banking supervisors allow banks to use, under certain conditions, internal risk measurement models (value-at-risk (VAR) models) to set the necessary own funds instead of the formal capital requirements. The Amended Basle Accord will be fully effective at the end of 1997 and will be incorporated in EU legislation through an amendment to the Capital Adequacy Directive for investment firms and credit institutions (CAD). The emphasis on internal controls has recently been taken a step further in the USA with the 'pre-commitment approach', which devises an incentive contract between banks and their regulators. It stipulates that a bank or investment firm has to pre-commit to its regulator not to exceed a certain portfolio loss over a certain period. This pre-commitment approach, which should be determined using the institution's own internal VAR models, is at the same time its regulatory market risk capital requirement. If it violates this commitment, then it will face a regulatory penalty.

Some recent international bank failures and financial problems have highlighted the global interdependence of financial markets and the need for solutions at that level. The collapse of the British Barings banks (February 1995) was provoked by uncovered positions taken by one trader in Singapore. Daiwa incurred a loss of US$1.1 billion as a result of the fraudulent transactions of a trader in its New York branch (August 1995). The G-7 discussed the issue at its three meetings in 1995–7. The Halifax G-7 meeting (June 1995) called for an integrated approach to potential systemic risks and closer international cooperation in the regulation and supervision of financial institutions and markets. It invited the Basle Committee on banking supervision and IOSCO, the International Organisation of Securities Commissions, to work closely together in addressing the major issues in this area, to examine the desirable steps to address identified problems and to report back. At the Lyon G-7 meeting (June 1996), the heads of state and government called for enhanced cooperation across markets and sectors to reinforce supervision: they welcomed the proposals of the Basle Committee and IOSCO, which concretized the international cooperation between supervisors through the appointment of a lead supervisor for globally active firms. They gave support to the joint forum on financial conglomerates, comprised of banking, securities and insurance supervisors. They invited the strengthening of prudential standards in emerging markets; the encouragement of private sector efforts to enhance market transparency; the improvement of reporting and disclosure of derivatives activities; and the enhancement of cooperation among exchanges and securities supervisors for information-sharing arrangements.

Against this background, the EU supervisory system might be well adapted. Further to the single market legislation, prudential control of financial market actors in the EU rests with the home-country supervisors. Market liberalization was achieved through the harmonization of essential rules in the Community directives and the mutual recognition of additional requirements. Hence a licence obtained in one member country is valid throughout the EU. The control of compliance with these rules rests with the home-country supervisors, who are in charge of controlling the operations of the financial institution throughout the Community. This principle was applied equally for the three groups of financial market players, banks (1992), insurance companies (1994) and investment firms (1996). For EU supervisors, the designation of a lead supervisor, as internationally proposed to reinforce supervision, is a prolongation of European practice. Moreover, EU legislation establishes that the 'home country' should be the country where a financial institution has its most important operations, as was decided further to the BCCI failure.

The constitution limiting the ECB's functions to monetary ones coincides with a trend which is generally discernible and suits the home-country-control principles of the single market. Involvement of the ECB in bank supervision could force it to act as a lender of last resort, which could be difficult to reconcile with the task of maintaining price stability and compromise its independence. On practical grounds, bank supervision can be better executed at the local level, because of the availability of specific expertise and the knowledge of the local market. Since the participating national central banks will be involved in open market and credit operations with banks, they will have hands-on experience with financial markets and institutions and information on market conditions. Nevertheless, strong and swift communication lines should be established between national central banks and supervisors and the ECB to assess liquidity crises in European financial markets. The ECB would be a useful device to constrain the use of lender-of-last-resort operations at the local level. Only when a crisis has the potential to become systemic would the ECB intervene. The ECB should therefore develop a capacity to systematically monitor financial markets and to assess financial stability.

4.2. Payment systems issues

In order to execute the joint monetary policy, the national central banks in the ESCB will link their different domestic settlement systems in the TARGET system. The system will also be open for private cross-border payments and will deal with wholesale transactions in real-time gross settlement (RTGS), meaning that payments are settled immediately without daylight exposure. RTGS has the advantage of reducing systemic risk, but requires the explicit provision of intraday liquidity so as to prevent gridlocks.[17] European central banks are currently in various phases of developing RTGS payment systems. TARGET will also be open to the central banks which are not in the monetary union to process the euro as a foreign currency.

For commercial cross-border payment business, the TARGET system will compete with other payment systems such as correspondent banking and net settlement systems, including the ECU clearing system of the ECU Banking Association (EBA).[18] Its services in that area will be priced at market rates, and are expected to be competitive for wholesale payments. The EBA's net settlement system will have the additional cost advantage that the need for collateral is much reduced. Under the current plans, a transfer through TARGET should be several times as expensive as a transfer under the EBA system. One could expect that the latter system should take care of middle-sized payments, whereas TARGET could be used for large transfers, those exceeding euro 10 million. The EBA expects TARGET and correspondent banking to have each a 20 per cent share, while the EBA system would have 30 per cent. With the gradual extension

---

[17] For a detailed analysis of the different forms of payment systems and the cost of RTGS, see Schoenmaker (1994) and Folkerts-Landau *et al.* (1996).

[18] ECU Banking Association, 'From ECU to Euro—The EBA's Future Business Potential', 13 December 1996.

of the use of the euro, TARGET and EBA systems are likely to replace correspondent banking arrangements between banks in the monetary union, and between banks outside to banks inside for transactions in euros. Some even expect that correspondent banking will totally disappear in the euro zone, as it has almost disappeared within all EU member states.

Most wholesale payment systems will be converted to the euro from the start of Stage 3A onwards. Systems that operate both wholesale and retail or only retail will have to deal with both currencies. Member states are preparing their payment systems in different ways for this situation.[19] The existence of different standards for payment orders in the member states will, however, continue to hamper cross-border integration.

There has been much discussion in the recent past about access of non-EMU Community countries to TARGET. Although the details are complicated, the principle that underlies this debate should be clear. TARGET will link national payment systems to execute the single monetary policy in the euro area and generally promote the use of RTGS in EU cross-border payments. Within the euro area, the national central banks are only agents of the ECB and must be treated as such. It is also apparent that there is no reason to establish special links between the ECB (i.e. TARGET) and the central banks from outside the EU. Should one consider a 'half-way house' for central banks that are members of the EU, but not part of EMU? This would be difficult to realize in practice because monetary policy cannot be divided. Although the 'out' central banks are unlikely to undermine the monetary policy of the ECB (they also have a Treaty obligation not to do this), there is no reason why they should be given special treatment. At present, national central banks deal with other central banks at arm's length. No central bank in the world allows other central banks to create its own money or gives other central banks privileges in its payment system. This does not imply, however, that TARGET should discriminate against commercial banks headquartered in 'out' countries, which are members of the same single market.

The TARGET debate often overlooks the fact that its system will be only one of many that will compete in the euro area, as indicated above. This availability of low-cost alternatives is also the reason why the implications of such an arm's-length treatment of non-EMU members (central and commercial banks) and financial centres should be limited. London has established itself as a financial centre for many currencies, despite the fact that commercial banks in London (and the Bank of England) never had privileged access to the two US payment systems. There is therefore no reason why the lack of privileged access should prove an impediment to achieving an important role in the 'euro' Euromarket.

If the EBA system is widely accepted, one could imagine a situation whereby that system is used for a majority of transactions and TARGET just handles the payments

---

[19] See e.g. the Master agreement on the execution of interbank domestic payments for the introduction of the euro currency, concluded between the Bundesbank and the German banking associations on 26 April 1996, which allows for both euro and DEM payments in the German payment system, depending on the instruction given at the start.

that arise after netting. This would further reduce the disadvantage of 'out' banks, who would anyway not need to make large euro payments for the common monetary policy.

In an August 1996 report, the EMI gave further details about the functioning of TARGET, the preparations and opening hours.[20] Liquidity in the system will be provided by making use of fully collateralized intraday overdrafts, reserve requirements imposed for monetary policy purposes and remunerated free reserves. Collateral could be mobilized and used on a cross-border basis in EMU as well, which will ease remote access to other EMU countries' payment systems (for banks in the EMU zone). The system will have long operating hours (from 7am until 6pm European Central Time) to facilitate the implementation of the monetary policy and to ensure a level playing field for credit institutions.

The question of the options for intraday credit in euros to non-EMU central banks or the access by non-EMU commercial banks has not been settled yet. The essential problem is as follows: equal access has to be assured for 'outs' as for 'ins', but difficulties with the settlement of an intraday credit might at the end of the day spill over into an overnight credit. The latter form of credit is not a payments system matter, but rather a monetary policy issue, since it might disturb euro monetary policy. This is at the same time the border where the difference between the two groups starts. Possible solutions that are being investigated at the moment include an earlier closing time for payments in TARGET for 'outs'; a common cut-off time with higher overdraft penalties for the 'outs'; and the setting of a maximum credit in euros that 'outs' can have, based on their euro reserves.

At the payment systems level, 'out' financial institutions will be hampered in setting up optimal operational structures to make full use of the single market. They will have to maintain a dual set of accounts with their central bank, in euros and in national currency, if they want to work in euros. They will need to put up additional collateral for remote access to payment systems in EMU countries; or they will need to set up a separately capitalized entity (subsidiary) in the euro zone if they want equal access to TARGET as enjoyed by EMU banks.

The issue of collateral should not be exaggerated, however. As can be seen from Table 2.8, collateral in the UK CHAPS, a national RTGS payment system, should be at most ECU 12.9 billion, or about 2 per cent of the total deposits, or 1 per cent of the balance sheet total of UK commercial banks. One-tenth of the daily turnover is the highest level of collateral an RTGS system is expected to need. Normal levels are thought, however, to be much lower, at around one-fiftieth of daily turnover.

The real question is what amount of additional collateral the 'out' (e.g. UK) commercial banks would have to pledge in order to obtain access to TARGET and at what cost. 'Out' commercial banks would make this financial outlay only if the cost is lower than the (low) cost of using the existing correspondent banking channels or other

---

[20] EMI Working Group on EU Payment Systems, *First Progress Report on the TARGET Project*, August 1996.

Table 2.8. Daily turnover and collateral in the UK CHAPS, 1994 (ECU bn.)

Reserves with central bank	1.8
Collateral	11.1
Intraday liquidity	12.9
Daily turnover	128.9
Bank deposits	648.1
Balance sheet total	930.3

Sources: Folkerts-Landau *et al.* (1996), OECD (1996).

private sector alternatives, such as the net payment system run by the ECU Banking Association, which has a much lower demand for collateral.

What will be the size of the flows for which TARGET might be used? Cross-border payment flows are usually much smaller than domestic ones. Trade with the EU amounts to about 10 per cent of UK GDP. Assuming a similar proportion applies to turnover in payments between the UK and the EU, cross-border transactions in the EU should be around euro 13 billion daily. (This implies an annual turnover of about euro 2,860 billion: UK–EU trade amounts to about euro 100 billion; the ratio of 30 of turnover to trade is within the range observed in other currency markets.)

These calculations suggest that the additional collateral required would be about ECU 1.3 billion. This collateral would be remunerated at market rates. Folkerts-Landau *et al.* (1996) estimated that the upper limit of the opportunity cost of pledging collateral is 0.25 per cent, a consequence of the fact that eligible securities are high quality and very liquid but no longer available to the bank for other purposes. This would imply that the cost of pledging additional collateral would be only ECU 3.25 million per annum (ECU 13 billion × 0.1 × 0.0025) for the entire UK banking system! This would be the maximum under a scenario of double collateral and still the sum is negligible if compared to gross income, profits, costs or any other indicator of the size of the UK banking system. Similar considerations apply to the other potential 'out' countries.

5. Conclusions: Implications for Capital Markets

EMU will be a further quantum step in the integration of European capital markets, although they will remain different for some time to come. Within the US monetary union it does not make sense to speak of different regional capital markets. Nothing differentiates the New York from the Californian market, except that some market participants are located (and deal) in New York and some others deal primarily in California. This will not be the case in Europe. Even after the introduction of the euro capital markets will retain a strong 'national' flavour. This does not apply to all market segments, but to most of the important ones. There are many reasons for this. They can best be observed by distinguishing between the retail and the wholesale levels.

At the retail level the reasons for differentiation are clear. National regulations and the habits of consumers mean that in each country different instruments are used. For example, in some countries simple savings accounts are still very popular (and protected by legislation) whereas in others they have been supplanted by money market certificates. Another example is mortgages, which show large differences from country to country (see Box 2.7). In Germany, mortgages are long-term fixed-rated

---

Box 2.7. Mortgage lending in the EU

European mortgage markets show a wide diversity in mortgage contracts and in refinancing methods. At the retail level, the interest rate can be variable or fixed over a long term. At the wholesale level, mortgage loans can be refinanced through short-term deposits or through long-term loans, namely mortgage-backed securities. These differences coincided in the past with country-specific patterns, with at the two extremes the building societies in the UK, using variable rates financed by short-term deposits, and the *Hypothekenbanken* in Germany, using fixed rates financed by long-term *Pfandbriefe*. A reason for the differences was the much higher level and variability of inflation in the UK during the 1970s and 1980s. The real rate paid by borrowers would have been extremely variable if nominal interest rates on mortgage loans had been fixed for five to ten years, as is customary in Germany. More recently, variable rates are also offered in Germany, so that the differences are not as stark as before. Large differences continue, however, and regulatory barriers remain to a truly integrated market. They comprise differences in securities, consumer protection, bankruptcy and tax legislation. Further Community action in these areas is not immediately foreseen, which implies that European mortgage markets will continue to be fragmented for some time to come.

Mortgage lending is one of the activities which can be exercised on a cross-border basis as laid down by the second banking directive, subject to home-country supervision only. Loopholes in the latter directive, such as the 'general good' clause, and remaining differences in tax and securities legislation have, however, proven to be a serious barrier to the cross-border exercise of mortgage services, and have left the host-country authorities with considerable scope for control: sometimes long-term refinancing was not possible in the host country, or otherwise additional host-country authorizations were required. Hence it follows that certain, possibly competitive forms of mortgage lending could not yet sufficiently spread at a Europe-wide level. From a capital markets perspective, this implies that long-term private debt instruments, such as the German *Pfandbriefe*, could not yet develop further.

Monetary union should further reduce these remaining barriers. The unification of monetary policy, the disappearance of currency risk and the harmonization of securities instruments (in the regulation on the legal status of the euro and the rules on collateral for monetary policy operations of the ECB) should provide host-country authorities with less scope for additional control. The impetus which has recently been given to harmonize capital income taxation should remove another important barrier. Given the price stability objective of the ECB and the expected stable short-term interest rate environment, fixed-rate long-term mortgage loans may increase in EMU, and with them long-term refinancing.

loans, which are repackaged and sold on capital markets as *Pfandbriefe*. In the UK, mortgage loans vary with changes in short-term interest rates. These idiosyncrasies at the retail level are not the focus of the present chapter. They might, however, affect even the wholesale level, since in some cases they can affect the preferred mode of refinancing of local financial institutions. For example, in Germany banks need a stable deposit base at long-term fixed rates. UK banks in contrast can live with a higher proportion of short-term deposits.

The consequences of these national idiosyncrasies for monetary policies can be seen in the size and composition of the main monetary aggregates. Table 2.5 above shows the composition of M3 for France and Germany (data for the UK are not easily available) and the shares held by households and the corporate sector. Demand deposits form a larger proportion (40.7 against 33.2 per cent of total M3) in Germany than in France. However, in both countries the share held by households, about 61 per cent, is the same. For time deposits (which account for about 20–26 per cent of the total) the shares held by households are, however, completely different: in Germany the corporate sector still holds about a quarter of all time deposits, whereas in France it holds almost none. With these differences in the deposit base it is likely that banks in different countries will continue to have different lending patterns as well. This implies also that a given change in euro interest rates might impact them quite differently. Moreover, to the extent that the funding pattern of the corporate sector continues to differ the same applies to the overall impact of monetary policy.

If one combines this finding with the leeway given to national central banks in the execution of the common monetary policy it reinforces the suspicion that even monetary policy will retain a national 'nuance'. Some national central banks might argue that a given increase in interest rates decided upon by the ECB in Frankfurt would have an unduly restrictive impact on their own country and might therefore feel justified in doing everything they can still do to soften the impact on their 'own' banking system. It is only to be hoped that the ECB will not allow such practices to get out of hand.

The government debt market is likely to become unified at the wholesale level, but a sizeable proportion of government is still sold in paper form to households in a number of member states. These papers are often geared to specific national circumstances like savings habits and tax regulations. While this way of financing the government is likely to become marginal in the very long run it will continue to constitute a sizeable part of the market until then.

There is general agreement that the financing structure of enterprises, which differs so strongly from country to country, is to a large extent determined by the structure of national tax systems (corporate taxation, personal taxation, etc.). These differences will not be affected by EMU and constitute another reason why capital markets will retain a national flavour.

The only broad-based change in financial markets that is likely to come as a consequence of EMU is some increase in securitization. Within the large market (at the wholesale level) that will be created the non-financial enterprises will find it more convenient to make the necessary effort to be able to issue commercial paper on their own instead of relying on bank loans. These economies of scale might also appear in other parts of the market and should in general favour large organized markets. One of the initial consequences of EMU might therefore be an increasing dichotomy between (mainly national) retail markets and a more and more unified wholesale market whose sheer size favours securitization and hence large organized exchanges.

At the wholesale level the reasons why some national idiosyncrasies are likely to persist are more subtle. The legal environment will continue to be different. A repo agreement in one member country might still have some different legal aspects from a similar agreement in another member country. Regulation of primary dealers is still subject to different national criteria. An additional reason, which is not always recognized, is that the common monetary policy might not be totally uniform. The reason for this lies in the federal organization of the ESCB, which leaves some room for differentiation by the national central banks which will continue to exist. A clear understanding of the structure and functioning of the ESCB is therefore required.

References

Arrowsmith, John (1996), 'Economic, Financial and Legal Aspects of the Transition to a Single European Currency', written evidence to the Treasury Committee of the House of Commons, UK (January).

Begg, David, Francesco Giavazzi, Jürgen von Hagen and Charles Wyplosz (1997), *EMU—Getting the End-Game Right*, Monitoring European Integration no. 7, London: Centre for Economic Policy Research (February).

Bishop, Graham (1990), 'Separating Fiscal from Monetary Sovereignty in EMU—A United States of Europe Is not Necessary', London: Salomon Brothers (November).

Dermine, Jean (1996), 'European Banking with a Single Currency', mimeo, INSEAD (March).

European Commission (1997), 'The Impact of the Introduction of the Euro on Capital Markets' (July).

European Monetary Institute (1996), 'First Progress Report on the TARGET Project', Working Group on EU Payment Systems (August).

European Monetary Institute (1997), 'The Single Monetary Policy in Stage III of EMU—Specification of the Operational Framework' (January).

European Mortgage Federation (1997), 'Mortgage Credit in the EU in 1996'.

Folkerts-Landau, David and Peter Garber (1992), 'The ECB: A Bank or a Monetary Policy Rule?', in M. Canzoneri, V. Grilli and P. Masson (eds.), *Establishing a Central Bank: Issues in Europe and Lessons from the US*, Cambridge: Cambridge University Press.

Folkerts-Landau, David, Peter Garber and Dirk Schoenmaker (1996), 'The Reform of Wholesale Payment Systems and Its Impact on Financial Markets', Group of Thirty, Occasional Paper no. 51.

Gantner, Anita (1997), 'Will the Ecofin Be Credible', *CEPS Review*, 4.

Goodhart, Charles and Dirk Schoenmaker (1995), 'Should the Functions of Monetary Policy and Banking Supervision Be Separated', *Oxford Economic Papers*, 47: 539–60.

Goodhart, Charles *et al.* (1997), 'Financial Regulation: Why, How and Where Now?' Monograph for the Central Bank Governors Meeting, Bank of England (June).

Grilli, Vittorio, Donato Masciandaro and Guido Tabellini (1991), 'Political and Monetary Institutions and Public Financial Policies in the Industrial Countries', *Economic Policy*, 13: 341–92.

Gros, Daniel (1996), 'Towards Economic and Monetary Union: Problems and Prospects', CEPS Paper no. 65.

Gros, Daniel and Karel Lannoo (1996), 'The Passage to the Euro', CEPS Working Party Report no. 15, Brussels (November).

Gros, Daniel and Niels Thygesen (1992), *European Monetary Integration: From the European Monetary System to European Monetary Union*, London: Longman (2nd rev. edn. forthcoming).

IMF (1996), *World Economic Outlook*, Washington, DC.

Monticelli, Carlo and Ugo Papi (1996), *European Integration, Monetary Coordination, and the Demand for Money*, Oxford: Clarendon Press.

OECD (1996), *Banking Profitability Statistics*.

Orr, Adrian, Malcolm Edey and Michael Kennedy (1995), 'The Determinants of Real Long Term Interest Rates: 17 Country Pooled Time Series Evidence', OECD Working Paper no. 155.

Romer, David (1988), 'What Are the Costs of Excessive Deficits?', *NBER Macroeconomics Annual 1988*, vol. 3.

Schoenmaker, Dirk (1994), 'Externalities in Payment Systems: Issues for Europe', CEPS Research Report no. 15.

Schoenmaker, Dirk (1995), 'Banking Supervision in Stage III of EMU', in *The Single Market in Banking: From 1992 to EMU*, CEPS Research Report no 17.

von Hagen, Jürgen (1997), 'Monetary Policy and Institutions in the EMU', *Swedish Economic Policy Journal*, 4(1), Spring: 51–116.

3
An International Role for the Euro?

CHARLES WYPLOSZ

Introduction

The international role of the euro is the hidden agenda of Europe's long-planned adoption of a single currency. Some Europeans long to regain monetary leadership, either for political symbolism or because they believe that it is financially profitable. Some in the USA are concerned for exactly symmetric reasons. Central bankers, as usual, worry that they may lose control but relish the thought of the impact that their cryptic pronouncements might have on markets all over the world. Markets wonder if there is money to be made by moving faster than officialdom. In the crime and underground business, this may be seen as yet another opportunity for evading detection, although there are risks ahead. This chapter reviews and assesses the so far limited literature on the issue.

The next section puts the emergence of the euro into historical perspective. It recalls the replacement of sterling by the dollar. Section 2 analyses what are the defining characteristics of a world currency. Section 3 evaluates the euro's chance of reaching this status. Whether it is a desirable outcome or not for Europe is discussed in Section 4, while Section 5 speculates on the implications of a bipolar international monetary system. The last section briefly concludes.

1. A Brief Historical Overview

1.1. What is a world currency?

It is customary to look at an international currency from the viewpoint of the functions traditionally ascribed to a national currency: medium of exchange, unit of account and store of value.[1] Table 3.1, from Krugman (1991), summarizes the situation, distinguishing private from public use. By and large, the private use of an international currency is no different from the private use of a national currency: it is

---

[1] For more details on the history of the international monetary system, see Eichengreen (1994) and Burda and Wyplosz (1997).

Table 3.1. Functions of an international currency

Function	Private use	Official use
Medium of exchange	Vehicle currency	Intervention currency
Unit of account	Quotation currency	Pegging currency
Store of value	Investment currency	Reserve currency

Source: Krugman (1991).

used to carry out transactions, to price goods, services and assets, and to be held as an asset. The only exception concerns the fact that, internationally, currencies can be exchanged against each other. When financial markets choose to make quotations in one particular currency, that currency acquires international status. The most popular view of an international currency is when it is widely used as a medium of exchange (Italian tourists take dollars when they travel to Indonesia).

What is specific to an international currency is its official use. Domestically, a currency typically has sole legal tender status. There is no similarly internationally recognized legal tender status but monetary authorities have various ways of raising a currency's status above the rest of the crowd. This can be done by using systematically one currency to trade on foreign exchange markets or by holding it as foreign exchange reserves. The most formal step is to choose a currency to which one's own currency is attached, either through a fixed peg or through more flexible arrangements ranging from a crawling peg to targeting.

There is no magic threshold that separates a plain from an international currency. The six cells in Table 3.1 allow us to assess the degree of internationalization of a currency. Of course, there are links between the various functions. For example, it is because the US dollar (henceforth, dollar for short) is widely used as a medium of exchange that people hold it as a store of value. The dollar is the only currency that currently performs all six functions. The DM and the yen perform these functions, but to a lesser degree and only in some regions.

1.2. How the dollar won the world

The first world currency (in modern times) was sterling. Sterling ruled the financial world at the end of the nineteenth century and up to the First World War. This was the time of the Gold Standard. Paper money was spreading fast but remained fully convertible into gold. In that sense, paper currencies were just titles to gold. So what does it mean that sterling was *the* world currency? In terms of Table 3.1, sterling was widely used as a unit of account for international transactions, as well as as an investment and reserve currency. The City of London was by far the largest financial centre. More importantly perhaps, the Bank of England's setting of its own interest rate affected the cost of money in the rest of the world. The Bank was able to control interest rates by engaging in liquidity management, thus departing from full gold coverage of sterling paper. The Bank's influence was related to its reputation: departures from full backing were not seen as a threat by holders of sterling paper. Interest rates in other countries followed the sterling interest rate owing to the widespread use of sterling as private and official store of value.

Following the First World War, Britain considered that, to retain its central role, sterling would have to recover its gold value, which had been suspended at the outset of hostilities. The Chancellor of the Exchequer, Winston Churchill, mistakenly associated reputation with continuity. The problem was that from 1913 to 1920 prices had increased by 150 per cent in Britain. Having only depreciated by 30 per cent, sterling was already overvalued. Returning to the prewar parity resulted in a major loss of competitiveness and trade deficits. The situation was not sustainable and sterling started to fade away as a store of value. It remained a unit of account until the Second World War, but alongside the dollar, which gradually took over status of world currency.

The USA emerged from the Second World War with a strong economy and political supremacy. The Marshall Plan well illustrates the imbalance between the UK and the USA at that time. The Gold Exchange Standard adopted in Bretton Woods in 1944 put the dollar squarely centre stage. All currencies were to be pegged to the dollar and the dollar would be pegged to gold. The dollar proceeded to fill all the functions shown in Table 3.1.

The demise of the Bretton Woods system partly weakened and partly strengthened the dollar. The Jamaica 1973 agreement formally marked the end of compulsory pegging to the dollar. In that sense the dollar has partly lost its function as official unit of account. The number of countries that continue to peg to the dollar has continuously decreased since then. Table 3.2 shows that only 21 of the 181 members of the International Monetary Fund (IMF) are pegged to the dollar. Yet the table understates the role of the dollar, since many of the currencies classified as having chosen 'other pegs' in fact use currency baskets in which the dollar figures prominently. On the other side, since 1971 gold has essentially lost all monetary function, leaving the dollar as *the* ultimate unit of account.

Table 3.2. Exchange rate regimes (no. of countries)

Regime	1975	June 1997
Fixed exchange rate		
Pegged to:		
US dollar	46	21
French franc	13	14
Sterling	8	0
Other	32	31
Limited flexibility	13	51
Freely floating	15	64
Total	127	181

Source: IMF.

1.3. Europe's slow rise

Since 1973, the dollar has ceased to enjoy a legal advantage over potential competitors. In effect, its role has been declining, albeit very slowly. This evolution is illustrated by the evolution of foreign exchange reserves (the store of value official function). Table 3.3 shows that the dollar's share has been gradually eroded since 1973. The newly emerging currencies are the DM and the yen, with some limited role for ECU-denominated assets.

Table 3.3. Currency composition of foreign exchange reserves[a]

	1973	1987	1995
US dollar	84.5	66.0	56.4
Sterling	5.9	2.2	3.4
DM	6.7	13.4	13.7
French franc	1.2	0.8	1.8
Swiss franc	1.4	1.5	0.1
Yen	—	7.0	7.1
ECU	—	5.7	6.5
Others		3.4	9.7

[a] Percentage of total, all countries, end of year.

Sources: Alogoskoufis and Portes (1992), Masson and Turtelboom (1997).

This pattern is quite general across the diverse functions of what makes an international currency. In particular, the DM and the ECU have won the beginning of an international recognition, cutting into the dollar's domination. Part of the reason lies in Europe. The existence of a fixed exchange rate arrangement, the European Monetary System (EMS), has prompted member central banks to intervene increasingly in common currencies. This in turn has led to holding foreign exchange reserves in European currencies. Another, more important, explanation is the emergence of the DM as the European currency.

Up until the mid-1980s, the Bundesbank was known as a highly reputable central bank which had shielded Germany from the boom-and-bust swings that followed the two oil shocks. Yet, the DM was one member of the EMS among others. Certainly, the DM was a currency that no one would ever expect to see depreciated, but that is how far it could be singled out. By the end of the 1980s, the EMS came to be known as a DM area and Fed-watchers started to train to become Bundesbank-watchers as well. Nowadays no one remotely interested in international finance can afford to ignore on which day the Council of the Bundesbank meets and Mr Tietmeyer is almost as well known to the broad public as Mr Greenspan. What happened?[2]

---

[2] The history of the emergence of the DM as the prime EMS currency has been described by many authors. See e.g. Giavazzi and Giovannini (1989), Begg and Wyplosz (1993), Burda and Wyplosz (1997).

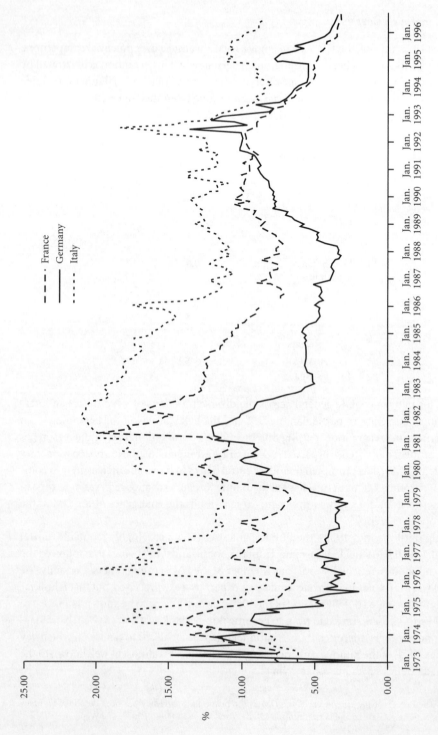

Figure 3.1. Short-term interest rates
Source: IMF.

The DM has become the currency against which other currencies can only depreciate. Its interest rates have naturally become the base from which interest rates elsewhere in Europe are set. In the other EMS countries, the interest rate is the German rate *plus* expected depreciation *vis-à-vis* the DM over the relevant horizon. Any move by the Bundesbank that affects the German interest rate is immediately followed by similar changes in other EMS interest rates. The link was made increasingly tighter as restrictions on capital movements, widespread in the 1970s and early 1980s, were gradually eliminated, being outlawed as of July 1990 by the Single Act (Figure 3.1). This evolution has meant that the Bundesbank *de facto* controls all interest rates in the EMS, giving the DM a weight far larger than justified by the economic size of Germany.

2. What Do We Know about World Currencies?

This section will look at various possible reasons why a currency becomes international. Two main theories have been proposed. One concerns the means of payments function, the other the store of value function. We look at each theory separately and then draw a number of implications.

2.1. Vehicle currencies

2.1.1. *Invoicing*

Trade can be paid for in the exporter's currency, in the importer's currency, or in a third, vehicle currency. Since the seminal work of Grassman (1973), it is known that trade tends to be invoiced in the exporter's currency. If that were always the case, then invoicing would be proportional to the volume of exports country by country. The recent estimates shown in the right panel of Table 3.4 broadly confirm this result, but the rule is not very robust. Only in the USA does it come close to being exactly satisfied. In the other countries a significant and often growing proportion of exports is not invoiced in the domestic currency. For smaller countries it is not even a tendency.

Table 3.4. Trade invoicing

	% Of world trade			% Of national exports	
	1980	1987	1992	1980	1987
US dollar	56	48	48	97	92
DM	14	16	15	83	77
Yen	2	4	5	29	40
Sterling	7	6	6	76	62
French franc	6	7	6	61	55

Source: Bénassy-Quéré (1996), based on EU Commission estimates.

The left panel of the table confirms the special status of the dollar. In 1992, 48 per cent of all international trade was invoiced in dollars. This is 3.6 times the share of the USA in world trade. The only other currency whose share of invoicing exceeds the country's trade share is Germany (1.4 times), while the ratio is exactly 1 for sterling and the franc, which appear to be minor invoicing currencies. The weight of the USA has declined since 1980 but this is almost entirely explained by the decline of oil in world trade (owing to the fall of oil prices after 1986). When this factor is accounted for, the role of various currencies has hardly changed since 1980.

It is not easy to explain these facts by appealing to commercial practices. Some authors (e.g. McKinnon, 1979) have argued that sellers of differentiated goods use their market power to impose invoicing in their own currency and thus avoid currency risk. Indeed Tavlas (1991) shows that trade invoicing is linked to exports of specialized products and to the extent of trade with developing countries. However Rao and Magee (1980) have shown an exporter should be indifferent between charging a lower price for invoicing in one's own currency or a higher price to compensate for the exchange risk when invoicing is in a foreign currency. Given this equivalence, we are left with no good reason why exports tend to be invoiced in the exporter's currency. The explanation must lie elsewhere.

2.1.2. *Transaction costs*

A more promising explanation takes into account the costs of transactions in foreign currencies. A number of authors (Niehans, 1969; Krugman, 1980) have looked into the possibility that the cost of exchanging currency, which must be borne by one of the two parties,[3] may differ according to the currencies involved. For example, when goods are exported from Denmark to the Netherlands, either the exporter or the importer will have to face the cost of changing guilders into krone. The choice must be, implicitly at least, part of the negotiation on the price of the deal. In that case both parties stand to benefit from lower transaction costs.

What if it is cheaper to go from guilders into dollars and then from dollars into krone? In that case it is easier and cheaper to invoice the deal in dollars. The Dutch importer will face one transaction cost as she buys the dollars, and the Danish exporter will face another cost in selling the dollars for krone. Both will be better off, and will not even have to bargain on the currency used in invoicing.

Transaction costs are related to three services that foreign exchange market intermediaries must perform. First is order processing. To execute orders for their customers, intermediaries must be continuously present in the market and subscribe to information and trading systems. This includes finding counterparts. Second come inventory costs. As they must hold adequate amounts of currencies, intermediaries face costs of unbalanced portfolios and the risk of capital losses. The last cost is that of acquiring the information needed to price currencies. Clearly, at least for order processing and information costs, there exist increasing returns to scale, so that larger

---

[3] This is not quite true, as will become clearer soon.

Table 3.5. Transaction costs in foreign exchange markets, April 1992

	Spread	Volume	Volatility
DM/dollar	4.56	87.9	0.31
FF/dollar	3.77	3.0	0.32
FF/DM	1.11	6.7	0.04
Guilder/dollar	3.65	1.1	0.03
Guilder/DM	0.85	8.5	0.00

Notes: Spread is measured in basis points; volume is billion dollars, daily average; volatility is measured in basis points.

Source: Hartman (1996a).

markets should lead to lower costs. The second cost is related to the volatility of exchange rates (more generally to the risk/return characteristic of currencies, which includes correlations with wider market returns).

Increasing returns to scale imply that transaction costs should naturally lead to a few large wholesale markets for the main currencies, while the other currencies should be dealt with on smaller retail markets. Recent statistical work (Hartmann, 1996a) broadly confirms both the theoretical prediction and earlier empirical studies, but it also indicates that there is much more to it. Table 3.5 shows a couple of examples. The costs of transaction of the largest wholesale foreign market, between the dollar and the DM, appear larger than for two retail markets, the franc and guilder *vis-à-vis* the DM. Part of the explanation has to do with exchange rate volatility, which is clearly lower for the guilder–DM rate. Another part of the story is that transaction costs are not well known. The table reports inter-dealer spreads quoted on Reuters. These are quotes, not transactions. They refer to the inter-dealer market, not to transactions affecting end-users. The European Commission report (1990) had publicized enormous costs for the retail market, between 200 and 300 basis points.

The conclusion is that increasing returns are present on foreign exchange markets. *Ceteris paribus*, this should lead to a limited number of wholesale markets involving a few vehicle currencies. In particular the dollar is often used as third currency for transactions between countries with 'minor' currencies. The DM could also be fulfilling this function within Europe.

2.1.3. *Foreign exchange reserves and central bank interventions*

So far we have looked at the size of the market as explained by private behaviour. Two of the attributes of an international currency are official store of value and use as means of payment in official transactions. Central banks are occasionally present on foreign exchange markets. Even in countries like the USA, Japan and the UK which do not have a formal exchange rate target, central banks are known to be keen to restrain volatility (Funabashi, 1988).

Little is publicly known of interventions in general, and of the currency in which they are undertaken in particular. What is better known is the currency denomination of officially held foreign exchange reserves. The US dollar represents about 56 per cent of world exchange reserves. At about 14 per cent the DM is a distant second, leaving several other currencies (sterling, SDRs, ECUs, French and Swiss francs) to share the rest. The dominance of the dollar is linked to its role as vehicle currency for trade: central banks care about exchange rates partly because they are concerned that fluctuations may affect competition in goods and services. It matters for them to limit volatility of the currencies used in international trade.

Foreign exchange reserves are directly associated with trade in developing countries whose currencies are not convertible, or at least not widely traded. These countries consider that they need reserves to face their import expenses. There is natural tendency for them to hold as reserves the same currencies that they use in trading with the rest of the world. This establishes another link from vehicle currency to official currency.

2.1.4. *Summary*

We have encountered two main reasons for a currency to be used as a vehicle for international transactions: low cost and official use. Yet, these two factors too need to be explained. This is left for Section 2.3 below.

2.2. Store of value and portfolio diversification

The analysis so far concerns currencies defined as cash, that is, liabilities of the central banks. As a store of value, however, what matters really are not holdings of cash but holdings of interest-yielding assets. Some of these assets are issued by the public sector (Treasury bills and bonds) others by the private sector. In fact, this is where the big numbers are.

2.2.1. *Country size*

Looking first at internationally held bonds (issued by public and private borrowers as well as by international organizations), estimates by the BIS for end-1996 report a total of about US$3,200 billion. Table 3.6 shows that some US$1,200 billion was denominated in dollars, US$520 billion in yen and US$315 billion in DM. These numbers could just reflect the size of public debts in the largest countries. Table 3.6 relates the two

Table 3.6. International bonds (US$ bn.)

(1) Internationally held bonds denominated in		(2) Gross national public debt		Ratio (1)/(2)
Dollars	1,207	USA	4,822	0.25
DM	315	Germany	1,471	0.24
Yen	519	Japan	1,641	0.14

Sources: Artus (1997) and *European Economy*, 62 (1996).

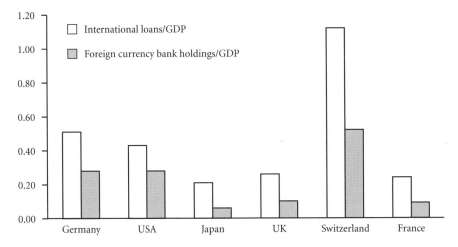

Figure 3.2. Currency internationalization compared to GDP

Sources: Artus (1997); IMF; *European Economy*, 62 (1996); and author's calculations.

measures and partly confirms this interpretation: internationally held bonds in the domestic currency represent about 25 per cent of the US and German public debts. There are indications (Bénassy-Quéré and Deusy-Fournier, 1995) that a significant share of internationally held dollar and DM bonds is public debt while, in the case of the yen, most of the foreign-held bonds are private issues.

Does country size matter? Figure 3.2 relates two measures of currency internationalization to GDPs. The first measure is the value of international loans (loans from a country's resident to a resident of another country) by currency of denomination. The BIS reports for end-1996 international loans amounting to US$7,600 billion, with US$3,260 billion denominated in dollars, US$1,150 billion in DM and US$875 in yen. The second measure is the currency denomination of cross-border bank holdings. The Swiss franc clearly plays a special role, but it has declined considerably since the liberalization of capital flows in Europe in the mid-1980s. The figure shows again that the dollar and the mark rank about equally, ahead of France, Japan and the UK.

These numbers conceal a well-known result from the international finance literature: there is surprisingly little portfolio diversification across borders.[4] The phenomenon of 'home-country bias' concerns the two definitions of 'foreign assets': individuals and financial institutions alike tend to hold mostly assets issued by fellow residents, and they also tend to hold assets mostly denominated in their home currency. The many explanations offered to explain this phenomenon go far beyond the brief of the present chapter. The three main ones are: (1) a preference for domestically produced goods; (2) information asymmetries, the fact that it is easier to know about the credit-worthiness

---

[4] See Solnik (1974), Tesar and Weber (1992), Dumas (1994).

of resident than foreign borrowers; (3) regulations, ranging from capital controls to restrictions on pension fund portfolios. Thus, to become an international store of value, a currency must climb a steep hill. It is unlikely that the world will support more than one, maybe two or three genuine world currencies.

2.2.2. *Market effects*

Empirical work suggests that, beyond size, stability in terms of inflation and exchange rates affects the use of a currency in international portfolios. Most important, maybe, is the existence of wide and deep financial markets on which assets can be traded and currencies exchanged.

Yet, market location does not determine the influence of currencies, as can be seen from Table 3.7. London is by far the largest foreign exchange market but sterling plays a relatively minor role. On the other side, the DM is the second most traded currency while Frankfurt is a rather small market. Developments in financial market technologies increasingly allow for location to matter less. This concerns the origin of assets: stocks of a given company can be simultaneously traded on exchanges world-wide, whether the stocks themselves or derivatives. Thus the size of the country, a rough measure of the volume of stocks issued in that country, matters little, and will matter less. The same is true regarding the currency. As illustrated in Table 3.7, London still maintains its two-century-old supremacy as financial centre of the world (this applies to the foreign exchange market, not to the stock exchange), but sterling has long lost its status of world currency. It has lost it, we have seen, partly because of policy mistakes: deflation policies in the 1920s, inflationary policies in the 1950s and 1960s. Conversely, the DM has emerged as the prime European currency first, and as a major world player despite a fairly repressed financial market. Its strength is stability: guaranteed low inflation and a long-run tendency to appreciate.

Table 3.7. Exchange markets, April 1995

	Total average daily market turnover (US$ bn.)							
	London	New York	Tokyo	Singapore	Hong Kong	Zurich	Frankfurt	Paris
April 1989	184	115	111	55	49	56	55	23
April 1995	465	244	161	105	90	87	76	58

	Use of currency on one side of transaction (total = 200%)							
	Dollar	DM	Yen	Sterling	French franc	Swiss franc	ECU	Other EMS
April 1989	90	27	27	15	2	10	1	3
April 1995	83	37	24	10	8	7	2	13

Source: BIS (1996).

2.2.3. *Summary*

This section leaves us some more clues. Size is a necessary condition for a currency to achieve world-class status. Size matters because there is not enough portfolio diversification. Both issuers of liabilities and holders of assets prefer the home currency. A favourable environment for financial markets is neither sufficient (viz. sterling) nor necessary (viz. the DM) for internationalization. Stability-oriented policies are a necessary condition: the DM has emerged as a serious contender as the dollar declined following two decades of lax policies in the USA.

2.3. Synergies and inertia

The many clues accumulated so far still do not add up to a complete interpretation. The true story seems to be dynamic: an already widely used currency accumulates the characteristics that make it even more attractive internationally. Put differently, something must trigger a virtuous cycle which strengthens a currency's appeal. This interpretation has long been identified and recently more firmly established (Hartmann, 1996a). It links market size and transaction costs.

Section 2.1 has argued that for a currency to be widely used, transaction costs must be low. But what makes transaction costs low? Mostly, size. It is easy to see, then, that if a currency benefits from a large market (exchange market, bond market, stock exchange) with low transaction costs, it will attract traders and investors from elsewhere. The markets grow and transaction costs further decline, which attracts more business. Further synergies come into play. The vehicle currency function leads to large exchange markets where costs are low and encourage using the currency as a vehicle for triangular operations. This interpretation carries a number of important implications.

First, history matters. A currency that has somehow managed to lift itself to world rank has a good chance of staying there, at least for a while. This obviously fits well the case of sterling. Conversely, a currency which might claim world status may be unable to challenge the incumbent. This could apply to the euro.

Secondly, and as a consequence, specific events may be needed to jump-start a change of guard. The two world wars did it for the dollar.

Thirdly, size is even more important than initially noted. To be international, a currency must start from a large home base where transaction costs decline sufficiently for the currency to start moving up the world ladder. The DM has gone quite far owing to its intrinsic quality, but it could not have gone much further had EMU not happened. The same applies for the yen. One can of course start wondering about the Chinese yuan or the Indian ruppiah.

Fourthly, low and declining costs are a necessary condition. Competition responds to razor-thin differences. Financial market costs partly depend on the uncertainty that underpins financial products. A stable economic and political environment is needed to achieve that extra cost reduction which makes a huge difference.

Fifthly, the authorities have a role to play, if they wish. They affect costs through regulation. Regulation matters because, in principle, it reduces uncertainty, but it is costly. The challenge is to find the proper balance between a regulation which is so light that it fails to limit risk and a regulation that becomes too heavy and costly.

Sixthly, the authorities also affect the size of markets as they are participants themselves. This applies not just to buying and selling for their own needs, but also to the exchange rate regime. More stability may give the currency a competitive edge, but misguided efforts at defending an exchange rate parity may backfire.

Finally, we are looking at a very slow process. The virtuous cycle of declining costs and growing market size is unlikely to unfold fast. The time-scale is measured in decades, not in months. Yet, because of its inherent inertia, evolution is likely to take the form of leaps, not smooth shifts, a reminder of the Darwinian evolutionary process.

3. The Euro's Prospects

We now apply the previous conclusions to investigate the central question: what international role for the euro? We start by looking at Europe's size and find that indeed the euro has a fighting chance. We next look at the stability of the currency and conclude that this is where the euro's main comparative advantage may lie. We then discuss the issue of transaction costs and financial market structure, coming up with a sombre assessment. Finally, we consider briefly the euro's potential role as the world's underground currency.

3.1. Size and trade

Europe is big and rather closed, much as the USA. Table 3.8 makes that point. The first two columns present the economic size as measured by GDP in 1991. The first column uses GDPs converted into dollars at the actual exchange rate. The second column corrects for differences in cost of living, using purchasing power parity (PPP)-adjusted exchange rates. On the second measure the European Union and the USA each represent about 22 per cent of world GDP. This is big.

The third column shows European exports as a percentage of world exports in 1992. Europe is often described as very open because so far we have looked at intra-European exports of each member country: on that count, European exports represent 43.2 per cent of world exports. However, in EMU intra-European exports will become intra-euro-area transactions, much like trade between Texas and Minnesota. When the transactions are netted out we are left with a significantly lower share of 16.9 per cent.[5] This is larger than the US share, but not much larger. Since exports tend to be invoiced in the exporter's currency, the euro will have an advantage over the dollar, but not a significant one.

---

[5] For this calculation intra-European exports are not netted out of world exports.

Table 3.8. The European Union: size and openness (% of world figure)

	GDP at market prices	GDP at PPP	Exports at market prices
EU15 (external trade)	30.1	22.0	16.9
EU15 (internal trade)			26.3
USA	24.5	21.7	12.3
Japan	14.6	9.1	9.3
Germany	7.4	5.0	11.8

Source: Hartmann (1996*b*).

An interesting back-of-the-envelope calculation performed by Hartmann (1996*b*) assumes that trade patterns and invoicing practices remain unchanged. Using 1992 as a benchmark, he finds that the share of world trade invoicing in dollar will grow from 47.6 per cent to 59.4 per cent. This corresponds to the 'elimination' of about 26 per cent of world trade when intra-European trade becomes internal transactions. The share of the euro is 25.2 per cent. These are just indicative numbers, of course, based on specific assumptions. Three corrections are in order.

First, not all EU15 will participate in EMU. The UK, Sweden, Denmark and Greece could join later. In that case the exports of the euro area will be larger, of the order of 20 per cent.[6] Paradoxically, therefore, the narrower the initial group of EMU members the larger will be the share of euro area exports. This advantage should not be overblown, however. It has been noted already that the emergence of a vehicle currency is a very slow process. It is likely that, long before the euro has displaced the dollar, EMU will have expanded to include not only all fifteen current EU members, but probably some more countries in the East or the South.

Secondly, this is a static view. Some areas of the world grow faster than others and such unequal development may affect trade patterns over the next decade or two. In particular, Asia is the growth market of the world, one where Europe is often seen as being at a comparative disadvantage relative to the USA and Japan. This is not quite correct. Between 1980 and 1992, the US share of OECD exports to Asia declined (from 34.7 per cent to 29.3 per cent), Japan's share rose slightly (from 26.5 per cent to 29.6 per cent), while it is Europe that most progressed (from 20.6 per cent to 24.6 per cent).[7] That trend may not continue, but at least the Asian growth miracle does not require that the previous conclusion be qualified.

Thirdly, Eastern Europe and possibly the former Soviet Union are likely to undergo many years of relatively fast growth. This is the euro's turf. Already eight countries[8]

---

[6] EU exports to the UK, Denmark, Sweden and Greece represent some 10% of total EU15 exports. This figure increases to 15% when Italy is added.

[7] Europe here corresponds to the twelve EU countries before Austria, Finland and Sweden joined in.

[8] Bulgaria, the Czech Republic, Estonia, Hungary, Lithuania, Poland, Slovakia and Slovenia.

have tied, officially or not, their currencies to the DM or to baskets where the DM or the ECU plays a significant role.

3.2. Stability and strength

3.2.1. *Principles*

Stability is seen as a necessary condition for a currency to acquire an international role. What does stability mean exactly? Going back once again to Table 3.1, it is clear that two characteristics matter. For the unit of account function the amount that one unit of the currency can buy must remain stable; that is, inflation must be low and predictable. For the medium of exchange and store of value functions, a world currency is used as a temporary abode. It may last a few seconds as the vehicle currency is used for exchange between third currencies, but it may last longer as money is stacked away for honest or dishonest reasons. In that case, it matters that the value of the currency not be expected to be eroded. Holders want to know that whenever they sell the world currency to go into a currency of their choice, they will not have to suffer a capital loss. The currency must be 'strong', meaning that it is expected to secularly appreciate and not to undergo too-important depreciations, even if temporary. Thus necessary conditions are low and predictable inflation as well as an exchange rate tendentially appreciating and rarely depreciating.

Finance theory would add another consideration. Capital asset pricing theories emphasize that an asset is desirable either because it provides high returns or because the returns are not risky. An international currency supports non-interest-bearing cash as well as interest-bearing assets. In the former case, inflation means a negative return, so the lower inflation the more attractive the currency. In the latter case, the low interest rates which usually accompany low inflation may seem a hindrance. In fact these low interest rates owing to low inflation become a benchmark against which asset returns in more inflation-prone countries are measured. Active asset managers will often leave the low-interest currency to take advantage of better yields elsewhere, but they will always stay on the alert and remain ready to return to the safety of low returns. This has been the case for a long time; recently assets invested in Mexico and the rest of Latin America were suddenly converted back into dollars in 1994–5, and yet again from Thailand and many Asian countries in 1997. Low interest rates therefore do not prevent a currency from being used as a store of value, a sort of base from which front-line attacks can be carried out. As for risk, it is measured by the degree of correlation with the world portfolio: *ceteris paribus* 'contrarian' assets are more desirable. A true world currency, though, is bound to weigh heavily in the world portfolio, so that it is a bad candidate for low risk in the finance-theoretical sense. Simply put, one cannot be the benchmark and sit on the fence.

The twin characteristics of low inflation and a strong currency are related, and ultimately derive from monetary policy. In addition, low inflation empirically means stable inflation. Lower inflation than in other countries typically translates into a long-run trend of appreciation even if shorter-run depreciations cannot be ruled out. The source of price stability and exchange rate strength is monetary policy. A central bank that squarely focuses on a price or inflation target[9] and is ready to tolerate output and employment fluctuations to achieve its target is bound to deliver what it seeks. In addition the central bank acquires a reputation which affects the behaviour of firms as they set prices for their products, workers and their trade unions as they negotiate over wages, and market traders as they operate on foreign exchange markets.

3.2.2. *The European Central Bank: average weight vs. institutions*

Can we guess what will be the track record of the ECB? Two main views have been advanced, with radically different conclusions. The first view focuses on the governing body of the ECB, the Governing Council. The Council will include the governors of all member central banks (which will lose all independent monetary policy power) as well as the members of the Executive Board, namely the President and the Vice-President and (up to) four appointed members. It is natural to wonder what will be the mix of opinions within this body.

According to Currie *et al.* (1990), each governor will tend to represent the particular views of her country. For example, German citizens are known to harbour a profound repulsion towards inflation and to be ready to suffer recessions and rising unemployment if that is what it takes to curb inflation. Conversely, Club Med citizens are presumed to be less allergic to inflation and willing to compromise to avoid a recession. In that view, the position of the ECB and the strength of the euro will depend on which countries are part of EMU. At the beginning, the ECB will be an untested authority and will have to establish its own reputation form scratch. The logical conclusion is that only a narrow EMU will stand a chance of producing a currency apt to inherit the DM's emerging international status. Put differently, the ECB will be the average of its members, and the strength of the euro—and price stability in EMU—will be the average strength of the currencies which are being replaced by the euro.

This 'average weight' view carries considerable support among some central banks and on financial markets. Yet it is not based on solid principles. To start with, it ignores the constitution of the ECB, a point to which we soon return. Next, it assumes that each governor will represent her home-country public opinion. Governors of the national central banks will enjoy total independence from their authorities. The question therefore is the degree to which they will see it as their mandate to represent within the Council views held by public opinions back home. Then there is the question of whether there really exist national preferences. It is unclear why, placed in the same conditions and with the same understanding of the economic mechanism, Italian citizens would be more tolerant towards inflation than German citizens. One possibility is that economic conditions differ, with different incentives. This is precisely what the convergence criteria were meant to homogenize.

---

[9] Recent work by Svensson (1996) considers the distinction between a price level target and an inflation (rate of growth of the price level) target.

The other possibility is that perceptions of the economic mechanism differ across countries, but then scientific humility requires us to admit that no one can say who is right.[10] At least, it is interesting to note what revealed preferences show: according to the recent study by Clarida *et al.* (1997) the Bundesbank itself targets a combination of inflation and output. They further show that the behaviour of the Bundesbank's approach does not differ significantly from that of the Federal Reserve Bank or that of the Bank of Japan. This suggests that popular caricatures may be fun, but are seriously misleading. Finally, we need to consider the personal incentives that governors will face when sitting in the Governing Council. Will their subsequent career depend upon catering to domestic interests or rather upon being influential within the Council? On one side, they may indeed plan to take on other official positions at home which would lead them to use their chair at the Governing Council to trumpet their attachment to the homeland. On the other side, the profession's most coveted job will be to become President of the ECB. This position is more likely to go to a team-player than to a maverick populist. It should also be noted that governors will certainly be chosen in the future for their skills in becoming influential within the Governing Council, a profile which fits conservative leanings better than national-champion zeal.

The second view emphasizes institutions. It notes the unambiguous mission laid out for the ECB in the Maastricht Treaty: 'The primary objective of the ESCB shall be to maintain price stability. Without prejudice to the objective of price stability, the ESCB shall support the general economic policies in the Community' (Art. 105(1)).[11] The 'institutions matter' view also observes that of the two governing bodies, the Executive Board will be in charge of day-to-day operations while the Governing Council will have a broader mission. Without denying that the Governing Council will have a say in setting policy, it is likely that only under exceptional circumstances will the Council be ready to disagree with the six-person Executive Board. This matters because the Executive Board members will not be employed by national central banks, providing them with some 'distance' from national purviews.

Under the 'institutions matter' interpretation, the ECB will be even more independent from political pressure than the Bundesbank. Its mandate being the same as the Bundesbank's, the presumption is that the ECB will implement policies which will be at least as much geared to price stability as the Bundesbank's. In addition, it is argued, the ECB will not start without reputation. Its constitution is clearly inspired by the Bundesbank's, it will be located in Frankfurt, and its first President brings with him a solid reputation of inflation-fighter.

Critics of the 'institutions matter' view note that the formal independence of a

---

[10] A very interesting review of existing macroeconomic models led by Bryant *et al.* (1993) reveals profound divergences.

[11] The Treaty draws a formal distinction between the ECB and the European System of Central Banks (ESCB). The ESCB is composed of the ECB and national central banks. In fact, the ECB is where decisions will be taken: 'The ESCB shall be governed by the decision-making bodies of the ECB' (Art. 8 of the Protocol laying down the statutes of the ESCB). For this reason we mention ECB where, occasionally, the Treaty refers to the ESCB.

central bank is limited by powerful if implicit democratic checks and balances. The Bundesbank always emphasizes that it can pursue tough policies only when it has the support of German public opinion. The ECB will face a public opinion which can be seen as the average of the national public opinions, an observation which reinforces the 'average weight' view. One answer is that, in contrast to national central banks, which face one government and one (possibly diverse) public opinion, the ECB will face several governments and public opinions. These pressure groups are unlikely to agree, and especially to forge an alliance to oppose the ECB. Indeed, should the ECB pursue a policy perceived as too strict in some quarters, unless the policy is clearly misguided there will be other governments which will want to support the ECB. Put differently, public opinions will not average out but disagree and the ECB will find it easy to divide and conquer.

3.2.3. *External value of the euro*

Low inflation implies a strong currency. Strong currency status, on the other side, does not ensure that the currency will not occasionally depreciate. Strong currencies are known to exhibit long-lasting swings which are related to macroeconomic cycles and associated financial swings.

Monetary authorities are not completely powerless in the face of these cycles. Much depends on how they carry out policy. More precisely, central banks contemplate a menu of intermediate targets: money growth, interest rates, the exchange rate or (expected) inflation. The choice of an intermediate target is a complex and much-studied issue. Most central banks have moved to a fairly flexible approach, opportunistically using all intermediate targets. The creation of EMU is prompting a re-think, concerning in particular the question of what to do with the euro, as surveyed in Giavazzi *et al.* (1997).

In particular, it is asked whether the euro will be more or less stable than the DM. As a major currency, the evolution of the euro will not depend solely on European conditions. The external value of the euro will be sized up against the dollar, possibly the yen too. But one can view the dollar–euro exchange rates as a measure of the external value of the dollar as much as of the euro. There is no absolute benchmark here. The proper question will therefore be: how will the main currencies of the world be managed once the euro is born? At present, there is no unanimous answer.

Benign neglect. It is often believed that volatility among the main currencies will increase because of benign neglect. Exchange rate fluctuations can be dampened by the monetary authorities. Exchange market interventions play a role in smoothing out short-term fluctuations, but they lose their effectiveness over the longer run, say, from one month to three years. Over this longer horizon—the one that matters most for trade and non-speculative investment—to exert a dominating influence central banks must put a clear priority on the exchange rate target, at the expense of domestic targets. In a world dominated by three large and relatively closed currency blocks (dollar, euro and yen) the main central banks will be quite reluctant to sacrifice domestic targets to the exchange rate target since the latter will exert limited effects on the economy. Such benign neglect has often been ascribed to the behaviour of the USA. Other, more open countries, chiefly in Europe, have felt compelled to carry out interventions to bring some degree of stability to their dollar exchange rates. Equipped with the euro, Europe will resemble the USA and could well indeed adopt a benign neglect approach to the external value of the euro. This would mean more volatility than that exhibited by the DM.

Currency substitution. If the dollar and the euro share the role of world currency, they will become alternatives to millions of operators. This may lead to the phenomenon of currency substitution, often described, never seen so far.[12] When two currencies are (perfect) substitutes, demand for the sum of the two is well defined, but the breakdown into one or the other is pretty much arbitrary and therefore quite volatile. International currency operators will each tend to prefer using just one currency, but will not care too much which one as long as it performs the same services. Being indifferent, they will be willing to jump ship whenever the breeze tells them to. The proponents of the currency substitution view assert that the result will be unstable demand for the world currencies which will translate into high exchange rate volatility. Indeed, the only way to limit instability would be for supply to promptly respond to demand. Given the uncertainty that is bound to surround these shifts it is highly unlikely that the monetary authorities will stand ready to accommodate such whims.

More stability? Other arguments suggest less volatility. To start with, exchange rates are buffeted by various shocks, some of which are home-made. EMU, being large, may well suffer from less macroeconomic shocks, as the law of large numbers suggests that local (i.e. national or regional) shocks will have a tendency to offset each other. Secondly, measuring openness as percentage points of GDP may hide the qualitative nature of trade links. Europe will have a number of trade partners that are close neighbours, in contrast to the USA, which mostly trades with distant partners. This may work against benign neglect. Finally, the USA could largely ignore the dollar in part because other monetary authorities were 'minding the store'. Either through exchange market intervention or by adapting their monetary policies, central banks in Europe and Japan have shown concern for the dollar value of their currencies. In a bipolar world with two large currencies, the situation is bound to change. Large fluctuations in the euro will sizeably affect the value of the dollar. Benign neglect would lead to transatlantic conflicts, and cannot therefore be benign.

Assessment. Given the prospective nature of the question, there is no way of deciding which of these arguments will carry more weight. According to the evidence provided by Martin (1997) there exists a hump-shaped relationship between country size and

---

[12] A standard reference to the literature on currency substitution is Giovannini and Turtleboom (1991).

exchange rate volatility. Very small countries tend to be open and thus are very sensitive to exchange rate movements; their monetary authorities actively stabilize the exchange rate, which they view as a more important target than purely nominal variables. At the other end of the spectrum, large countries are too closed to use the exchange rate as a policy tool. This evidence is too preliminary to be taken at face value, but it suggests that the euro could be less volatile *vis-à-vis* the dollar than current European currencies.

3.3. Transaction costs and financial markets

Of all the characteristics of an international currency, the existence of wide and deep markets with low transaction costs seems to be the most crucial. Will the existence of the euro provoke the emergence of a market where size and competition are combined to drive down transaction costs below those found on dollar markets? The answer depends essentially on the effects that the euro will have on European banks and financial markets. This is an issue beyond the scope of the present chapter. Consequently, we simply offer here a few remarks.

It is generally expected that the euro will trigger a wave of profound changes in Europe. The long-run result should indeed be highly competitive transaction costs. Under that scenario, the euro has a serious chance of challenging the dollar as a world currency. This concerns first the store of value function, but can spread to the other private and public functions as well. Much will depend on direct costs but also on indirect costs such as taxes, regulations and risk. The authorities will have a crucial role to play here. In Section 4 we consider the question of whether they should take steps to favour the adoption of the euro as a world currency.

The transition to highly efficient markets may be difficult, however. To start with, banks are not everywhere competitive. A shake-up may be desirable in the long run, but fairly devastating in the shorter run. Similarly, there might not be room for as many financial centres as we currently have. Hopefully the evolution can take the form of a soft landing, but that is not guaranteed. This may have an impact on the international future of the euro.

As noted in Section 2.3 above, the status of a currency is history-dependent. The emergence of a world currency requires a triggering factor. It may be an adverse evolution of the reigning currency, or it may be a favourable shock on the challenger. The well-publicized and highly dramatized birth of the euro can play the role of favourable shock. Certainly markets are well aware of the impending changes and ready to jump on the bandwagon should it get rolling. If, as the euro starts its ascent, a series of serious financial and/or banking crises occurs, the bandwagon will turn into a snail retreating inside its shell. Much of the initial favourable effect will have been lost. Even if banks and financial markets eventually emerge considerably strengthened, the initial kick will have been wasted and, pending further major shocks (always possible), the euro will have to climb the ladder one step at a time. As matters go in this area, this could mean several decades.

3.4. A shadowy money?

So far it has implicitly been assumed that cash matters for medium of exchange (transaction and official intervention) purposes while interest-yielding assets matter for the store of value function. Indeed, cash is a very poor asset. Yet, cash is used as a store of value and, in fact, increasingly so. It is the store of value for criminal activities, including tax evasion.

By definition, little is known of the use of cash in the underworld, and on currency holdings in general. Rogoff (1998) presents estimates from a number of studies mainly carried out by monetary authorities. He concludes that the main currencies used in cash form are the dollar (US$250 billion held abroad), the yen (US$80 billion held abroad), the DM (US$50 billion) and the Swiss franc (US$12 billion).[13] Table 3.9 shows that this represents a very sizeable proportion of these currencies' supply. For the other currencies, the amounts held abroad seem much smaller.

Table 3.9. Who holds the cash? (currency held outside banks)

	USA		Germany		Japan		Switzerland	
	1980	1995	1980	1995	1980	1995	1980	1995
Currency[a] (% of GDP)	8.1	9.5	5.7	6.9	7.3	9.7	14.9	9.1
Currency held abroad (% of total)	40	70	—	20	—	25	—	50(?)
Large denomination[b] (% of currency)	40	60	25	45	85	85	60	60

  [a] Currency outside banks.

  [b] Large denomination is: US$100 notes in the USA; DM 200, 500 and 1,000 notes in Germany; yen 10,000 notes in Japan; SFr 500 and 1,000 in Switzerland.

Source: Rogoff (1998).

What will be the euro's share of this market? Starting from the DM's share, the euro may be a serious competitor.[14] Presumably, the characteristics that make a currency appealing for this particular function are similar to those already surveyed. One characteristic is specific to underground demand, though. The availability of large denomination banknotes must be an advantage, for both storage and large 'business' transactions.

The estimates reported in Table 3.9 show that large denomination notes are already, or are becoming, the most popular denomination. Indeed, as transaction technology

---

  [13] In the case of the Swiss franc, Rogoff (1998) reports beliefs that much of it is held in cash in vaults in banks in Switzerland.

  [14] One interesting question is how foreign holders of DM and other European banknotes will convert them into euros in 2002. Will receipts from tourism temporarily swell? Will the authorities keep a watch?

(and street mugging) has rendered cash an increasingly less attractive vehicle for settling payments, including at the retail level, it may seem surprising to observe that currency holding is growing as fast as GDP throughout the OECD area. The fact that most of the growth in cash lies in large denomination notes suggests that an increasing share of currency is actually held in the underground, both at home or abroad (Rogoff puts the share at 70–80 per cent in the OECD countries).

On this ground, the euro seems to be well poised. While the largest denomination available in dollars is US$100, it has been decided that the ECB will issue notes of euro 100, 200 and 500. The euro 500 notes will be in the league of the DM and the Swiss franc, far above the dollar, but still lower than the Canadian $1,000 notes.

There is a hitch, though. Those in the underground who currently hold European currencies will have to exchange them into euros in 2002. If the amounts are very large, as suggested by the above estimates, underground cash-holders will want to spread this operation over time for obvious reasons. To avoid being trapped in the limited period anticipated for the euro changeover, they will probably want to start selling their cash as soon as EMU is decided. The natural currencies to get into, at that stage when euro notes do not yet exist, will be the dollar and the Swiss franc. Will they then shift back to euros, or will the dollar have received a permanent advantage?

4. Pros and Cons of a World Currency

Having reviewed the potential for the euro to become a world currency, it is about time to ask whether this is a desirable outcome at all. At the superficial symbolic level, the answer is yes. As economist Mundell (1993) noted, 'great powers have great currencies'. While some people take pride in seeing the pictures of their national heroes on bank-notes, this privilege will be denied to European citizens, who will only see carefully de-identified architectural objects. So the euro will not be, *per se*, the symbol of Europe's greatness. Of course, the knowledge that the euro is commonly used in remote corners of the planet might make up for this loss of identity. Yet, it is unlikely that national pride will be the main benefit of the single currency. Benefits and costs lie elsewhere.

4.1. Transaction costs

The main benefit from an international currency is that domestic residents enjoy savings on their transaction costs. At the more mundane level, travelling abroad is easier if your currency is widely recognized and accepted. Many payments can be made directly in the vehicle currency; when payments must be made in the local currency, exchange can be direct rather than triangular (through the vehicle currency). This is more comfort than significant cost reduction.

More economically significant is the fact that large transactions in both the foreign exchange and financial markets lead to low transaction costs and the certainty that any deal will be bilateral and not triangular. This direct saving also has an indirect effect on trade in goods and financial instruments. One way or another currency exchange costs affect the price of exports. Lower costs mean lower prices. Similarly financial asset transactions benefit from cost savings. If domestic financial institutions have a comparative advantage in dealing in the domestic currency, they stand to benefit from larger world market shares as the domestic market becomes in fact a significant share of the world market. In addition demand from a very large customer base is likely to be more stable than local demand, leading to lower operation costs, which benefit both the financial institutions and their customers.

It is not known how significant this advantage may be. Casual observation is that it cannot be very large. Under proper circumstances, however, it may be of strategic importance. For example, to compete with Boeing, Airbus must sell in dollars while most of its costs are in European currencies. Fluctuations in the dollar translate into profit volatility, which in turn imposes financial costs which are not borne by Boeing. Airbus frequently complains about this effect.

Of course, there is some circularity in the argument. Having a vehicle currency leads to low transaction costs, but low transaction costs are a necessary condition for a currency to assume a world status. So which comes first? As noted above in Section 2.3, there is indeed a virtuous circle, and this is why the status of world currency is subject to considerable inertia.

4.2. Seigniorage

The most frequently quoted benefit is seigniorage. Since misconceptions are frequent in this area, it is worth clarifying what is seigniorage and what is not. Seigniorage accrues when currency (more precisely the money base) is produced at virtually zero cost by the monetary authorities. The private sector provides goods and services (including work by civil servants) in exchange for fresh currency: seigniorage is the value of these goods and services.

This is very different from money held in the form of bank accounts, by far the largest component of the commonly used monetary aggregates (M1, M2, M3, etc.). Like the monetary authorities, commercial banks create this form of money 'at zero cost'. To do so, however, they need to grant credit, which means attracting customers, taking a commercial risk and providing a range of banking services sometimes below cost. What banks earn on this activity is simply their profits. Crucially, in contrast with the central bank, which enjoys a monopoly on the production of currency, the use of which is compulsory for some transactions, money created by banks is the object of competition so that customers get something in return, including interest payments on deposits.

It is also important to note that seigniorage accrues only on cash, because no interest is served. If interest is served at the market rate, as is the case of Treasury bills, there is no seigniorage. Unlike holders of greenbacks, foreign holders of bonds denominated in dollars, for example, get their market value's worth of interest income. This applies *inter alia* to foreign exchange reserves held around the world by central banks. Central banks almost never hold dollars in cash, or only hold trivial amounts of cash for everyday use. The bulk of foreign exchange reserves is held in dollars (Table 3.3), but this is not a source of seigniorage since most of these reserves are in US Treasury bills on which the US government pays interest. The only gain, maybe, is that the reserve function of the dollar sustains a higher demand for Treasury bills, and therefore lower interest costs, than would be the case otherwise.

Still, the rest of the world holds some US$250 billion worth of greenbacks. This looks like a very good deal for the USA. It certainly is. It amounts to a present from the rest of the world to the USA worth some 3.3 per cent of US GDP. Yet, these numbers are deceptive, because the stock of dollars held abroad has been accumulated over a very long period of time. Rather than a once-off present it is a tiny benefit that trickles down year in and year out. Numbers produced by Alogoskoufis and Portes (1992) and Rogoff (1998) suggest that the annual revenue from seigniorage for the USA is worth some 0.2 per cent of GDP.

4.3. Money demand instability

It is often feared that demand for an international currency may be volatile, or at least subject to unpredictable rapid shifts. US residents hold dollars because the dollar is the sole legal tender within the USA. Everyday transactions must be carried out using dollars. Russians and Bolivians hold dollars because they trust more this currency than their own. If, however, the rouble or the peso were to become suddenly reliable—not a far-fetched possibility—Russians and Bolivians would have no reason to keep holding dollars. This example illustrates the deep difference in the demand for dollars by US residents and by non-residents. Non-resident demand is *potentially* unstable.

This source of instability has long led monetary authorities in Germany and Japan to discourage an international role for their currencies. They have done so by various means, including at some point (until the early 1980s in Japan) restrictions on capital movements. What the Bundesbank fears is a rapid change of fortune, taking the form of large sales of the DM. Either this leads to a depreciation of the DM, with inflationary consequences, or it forces the Bundesbank to intervene and buy back DMs with the risk that foreign exchange reserves be depleted.

There is another, more subtle, risk. All over the world, commercial banks offer accounts, and sometimes loans too, in dollars to their customers. What happens if a major bank collapses, possibly followed by the whole banking system? It is usually understood that central banks stand ready to exercise the lender-of-last-resort function: they prevent bank runs by guaranteeing that deposits will be honoured. In effect they stand ready to create whatever amount of currency is needed to pay back anxious depositors. Because bank deposits exceed the money base by a factor of five or ten, the amount of cash that has to be injected in a crisis situation can be truly enormous, possibly larger that the existing stock of currency. The result might be a surge of inflation. Since each central bank well understands that it lives under that threat, it faces the right incentives for careful bank regulation and oversight.

Bank regulators, however, only monitor national banks. Foreign banks which deal in dollars in a foreign country are beyond the jurisdiction of US institutions. If a bank fails, the local central bank may not have enough dollars to reimburse depositors. In that case the Federal Reserve Bank may come under pressure to 'do something', which means to print currency. This implies that the Fed intervenes to guarantee a risk that is not monitored by any US agency. Incentives can be perverse.

4.4. Conclusion

Owning the world currency entails a few benefits and a few costs. Beyond political symbolism—a potent motivation—the benefits are small. Seigniorage does not amount to very significant amounts. Transaction costs are likely to be lower, providing exporters and financial houses with some comparative advantage. However, the amounts involved are likely to be small. Costs, too, are unlikely to be sizeable. They mostly take the form of potential risks. The US-led rescue of Mexico in 1994–5 is one instance where dollar assets were involved, but this is a rare event. In sum, therefore, the balance of pros and cons is rather inconclusive, and the stakes limited anyway.

5. The International Monetary System

Will the emergence of a second world currency change the operation of the international monetary system? Since 1945 we have been living in a world with one international currency and one economic superpower. The US supremacy may have declined, yet it has not been seriously challenged so far. Can the euro undermine the existing equilibrium? The size of EMU will be similar to that of the USA, as will be its economic and financial structure. The main difference will be the lack of political unity in Europe. This difference is crucial.

This chapter has argued that the euro will not become any time soon the dollar's *alter ego*, and is even less likely to replace it as the world currency. If, however, the euro were to become an international currency, a number of interesting issues emerge.

First comes the question of the stability of the dollar–euro exchange rate, which matters for the operation of the future international monetary system. The conclusion from Section 3.2.3 is that there are as many good reasons to expect more exchange rate volatility as there are reasons to anticipate quite some stability. A key issue is the incentive of the national monetary authorities to give up some of their domestic objectives to seek exchange rate stability. A priori, we expect the incentive to be weak. This is where the international monetary system comes into play. Two oxen that pull the same cart need to remain in step. If both currencies are simultaneously used as vehicles for international trade and financial transactions, a high degree of volatility of their bilateral exchange rate could become a serious inconvenience. Pressure will build up on the Federal Reserve and the ECB to do something about it.

What are the possibilities for cooperation? Current international institutions with relevant responsibilities include the IMF, OECD ministerial meetings and the G-7. All these channels of communication play an important role in exchanging information and sharing views. Undoubtedly the main official players (central bank and Treasury officials) know each other well and are able, when the need arises, to quickly work out a common approach. This was the case when the dollar became massively overvalued in 1985 (the Plaza and Louvre agreements), when the Mexican peso collapsed at the end of 1994, and more recently when Asian currencies came under attack. In their own cooperative efforts, the Europeans were less successful when they first failed to fully recognize the implications of German unification, and then let the EMS be dismantled bit by bit in 1992–3.[15]

These institutions are multilateral, however. Cooperation is a gentlemen's club affair, but one where there is a clear leader, the USA. Willy-nilly (and here there is a gulf between British approbation and Gallic contrarian efforts) the rich countries turn to the USA to broker arrangements. This reflects well the post-Second World War status of the dollar. With the euro becoming a more equal partner, the situation might become more complicated. Analysing the interwar period when the dollar was overtaking sterling, Eichengreen (1989) argues that the international monetary system works better when one country has hegemonic power than when more than one country share leadership. The idea is that, when managing world affairs, each leader country is tempted to look for outcomes which serve its own interests and to let the other leader shoulder the costly parts. In world monetary affairs too many cooks spoil the broth.

If this diagnostic is correct, the international monetary system will enter a period of turbulence. In particular, existing institutions will become ill adapted to a bipolar world. Things could get even more complicated if the yen were to emerge as yet another world currency. One solution that is most likely ruled out is a return to fixed exchange rates *à la* Bretton Woods. The large and relatively closed blocs which are likely to dominate the international monetary system over the next decades have little interest in committing monetary policy to an external target. Nor would a return to gold be acceptable. Rather, the question will be whether some limits to flexibility should be put in place, in the form of (possibly soft) target zones.

Questions will also arise concerning the IMF and the G-7. There are talks, already, of a G-3. The loser would be Canada. Anyway, it would have to wait until Italy and the UK both join EMU. Even so, if the yen remains a junior partner, there will be the need for bilateral links between the USA and Europe. This could be politically difficult.

6. Conclusion

Thinking ahead to what the monetary and financial world will look like with the euro leaves us with few certainties, but a number of conclusions seem robust. They are summarized in this section.

---

[15] Analyses of this period are e.g. Eichengreen and Wyplosz (1993) and Buiter *et al.* (1998).

The euro will not wash away the dollar over the next decade or two. It has taken decades for the dollar to assume its current dominating status and it does not currently suffer from any major weakness. The euro will be born with many of the necessary attributes of a world currency, but it will face stiff competition and will have to climb the ladder one step at a time.

Yet the euro will possess many of the characteristics which lead a currency to be adopted world-wide for both transactions and savings: size of internal market, share of world trade, size of financial markets, low and steady inflation. Working against the euro will be the dollar's domination in the fast-growing countries of Asia and South America.

The European authorities can play a role in promoting the euro, mainly through the regulation of banks and other financial institutions. Their decisions regarding the exchange rate regime will also matter. More exchange rate stability will help, but misguided efforts at defending an exchange rate parity may backfire.

It is not clear that the ECB will champion the euro. Beyond glamour, there are few benefits. Seigniorage does not amount to very significant amounts. Transaction costs are likely to be lower, providing exporters and financial houses with some comparative advantage. However, the amounts involved are small. Over the first few years, it is likely that the ECB will focus on internal stability and be, at least, unsupportive of a large external role for its currency.

Independently of the ECB's own objectives, there remains the question of whether the currency of a large entity tends to be more or less stable than the current currencies of medium-sized countries. Smaller countries, being usually open, are sensitive to exchange rate movements and typically attempt to achieve some degree of stability. This argument suggests that the euro might follow the same kind of wide and long-lasting swings as are observed for the yen, sterling or the dollar.

Surprisingly maybe, the euro's main competitive advantage may lie in the use of cash, mostly in underground currency. It will be issued in denominations much larger than the US$100 bills currently widely used for shady operations. The euro 500 notes will be in the league of the DM and the Swiss franc, far above the dollar, but still lower than the Canadian $1,000 notes.

When and if the international monetary system becomes more bipolar, it could well be more turbulent. Things could get even more complicated if the yen were to emerge as yet another world currency. A return to fixed exchange rates *à la* Bretton Woods will be even less likely than now because neither Europe nor the USA will wish to commit itself to an exchange rate target. The most likely effort would consist in agreeing upon limits, possibly in the form of target zones.

References

Alogoskoufis, George and Richard Portes (1992), 'European Monetary Union and International Currencies in a Tripolar World', in M. B. Canzoneri, V. Grilli and Paul R. Masson (eds.), *Establishing a Central Bank: Issues in Europe and Lessons from the US*, Cambridge: Cambridge University Press.

Artus, Patrick (1997), 'Est-il sûr que l'euro va devenir une monnaie internationale?' Etude no. 97.08, Paris: Caisse des Dépôts et Consignations (April).

Begg, David and Charles Wyplosz (1993), 'The European Monetary System: Recent Intellectual History', in *The Monetary Future of Europe*, London: Centre for Economic Policy Research.

Bénassy-Quéré, Agnès (1996), 'Potentialities and Opportunities of the Euro as an International Currency', Economic Papers no. 115, Brussels: European Commission (July).

Bénassy-Quéré, Agnès and Pierre Deusy-Fournier (1995), 'Le Rôle international des grandes devises: 1974–1994', *Bulletin Economique et Financier*, 42: 13–32, Banque Internationale à Luxembourg.

BIS (1996), *Central Bank Survey of Foreign Exchange and Derivative Market Activity*, Basle.

Bryant, Ralph, Peter Hooper and Catherine Mann (1993) (eds.), *Evaluating Policy Regimes: New Research in Empirical Macroeconomics*, Washington, DC: The Brookings Institution.

Buiter, Willem, Giancarlo Corsetti and Paolo Pesenti (1998), *Financial Markets and European Monetary Cooperation*, New York: Cambridge University Press.

Burda, Michael and Charles Wyplosz (1997), *Macroeconomics: A European Text*, 2nd edn., Oxford: Oxford University Press.

Clarida, Richard, Jordi Gali and Mark Gertler (1997), 'Monetary Policy Rules in Practice: Some International Evidence', unpublished paper, Columbia University.

Currie, David, Paul Levine and John Pearlman (1990), 'European Monetary Union or Hard-EMS', CPER Discussion Paper no. 472, London: CEPR.

Dumas, Bernard (1994), 'Partial-Equilibrium vs. General-Equilibrium Models of International Capital Market Equilibrium', in F. van der Ploeg (ed.), *Handbook of International Macroeconomics*, Oxford: Basil Blackwell.

Eichengreen, Barry (1989), 'Hegemonic Stability Theories of the International Monetary System', in R. N. Cooper (ed.), *Can Nations Agree? Issues in International Economic Cooperation*, Studies in International Economics series, Washington, DC: The Brookings Institution, pp. 255–98.

Eichengreen, Barry (1994), *International Monetary Arrangements for the 21st Century*, Washington, DC: The Brookings Institution.

Eichengreen, Barry and Charles Wyplosz (1993), 'The Unstable EMS', *Brookings Papers on Economic Activity*, 1: 51–144.

European Commission (1990), 'One Market, One Money', *European Economy*, 44 (October).

Funabashi, Yoichi (1988), *Managing the Dollar: From the Plaza to the Louvre*, Washington, DC: Institute for International Economics.

Giavazzi, Francesco and Alberto Giovannini (1989), *Limiting Exchange Rate Flexibility*, Cambridge, MA: MIT Press.

Giavazzi, Francesco, David Begg and Charles Wyplosz (1997), 'Options for the Future Exchange Rate Policy of the EMU', report to the European Commission (September).

Giovannini, Alberto and Bart Turtleboom (1992), 'Currency Substitution', NBER Working Paper no. 4232 (December).

Grassman, Sven (1973), 'A Fundamental Symmetry in International Payments Patterns', *Journal of International Economics*, 3: 105–16.

Hartmann, Philipp (1996a), 'Vehicle Currencies in the Foreign Exchange Market', unpublished doctoral dissertation, Paris: Ecole des Hautes Etudes en Sciences Sociales.

Hartmann, Philipp (1996b), 'The Future of the Euro as an International Currency', Research Report no. 20, Brussels: CEPS (December).

Krugman, Paul (1980), 'Vehicle Currencies and the Structure of International Exchange', *Journal of Money, Credit and Banking*, 12(3): 513–26.

Krugman, Paul (1991), *Currencies and Crises*, Cambridge, MA: MIT Press.

McKinnon, Ronald (1979), *Money in International Exchange*, New York: Macmillan.

Martin, Philippe (1997), 'The Exchange Rate Policy of the Euro: A Matter of Size?', unpublished paper, Geneva: Graduate Institute of International Studies.

Masson, Paul R. and Bart G. Turtelboom (1997), 'Characteristics of the Euro, the Demand for Reserves, and Policy Coordination Under EMU', IMF Working Paper, Washington, DC: International Monetary Fund (April).

Niehans, Jürg (1969), 'Money in a Static Theory of Optimal Payment Arrangements', *Journal of Money, Credit and Banking*, 1(4): 706–26.

Rao, Ramesh K. S. and Stephen P. Magee (1980), 'The Currency of Denomination of International Trade Contracts', in R. Levich and C. Wihlborg (eds.), *Exchange Risk and Exposure: Current Developments in International Financial Management*, Lexington.

Rogoff, Kenneth (1998), 'Foreign and Underground Demand for Euro Notes: Blessing or a Curse?' *Economic Policy*, 26: 261–303.

Solnik, Bruno (1974), 'Why Not Diversify Internationally Rather than Domestically?' *Financial Analyst Journal*, 20: 48–54.

Svensson, Lars. E. O. (1996), 'Price-level Targeting versus Inflation Targeting: A Free Lunch?' CEPR Discussion Paper no. 1510, London: CEPR.

Tavlas, George S. (1991) 'On the International Use of Currencies: The Case of the Deutsche Mark', Essays in International Finance no. 181, Princeton University.

Tesar, Linda and Ingrid Weber (1992), 'International Equity Transactions and US Portfolio Choice', in J. Frankel (ed.), *The Internationalization of Equity Markets*, Chicago: Chicago University Press.

Part II

The Fixed-Income Markets

4
Yield Spreads and Optimal Public Debt Management under the Single Currency

LARS TYGE NIELSEN

1. Introduction

This chapter examines issues of optimal debt management and the determinants of default risk on government bonds issued by member countries of the future European Monetary Union.

In the context of a theoretical model of public finance, optimal default, and optimal debt management, we discuss how inflation and taxation, default probabilities, and the optimal currency composition of the public debt are affected by EMU.

In particular, we consider the argument that the loss of monetary independence by member countries of the EMU will necessarily increase their default risk. According to this argument, when nations have their own currencies, they can avoid default essentially by printing the money they need to pay back their debt. EMU member countries will not be able to do this. We evaluate and reject the argument within a model of optimal default. The fact that a country is able to avoid default by printing money does not imply that it is optimal for it to do so.

The analysis highlights some problems of public debt management under EMU. They have to do with the incentives for member countries to issue non-euro-denominated debt rather than nominal euro-denominated debt. Doing so will lower the steady-state inflation rate in the EMU, because such debt functions as a commitment device. This benefit is low for each country and is shared by all. Other benefits and costs of issuing such debt are borne by the individual issuing country, however. This implies that there is a need for a mechanism for coordinating the debt management policies of the member countries.

2. Yield Spreads

Different European countries pay different interest rates on their public debts denominated in domestic currencies. For example, the yields on French government bonds, denominated in French francs, are different from the yields on German government bonds, denominated in German marks.

There are a number of possible reasons for these differences.

The major reason is potential exchange rate movements. Investors recognize that exchange rates may change, and they demand compensation for any expected changes in exchange rates. Roughly speaking, if investors expect a depreciation of the French franc relative to the German mark of 1 per cent per year, then they will demand compensation in the form of an excess yield on French bonds of about 1 per cent.

In addition to compensation for expected changes in exchange rates, investors may require an exchange rate risk premium, which is a compensation for taking on exchange rate risk.

Whether the exchange rate risk premium is positive or negative cannot be determined a priori. Investment in German bonds and investment in French bonds are both risky. An investor who evaluates his returns in German marks will find French bonds risky, while an investor who evaluates his returns in French francs will find German bonds risky. They cannot both get a positive exchange rate risk premium.

Under EMU, the potential for exchange rate movements disappears and will no longer give rise to yield spreads.

A second source of yield spreads, which we focus on in this chapter, is credit risk or default risk. This is the risk that the issuing government may not in the end pay the promised cash flows or may not pay them at the promised time.

To the extent investors believe that the issuing government may not make the promised payments, they will demand compensation for the expected shortfall. They will mark down the price of the bond accordingly and raise its yield. They may raise the yield even further, as compensation for taking the risk that the actual shortfall may differ from the expected shortfall.

What we shall call the *default premium* is the entire difference in yield between defaultable and default-free debt. It includes compensation both for the expected shortfall and for the uncertainty associated with that shortfall. Notice the difference in terminology: the exchange rate risk premium includes compensation only for the uncertainty associated with exchange rate movements, not for expected exchange rate movements. Also notice that the *credit spread* or *default spread* between two bonds equals the difference in their default premia.

There are four major reasons why membership of EMU may affect the default premia. Probably the most important one is the budgetary discipline imposed by EMU on the member countries, which will lower their risk of default. A second reason why membership of EMU may affect the default premia is that financial markets may believe that if a member country comes close to default, the EMU or the other EMU member countries will bail it out. Such intervention is explicitly ruled out by the Maastricht Treaty, but this clause may not be credible, in which case the default premia will be affected. The third reason is that membership of EMU may change the costs or penalties that a country will face if it defaults. The fourth reason is that individual member countries lose control of their monetary policy.

Common sense says that when nations have their own currencies, they can avoid default on their domestic currency debt essentially by printing the money they need to pay it back. The government can borrow the money in the central bank and use it to service the debt. Alternatively, the central bank can buy up government bonds in the open market in exchange for money.

These operations will lead to an increase in the money supply and to inflation, which reduces the real value of the remaining domestic currency debt. Printing money to service or buy back government debt is not likely to be consistent with a fixed exchange rate. The increase in the money supply will lead to a depreciation of the foreign exchange value of the currency.

A country in the EMU will not be in control of its own monetary policy. It cannot issue money, and it will not be allowed to borrow directly from the ECB, although the ECB may well buy up bonds issued by a member country in the open market. It has been hypothesized that the loss of control over monetary policy will raise the probability of default and the default premium on the debt of the EMU member countries.

The analysis in this study does not agree with that hypothesis. We argue that countries decide to default as a consequence of a trade-off between the benefits and the costs of default. They default when it is optimal for them to do so. Even if a country were able to avoid defaulting by printing money, it might not want to do so, because the resulting inflation would be worse than any penalty for default. Whether the loss of monetary independence for EMU member countries will raise or lower their probability of default depends on how it affects the attractiveness of what they can achieve without defaulting.

In addition to exchange rate movements and default risk, there are a number of other potential reasons for the existence of yield spreads between bonds issued by different governments or denominated in different currencies. They include the cash flow structure of the bonds, market segmentation and taxation, and liquidity. They are mentioned here only in order to distinguish them from exchange rate movements and default risk, which are the focus of the analysis.

Bonds issued by different governments will typically have different cash flow structures, and in particular different timing and size of coupon payments. To account for this, one would calculate and compare the implied zero-coupon yields.

Market segmentation means that investors from different countries face different constraints on their portfolio choice, or that they have different preferences for reasons other than differences in risk-aversion. These constraints and preferences may depend, for example, on the tax regime and on official regulations. To the extent that they influence the demand for different categories of government bonds, they may give rise to yield spreads.

The liquidity of a bond issue depends on its size, the volume of trade in the bonds, whether they are deliverable in a futures contract, and whether the issue functions as a benchmark issue. The lower the liquidity, the lower will the price typically be and the higher the yield. Liquidity may well differ among different categories of government bonds and hence give rise to yield spreads between them.

3. Inflation, Devaluation and Default

The question of how EMU affects inflation, taxation, default, and debt management will be analysed in the context of a model which is explained in detail in the Appendix. It is an expanded version of the model of Miller (1997).

We shall not analyse the borrowing decision in detail, except that we assume the real value of the total public debt to be constant. The decomposition of the debt into domestic currency and foreign currency debt is a separate matter. Similarly, we abstract from the effects of economic growth and assume that the money demand, and hence the money supply, is constant in real terms.

Government expenditures can be partially financed by an inflation tax in the following way. Inflation will reduce the real value of domestic bonds and the domestic money stock. This means that the government can issue new debt and increase the nominal money supply, while keeping the debt and the money supply constant in real terms. In other words, it can print money (and bonds) to help pay for its expenditures.

We assume purchasing power parity. This implies that any inflation (in excess of foreign inflation) corresponds to depreciation of the currency.

To the extent that government expenditures are not financed by an inflation tax, they have to be financed by ordinary taxation. Both inflation and taxation involve social costs. These may be political or economic in nature. For example, taxation beyond a minimum level is likely to be distortionary and lead to economic costs. To finance its budget, a government may have to resort to both taxation and inflation, but it will trade off the social costs of taxation against the social costs of inflation.

The assumption that the government's objective is a function of taxation and inflation is not uncommon in the public finance literature. It is made, for example, in studies on public finance, including Mankiw (1987), Miller (1997), and Missale and Blanchard (1994). Kydland and Prescott (1977) and Barro and Gordon (1983) assume that the government's objective is a function of inflation and unemployment. Another approach is to assume that the government maximizes the utility of a representative consumer. This is done, for example, in Bohn (1988, 1990), Canzoneri and Rogers (1990), Calvo (1978), and Persson *et al.* (1987).

The choice between inflation and taxation may be made differently by different countries. In other words, some will choose relatively high taxation and relatively low inflation, while others will make the opposite choice. The choice is likely to depend on the efficiency with which the country is able to generate tax revenue. Everything else being equal, countries that have more difficulty raising taxes will choose a higher level of inflation and a lower level of taxation.

This is not the end of the story, because the financial markets will second-guess the government's decisions. In particular, the markets will forecast the inflation rate and use this information in setting the interest rate on the nominal domestic currency debt. If the markets expect the government to raise the inflation rate, then they will compensate for it by raising the interest rate. This means that to the extent inflation is expected in advance, the government will not get any net budget relief from the inflation tax on domestic bonds. The only budget relief from inflation will come from the inflation tax on the money stock.

This feedback loop between inflation and the interest rate on the nominal domestic debt implies that the government is in fact not completely free to set the inflation rate. The larger the domestic currency debt as a fraction of the total debt, the more incentive will the government have to inflate. Hence, the more inflation will be expected, and the higher will be the interest rate.

In this sense, the government can use foreign currency debt as a commitment device. The more foreign currency debt it has, the less incentive does it have for inflation, and hence the lower will inflation expectations and actual inflation be.

The argument that debt creates an incentive for inflation builds on Kydland and Prescott (1977) and Calvo (1978). Persson *et al.* (1987) and Missale and Blanchard (1994), among others, have analysed how a careful choice of the composition of the debt can alleviate the problem.

4. Optimal Default

In order to understand how default premia are determined, it is useful to analyse the situations where it may be optimal for a sovereign government to default on its debt.

Presumably, what induces sovereign governments to service their debt is that there is some real or perceived cost of defaulting. For example, the country may be subject to various kinds of sanctions and pressure. Creditors may be able to seize a part or all of the defaulting country's assets abroad. The country's reputation may be damaged in such a way that it is no longer able to access the international financial markets. These issues have been discussed in the literature on LDC debt (see Eaton (1996) and the references therein).

To keep things simple, we assume that there is a fixed cost of default which is independent of the amount of the default. This cost is a utility cost or a social cost, in the sense that it is comparable to the social cost of taxation and inflation.

The fixed cost may differ depending on whether the country defaults on only the domestic debt, only the foreign debt, or on both. With fixed costs like this, there will be no partial default within a debt category. If the country defaults on a particular category of debt, then it might as well repudiate it completely.

The main fiscal effect of default is that interest will no longer be paid on the debt which is in default. This gives a measure of fiscal relief. The same government expenditures can be financed by less tax revenue or less inflation. This means that the social cost of taxation and inflation will go down as a result of the default.

Given the country's fiscal situation, its government considers the possibility of defaulting on either the domestic debt, the foreign debt, or both. For each of those possibilities, it calculates the net reduction in social cost resulting from debt relief and paying the fixed cost of default. It then chooses either no default or one of the three default possibilities.

It follows from this description of default that the higher the fixed cost of default on any category of debt, the lower the probability of default on that debt, and hence, the lower the default premium.

It is plausible that the cost for the government of default on domestic currency debt is generally higher than the cost of default on foreign currency debt. Domestic currency debt is primarily held by domestic residents, who can punish the government politically. It is also held by the domestic banking system, and therefore default could lead to a financial crisis. If indeed the cost of default is higher for domestic currency debt, then the theory predicts that the probability of default is lower for domestic currency debt than for foreign currency debt, and that the default premium will also be lower. This is consistent with the fact that the ratings agencies generally rate a country's domestic currency debt higher than its foreign currency debt.

The likelihood of default and the default premium on each category of debt will also be affected by the size of that debt as a fraction of the total debt. The larger a given category of debt, the larger the potential budgetary relief for the government from default on that debt, and hence, the higher the probability of default and the default premium.

A change in the composition of the debt will typically change the default premium on both components in opposite directions. It is, however, also useful to know how the default premium on the total debt is affected. We shall consider two possibilities.

First, suppose the cost of default is higher on domestic currency debt than on foreign currency debt, and the cost of defaulting on both categories of debt is even higher than that. When the domestic debt is less than half the total, the country will never default on the domestic debt alone. If it defaults, it will default either on the foreign debt or on both. As the share of domestic debt increases from zero towards a half, the probability of default and the default premium on the domestic debt will not be affected. However, the attractiveness of defaulting on the foreign debt alone decreases. Hence, as the share of domestic debt increases, the probability of default and the default premium on the foreign debt will go down. Therefore, the default premium on the total debt will go down.

Secondly, if the cost of default is the same for foreign and domestic currency debt, and if it is independent of whether the country defaults on only one of those categories or on both, then the default probability and the default premium on the total debt will be independent of the composition of the debt.

5. Optimal Debt Management

If we disregard uncertainty, and if we disregard the possibility of default, then the analysis predicts that it is optimal for the government to have only foreign currency debt and no domestic currency debt. This is true even when default is taken into account, provided that the total default premium on the debt is independent of its currency composition. As we have argued, this will be the case if the cost of default is independent of whether the country defaults on the domestic debt, the foreign debt, or both.

The reason for this result is as follows. If the government has no domestic debt, then its budget is unaffected by the domestic interest rate and hence unaffected by any link between the interest rate and inflation. It is therefore free to choose the inflation rate which optimally trades off the cost of inflation and the cost of taxation.

If, on the other hand, the government does issue domestic debt, then at each given interest rate on the domestic debt, it is optimal to use a higher level of inflation. But the markets will foresee the higher inflation and raise the interest rate. In equilibrium, the fiscal effects of higher inflation and a higher interest rate offset each other, and there is no budget relief from the inflation tax on bonds. But the government loses control of the inflation rate and is no longer free to choose it so as to optimally trade its cost off against the cost of taxation.

So if the government is only concerned with minimizing the steady-state level of inflation, it should choose to have zero domestic debt. Since governments do have positive domestic debt, we need to look for alternative motives for domestic debt. We shall analyse two such motives. The first is to hedge against unexpectedly high government expenditures, and the second is to lower the default premium paid on the debt.

First, consider the possibility of surprises in government expenditures. The government chooses the composition of its debt before knowing the level of government expenditures. An unexpected increase in expenditures will give rise to unexpected increases in inflation and taxation. If there is some domestic debt outstanding, then it will be taxed by the inflation tax. This helps finance the expenditures and lowers the required increase in inflation and taxes. Therefore, domestic debt can lower the variability of the social cost of inflation and taxation. The government takes on domestic debt in order to benefit from the inflation tax when it unexpectedly needs it. Versions of the hedging motive for nominal domestic currency debt have been pointed out by Bohn (1988, 1990) and Miller (1997).

A second motive to take on domestic debt may be a desire to pay a low default premium. This requires that the total default premium paid on the debt should be a decreasing function of the fraction of the debt that is denominated in domestic currency. We have argued above, in the context of the analysis of optimal default, that this will be the case for low values of domestic debt if the fixed cost of default on domestic debt is higher than the fixed cost of default on foreign debt.

The model implies that it is now optimal to take on a positive amount of domestic currency debt. In doing so, the country makes a trade-off between the benefit of domestic debt, which is that it carries a lower default premium, and the benefit of foreign debt, which is that it functions as a commitment to low inflation.

6. Inflation and Default under EMU

To see how inflation, default, and debt management will be affected by EMU, we assume that monetary policy under EMU will be conducted with a view to the interests of all the member countries—specifically, that it will minimize a population-weighted average of the social costs of inflation and taxation borne by the members. This is of course not the only possible assumption, but a detailed analysis of the political economy of EMU is beyond the scope of this study.

It turns out that the equilibrium inflation rate under EMU will be a weighted average of the inflation rates that would have prevailed in the member countries had they stayed outside EMU and allowed their exchange rates to float freely.

Thus, EMU results in a unique combination of inflation and taxation. Each country can compare this combination with what it could achieve by staying out of EMU. If the combination of inflation and taxation that it can achieve inside EMU is better than what it can achieve outside, and if everything else including the fixed costs of default is the same, then the probability of default will be higher inside EMU. For some countries, the probability of default will be higher in EMU, for others it will be lower.

In other words, the fact that countries lose control of their monetary policy when they join EMU does not necessarily imply that their probability of default goes up. If EMU helps them reach a superior combination of inflation and taxation, then their probability of default goes down.

For concreteness, suppose all the countries were identical except for the efficiency of their taxation. For countries where the relative social cost of taxation is higher than the EMU average, the inflation rate under EMU will be lower than it would be if the country was not a member, all else being equal. For countries where the social cost of taxation is lower than the average, the opposite is true. If the countries all have the same social cost of taxation, then EMU does not affect the equilibrium inflation rate, all else being equal.

7. Optimal Debt Management under EMU

The optimal debt policy under EMU depends, in general, on the relative sizes of the countries, their debts, government expenditures, etc. Again for concreteness, consider the hypothetical case where all the countries are identical except possibly for the efficiency of their taxation.

First, disregard uncertainty, and disregard the possibility of default. If in fact the countries are identical in all respects, including the efficiency of their taxation, then they will all agree that the total domestic debt of the union should be zero, because this will commit the EMU to low inflation. If any one country sees that the aggregate domestic debt of the other member countries is positive, then it will want to buy up that debt for money it borrows in non-euro currencies, thereby adjusting the net euro-denominated debt of the union to zero. That will result in an optimal situation for all members.

If the countries differ in their relative social costs of taxation, then they will not agree on the optimal aggregate euro-denominated debt for the union. Any given fraction of the debt denominated in euros is likely to be found too high by some and too low for others. For example, if the net euro debt is zero, then countries with high social cost of taxation will have an incentive to issue more such debt in order to raise the inflation rate. On the other hand, countries with low social cost of taxation will find the EMU inflation rate to be higher than they would like, and they can lower it by issuing less euro debt, or even having a negative euro debt, which they can achieve by buying up euro-denominated debt financed by non-euro borrowing.

This exemplifies the potential need for a mechanism that would coordinate the debt management policies of the EMU member countries.

Now consider the incentive to issue euro-denominated debt in order to hedge against unexpected government expenditure requirements. We have seen that for a country outside EMU, it is optimal to issue some domestic debt as a hedge. If government expenditures unexpectedly increase, then inflation will go up. Since the increase in inflation is unexpected, it inflates away part of the real value of the domestic debt, and thus it helps finance the expenditures. The incentive to issue domestic debt is tempered by the commitment effect: the steady-state inflation rate will be higher than without the debt. The government will then attempt to make an optimal trade-off between these two effects.

A country in EMU will also face a trade-off between the hedging incentive and the commitment effect. However, a coordination problem arises from the fact that the hedging benefit from issuing euro debt accrues only to the issuing country, whereas the resulting increase in equilibrium inflation affects every member.

If a member country issues euro-denominated debt to hedge against surprises in government expenditures, then it raises the aggregate euro debt in the union, and hence, it raises the steady-state inflation rate. But it does not itself bear the full cost of this increase in inflation. If the country accounts for one-tenth of the EMU, and if it changes its debt from all non-euro currency to all euros, then it raises the proportion of euro debt in the aggregate EMU debt by only 10 per cent. The effect on inflation will be much smaller than if the country was outside the EMU. However, the cost of that inflation is borne by every member country. Similarly, any effect on the variance of inflation will be felt equally by every member country.

The potential hedging benefits accrue only to the country which issues the euro-denominated debt. The debt may lower the variance of the required tax revenue for that country, but not for the others.

So the inflation cost is borne by everybody and relatively small for each country, while the potential hedging benefit in the form of reduced variance of the required tax revenue accrues only to the issuing country. This implies that the optimal composition of debt for each country may not lead to an optimal composition for the EMU as a whole. Again, this points to the desirability of coordination of the member countries' debt management policies.

Next, consider the default motive to issue euro-denominated debt. We have argued that for a country outside EMU, it may be optimal to issue some domestic currency debt in order to lower the total default premium paid on the debt. This will be the case if the total default premium is a decreasing function of the fraction of the debt denominated in domestic currency, at low values of that fraction. This will be true if the fixed cost of default on domestic currency debt is higher than the fixed cost of default on foreign currency debt. The incentive to issue domestic debt to lower the total default premium has to be balanced against the commitment effect of having debt in foreign currency, which lowers the steady-state inflation rate.

Suppose that for countries in EMU, the total default premium on their debt is an increasing function of the fraction of the debt which is denominated in euros rather than in non-euro currencies. This will be the case if the fixed cost of default on euro debt is higher than the fixed cost of default on debt denominated in non-euro currencies. A member country which issues euro-denominated debt can then lower the default premium it pays by issuing some euro-denominated debt. This incentive has to be balanced against the increased euro inflation that results from issuing euro debt. However, as in the case of hedging, the inflation effect will be small and will be borne by all member countries, while the benefit in the form of a lower default premium will be reaped only by the country which issues the euro debt.

Again, the inflation cost is borne by everybody and is relatively small for each country, while the benefit in the form of a reduced default premium is reaped only by the issuing country. This implies that each country has a default-related incentive to issue more euro-denominated debt and less non-euro-denominated debt than is socially optimal. The result will be a higher steady-state inflation rate than would be possible if the EMU were to coordinate the countries' debt management policy.

8. Conclusions

This chapter has examined the optimal management of the public debt and the determinants of default risk on government bonds inside and outside European Monetary Union. The budgetary discipline imposed by EMU will lower the default risk and default premia on government bonds. We have rejected the argument that the loss of monetary independence by the individual member countries will necessarily increase their default risk. A country's default probability may decrease if EMU helps it reach a combination of taxation and inflation which is better than it could achieve on its own. Individual countries will have incentives to issue a package of euro-denominated and non-euro-denominated debt that differs from what is socially optimal for the EMU as a whole. This points to a need for a mechanism to coordinate the public debt management of member countries.

Appendix: Formal Analysis

A.1. The model

We use a model of debt management which is adapted from Miller (1997) and expanded with a model of optimal default and an analysis of different exchange rate regimes, including EMU.

Miller's model is formulated in discrete time. This leads to a fairly complicated form of the government budget constraint, which is then simplified by a first-order Taylor approximation. Here, we avoid the Taylor approximation by expressing all flow variables, as well as all interest rates, inflation rates, and rates of appreciation, as instantaneous rates.

The model abstracts from fluctuations in money demand and assumes that the real money stock is kept constant. It also abstracts from the effects of economic growth and assumes that the government keeps a constant level of debt measured in real terms. A part of this debt will be denominated in domestic currency and a part of it in foreign currency. The foreign currency bonds could alternatively be interpreted as inflation-indexed bonds.

The central part of the model is the government's flow budget constraint:

$$x = g + b(i - \pi) + b^*(i^* - \pi^*) - m\pi,$$

where x is real tax revenues; g is real expenditures (excluding interest payments); b is the real value of home currency denominated debt; b^* is the real value of foreign currency denominated debt; i is the nominal interest rate on home currency denominated debt; i^* is the nominal interest rate on foreign currency denominated debt; and m is the real money stock.

To understand the logic behind this budget constraint, first note that there is no ambiguity in measuring both domestic and foreign debt in real terms, because we assume absolute purchasing power parity:

$$EP^* = P,$$

where E is the exchange rate, the price of foreign currency in terms of home currency; P^* is the foreign price level; and P is the domestic price level.

Because of purchasing power parity, the nominal foreign currency value of foreign currency denominated debt can be measured in real terms in two equivalent ways. It can be divided by the foreign price level P^* or it can be translated into nominal home currency by multiplying by the exchange rate and then dividing by the home price level P.

The terms $(i - \pi)$ and $(i^* - \pi^*)$ are the real interest rates paid on domestic and foreign debt, respectively.

The budget constraint assumes that the government issues new money and new debt so as to keep the real values of the money stock and the foreign and domestic debt constant. In fact, $b\pi$, $b^*\pi^*$, and $m\pi$ are the real value of new issues of domestic debt, foreign debt, and money, respectively.

To see this, observe that the nominal change in the money stock is

$$M' = \mu P,$$

where M is the nominal value of the domestic money stock; and μ is the new issuance of money, in real terms.

The change in the real value of the money stock is

$$\left(\frac{M}{P}\right)' = \frac{M'P - MP'}{P^2} = \frac{M'}{P} - \frac{M}{P}\frac{P'}{P} = \mu - m\pi.$$

To keep the real value of the money stock constant, it has to be that

$$\mu = m\pi.$$

The same argument holds for the debt:

$$\beta = b\pi.$$

and

$$\beta^* = b^*\pi^*,$$

where β is the net new issuance of home currency debt, measured in real terms; and β^* is the net new issuance of foreign currency debt, measured in real terms.

We can also think of $b\pi$ and $m\pi$ as the real revenue from the inflation tax on domestic bonds and on money, respectively.

We can now write the budget constraint as

$$x + b\pi + b^*\pi^* + m\pi = g + bi + b^*i^*.$$

The right-hand side is real expenditures plus interest payments on domestic and foreign currency denominated debt, measured in real terms. The left-hand side is real tax revenues plus net new issuance of domestic and foreign currency denominated debt and domestic money, measured in real terms.

The government minimizes a social loss function of the form

$$Ax^2 + \pi^2$$

subject to the budget constraint. We may also refer to the social loss as social cost or social disutility.

The interpretation is as follows. Both taxation and inflation are socially or politically costly. To meet its budget constraint, the government may have to resort to both of them, but it will trade off the social disutility of taxation against the social disutility of inflation. The constant A is interpreted as the relative cost of taxation.

A.2. A flexible exchange rate system

In a flexible exchange rate system, the government jointly chooses the inflation rate π and the level x of real tax revenues, given g, b, i, b^*, i^*, π^*, and m. Alternatively, given those variables, the budget constraint expresses x as a function of π, and the government simply chooses π.

The first-order condition for solving the minimization problem says

$$
\begin{aligned}
0 &= \frac{\delta}{\delta\pi}\left(\frac{1}{2}Ax^2 + \frac{1}{2}\pi^2\right) \\
&= Ax\frac{\delta x}{\delta\pi} + \pi \\
&= -Ax(b+m) + \pi \\
&= -A(b+m)[g+b(i-\pi)+b^*(i^*-\pi^*)-m\pi] + \pi \\
&= -A(b+m)[g+bi+b^*(i^*-\pi^*)] + \pi[1+A(b+m)^2].
\end{aligned}
$$

The solution for the optimal inflation rate is

$$
\pi = \frac{A(b+m)}{1+A(b+m)^2}[g+bi+b^*(i^*-\pi^*)].
$$

We can also find the optimal level of taxation:

$$
\begin{aligned}
x &= g+b(i-\pi)+b^*(i^*-\pi^*)-m\pi \\
&= g+bi+b^*(i^*-\pi^*)-(b+m)\pi \\
&= [1-(b+m)\pi][g+bi+b^*(i^*-\pi^*)] \\
&= \left[1 - \frac{A(b+m)^2}{1+A(b+m)^2}\right][g+bi+b^*(i^*-\pi^*)] \\
&= \frac{1}{1+A(b+m)^2}[g+bi+b^*(i^*-\pi^*)]
\end{aligned}
$$

Both inflation and taxation are increasing functions of government expenditures. They are also increasing functions of the domestic interest rate i. The government uses both increased taxation and increased inflation to finance an increase in government expenditures or in interest payments on the debt. Inflation is also an increasing function of A, the relative cost of taxation, while taxation is a decreasing function of A. Everything else being equal, countries that have more difficulty raising taxes will choose a higher level of inflation and a lower level of taxation.

This is not the end of the story, because the financial markets will second-guess the government's decisions. In particular, the markets will forecast the inflation rate and use this information in setting the interest rate on the debt. If the markets expect the government to raise the inflation rate, then they will compensate for it by raising the interest rate. This means that the government will not get any net budget relief from the inflation tax on domestic bonds. The only budget relief from inflation will come from the inflation tax on the money stock.

To demonstrate how the feedback from inflation expectations to the interest rate works, it is useful to rewrite some of the variables in terms of expected values. First of all, absolute purchasing power parity implies relative purchasing power parity:

$$e + \pi^* - \pi = 0,$$

where $e = E'/E$ is the rate of appreciation of the foreign currency; $\pi = P'/P$ is the domestic inflation rate; and $\pi^* = (P^*)'/P^*$ is the foreign inflation rate.

Now let e^e, π^e, and π^{*e} denote the expected, as opposed to realized, values of e, π, and π^*. Since relative purchasing power parity is expected to hold,

$$\pi^e = \pi^{*e} + e^e.$$

We assume that uncovered interest rate parity holds for default-free interest rates:

$$r = r^* + e^e,$$

where r is the nominal interest rate on default-free debt in home currency; and r^* is the nominal interest rate on default-free debt in foreign currency. Then,

$$i = d + r$$

and

$$i^* = d^* + r^*,$$

where d is a default premium on government debt denominated in domestic currency; and d^* is a default premium on government debt denominated in foreign currency.

Finally, we assume that the expected foreign real interest rate on default-free debt is a constant which, for analytical purposes, we can conveniently set to zero:

$$0 = r^* - \pi^{*e} = r - e^e - (\pi^e - e^e) = r - \pi^e.$$

Hence,

$$i^* = d^* + r^* = d^* + \pi^{*e}$$

and

$$i = d + r = d + \pi^e.$$

We can rewrite the equation for the optimal inflation rate in terms of expectations:

$$\pi = \frac{A(b+m)}{1 + A(b+m)^2}[g + bd + b^*d^* + b\pi^e + b^*(\pi^{*e} - \pi^*)].$$

Next, we impose rational expectations. The financial markets have the same information as the government has when it chooses the inflation rate, and they know the government's incentives. Therefore, after g has been observed, the markets can perfectly predict the inflation rate:

$$\pi^e = \pi.$$

This is the assumption of rational expectations. We assume that this holds also abroad

$$\pi^{*e} = \pi^*.$$

The rational expectations inflation rate π is determined by substituting $\pi^{*e} = \pi^*$ and $\pi^e = \pi$ into the equation for optimal inflation above:

$$\pi = \frac{A(b+m)}{1+A(b+m)^2}(g+bd+b^*d^*+b\pi).$$

This implies

$$0 = \frac{A(b+m)}{1+A(b+m)^2}(g+bd+b^*d^*) - \left[1 - b\frac{A(b+m)}{1+A(b+m)^2}\right]\pi,$$

and, hence, the rational expectations level of inflation is

$$\begin{aligned}
\pi &= \frac{A(b+m)(g+bd+b^*d^*)}{1+A(b+m)^2 - bA(b+m)} \\
&= \frac{A(b+m)(g+bd+b^*d^*)}{1+A(b+m)m} \\
&= L(g+bd+b^*d^*),
\end{aligned}$$

where

$$L = \frac{A(b+m)}{1+A(b+m)m}.$$

Note that L is an increasing function of both A and b. If the total default premium $bd + b^*d^*$ is an increasing function of b, then so is the inflation rate. The inflation rate is also an increasing function of the relative cost of taxation, A.

In rational expectations equilibrium, the government budget constraint reduces to

$$x = g + bd + b^*d^* - m\pi.$$

There is in fact no fiscal benefit from inflating to reduce the real value of the domestic debt. Any inflation will be expected by the market and will therefore give rise to an offsetting increase in the interest rate paid on the debt. The only fiscal effect of inflation comes from the reduction in the real value of the money stock.

The rational expectations level of tax revenue is

$$\begin{aligned}
x &= g + bd + b^*d^* - m\pi \\
&= (1 - mL)(g + bd + b^*d^*)
\end{aligned}$$

$$= \frac{1}{1 + A(b+m)m}(g + bd + b^* d^*).$$

Given g, we can calculate the equilibrium value of the social loss function:

$$
\begin{aligned}
Ax^2 + \pi^2 &= A(g + bd + b^* d^* - m\pi)^2 + \pi^2 \\
&= A[g + bd + b^* d^* - mL(g + bp)]^2 + L^2(g + bd + b^* d^*)^2 \\
&= (g + bd + b^* d^*)^2 [A(1 - mL)^2 + L^2] \\
&= (g + bd + b^* d^*)^2 A \frac{1 + A(b+m)^2}{[1 + A(b+m)m]^2}.
\end{aligned}
$$

A.3. A fixed exchange rate system

If the government fixes its exchange rate, then it is not free to choose the inflation rate. Provided that the fixed exchange rate is credible, $e^e = 0$, the inflation rate will equal the foreign inflation rate:

$$\pi = \pi^*$$

and

$$\pi^e = \pi^{*e}.$$

Assume that foreign inflation is perfectly foreseen,

$$\pi = \pi^e = \pi^{*e} = \pi^*.$$

The government budget constraint is

$$x = g + b(i - \pi) + b^*(i^* - \pi^*) - m\pi = g + bd + b^* d^* - m\pi^*.$$

Thus, the fixed exchange rate system, like the flexible exchange rate system in rational expectations equilibrium, gives a unique combination of inflation and taxation. The systems can be compared on the basis of the social disutility of these two combinations.

If the social disutility would be lower in a flexible than in a fixed exchange rate system, then the government has an incentive to move to flexible exchange rates. The fixed exchange rate system will lose some or all of the credibility it might have had.

In a credible fixed-rate system, there is no issue of optimal debt management for the purpose of committing to low inflation or hedging against fluctuations in domestic government expenditures. However, there may be an issue of optimal debt management for the purpose of lowering the default premium paid on the public debt.

A.4. Optimal default

In this section, we expand the public finance model with a tentative and rudimentary model of optimal default.

We assume that there is a fixed cost of default. This cost is a utility cost or a social loss, in the sense that it is comparable to the social loss function of taxation and inflation.

The fixed cost may differ depending on whether the country defaults on only the domestic debt, only the foreign debt, or on both. Let the costs be F, F^*, and F^{**} for defaulting on the domestic debt, the foreign debt, and both, respectively. With fixed costs like this, if a country defaults on a particular category of debt, then it might as well repudiate it completely. There will be no partial default within a debt category.

If the domestic debt is repudiated, then the term bi in the government budget constraint is set to zero. If the foreign debt is repudiated, then the term b^*i^* is set to zero. In both cases, the same government expenditures can be financed by less tax revenue or less inflation, and the value of the social loss function will decline as a result of the default. However, now the fixed utility cost of default has to be added to the social loss.

Given the country's fiscal situation, its government considers the possibility of defaulting on either the domestic debt, the foreign debt, or both. For each of those possibilities, it calculates the net reduction in social loss resulting from debt relief and paying the fixed utility cost. It then chooses either no default or one of the three default possibilities.

The higher the country's social loss, the smaller the debt relief it needs in order to justify paying a given fixed cost of default. This is because of the increasing marginal social cost of taxation and inflation. The higher the taxation and inflation would be without default, the bigger the benefit of reducing them. Hence, the higher the country's taxation and inflation, the smaller the reduction in taxes and inflation required in order to justify a fixed utility cost of default.

Which of the three default options the government chooses will depend on the various exogenous variables of the model. Government expenditures g is the main exogenous variable whose random fluctuations will give rise to random fluctuations in required tax revenue and in inflation, and hence in social loss.

Without further assumptions about the costs of default, we can say the following about the risk of default and the default premium. The higher the variability of government expenditures, the higher the probability of default. The higher the fixed cost of default on any category of debt, the lower the probability of default on that debt, and hence, the lower the default premium. The larger a given category of debt as a fraction of total debt, the larger the debt relief from default on that debt, and hence the higher the probability of default and the higher the default premium.

It will be important to know how the total default premium $bd + b^*d^*$ paid on the debt depends on the composition of the debt, given the total debt $b + b^*$. Let θ be the fraction of domestic debt in total debt:

$$\theta = \frac{b}{b + b^*}.$$

Then d, d^*, and the total default premium

$$bd + b^*d^* = [\theta d + (1 - \theta)d^*](b + b^*)$$

may be functions of θ.

Consider the case where $F = F^* = F^{**}$. If the country defaults, it will default on all the debt. The probability of default will be the same for both categories of debt and will be independent of the composition of the debt.

Consider next the case where $F^* < F < F^{**}$.

Suppose $0 \leq \theta \leq 0.5$. When the foreign debt is half the total, or more, the country will never default on the domestic debt alone. It will either default on the foreign debt alone or on both. Therefore, the premium on the foreign debt will be higher than that on the domestic debt: $d \leq d^*$.

For $0 \leq \theta \leq 0.5$, d is constant as a function of θ. As the domestic debt increases, the probability of defaulting on it does not change, because it equals the probability of defaulting on all the debt. Since it becomes less and less favourable to default on the foreign debt alone, the default probability on the foreign debt decreases. Hence, d^* decreases, and $\theta d + (1 - \theta)d^*$ decreases.

The case where $F < F^* < F^{**}$, is of course symmetric.

A.5. Optimal debt management

Given the total real value $b + b^*$ of the debt, the government has a decision to make about how large b should be.

Consider an individual country under a flexible exchange rate regime.

Consider first the case where, for a given total debt $b + b^*$, the total default premium $bd + b^* d^*$ is independent of b. We have argued above that this will be the case if the cost of default is a single fixed cost which is independent of whether the country defaults on the domestic debt, on the foreign debt, or on both: $F = F^* = F^{**}$.

In this case, to minimize the social loss function it suffices to minimize the expression

$$A(1 - mL)^2 + L^2$$

as a function of L. The derivative with respect to L is

$$2A(1 - mL)(-m) + 2L = -Am + (1 + Am^2)L,$$

which is zero at

$$\overline{L} = \frac{Am}{1 + Am^2}.$$

This is the value of L which minimizes the cost function. It is an increasing function of Am. The higher the relative cost of taxation and the larger the benefit of inflation, the higher is the optimal inflation rate.

Given the total real value $b + b^*$ of the debt, the optimal value of b is where

$$L = \frac{A(b + m)}{1 + A(b + m)m} = \frac{Am}{1 + Am^2} = \overline{L},$$

which implies $b = 0$. It is optimal to have zero domestic debt and to have all debt denominated in foreign currency.

Notice that $b = 0$ minimizes inflation and maximizes taxation across rational expectations equilibria.

So, if the government is only concerned with minimizing the steady-state level of inflation, it should choose to have zero domestic debt.

Next, consider the possibility of surprises in government expenditures. For the purpose of this analysis, we simplify the model by setting the default premia to zero. This is actually immaterial, so long as the total default premium paid on the debt is independent of the composition of the debt.

Before g is known, the expected inflation will be

$$\pi^e = Lg^e.$$

This expected inflation feeds into the interest rate, which affects the optimal inflation rate:

$$
\begin{aligned}
\pi &= \frac{A(b+m)}{1+A(b+m)^2}[g+b\pi^e+b^*(\pi^{*e}-\pi^*)] \\
&= \frac{A(b+m)}{1+A(b+m)^2}(g+bLg^e) \\
&= \frac{A(b+m)}{1+A(b+m)^2}[g-g^e+(1+bL)g^e] \\
&= \frac{A(b+m)}{1+A(b+m)^2}(g-g^e)+\frac{A(b+m)}{1+A(b+m)m}g^e,
\end{aligned}
$$

ignoring inflation surprises from abroad.

The corresponding tax revenue will be

$$
\begin{aligned}
x &= g+b(i-\pi)+b^*(i^*-\pi^*)-m\pi \\
&= g+b(\pi^e-\pi)-m\pi \\
&= g+b\pi^e-(b+m)\pi \\
&= g+bLg^e-(b+m)\frac{A(b+m)}{1+A(b+m)^2}(g-g^e)-(b+m)\frac{A(b+m)}{1+A(b+m)m}g^e \\
&= \left[1-(b+m)\frac{A(b+m)}{1+A(b+m)^2}\right](g-g^e)+\left[1+bL-(m+b)\frac{A(b+m)}{1+A(b+m)m}\right]g^e \\
&= \frac{1}{1+A(b+m)^2}(g-g^e)+\frac{1}{1+A(b+m)m}g^e.
\end{aligned}
$$

Both inflation and tax revenue are positively related to g^e, and they are perfectly correlated.

The government chooses the composition of the debt before the level g of expenditures is known. In this case, assume that it minimizes the expectation of the social loss function:

$$
\begin{aligned}
E[Ax^2 + \pi^2] &= A[\mathrm{var}(x) + (Ex)^2] + \mathrm{var}(\pi) + (E\pi)^2 \\
&= A\frac{1}{[1 + A(b+m)^2]^2}\sigma^2 + A\frac{1}{[1 + A(b+m)m]^2}(g^e)^2 \\
&\quad + \frac{[A(b+m)]^2}{[1 + A(b+m)^2]^2}\sigma^2 + \frac{[A(b+m)]^2}{[1 + A(b+m)m]^2}(g^e)^2 \\
&= \frac{A}{[1 + A(b+m)^2]^2}\sigma^2 + \frac{A[1 + A(b+m)^2]}{1 + A(b+m)m}(g^e)^2,
\end{aligned}
$$

where σ^2 is the variance of government expenditures.

At $b = 0$, the derivative of the first term is negative, while the derivative of the second term is zero. Hence the derivative of the whole expression is negative. This implies that the optimal level of b is positive.

We have shown that the desire to minimize fluctuations in the social loss function resulting from fluctuations in government expenditures gives the government an incentive to issue domestic debt. The reason is that unexpectedly high expenditures will be partially financed by unexpectedly high inflation, which inflates away some of the real value of the domestic debt.

A second motive to take on domestic debt may be a desire to pay a low default premium. For the purpose of this analysis, we disregard the hedging motive and assume that the total default premium $bd + b^*d^*$ paid on the debt is a decreasing function of the amount b of domestic debt, at least at low levels of b. We have argued above that this will be the case if the fixed cost of default on the domestic debt is higher than the cost of default on the foreign debt and lower than the cost of defaulting on both: $F^* < F < F^{**}$.

We have shown above that given g, the rational expectations equilibrium value of the social loss function will be

$$
Ax^2 + \pi^2 = (g + bd + b^*d^*)^2 \frac{A[1 + A(b+m)^2]}{[1 + A(b+m)m]^2}.
$$

Again, given the total real value $b + b^*$ of the debt, the government decides how large b should be.

We showed earlier that if the total default premium $bd + b^*d^*$ is independent of b, given the total debt $b + b^*$, then the social loss is minimized at $b = 0$. This implies that the derivative of the expression

$$
\frac{A[1 + A(b+m)^2]}{[1 + A(b+m)m]^2}
$$

with respect to b is zero at $b = 0$ and positive at $b > 0$.

In the present case, where the total default premium $bd + b^*d^*$ is a decreasing function of the amount b of domestic debt, at low levels of b, its derivative with respect to b is negative at $b = 0$. This implies that the derivative of the social loss function with respect to b at $b = 0$ is also negative. Hence, the level of b that minimizes the social loss is positive.

A.6. Inflation and taxation under EMU

Assume that there are n countries in EMU, $j = 1, \ldots, n$. The government budget constraint still holds for each of the countries, as well as for the EMU as a whole, with union aggregate values.

The budget constraint for country j says

$$x_j = g_j + b_j(i - \pi) + b_j^*(i^* - \pi^*) - m_j \pi.$$

Here, m_j is the real value of country j's share of the equity capital of the ECB, which will back the euro. As explained by Sinn and Feist (1997), the value of this share of equity capital may be quite different from the value of the country's monetary base or 'seigniorage wealth' before entering into EMU. This is so because the seigniorage wealth will be socialized and redistributed according to the member countries' population and GDP shares. In brief, a country's m_j may be directly affected by whether it enters EMU or stays out.

Similarly, b_j and b_j^* are the real values of country j's net debt in euros and in non-euro currency, respectively. To the extent the ECB holds bonds, country j's share of these bonds has to be netted out in calculating its euro- and non-euro-denominated net debt.

Country j accounts for a fraction w_j of the population of the EMU. The social loss of each country is a function of inflation and of real taxation x_j:

$$A_j x_j^2 + \pi.$$

Assume that EMU minimizes a weighted average of the social disutility functions, where the weights are the population weights w_j:

$$\sum_{j=1}^{n} w_j (A_j x_j^2 + \pi^2) = \sum_{j=1}^{n} w_j A_j x_j^2 + \pi^2 = \sum_{j=1}^{n} c_j x_j^2 + \pi^2,$$

where $c_j = w_j A_j$.

The increasing marginal social disutility from taxation implies that a given amount of taxation is less painful if it is spread out among many countries than if it is concentrated on a few.

The EMU-wide budget constraint says

$$x = g + b(i - \pi) + b^*(i^* - \pi^*) - m\pi$$

as before, but now

$$x = \sum_j w_j x_j$$

$$g = \sum_j w_j g_j$$

$$b = \sum_j w_j b_j$$

$$b^* = \sum_j w_j b_j^*$$

and

$$m = \sum_j w_j m_j$$

The first-order condition for minimizing the social disutility subject to the budget constraint says

$$0 = \frac{\delta}{\delta\pi}\left(\frac{1}{2}\sum_j c_j x_j^2 + \frac{1}{2}\pi^2\right)$$

$$= \sum_j c_j x_j \frac{\delta x_j}{\delta\pi} + \pi$$

$$= -\sum_j c_j x_j (b_j + m_j) + \pi$$

$$= -\sum_j c_j (b_j + m_j)[g_j + b_j(i-\pi) + b_j^*(i^*-\pi^*) - m_j\pi] + \pi$$

$$= -\sum_j c_j (b_j + m_j)[g_j + b_j i + b_j^*(i^*-\pi^*)] + \left[1 + \sum_j c_j (b_j + m_j)^2\right]\pi.$$

The solution for the optimal inflation rate is

$$\pi = \frac{\sum_j c_j (b_j + m_j)[g_j + b_j i + b_j^*(i^*-\pi^*)]}{1 + \sum_j c_j (b_j + m_j)^2}.$$

We can rewrite the equation for the optimal inflation rate in terms of expectations:

$$\pi = \frac{\sum_j c_j (b_j + m_j)[g_j + b_j d_j + b_j^* d_j^* + b_j \pi^e + b_j^*(\pi^{*e} - \pi^*)]}{1 + \sum_j c_j (b_j + m_j)^2},$$

where d_j and d_j^* are the default premia paid on country j's euro-denominated and non-euro-denominated debt, respectively.

Next, we impose rational expectations:

$$\pi = \frac{\sum_j c_j (b_j + m_j)(g_j + b_j d_j + b_j^* d_j^* + b_j \pi)}{1 + \sum_j c_j (b_j + m_j)^2}$$

$$= \frac{\sum_j c_j (b_j + m_j)(g_j + b_j d_j + b_j^* d_j^*)}{1 + \sum_j c_j (b_j + m_j)^2} + \frac{\sum_j c_j (b_j + m_j) b_j}{1 + \sum_j c_j (b_j + m_j)^2} \pi.$$

This implies

$$\frac{\sum_j c_j (b_j + m_j)(g_j + b_j d_j + b_j^* d_j^*)}{1 + \sum_j c_j (b_j + m_j)^2} = \pi \left[1 - \frac{\sum_j c_j (b_j + m_j) b_j}{1 + \sum_j c_j (b_j + m_j)^2} \right]$$

$$= \pi \frac{1 + \sum_j c_j (b_j + m_j) m_j}{1 + \sum_j c_j (b_j + m_j)^2}.$$

Hence, the rational expectations inflation level is

$$\pi = \frac{\sum_j c_j (b_j + m_j)(g_j + b_j d_j + b_j^* d_j^*)}{1 + \sum_j c_j (b_j + m_j) m_j}$$

$$= \sum_j \frac{c_j (b_j + m_j)}{1 + \sum_j c_j (b_j + m_j) m_j} (g_j + b_j d_j + b_j^* d_j^*)$$

$$= \sum_j L_j (g_j + b_j d_j + b_j^* d_j^*),$$

where

$$L_j = \frac{c_j (b_j + m_j)}{1 + \sum_j c_j (b_j + m_j) m_j}.$$

The rational expectations level of taxation in country j is

$$x_j = g_j + b_j d_j + b_j^* d_j^* - \pi m_j$$

$$= g_j + b_j d_j + b_j^* d_j^* - m_j \left[L_j (g_j + b_j d_j + b_j^* d_j^*) + \sum_{k \neq j} L_k (g_k + b_k d_k + b_k^* d_k^*) \right]$$

$$= (1 - m_j L_j)(g_j + b_j d_j + b_j^* d_j^*) - m_j \sum_{k \neq j} L_k (g_k + b_k d_k + b_k^* d_k^*).$$

Thus, EMU results in a unique combination of inflation and taxation.

Consider the case where all countries are identical, except that they may have different relative costs of taxation: $c_j = A_j/n$, $d_j = d$, $b_j = b$, $d_j^* = d^*$, $b_j^* = b^*$, $m_j = m$, $g_j = g$. In this case,

$$
\begin{aligned}
L_j &= \frac{c_j(b_j + m_j)}{1 + \sum_j c_j(b_j + m_j)m_j} \\
&= \frac{A_j(b+m)/n}{1 + \sum_j A_j(b+m)m/n} \\
&= \frac{1}{n}\frac{A_j(b+m)}{1 + A(b+m)m},
\end{aligned}
$$

where

$$
A = \frac{1}{n}\sum_j A_j
$$

is the average cost of taxation.

The equilibrium inflation rate is

$$
\begin{aligned}
\pi &= \sum_j L_j(g_j + b_j d_j + b_j^* d_j^*) \\
&= \sum_j \frac{1}{n}\frac{A_j(b+m)}{(1 + A(b+m)m/n)}(g + bd + b^*d^*) \\
&= \frac{A(b+m)}{1 + A(b+m)m}(g + bd + b^*d^*) \\
&= L(g + bd + b^*d^*),
\end{aligned}
$$

where

$$
L = \frac{A(b+m)}{1 + A(b+m)m}.
$$

The equilibrium level of taxation in every country is

$$
\begin{aligned}
x &= g + bd + b^*d^* - m\pi \\
&= (1 - mL)(g + bd + b^*d^*) \\
&= \frac{1}{1 + A(b+m)m}(g + bd + b^*d^*).
\end{aligned}
$$

These formulas are identical to those for countries outside EMU, except that A is now the average cost of taxation rather than the cost of taxation in the individual country.

For countries whose cost of taxation is higher than the average, the inflation rate under EMU will be lower than it would be if the country was not a member, all else being equal. For countries with cost of taxation lower than the average, the opposite is true.

If the countries all have the same cost of taxation, then EMU does not affect the equilibrium inflation rate, all else being equal.

For the individual country j, the value of the social disutility function is

$$A_j x^2 + \pi^2 = [A_j(1-mL)^2 + L^2](g+bd+b*d*)^2$$
$$= \frac{A_j + A^2(b+m)^2}{[1+A(b+m)m]^2}(g+bd+b*d*)^2.$$

Outside of EMU, country j would achieve a social disutility of

$$A_j x^2 + \pi^2 = \frac{A_j + A_j^2(b+m)^2}{[1+A(b+m)m]^2}(g+bd+b*d*)^2.$$

Hence, a country which has lower cost of taxation than the EMU average would do better by staying out of EMU.

A.7. Optimal debt management under EMU

Go back to the general case where the countries are not assumed to be identical. Each country in EMU is able to influence the equilibrium inflation rate π through its debt policy. As a function of π, country j's loss function is

$$A_j(g_j + b_j d_j + b_j^* d_j^* - \pi m_j)^2 + \pi^2.$$

The derivative with respect to π is

$$-2A_j m_j(g_j + b_j d_j + b_j^* d_j^* - \pi m_j) + 2\pi,$$

which is zero if and only if $\pi = \pi_j$, where

$$\pi_j = \frac{A_j m_j}{1+A_j m_j^2}(g_j + b_j d_j + b_j^* d_j^*).$$

This is the value of π which country j would like to reach through its debt policy. It is the same inflation as it would reach outside of EMU by having zero domestic currency debt. In EMU, it can reach this level of inflation by choosing b_j, and hence L_j, so as to solve

$$\pi_j = L_j(g_j + b_j d_j + b_j^* d_j^*) + \sum_{k \neq j} L_k(g_k + b_k d_k + b_k^* d_k^*),$$

where we recall the assumption that the total default premium $b_j d_j + b_j^* d_j^*$ is independent of the composition of country j's debt.

In the case where all countries are identical except for their relative cost of taxation, the optimal value of L_j is

$$L_j = \bar{L}_j = \frac{A_j m}{1 + A_j m^2}.$$

This expression is an increasing function of A_j. This implies that countries with higher A_j want higher $\bar{L}_j$ and higher inflation.

The value of $b + m$ which is optimal for country j is where

$$\frac{A(b+m)}{1 + A(b+m)m} = L = \bar{L}_j = \frac{A_j m}{1 + A_j m^2}.$$

If all A_j are identical, then this implies $b = 0$. All countries agree that the total domestic debt of the union should be zero. If any one country sees that the aggregate domestic debt of the other member countries is positive, then it will want to buy up that debt for money it borrows in non-euro currencies. That will make everybody happy.

If the A_j are not identical, then the countries will not agree on the optimal aggregate domestic debt for the union. Any given b is likely to be found too high by some and too low for others. For example, if $b = 0$, then countries with $A_j < A$ would like to lower L by lowering b. The EMU inflation rate is higher than they would like, and they can lower it by issuing less euro debt, or even having a negative euro debt, which they can do by buying up euro-denominated assets. On the other hand, countries with high cost of taxation would want to raise the EMU inflation rate by increasing the aggregate domestic debt.

So this is a game without an equilibrium. There is a need for a coordination mechanism.

Next, consider the motive for hedging against surprises in government expenditures. An unexpected increase in a country's government expenditures will give rise to unexpected increases in union-wide inflation and in taxation in the country in question. Because the country's government expenditures are only a fraction of aggregate government expenditures, the inflation effect will be smaller and the taxation effect larger than if the country had been outside the union.

If the country has some euro-denominated debt outstanding, then this debt will be taxed by the inflation tax. This helps finance the expenditures and lowers the required increase in other taxes. Thus, euro-denominated debt can lower the variability of the social cost function. This effect will be stronger if government expenditures are positively correlated across countries, because then the inflation effect will tend to be stronger.

If a country's government expenditures are uncorrelated with the government expenditures in other member countries, then it may see an unexpected decrease in inflation owing to unexpected decreases in government expenditures in other countries. This lowers the revenue from the inflation tax on real money balances and increases the required level of other taxation. The country can hedge against this possibility by accumulating euro-denominated net assets, partially financed by borrowing in currencies other than the euro.

A second motive to take on euro-denominated debt may be a desire to pay a low default premium, assuming that the total default premium $b_j d_j + b_j^* d_j^*$ that a country pays on its debt is a decreasing function of the amount b_j of euro-denominated debt, at least at low levels of b_j. We have argued that this will be the case if the fixed cost of default on the euro-denominated debt is higher than the cost of default on debt denominated in other currencies and lower than the cost of defaulting on both.

References

Barro, R. J. and D. B. Gordon (1983), 'A Positive Theory of Monetary Policy in a Natural Rate Model', *Journal of Political Economy*, 91: 589–610.

Bohn, H. (1988), 'Why Do We Have Nominal Government Debt?' *Journal of Monetary Economics*, 21: 127–40.

Bohn, H. (1990), 'A Positive Theory of Foreign Currency Debt', *Journal of International Economics*, 29: 273–92.

Calvo, G. (1978), 'On the Time Consistency of Optimal Policy in a Monetary Economy', *Econometrica*, 46: 1411–28.

Canzoneri, M. and C. A. Rogers (1990), 'Is the European Community an Optimal Currency Area: Optimal Taxation versus the Cost of Multiple Currencies', *American Economic Review*, 80: 419–33.

Eaton, J. (1996), 'Sovereign Debt, Repudiation, and Credit Terms', *International Journal of Finance and Economics*, 1: 25–36.

Kydland, F. E. and E. C. Prescott (1977), 'Rules rather than Discretion: The Inconsistency of Optimal Plans', *Journal of Political Economy*, 85: 473–92.

Mankiw, G. N. (1987), 'The Optimal Collection of Seigniorage: Theory and Evidence', *Journal of Monetary Economics*, 20: 327–41.

Miller, V. (1997), 'Why a Government Might Want to Consider Foreign Currency Denominated Debt', *Economics Letters*, 55: 247–50.

Missale, A. and O. J. Blanchard (1994), 'Inflation and Debt Maturity', *American Economic Review*, 84: 309–19.

Persson, M., T. Persson and L. E. O. Svensson (1987), 'Time Consistency of Fiscal and Monetary Policy', *Econometrica*, 55: 1419–31.

Sinn, H.-W. and H. Feist (1997), 'Eurowinners and Eurolosers: The Distribution of Seignorage Wealth in EMU', CEPR Discussion Paper no. 1747.

5

The Exposure of International Corporate Bond Returns to Exchange Rate Risk

GORDON DELIANEDIS AND PEDRO SANTA-CLARA

1. Introduction

This chapter looks at the effects of exchange rate variability on corporate bond returns, trying to ascertain the extent to which currency risk impacts the borrowing costs of companies. The relevance of this study becomes apparent in the context of European Monetary Union. In fact, one of the benefits of currency unification that has been touted is the reduction of financing costs to European companies, from decreasing exchange rate risk. This chapter examines the likelihood and extent of these potential gains.

Exchange rate changes may be correlated with corporate bond returns for two reasons: first, because the company's expected future cash flows may depend on exchange rates; secondly, because exchange rates may affect the required market discount rates on these cash flows. This change in the required discount rate can arise from changes in default-free interest rates or from changes in credit risk premia.

In this chapter, we try to isolate the changes in default-free interest rates in corporate bond returns and concentrate on the other sources of returns. With that purpose, we study *credit returns*, that is the returns on corporate bonds above the returns on risk-free bonds with the same promised payments. Credit returns are particularly interesting owing to the option-like pay-off of corporate bonds.[1] Since they just depend on changes in the solvency of the issuing company, credit returns are very sensitive to events that affect the future prospects of the company. Even more so than equity returns.

The riskiness of corporate credit returns has both idiosyncratic and systematic sources. However, only the latter may be priced and are thus of interest to us. Finding no covariation of credit spreads with such factors would be evidence that they are not priced. However, finding some covariation still leaves the question of whether the risk source is priced. We examine potential risk factors such as stock market returns,

Thanks are due to Jean Dermine for helpful comments.
[1] See Merton (1973).

default-free interest rate changes and exchange rate changes, with a special interest in this last factor, since it is the one that will be affected by monetary union.

The significance of exchange rate risk in explaining asset returns is an open, and insufficiently explored, question in the empirical asset pricing literature. Most papers have concentrated on stocks and default-free bonds, with mixed conclusions. Jorion (1991) finds little evidence of priced exchange rate risk in US stock returns, whereas Chow *et al.* (1997) do find evidence of exchange rate changes affecting the returns of US stocks and bonds, including long-term corporate bonds. This chapter adds to the literature by looking at a different asset class. Additionally, our sample extends coverage to include bonds denominated in several currencies, [2] and is thus informative about the effects of currency risk in a wide variety of firms.

Prior attempts at identifying the systematic factors of corporate bonds have primarily used portfolios of US dollar-denominated bonds organized on credit ratings. Chang and Huang (1990) find evidence for a two-factor latent-variable model using interest rate variables as the instruments. Fama and French (1989) find that future excess returns on stock and bond portfolios can be forecast by default spreads, term spreads, and dividend yields. These studies examine bonds' excess returns, that is, the return on a corporate bond less the risk-free interest rate for the holding period. This excess return is affected by two forces: movements in the riskless interest rate and changes in default premia. Our analysis focuses on credit returns in order to isolate changes in default premia.

Studies that have looked at credit returns explicitly are few in number. Sarig and Warga (1991) quantify the magnitude of credit returns for zero-coupon US corporate bonds while Litterman and Iben (1991) show how to extend the analysis to include coupon bonds. These studies do not address the dynamics of credit returns or try to identify the systematic factors that affect them.

Changes in exchange rates will affect asset returns in as much as their cash flows are not completely hedged within the firm. The effectiveness of exchange rate hedging is a function of the uncertainty and duration of future cash flows. Long-term cash flows will be harder to hedge than short-term cash flows owing to their increased uncertainty. Looking at short-horizon returns may understate exchange rate risk if firms can hedge their short-term cash flows effectively. But for future cash flows, where the long-term effects of exchange rate changes are difficult to ascertain, hedging effectiveness is doubtful. This is the motivation of Chow *et al.* (1997) in looking at long-horizon returns to assess whether exchange rate risk is priced. We therefore examine the exchange rate dependence of credit returns at different horizons.

The discussion is organized as follows. Section 2 outlines a simple model of corporate bond returns. Section 3 describes the data sources and the calculation methods used to construct the credit returns. Section 4 describes the empirical methodology along with the results. The approach is to regress credit returns on exchange rate changes, after controlling for other economic variables, to determine if exchange

---

[2] We consider four major European currencies and the Canadian dollar.

rate changes affect the credit returns of international corporate bonds. Section 5 concludes.

2. The Risk Exposures of Corporate Bond Returns

In this section we discuss the factors that affect returns to corporate bonds.

Previous research on corporate bonds has focused on explaining excess returns over short-term default-free interest rates. Unfortunately, this approach mixes the two effects of term-structure movements and default-spread movements. To examine changes in default spreads independently of movements in the term structure, we form *credit returns*, by taking the return to a corporate bond and subtracting the return to a riskless bond with the same promised payments. We believe this definition is more representative of actual movements in default spreads for corporations.

Corporate bonds are contingent claims on the value of the firms that issue them. The bond only receives the promised payments (coupon and principal) if the firm does not default. We can use a simple model to illustrate the determinants of corporate bond returns.

We assume that default happens when the value of the assets of the firm, V, falls below the value of its liabilities, K, with both processes assumed to follow diffusions. Default can then be modelled as the first time $X = \log(V/K)$ passes through 0. The dynamics of X can in general depend on any state variables that affect the assets or the liabilities of the firm.

If we further assume that the writedown in case of default is a constant fraction, W, of the price of a default-riskless bond with the same promised payments, the time t price of a zero-coupon corporate bond with maturity T has been shown by Saá-Requejo and Santa-Clara (1997) to be

$$C(t,T) = P(t,T)(1 - WQ(t,T)), \tag{1}$$

where $C(t, T)$ denotes the corporate bond price, $P(t, T)$ the default-riskless price and $Q(t, T)$ the forward risk adjusted probability that X will fall below 0 between dates t and T, that is, the probability of default before T.

The (continuously compounded) return to corporate zero-coupon bonds between dates t and s is given by

$$r_c(t,s,T) = \log C(s,T) - \log C(t,T)$$
$$= \log \frac{P(s,T)}{P(t,T)} + \log \frac{1-WQ(s,T)}{1-WQ(t,T)}. \tag{2}$$

We therefore write

$$r_c(t,s,T) = r_p(t,s,T) + r_x(t,s,T), \tag{3}$$

where the return to the corporate bond is decomposed into the return to a default-riskless zero-coupon bond with the same maturity and the credit return. We see that the credit return is due to changes in the forward risk adjusted probability of default.

This decomposition holds approximately with coupon bonds. The return to a coupon corporate bond can be decomposed into the return to a default-riskless zero-coupon bond with the same coupon rate and principal and the credit return.

The credit return depends on the evolution of the state variable X, which determines the probability of default. The dynamics of X depend on any systematic factors and idiosyncratic shocks that affect the assets and liabilities of the firm, which are left unspecified by the model.[3] Furthermore, the form of the dependence of credit returns on the risk factors is a priori unknown, since the forward risk adjusted probability of default depends on X generally in a nonlinear way, and the solvency ratio itself may vary nonlinearly with the factors.

The purpose of this chapter is to investigate and try to determine what systematic factors affect credit returns on corporate bonds.[4] We restrict the form of the dependence to linearity, which can of course be justified as a first-order approximation.

The variables which we use to explain credit spreads are stock market returns, changes in interest rates and changes in exchange rates. These variables have been studied before in other asset pricing studies and so we only briefly explain their use.

The return on the stock market is a standard explanatory variable in asset pricing models. This variable should have explanatory power for the variation in the value of the assets and the liabilities of the firm, and hence for changes in the probability of default and credit spreads.

Corporate bond returns are driven by changes in risk-free interest rates and changes in default premia. Campbell (1987) and others have shown that expected excess returns on stock and bond portfolios are related to changes in interest rates. Chang and Huang (1990) use interest rates as instruments for time-varying risk premia of corporate bond returns while Fama and French (1989) find evidence that the term premium (riskless long-term rate less the short-term rate) is related to excess returns of corporate bonds. The effect of interest rates on credit returns is not obvious because term-structure movements are removed with the matching bond.

Additionally, Saá-Requejo and Santa-Clara (1997) show that the forward risk adjusted probability of default depends on the volatilities of default-riskless interest rates and that these volatilities may depend on the interest rates themselves. Therefore changes in the probability of default should be related to changes in the yield curve.

Our interest in interest rate changes and stock market returns is residual. We are mainly interested in examining the exposure of corporate bond returns to exchange rate risk. We basically want to 'filter out' the effects of the former variables in order to assess the true impact of exchange rate changes.

Exchange rate changes will affect returns if the asset's cash flows are not completely

---

[3] The forward risk adjustment of the process X introduces bond volatilities in the drift. Changes in interest rates can therefore still have an impact on credit returns.

[4] We are only interested in systematic factors, since these are the only ones that may be priced.

hedged. Given the possibility of default, perfect currency hedging of corporate bonds is not possible. Whether the residual exchange risk can be diversified away or not is an open question.

Chow *et al.* (1997) argue that the lack of empirical evidence for priced exchange rate risk may arise from holding periods being too short. They claim that if exchange rate risk is priced, it should show up in long-term returns. The rationalization for the existence of long-horizon exchange rate exposure is that short-term cash flows can be effectively hedged whereas the effect of long-term exchange rate exposure on future cash flows is uncertain, making hedging less effective. If this conjecture is true, we should expect to see the significance of exchange rate exposure increase with the holding period length.

3. Data

The data for this study are provided by Datastream, which provides extensive coverage of financial and economic variables for a large cross-section of countries. Our interest is in the more developed markets, where liquidity is higher and pricing is more reliable. For this reason, we concentrate on bonds denominated in the currencies of France, Germany, Switzerland, and Great Britain, as well as the United States and Canada. These currencies provide the bulk of the bonds tracked and produce a sufficient sample size for each currency. The above currencies correspond to the major Eurobond markets.

Datastream tracks bonds which are alive as of the current day. It is not a historical database with prices for matured or defaulted issues, so the issue of sample selection bias may be important. The bias, if any, is mitigated by the fact that both bonds which have defaulted and bonds which have matured and paid off are not included in the present sample. These offsetting forces make the source of bias hard to sign and presumably insignificant.

The requirement that bonds be alive at the end of the sample makes the sample shrink as we recede back in time. As the sample starting point we choose December 1992, trading off the size of the cross-sections against the length of the time-series. We end our sample as of July 1997, giving a total of 239 weekly observations.

3.1. Corporate bond data

Corporate bond data are obtained from Datastream's bond database. The database includes a price history for the individual issues and their associated characteristics such as coupon rate, derivative features, and time to maturity. We start with all bonds in the database and eliminate bonds which are issued by the government, public authorities, supranationals, or any other public entity. The remaining bonds have been issued by private companies subject to credit risk.

A complication that arises from using corporate bonds is the presence of embedded options. Embedded options change the return decomposition from the model shown in the previous section. We therefore eliminate callable bonds, bonds with warrants, convertible bonds, putable bonds, and bonds with sinking fund provisions. This restriction lets us avoid evaluating the embedded options, which would be difficult given their variety and complexity.

It is well known that corporate bonds do not trade very often and market prices are observed infrequently. In the absence of market prices, quoted bond prices come from either dealers' bid–ask sheets or from matrix pricing of similar bonds.[5] Datastream claims to use a sale price or a dealer bid–ask price for its quoted bond prices, although differentiation between market price and dealer bid–ask price is not provided.

An obvious manifestation of not having liquid market prices for bonds is that for some issues the price does not change very often. This implies that, with high probability, the issue was not traded or the dealer bid–ask quote was not updated. Either way, we alleviate this concern by screening the prices to eliminate the issues that exhibit stale prices. For each bond we calculate how many times the bond's price[6] remained constant from week to week and divide this number by the total number of price observations. If the ratio is less than 20 per cent, we include the bond in our sample; otherwise the bond is eliminated from the sample.[7] For example, if bond prices only moved monthly (every four weeks), we would see in any given month three prices which were the same and one bond price which changed. The ratio would equal 75 per cent and the bond would be eliminated from the sample.

Our final screen is to take bonds which have either a Moody's or Standard and Poor's rating. The Moody's rating is the primary rating used, because it covers more bonds than Standard and Poor's. When the two ratings differ we choose the Moody's rating, and only when Moody's does not rate an issue do we take the Standard and Poor's rating, if available. From the definitions of the ratings for the two systems, it is straightforward to map a Standard and Poor's rating into a Moody's rating. To limit the number of classifications, we ignore the modifiers '+' and '−', as well as '1', '2', and '3', and treat the modified ratings in the same manner as the basic rating. This leaves us with five risk categories: AAA, AA, A, BAA, and BA, where BA includes all bonds rated BA and below.

For a portfolio to be included in our analysis, we require that the portfolio be comprised of at least three bonds. This leaves us with twenty-four portfolios sorted by currency and credit rating.

The final tally is a sample of 777 bonds denominated in the six currencies. The number of bonds alive at the beginning of the sample in December 1992 is 282. The average number of bonds per portfolio ranges from 12 in the beginning of the sample to 32 at the final date. These numbers compare favourably to other studies, which have used samples ranging from 10 to 20 bonds on average.

---

[5] See Sarig and Warga (1989).

[6] Price refers to the clean price. The gross price, which includes accrued interest, would automatically increase each month even if the bond is not traded.

[7] The choice of the 20% cut-off is arbitrary. The number is chosen to ensure that there are no bonds which trade very infrequently and that we have a large enough sample.

For each bond we calculate the continuously compounded return from week to week. The clean price and the gross price are given for each bond. The gross price is comprised of the clean (quoted) price, $CP_{i,t}$, plus the interest, AI_t, accrued upto time t.

$$GP_{i,t} = CP_{i,t} + AI_t. \tag{4}$$

The return to the bond is calculated as the log of the ratio of the current gross price to the previous week's gross price. The weekly return, $r_c(t)$, is calculated as

$$r_c(t) = \log \frac{GP(t)}{GP(t-1)}, \tag{5}$$

where the gross price is augmented with the coupon at the first date following the coupon payment.

3.2. Default-free bond data

To compute the credit return we need to subtract from the return of the corporate bond the return to a riskless bond with the same promised cash flows. We denote this constructed bond as the *default-free bond*. For each corporate bond, the coupon and redemption amounts and dates are known, so in order to compute the default-free bond prices, we only need to estimate the term structure of default-free zero-coupon interest rates.

As an approximation, we follow Coleman *et al.* (1992) and assume that the term structure can be modelled using a set of constant (continuously compounded) forward rates. We use eight forward rates denoted $f_0(t), \ldots, f_7(t)$, with (lower) nodes corresponding to $t_0 = 0$, $t_1 = 0.25$, $t_2 = 0.50$, $t_3 = 1$, $t_4 = 2$, $t_5 = 3$, $t_6 = 5$, and $t_7 = 7$ years. These default-free forward rates are estimated for every sample date and for every currency.

The forward rates are obtained by fitting Libor and swap data using least squares.[8] Denote the N-period swap rate by $S(t, N)$ and the N-period discount bond as $P(t, t + N)$. The valuation of the swap is akin to that of a coupon-paying bond. The estimated swap rate is the one that prices the swap at par and is denoted $\hat{S}(t, N)$,

$$\hat{S}(t,N) = \frac{1 - P(t,t+N)}{B(t, S(t,N), N)}, \tag{6}$$

where, assuming semi-annual swap payments,[9]

$$B(t,N,S(t,N)) = \sum_{j=1/2}^{2N} S(t,N)P(t,t+j) + P(t,t+2N) \tag{7}$$

---

[8] Grinblatt (1995) gives some justification for using swaps rather than Treasury bonds as default-free instruments. The swap rates, unlike some treasuries, are highly liquid and a constant maturity contract is available at each observation date.

[9] The frequency is different for different markets.

is the annuity factor associated with the swap coupon payments.

Finally, the zero-coupon bonds are priced by discounting the principal payment at the forward rates upto the maturity date:

$$P(t,T) = \exp\left(-\sum_{k=0}^{7} f_k(t)\max(\min(T-t-t_k,t_{k+1}-t_k),0)\right). \tag{8}$$

The default-free-bond pricing formula contains eight unknowns corresponding to the forward rates. We estimate these forward rates by minimizing the sum of squared errors between the observed and the computed swap rates. We use data on ten rates corresponding to the one-, three-, six-, and twelve-month Libor rates, and the two-, three-, four-, five-, seven-, and ten-year swap rates, denoted $S(t, N)$. For each period and for each currency, we estimate the unknown forward rates by minimizing the sum of squared errors:

$$\min_{\{f_i\}_{i=1}^{7}} L = \frac{1}{10}\sum_{i=1}^{10}(\hat{S}(t,N)-S(t,N))^2. \tag{9}$$

Figure 5.1 shows the evolution of the estimated term structures of forward rates for the f_2, f_5, and f_8. In general, there is an upward-sloping term structure for most currencies. Deviations from this pattern are small in magnitude and tend to occur at the short end of the term structure.

The prices of default-free coupon bonds are constructed as the sum of the cash flows times the riskless zero-coupon bond prices given in (8):

$$\hat{P}(t,N,\kappa) = \sum_{i=1}^{N} \kappa\hat{P}(t,t+i) + \hat{P}(t,t+N), \tag{10}$$

where κ is the coupon payment. Each price observation of each corporate bond in our sample is matched by one such default-free bond price. The return to the default-riskless coupon bond is then computed analogously to the risky corporate bonds as

$$r_p(t) = \log\frac{\hat{P}(t,N,\kappa)}{\hat{P}(t-1,N,\kappa)}, \tag{11}$$

where the bond price is augmented with the coupon at the first date following the coupon payment.

3.3. Credit returns

Credit returns are constructed by taking the return on corporate bonds and subtracting the returns from the matching default-free bonds. Equal-weighted portfolios are formed based on currency of denomination and credit rating. The selection of currency of issue as the portfolio formation criterion, is driven by the data availability. This criterion allows us to have sufficient observations in each portfolio. The portfolios

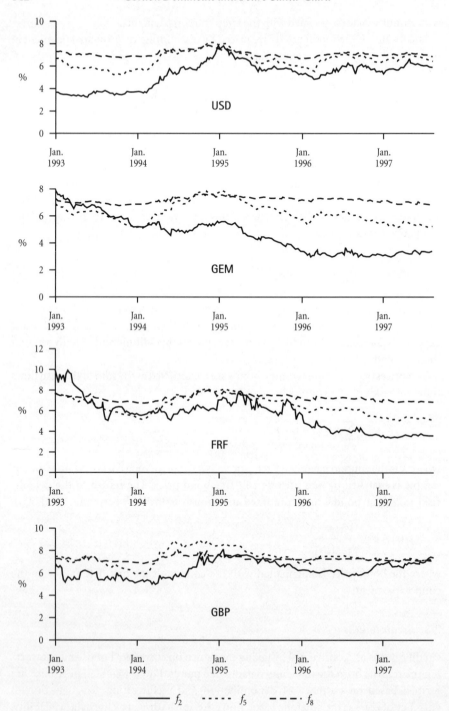

Figure 5.1. Forward rates

are zero-cost by construction and are formed each period. The credit ratings range from AAA to BA, but not all credit ratings are available for all currencies. We are left with a total of twenty-five portfolios denominated in the six currencies. Continuously compounded returns are computed for holding periods corresponding to one, four, thirteen, twenty-six, and fifty-two weeks.

Credit ratings are chosen as a sorting variable because they produce a wide dispersion in returns and they also group assets of similar risk into the same portfolios. Weinstein (1981) gives support to this choice by showing that credit ratings are related to bond betas. Our results show good dispersion in credit returns when we form portfolios based on credit ratings.

An alternative definition of default risk is the excess return. Excess returns are defined as the return on a corporate bond less the return on a riskless asset over the holding period. The excess return of a bond is composed of two components: riskless interest rate risk and default risk. The inclusion of riskless interest rate risk obscures the relationship between credit returns and default risk. Excess returns on corporate bonds have been studied previously and we report results for comparison purposes.

One issue with the data is that the portfolio maturity is changing over time. As bonds are added, the average maturity can increase or decrease depending on the bond's time to maturity relative to the portfolio. If no bonds are added during any period, the average maturity will decrease by one week, which is our observation interval. To check if maturing is a major factor, we regress the credit return and the excess return portfolios for the one-week horizon on the portfolio time to maturity. Table 5.1 shows the results from this regression. The results show no significant relationship between credit return and time to maturity. The excess returns show a weak negative relationship in the German and French currencies, with no discernible relationships in the other currencies. Using US corporate bonds, Sarig and Warga showed the term structure of credit spreads to be relatively flat for higher-rated bonds and negative for lower-grade bonds at the short and medium end of the term structure. With the regression results and the fact that our sample is primarily of higher-quality bonds, we believe the time to maturity issue is non-existent for our credit return results and is only a minor issue for the excess return results.

3.4. Explanatory variables

This section gives a brief description of the explanatory variables used to explain credit returns.

The term premium variable measures the excess return of a long-term default-free bond above the short-term interest rate for the holding period. We denote the term premium at time t by

$$TERM(t - T,t) = LB(t - T,t) - r(t - T,t), \tag{12}$$

where $LB(t - T, t)$ is the default-free long bond return from $t - T$ to t and where the short-term interest rate for horizon length T is denoted as $r(t - T, t)$. The return on the

Gordon Delianedis and Pedro Santa-Clara

Table 5.1. Credit spread and excess spread vs. time to maturity[a]

	β_{CS}	$t_{\beta_{CS}}$	β_{rf}	$t_{\beta_{rf}}$
USD				
AAA	.0660	.314	−.4192	−.003
AA	.1846	1.03	.1686	.192
A	.1878	.138	.1408	.128
BAA	.4789	.076	1.253	1.057
CAD				
AAA	.605	1.09	−.7509	−.105
AA	.483	1.32	−.7259	−.963
A	.480	1.28	−.5161	−.745
GEM				
AAA	−.3025	−.855	−1.319	−1.52
AA	−.0509	.206	−.5459	−.754
A	−.0837	.428	−.2906	−.551
BAA	.5021	.953	.6433	.822
BA	−.1562	−.302	−1.091	−2.40
FRF				
AAA	−.2386	−.604	−.2935	−.298
AA	−.1086	−.310	−2.336	−1.84
A	−.2330	−.612	−2.771	−2.06
BAA	−.1686	−.420	−3.362	−2.51
CHF				
AAA	−.0349	−.067	−.3559	−.557
AA	−.0473	−.098	−.1309	−.225
A	.3101	.895	.2066	.333
BAA	.226	.537	.1920	.326
BA	.3073	.610	.4762	.646
GBP				
AAA	.0551	.0865	.4727	.428
AA	.1148	.1479	.2720	.155
A	.7379	.8241	.8632	.511
BAA	.3581	.663	.6344	.618

[a] Regression of one-week credit and excess returns on time to maturity as measured in days ($\times 10^6$). The regression $CS_{i,t} = \alpha + \beta_i \, TM_t + \varepsilon_t$ is run where TM is the time to maturity, CS represents the credit return and rf represents the excess return. Heteroscedasticity and autocorrelation t-stats are given.

default-free long bond is taken to be the total return to a portfolio of government bonds of maturity greater than ten years. This series is constructed by Datastream and is provided for all six currencies.

The other interest rate variable relates to the slope of the term structure. We define the slope of the term structure by the return to the six-month bill minus the return to the one-month bill. The variable is denoted as

$$SLP(t - T,t) = r_{6M}(t - T,t) - r_{1w}(t - T,t), \tag{13}$$

where $r_{6M}(t - T, t)$ is the return on the six-month bill and $r_{1w}(t - T, t)$ is the continuously compounded one-week risk-free return.

We define the local stock market excess return associated with currency i as

$$STK_i(t - T,t) = \log \frac{S_{i,t}}{S_{i,t-T}} - r(t - T,t), \tag{14}$$

where $S_{i,t}$ is the stock index level of country i at time t. The stock market return is a Datastream-provided index, which is calculated to include all payouts, including dividends, for a subset of the assets in the local stock markets. We use the Datastream indexes to be consistent when measuring excess stock returns in different markets.

Exchange rate changes have to be defined relative to other currencies. We follow Chow *et al.* (1997) in constructing a trade-weighted exchange rate index which weights exchange rate returns by the volume of trade conducted with each country. For each country we construct the trade weights with the other five countries in our sample. The volume of trade is defined as the sum of imports and exports between the domestic country and the five other foreign countries. The reference year is chosen as the end of 1994 and the weights are held constant throughout the sample.[10] A summary of the weights is provided in Table 5.2. Except for Canada, which conducts over 90 per cent of its trade with the USA, the rest of the countries have significant trade with multiple countries.

The weekly exchange rate data is obtained from Morgan Stanley as supplied in Datastream. The excess return to exchange rate movements for currency i over the interval $t - T$ is defined as

$$XCH_i(t - T,t) = \sum_{j=1}^{6} w_{i,j} \log \frac{XCH_{i,j}(t)}{XCH_{i,j}(t - T)} - r(t - T,t), \tag{15}$$

Table 5.2. Trade-based exchange rate weighting[a]

	USD	CAD	GEM	FRF	CHF	GBP	X1	X2
USD	0	62	13	8	3	14	GEM	GBP
CAD	94	0	2	1	1	2	USD	GBP
GEM	24	2	0	36	16	22	USD	GBP
FRF	20	2	46	0	8	24	USD	GEM
CHF	15	1	53	19	0	12	USD	GEM
GBP	32	4	33	24	7	0	USD	GEM

a Percentage of trade between country i (left-hand column) and country j (top row). X1 and X2 represent the two currencies which exchange rate exposure is measured against.

10 The data are from the 1995 IMF *Directory of Trade*, which reports trade statistics for the previous year.

where $XCH_{i,j}(t)$ is the actual exchange rate between currency i and currency j at time t and $w_{i,j}$ is the trade-based weight given in Table 5.2.

As an alternative to the trade-based weighting scheme just described, we look at two different weighting schemes. The first scheme, denoted as $XCH1$, measures exchange rate exposure of each country relative to the average of two major currencies drawn from the US dollar, German mark, and British pound:

$$XCH1_i(t-T,t) = \sum_{j=1}^{2} 0.5 \left(r_j(t-T,t) - \log \frac{XCH_{i,j}(t)}{XCH_{i,j}(t-T)} \right) - r(t-T,t). \tag{16}$$

For example, for US dollar returns, we use as explanatory variables the changes in the German mark and British pound; while for Swiss franc returns, we consider changes in the German mark and US dollar. The two currencies which are used for each country are given in Table 5.2.

Secondly, we measure exchange rate exposure individually relative to two major currencies. For example, for the US dollar we define the exchange rate factor as either the German mark or the British pound. We check both exchange rates to see if credit returns are related to either of these exchange rates individually.

4. Descriptive Statistics

Table 5.3 provides summary statistics for the twenty-five credit return portfolios at different investment horizons. The table shows the credit returns to be generally increasing as the credit rating decreases. Deviations from strict monotonicity occur only in some French franc and US dollar portfolios. The credit returns for the French franc are all very small and thus the deviations are not very meaningful. The other deviation is the AA US dollar portfolio, which has a return too high relative to the other US dollar-denominated portfolios. It should be noted that the differences in means are not statistically different and thus the credit rating portfolios may be correctly ordered. The magnitudes of credit returns differ across currencies, where the highest (in local currency) are in US dollars and British pounds and the lowest are in French francs.[11] Plots of the three-month horizon AAA and A credit return portfolios are shown for four currencies in Figures 5.2 and 5.3.

The reported credit returns are all positive except for the AAA portfolios for the German mark and Swiss franc. The result would be troubling, because one would always invest in the riskless bond instead of the risky bond if the credit return were truly negative. The magnitudes of the discrepancies are, however, small and not statistically different from zero. Also, the downward slope in the German forward curves in the beginning of the sample might downward-bias the credit returns. Additionally, the

---

[11] As a comparison with other work, Sarig and Warga (1991) find credit yields of 0.25–1.5% for AAA through BAA credit ratings and 1.5–5% for BA credit ratings and below. These results are not directly applicable because the time-periods studied are different.

Table 5.3. Credit returns by currency and rating class[a] (%)

	Mean return/Horizon (weeks)					Standard deviation/Horizon (weeks)				
	1	4	13	26	52	1	4	13	26	52
USD										
AAA	1.146	1.164	1.136	1.177	1.168	1.187	.825	.574	.439	.421
AA	2.448	2.539	2.582	2.582	2.588	1.262	.853	.640	.614	.757
A	1.936	2.039	2.021	2.036	1.999	1.132	.771	.570	.547	.586
BAA	3.650	3.678	3.636	3.659	3.637	1.691	1.448	1.242	.811	.961
CAD										
AAA	.598	.536	.502	.547	.467	2.779	1.765	1.373	1.136	.956
AA	.868	.799	.736	.747	.664	2.766	1.707	1.302	1.055	.915
A	1.361	1.326	1.302	1.349	1.271	2.677	1.673	1.422	1.253	1.088
GEM										
AAA	−.176	−.208	−.106	−.097	−.070	1.968	1.267	.745	.625	.576
AA	.121	.028	.096	.139	.205	2.074	1.355	.931	.824	.770
A	.378	.354	.481	.508	.576	2.142	1.499	1.100	1.076	1.043
BAA	1.48	1.249	1.283	1.353	1.358	3.098	2.340	1.921	1.990	2.207
BA	2.876	3.041	3.164	3.095	3.179	3.356	2.911	2.710	2.617	2.379
FRF										
AAA	.077	.058	.002	.120	.232	2.184	1.479	1.163	.885	.546
AA	.034	.052	.046	.161	.267	2.124	1.376	1.056	.842	.419
A	.051	.112	.095	.164	.262	2.094	1.324	.972	.743	.458
BAA	.077	.074	.085	.038	.005	2.472	1.576	1.133	.891	.546
CHF										
AAA	−.265	−.254	.015	−.054	−.001	2.675	1.951	1.480	1.330	1.271
AA	.106	.013	.164	.133	.172	2.827	1.955	1.592	1.458	1.402
A	.850	.679	.734	.646	.669	2.402	1.781	1.497	1.426	1.403
BAA	1.716	1.698	1.846	1.792	1.789	3.576	2.654	2.088	1.972	2.050
BA	2.972	2.799	2.786	2.486	2.592	3.157	2.844	3.137	2.623	2.256
GBP										
AAA	1.574	1.755	1.567	1.394	1.136	2.794	1.918	1.466	1.354	1.164
AA	1.729	1.835	1.689	1.510	1.296	2.576	1.760	1.310	1.215	1.003
A	2.726	2.849	2.654	2.423	2.104	2.814	2.030	1.615	1.591	1.405
BAA	4.065	4.157	4.079	3.913	3.489	3.207	2.375	2.021	2.009	1.402

[a] Weekly bond portfolio returns from Jan. 1993 to July 1997. The first set of numbers are time-series means of bond portfolio returns. Returns are in excess of a similar riskless bond and are reported on an annual basis. The second set of numbers are the time-series standard deviations of the portfolio returns.

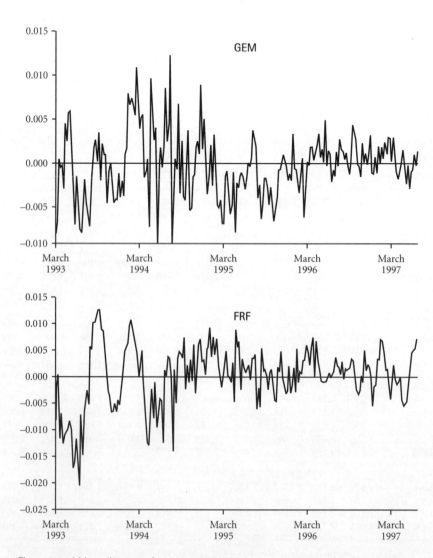

Figure 5.2. AAA credit returns for a three-month horizon

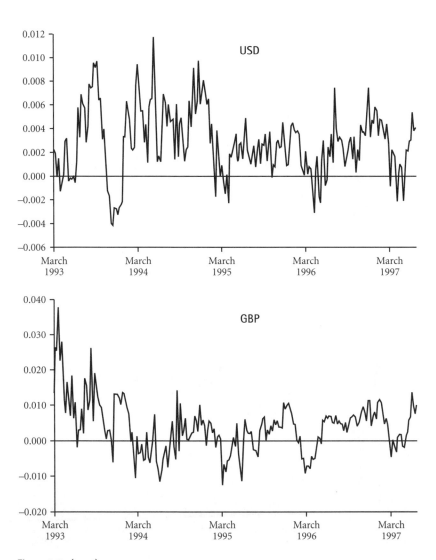

Figure 5.2. (*cont.*)

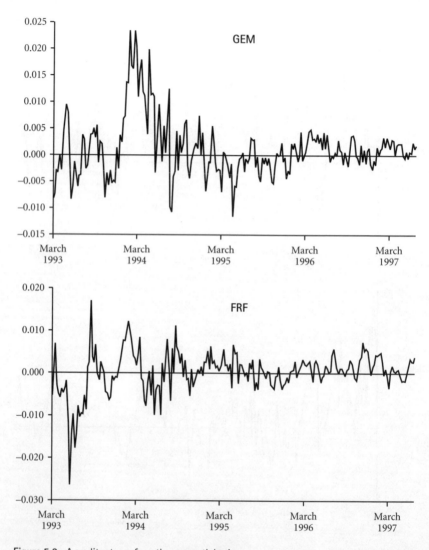

Figure 5.3. A credit returns for a three-month horizon

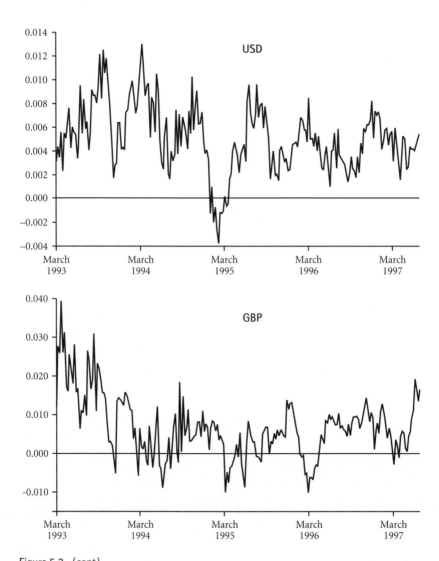

Figure 5.3. (*cont.*)

purpose of this study is to examine the dynamics of credit returns as opposed to explaining the actual credit return levels. Errors that affect the level of credit spreads may not affect inferences with respect to the effect of exchange rate risk or any other systematic risks on the dynamics of credit returns.

For comparison purposes, we also look at the excess returns of corporate bonds over the holding-period default-free interest rate. Summary statistics for the excess return portfolios are given in Table 5.4. The excess returns are positive for all portfolios. The analysis of returns by the credit rating of portfolios shows increasing returns as the credit quality increases. The exceptions occur in the French franc and US dollar. These are the same exceptions noted already for credit returns. Looking at the holding period length, we see that excess returns decrease as the holding period increases. The decrease reflects the fact that term structures of riskless interest rates are upward-sloping. Excess returns are calculated relative to the holding-period riskless return. With an upward-sloping term structure, the riskless interest rate increases with maturity and thus excess returns decrease.

Correlations for the credit returns and excess returns are reported in Tables 5.5–8. Table 5.5 reports the correlations of credit rating portfolios for each currency at one-week and three-month horizons. The results show considerable correlation among the higher-quality credit rating (AAA through A) portfolios and less correlation between these high-quality portfolios and the lower-quality portfolios (BAA and BA). Table 5.6 shows the correlation results for the excess returns. Correlations for excess returns are much higher than correlations for credit returns. The excess return is the difference between the return of the corporate bond and the risk-free return for the holding period. All excess return portfolios are measured relative to the same risk-free return and thus changes in the risk-free return will be highly correlated among credit rating portfolios.

Correlations between credit returns of the same credit quality, but different currency denomination, are reported in Table 5.7 (returns are stated in the local currency). The results show that credit returns of the same credit quality are not highly correlated across currencies. The low correlations suggest that default risk is not systematic across currencies, which may translate into unpriced exchange rate risk. The same correlations using excess returns are reported in Table 5.8. Here again we see substantial correlation across currencies. The high correlations result from the fact that riskless interest rates are correlated across currencies. Excess returns are measured relative to a riskless rate and if these rates are correlated across currencies, than one would expect excess returns to be correlated across currencies as we see in Table 5.8.

The correlation results highlight the difference between credit returns and excess returns. Credit returns are not as highly correlated as excess returns because they only measure default risk. Excess returns measure changes in riskless interest rates in addition to default risk and thus are much more correlated. The high dependence of excess returns on riskless interest rate moves shrouds the actual effect of default risk on corporate bonds. For this reason, we will focus on credit returns, which by construction are a more direct measure of default risk.

Table 5.4. Excess returns by currency and rating class[a] (%)

	Mean return/Horizon (weeks)					Standard deviation/Horizon (weeks)				
	1	4	13	26	52	1	4	13	26	52
USD										
AAA	3.035	2.803	2.066	1.725	1.136	4.730	4.865	5.587	5.908	5.528
AA	4.240	4.088	3.429	3.047	2.458	4.090	4.371	5.160	5.437	4.973
A	3.622	3.471	2.808	2.467	1.875	3.857	4.079	4.730	5.042	4.619
BAA	5.088	4.903	4.249	3.943	3.397	3.375	3.499	3.884	3.831	3.349
CAD										
AAA	4.171	4.224	3.638	3.244	2.260	4.811	4.814	5.585	5.631	4.915
AA	4.276	4.347	3.775	3.395	2.357	4.676	4.735	5.589	5.759	4.976
A	4.819	4.872	4.363	4.004	3.047	4.518	4.499	5.266	5.323	4.597
GER										
AAA	3.276	3.234	3.019	3.007	2.434	2.976	3.336	3.899	4.506	4.598
AA	3.360	3.254	3.015	3.041	2.535	2.327	2.937	3.510	3.988	4.012
A	3.599	3.568	3.404	3.423	2.935	2.280	2.753	3.270	3.776	3.718
BAA	4.744	4.493	4.221	4.276	3.735	2.373	2.477	2.977	3.251	3.026
BA	5.617	5.768	5.613	5.520	5.040	2.508	2.685	3.092	3.699	4.242
FRF										
AAA	4.748	4.533	4.172	3.930	2.875	4.748	4.911	5.723	6.865	7.034
AA	4.222	4.054	3.762	3.506	2.537	4.448	4.504	5.208	6.256	6.438
A	3.664	3.563	3.291	2.988	2.134	3.895	3.844	4.494	5.409	5.629
BAA	4.334	4.151	3.852	3.524	2.497	5.076	4.946	5.730	6.876	7.259
CHF										
AAA	3.948	3.980	3.629	3.380	2.666	2.331	3.051	3.547	4.076	3.928
AA	4.146	4.077	3.661	3.461	2.785	2.037	2.778	3.254	3.786	3.599
A	4.451	4.298	3.786	3.515	2.885	2.078	2.817	3.216	3.657	3.450
BAA	5.776	4.774	5.321	5.096	4.388	3.155	3.121	3.304	3.850	3.480
BA	6.885	6.722	6.095	5.608	5.000	2.729	3.427	3.938	4.319	4.685
GBP										
AAA	3.120	3.018	2.486	2.401	1.389	4.786	5.052	5.947	6.380	5.410
AA	3.270	3.097	2.605	2.507	1.554	4.648	4.828	5.669	6.084	5.144
A	4.275	4.118	3.586	3.427	2.353	4.889	5.066	5.854	6.314	5.219
BAA	5.726	5.540	5.128	5.042	3.816	5.262	5.497	6.500	7.058	5.843

[a] Weekly bond portfolio returns from Jan. 1993 to July 1997. The first set of numbers are time-series means of bond portfolio returns. Returns are in excess of a similar riskless bond and are reported on an annualized basis. The second set of numbers are the time-series standard deviations of the portfolio returns.

Table 5.5. Credit return correlations[a]

	One-week horizon					Three-month horizon				
USD	AAA	AA	A	BAA		AAA	AA	A	BAA	
AAA	1					1				
AA	.723	1				.545	1			
A	.784	.753	1			.510	.658	1		
BAA	.274	.236	.249	1		.114	.108	.325	1	
CAD	AAA	AA	A			AAA	AA	A		
AAA	1					1				
AA	.987	1				.966	1			
A	.976	.986	1			.937	.965	1		
GEM	AAA	AA	A	BAA	BA	AAA	AA	A	BAA	BA
AAA	1					1				
AA	.868	1				.813	1			
A	.851	.901	1			.779	.902	1		
BAA	.583	.713	.724	1		.569	.749	.894	1	
BA	.535	.670	.636	.582	1	.419	.503	.512	.578	1
FRF	AAA	AA	A	BAA		AAA	AA	A	BAA	
AAA	1					1				
AA	.919	1				.899	1			
A	.752	.787	1			.823	.868	1		
BAA	.736	.728	.689	1		.710	.752	.693	1	
CHF	AAA	AA	A	BAA	BA	AAA	AA	A	BAA	BA
AAA	1					1				
AA	.852	1				.921	1			
A	.817	.856	1			.903	.900	1		
BAA	.650	.573	.643	1		.758	.744	.759	1	
BA	.656	.682	.685	.511	1	.716	.712	.744	.668	1
GBP	AAA	AA	A	BAA		AAA	AA	A	BAA	
AAA	1					1				
AA	.988	1				.973	1			
A	.977	.988	1			.950	.957	1		
BAA	.882	.903	.912	1		.763	.783	.853	1	

[a] Correlations of credit return portfolios across credit ratings for individual currencies. One-week and three-month horizons are reported.

Table 5.6. Excess return correlations[a]

	One-week horizon					Three-month horizon				
USD	AAA	AA	A	BAA		AAA	AA	A	BAA	
AAA	1					1				
AA	.984	1				.994	1			
A	.982	.978	1			.991	.992	1		
BAA	.858	.849	.858	1		.911	.911	.933	1	
CAD	AAA	AA	A			AAA	AA	A		
AAA	1					1				
AA	.993	1				.996	1			
A	.988	.991	1			.996	.998	1		
GEM	AAA	AA	A	BAA	BA	AAA	AA	A	BAA	BA
AAA	1					1				
AA	.935	1				.988	1			
A	.911	.915	1			.982	.991	1		
BAA	.509	.545	.559	1		.889	.917	.923	1	
BA	.395	.436	.402	.244	1	.714	.718	.709	.715	1
FRF	AAA	AA	A	BAA		AAA	AA	A	BAA	
AAA	1					1				
AA	.979	1				.994	1			
A	.936	.947	1			.986	.993	1		
BAA	.946	.941	.928	1		.983	.989	.989	1	
CHF	AAA	AA	A	BAA	BA	AAA	AA	A	BAA	BA
AAA	1					1				
AA	.799	1				.981	1			
A	.821	.770	1			.974	.976	1		
BAA	.550	.387	.560	1		.916	.913	.921	1	
BA	.567	.531	.597	.373	1	.776	.788	.817	.785	1
GBP	AAA	AA	A	BAA		AAA	AA	A	BAA	
AAA	1					1				
AA	.996	1				.998	1			
A	.991	.995	1			.995	.996	1		
BAA	.968	.973	.975	1		.978	.981	.987	1	

[a] Correlations of excess return portfolios across credit ratings for individual currencies. One-week and three-month horizons are reported.

Gordon Delianedis and Pedro Santa-Clara

Table 5.7. Correlations of credit rating portfolios across currencies[a]

AAA	USD	CAD	GEM	FRF	CHF	GBP
USD	1					
CAD	.300	1				
GEM	.28	.088	1			
FRF	−.009	.093	.333	1		
CHF	.066	−.061	.316	.125	1	
GBP	.238	.261	.105	−.015	.083	1

AA	USD	CAD	GEM	FRF	CHF	GBP
USD	1					
CAD	.436	1				
GEM	.110	.068	1			
FRF	.068	.126	.434	1		
CHF	.099	.054	.422	.220	1	
GBP	.161	.214	−.013	−.013	.063	1

A	USD	CAD	GEM	FRF	CHF	GBP
USD	1					
CAD	.299	1				
GEM	.090	.036	1			
FRF	.051	.098	.413	1		
CHF	.044	.084	.474	.250	1	
GBP	.162	.168	.020	−.094	.092	1

BAA	USD	CAD	GEM	FRF	CHF	GBP
USD	1					
CAD	—	1				
GEM	.136	—	1			
FRF	.035	—	.291	1		
CHF	−.090	—	.339	.103	1	
GBP	.024	—	.012	.013	−.021	1

[a] Each panel represents a specific rating class. The results presented are for one-week horizons. Correlations are computed using returns quoted in the local currency.

Table 5.8. Correlations of excess return portfolios across currencies[a]

AAA	USD	CAD	GEM	FRF	CHF	GBP
USD	1					
CAD	.746	1				
GEM	.483	.536	1			
FRF	.492	.543	.795	1		
CHF	.276	.347	.653	.524	1	
GBP	.521	.553	.667	.709	.484	1

AA	USD	CAD	GEM	FRF	CHF	GBP
USD	1					
CAD	.729	1				
GEM	.490	.540	1			
FRF	.435	.521	.722	1		
CHF	.205	.248	.569	.361	1	
GBP	.513	.561	.645	.689	.324	1

A	USD	CAD	GEM	FRF	CHF	GBP
USD	1					
CAD	.760	1				
GEM	.447	.523	1			
FRF	.439	.523	.659	1		
CHF	.300	.346	.588	.436	1	
GBP	.521	.553	.602	.654	.387	1

BAA	USD	CAD	GEM	FRF	CHF	GBP
USD	1					
CAD	—	1				
GEM	.183	—	1			
FRF	.345	—	.388	1		
CHF	.084	—	.231	.206	1	
GBP	.445	—	.365	.682	.189	1

[a] Each panel represents a specific rating class. The results presented are for one-week horizons. Correlations are computed using returns quoted in the local currency.

Table 5.9. Factor statistics and correlations[a]

	Mean	S.D.	ρ_1	ρ_2	ρ_3	ρ_{13}	ρ_{26}	ρ_{52}
USD								
STK	13.66	10.62	−.088	−.025	.019	−.008	.013	−.062
XCH	−3.07	3.93	.066	.002	−.063	.000	−.048	.016
TERM	4.02	8.52	−.062	.069	.119	.100	−.041	−.020
SLOPE	.113	.3476	−.117	.057	.171	.136	.121	−.100
CAD								
STK	13.03	10.21	.027	.085	.027	−.033	.055	.022
XCH	−6.93	4.48	−.047	.090	−.138	−.033	−.027	−.036
TERM	6.96	8.91	−.051	.059	.155	.123	−.066	.029
SLOPE	.793	.852	−.181	.029	.107	.023	−.062	−.091
GEM								
STK	15.97	12.35	−.082	.068	.159	.085	.016	−.014
XCH	−7.25	4.16	−.022	.059	.125	.048	.000	−.070
TERM	6.96	9.21	−.122	−.062	.282	.115	.166	.032
SLOPE	.3901	.3209	−.079	.001	−.003	.016	−.189	.102
FRF								
STK	9.67	14.40	−.042	.001	.126	−.007	.023	−.052
XCH	−7.68	3.70	.005	−.045	.047	−.060	−.023	.108
TERM	2.27	8.93	−.112	−.017	.182	.014	.025	.010
SLOPE	.6204	.8653	−.093	.101	−.031	−.076	.064	−.035
CHF								
STK	20.56	12.57	−.020	.057	.062	.048	.133	.075
XCH	−2.10	4.93	.003	−.015	.035	−.023	.034	.094
TERM	5.48	4.74	.198	.084	.184	.022	.068	−.052
SLOPE	.476	.399	−.089	.187	.033	−.009	.007	.081
GBP								
STK	9.52	10.75	−.078	−.001	.015	−.017	.045	.040
XCH	−2.08	6.04	−.028	.031	.132	−.017	−.049	.046
TERM	5.05	8.66	−.092	−.066	.226	.049	.028	.015
SLOPE	.311	.382	.010	−.022	−.070	.086	.060	−.063

[a] Descriptive statistics for the explanatory variables of the credit returns and excess returns. *STK* is the return on the market portfolio less the risk-free rate, *XCH* is the return on a trade-weighted currency portfolio less the risk-free rate, and *TERM* is the return on a portfolio of long government bonds less the risk-free rate. The returns are reported for the one-week holding period with the mean and standard deviations being reported on an annual basis.

The final set of variables we present summary statistics for are the explanatory variables which are reported in Table 5.9. The means, standard deviations, and auto-correlations are all computed in local currency for a one-week holding period, with the means and standard deviations reported in annual units. The explanatory variables are constructed as zero-cost portfolios with the short side of the portfolio being the return on the risk-free asset. The table shows that the excess stock returns were high over this period, with the Swiss and German markets having the highest growth. The term spreads vary across currencies, from 2.27 per cent for the French franc to 6.96 per cent for the German mark and Canadian dollar.

Autocorrelations for the explanatory variables are reported for horizons of one-month to one-year. The table shows that most autocorrelations are less than 0.15 in absolute value for all the explanatory variables. Additionally there does not appear to be any pattern among the autocorrelations.

5. Regressions

This section describes the econometric method used and the results obtained. A regression framework is employed to explore the relationship between credit returns and a set of explanatory factors.

5.1. Econometric method

Credit returns are constructed by longing a corporate bond and shorting an equivalent default-free bond. A total of twenty-five portfolios are formed based on currency of issue and credit rating. Five different holding periods are examined, ranging from one week to one year. The number of weekly observations per portfolio ranges from 238 for the one-week-horizon portfolio down to 186 for the one-year-horizon portfolio.

The following ordinary least squares (OLS) regression is run for each portfolio at every horizon:

$$CS_i(t-T,t) = \alpha + \beta_{STK} STK_i(t-T,t) + \beta_{XCH} XCH_i(t-T,t)$$
$$+ \beta_{TERM} TERM_i(t-T,t) + \beta_{SLP} SLP_i(t-T,t) + \varepsilon_i(t-T,t). \qquad (17)$$

Our approach is to regress credit returns on contemporaneous realizations of a set of explanatory variables. The explanatory variables represent economic factors that can potentially explain the systematic risks inherent in credit returns. The β_i coefficients are assumed to be constant over the sample period. Since our data-set covers a relatively short period, 238 weeks, the assumption that factor loadings are constant is not too restrictive. The restriction to constant loadings does not preclude time-variability of the associated risk premia, and this assumption has been made in many other asset pricing tests. For example, Connor and Koraczyk (1989) extract factors from equity returns, assuming that factor loadings remain constant over a five-year horizon.

Since both returns and explanatory variables are formed as zero-cost portfolios, we can interpret these βs as factor loadings of a multi-factor asset pricing model. We do not address explicitly whether these sources of risk are priced. Pricing of risk would involve a second-stage cross-sectional regression of asset returns on the estimated factor loadings. The pricing of risk matters if we find a significant relationship between credit returns and the factors.

An econometric problem that we face comes from using overlapping observations for the longer-horizon returns. Overlapping observations induce autocorrelation in the residuals and will bias the standard errors computed under OLS. We adjust our standard errors using Hansen's (1982) generalized method of moments (GMM) procedure. Hansen's GMM procedure takes the OLS first-order conditions[12] and transforms them into a minimization problem of choosing β to minimize the following objective function:

$$\min_{\beta} g(\beta|x,y)'\hat{\Sigma}^{-1}g(\beta|x,y), \tag{18}$$

where $g(\beta|x, y)$ are the sample orthogonality conditions and $\hat{\Sigma}$ is the sample covariance matrix of the orthogonality conditions. The estimate of the covariance matrix under OLS is an identity matrix scaled by the residual variance. To account for autocorrelation and heteroscedasticity, Hansen shows that the covariance matrix takes the form

$$\hat{\Sigma} = \hat{\Gamma}_0 + \sum_{v=1}^{q}\left(1 - \frac{v}{q+1}\right)(\hat{\Gamma}_v + \hat{\Gamma}_v'), \tag{19}$$

where the sample autocorrelations are given by

$$\hat{\Gamma}_v = \frac{1}{T}\sum_{t=v+1}^{T}\varepsilon_t\varepsilon_{t-v}x_t x_{t-v}. \tag{20}$$

The weights which are applied to the lagged covariance matrices ensure the matrix is positive definite and were first proposed by Newey and West (1987). The resulting covariance matrix is shown to be consistent and efficient relative to OLS.

The covariance matrix estimate takes the order of autocorrelation into account in the number, v, of lagged covariance matrices, $\hat{\Gamma}_v$, to include. Each $\hat{\Gamma}_v$ represents the autocorrelation of order v. The number of lagged covariance matrices chosen depends on the autocorrelation structure of the problem. With overlapping observations, we choose the number of lags to equal the number of overlapping observations. For the one-week horizon, there are no overlapping observations and the covariance matrix simplifies to White's (1980) heteroscedasticity-consistent matrix. This result can be

---

[12] The OLS regression of $y = \beta X + \varepsilon$ produces the vector of orthogonality conditions $g(\beta|x, y) = E(y - x\beta)x) = 0$.

seen from (19), where when $v = 0$ the covariance matrix simplifies to $\hat{\Gamma}_0$, which is a diagonal matrix with the sample parameter variances as the diagonal elements.

Independent of the overlapping observations, there may be residual autocorrelation. To address this concern, we add an additional four lags to the covariance matrix to account for this autocorrelation.

5.2. Results

This section summarizes the regression results for the credit return portfolios. We look at the factors that affect credit returns to determine whether exchange rates affect credit returns. The regression results are shown in Tables 5.10–14 where each table represents a specific horizon length. We will refer to horizon lengths of one week and one month as *short term*, three- and six-month horizon lengths as *medium term*, and the one-year horizon as *long term*. Significance levels of the parameter estimates are given at the 5 per cent and 1 per cent level and are denoted by * and ** in the tables. When we refer to *significant coefficients* we are referring to coefficients significant at least at the 5 per cent level.

The primary explanatory variables that explain credit returns are the term spread and the slope of the term structure. Both these explanatory variables show a negative relationship with credit returns.

The term spread variable represents the difference between the return on a long-term government bond and the return on the short-term government bond. A significant relationship of the term spread factor with credit returns is found for a large majority of the portfolios. For the Canadian dollar, German mark, and Swiss franc, the term spread is negatively related to credit returns. This relationship is observed across the different horizons as well as the different credit ratings. It should be noted that not all portfolios at all horizons exhibit this negative relationship. The relationship of term spread to credit returns is reversed with respect to the British pound. The pound-denominated credit return portfolios show a significant positive relationship with the term spread. The relationship is evident at all horizons, with the shorter horizons showing a stronger relationship. The US dollar-denominated portfolios fail to show any significant relationship at any of the horizon lengths.

Whereas the term spread measures the height of the term structure, the slope variable measures the steepness of the term structure. Our regression results show a significant negative relationship between credit returns and the slope variable. The negative relationship is observed across most currencies and at most horizons. The Swiss franc and German mark show a significant relationship at all horizons. The Canadian dollar shows no relationship with the slope variable over any horizon, while the French franc shows a significant relationship primarily at the short- and medium-term horizons.

The final non-exchange rate variable we investigate is the excess return on the local stock market. The results are mixed as to the sign of the relationship between excess stock market return and credit returns. There appears to be little relationship at the

Table 5.10. Credit return regressions: one-week horizon[a]

	α	β_{STK}	β_{TERM}	β_{XCH}	β_{SLP}
USD					
AAA	0.0002**	−0.0017	−0.0036	−0.0183	0.0055*
AA	0.0005**	0.0083	−0.0399*	−0.0294	0.0010
A	0.0004**	0.0099	−0.0353	−0.0006	0.0023
BAA	0.0007**	0.0116	−0.0154	−0.0153	−0.0020
CAD					
AAA	0.0002	−0.0186	−0.0912*	0.0442	0.0039
AA	0.0003*	−0.0171	−0.1032*	0.0495	0.0041
A	0.0004**	−0.0172	−0.0957*	0.0422	0.0025
GEM					
AAA	0.0001	−0.0220*	−0.0282	0.0150	−0.0050
AA	0.0003**	−0.0269**	−0.0626**	0.0056	−0.0095
A	0.0003**	−0.0248*	−0.0606**	0.0232	−0.0113
BAA	0.0006**	−0.0168	−0.1154**	0.0176	−0.0180
BA	0.0010**	−0.0247*	−0.1184**	0.0752	−0.0279
FRF					
AAA	0.0001	−0.0092	−0.0226	−0.0358	−0.0054
AA	0.0001	−0.0135	−0.0176	−0.0552	−0.0041
A	0.0001	−0.0063	−0.0163	−0.0446	−0.0067
BAA	0.0001	−0.0263	−0.0009*	−0.0001	−0.0048
CHF					
AAA	0.0003*	−0.0288*	−0.0461	0.0149	−0.0203**
AA	0.0004**	−0.0320*	−0.1141**	0.0374	−0.0188**
A	0.0005**	−0.0268	−0.0516	0.0371	−0.0187**
BAA	0.0007**	−0.0203	−0.1923**	0.0273	−0.0116**
BA	0.0009**	−0.0284	−0.1053*	0.0923*	−0.0190**
GBP					
AAA	0.0003*	−0.0101	0.1141**	0.0096	−0.0091
AA	0.0003**	−0.0127	0.1207**	0.0048	−0.0092
A	0.0005**	−0.0132	0.1480**	0.0121	−0.0112
BAA	0.0007**	−0.0099	0.1679**	0.0337	−0.0182**

[a] Regression of credit and excess returns on a constant; STK = stock market excess return, XCH = exchange rate return, $TERM$ = return on long bond index less holding period riskless return, and SLP = one-year return less one-week return.

$$CS_t = \alpha + \beta_{STK} STK_t + \beta_{TERM} TERM_t + \beta_{XCH} XCH_t + \beta_{SLP} SLP_t$$

Table 5.11. Credit return regressions: four-week horizon[a]

	α	β_{STK}	β_{TERM}	β_{XCH}	β_{SLP}
USD					
AAA	0.0009**	−0.0036	0.0182	−0.0136	−0.0020
AA	0.0021**	−0.0071	−0.0125	−0.0087	−0.0041*
A	0.0016**	0.0028	−0.0091	0.0071	−0.0048*
BAA	0.0027**	0.0213	−0.0316	0.0058	−0.0065
CAD					
AAA	0.0006	−0.0106	−0.0285	0.0349	−0.0050
AA	0.0009**	−0.0065	−0.0429*	0.0358	−0.0048
A	0.0013**	−0.0096	−0.0494*	0.0308	−0.0050
GEM					
AAA	0.0000	−0.0070	−0.0106	0.0197	−0.0135**
AA	0.0003	−0.0029	−0.0347**	0.0086	−0.0151**
A	0.0007	−0.0012	−0.0477**	0.0052	−0.0205**
BAA	0.0017**	0.0077	−0.1120**	0.0030	−0.0301**
BA	0.0031**	−0.0233	−0.1151**	0.1710*	−0.0316**
FRF					
AAA	0.0001	0.0070	0.0003	−0.0153	−0.0089*
AA	0.0001	0.0041	−0.0003	−0.0022	−0.0079*
A	0.0002	0.0057	−0.0135	−0.0074	−0.0084*
BAA	0.0000	0.0010	−0.0084	0.0319	−0.0090*
CHF					
AAA	0.0004	0.0071	−0.1192**	−0.0137	−0.0228**
AA	0.0005	0.0170	−0.1642**	0.0298	−0.0172**
A	0.0010*	0.0120	−0.1120**	0.0252	−0.0201**
BAA	0.0022**	0.0048	−0.2060**	0.0608	−0.0129
BA	0.0028**	0.0091	−0.1577**	0.1532*	−0.0204*
GBP					
AAA	0.0009*	−0.0017	0.1140**	−0.0160	−0.0127*
AA	0.0009**	0.0010	0.1062**	−0.0225	−0.0105*
A	0.0017**	−0.0035	0.1296**	−0.0070	−0.0126*
BAA	0.0027**	−0.0026	0.1378**	−0.0168	−0.0122*

[a] See Table 5.10 for definitions.

Table 5.12. Credit return regressions: thirteen–week horizon[a]

	α	β_{STK}	β_{TERM}	β_{XCH}	β_{SLP}
USD					
AAA	0.0031**	−0.0127	0.0133	−0.0290	−0.0016
AA	0.0072**	−0.0236*	−0.0030	−0.0108	−0.0065**
A	0.0053**	−0.0066	−0.0098	−0.0199	−0.0087**
BAA	0.0093**	0.0041	−0.0471	0.0333	−0.0062
CAD					
AAA	0.0022*	−0.0317*	−0.0263	0.0668**	−0.0042
AA	0.0026**	−0.0220	−0.0370*	0.0702**	−0.0042
A	0.0043**	−0.0231	−0.0517*	0.0617	−0.0057
GEM					
AAA	0.0001	0.0005	−0.0187**	0.0077	−0.0189**
AA	0.0008	0.0108	−0.0411**	−0.0237	−0.0231**
A	0.0020*	0.0098	−0.0617**	−0.0101	−0.0233**
BAA	0.0035*	0.0632**	−0.1273**	−0.0568	−0.0317**
BA	0.0086**	0.0120	−0.1421**	0.2462**	−0.0367**
FRF					
AAA	−0.0003	0.0188	0.0145	−0.0484	−0.0099**
AA	−0.0001	0.0238*	0.0006	−0.0594	−0.0125**
A	0.0000	0.0212*	−0.0096	−0.0551	−0.0072**
BAA	−0.0006	0.0300*	−0.0172	−0.0049	−0.0070
CHF					
AAA	0.0013*	0.0145**	−0.1604**	0.0251	−0.0225**
AA	0.0014	0.0250**	−0.1897**	0.0522**	−0.0192**
A	0.0026*	0.0219**	−0.1470**	0.0149	−0.0275**
BAA	0.0059**	0.0284	−0.2348**	0.0509	−0.0127
BA	0.0075**	0.0489	−0.2424**	0.1562	−0.0353
GBP					
AAA	0.0028**	−0.0230	0.0975**	−0.0613*	−0.0045
AA	0.0031**	−0.0210	0.0899**	−0.0614*	−0.0044
A	0.0057**	−0.0379	0.1121**	−0.0564	−0.0052
BAA	0.0094**	−0.0569*	0.1429**	−0.0572	−0.0032

[a] See Table 5.10 for definitions.

Table 5.13. Credit return regressions: twenty-six-week horizon[a]

	α	β_{STK}	β_{TERM}	β_{XCH}	β_{SLP}
USD					
AAA	0.0071**	−0.0207*	0.0060	0.0056	0.0043
AA	0.0158**	−0.0490**	0.0004	0.0038	−0.0045
A	0.0117**	−0.0270*	0.0011	−0.0386*	−0.0107**
BAA	0.0215**	−0.0566**	0.0052	−0.0502*	−0.0143**
CAD					
AAA	0.0040**	−0.0116	−0.0510	0.0498	−0.0006
AA	0.0047**	−0.0020	−0.0565*	0.0502	−0.0003
A	0.0082**	−0.0011	−0.0796**	0.0498	−0.0004
GEM					
AAA	0.0001	0.0006	−0.0341	0.0382	−0.0113
AA	0.0020*	−0.0001	−0.0594**	0.0471*	−0.0136*
A	0.0037**	0.0144*	−0.0793**	0.0220**	−0.0150**
BAA	0.0071**	0.0717	−0.1644**	−0.0023	−0.0336*
BA	0.0184**	−0.0380	−0.1480**	0.4120**	−0.0385*
FRF					
AAA	0.0002	0.0074	0.0250*	−0.0682	−0.0033
AA	0.0002	0.0191	0.0040	−0.0877	−0.0039
A	0.0006	0.0103	−0.0039	−0.0446	−0.0023
BAA	−0.0011	0.0278*	0.0009	−0.0444	−0.0035
CHF					
AAA	0.0016*	0.0187**	−0.1721	0.0237*	−0.0158**
AA	0.0020*	0.0292**	−0.1935**	0.0314**	−0.0165*
A	0.0039*	0.0353**	−0.1772**	−0.0044	−0.0201*
BAA	0.0096**	0.0525**	−0.2557**	0.0077	−0.0090
BA	0.0123**	0.0582	−0.2515**	0.1189	−0.0334*
GBP					
AAA	0.0052**	−0.0285	0.1070**	−0.0528	−0.0100
AA	0.0062**	−0.0368	0.1056**	−0.0511*	−0.0090
A	0.0112**	−0.0560*	0.1361*	−0.0419	−0.0132*
BAA	0.0191**	−0.0958	0.1929**	−0.0545	−0.0057

[a] See Table 5.10 for definitions.

Table 5.14. Credit return regressions: fifty-two-week horizon[a]

	α	β_{STK}	β_{TERM}	β_{XCH}	β_{SLP}
USD					
AAA	0.0149**	−0.0301**	0.0046	0.0247	0.0045
AA	0.0340**	−0.0761**	0.0105**	0.0240	−0.0086**
A	0.0256**	−0.0484**	0.0086	−0.0624**	−0.0158**
BAA	0.0470**	−0.0953**	0.0254	−0.0400	−0.0188**
CAD					
AAA	0.0057**	0.0153	−0.0601**	0.1348**	−0.0002
AA	0.0080**	0.0145	−0.0663**	0.0960**	−0.0006
A	0.0145**	0.0218	−0.0914**	0.0987**	−0.0009
GEM					
AAA	0.0000	0.0073	−0.0476**	0.0575**	−0.0093
AA	0.0037**	0.0065	−0.0748**	0.0708**	−0.0147
A	0.0065**	0.0342	−0.0998**	0.0305	−0.0183
BAA	0.0122**	0.1135	−0.2043**	−0.0094	−0.0471**
BA	0.0369**	−0.0571	−0.1523**	0.5703**	−0.0407**
FRF					
AAA	0.0029**	−0.0187	0.0359**	0.0166	0.0038*
AA	0.0029**	−0.0053	0.0070	0.0071	0.0035
A	0.0037**	−0.0176	0.0080	0.0647*	0.0035
BAA	0.0003	0.0025	0.0134**	0.0492*	0.0033
CHF					
AAA	0.0021**	0.0244**	−0.1901**	0.0219**	−0.0210**
AA	0.0029**	0.0369**	−0.2182**	0.0266*	−0.0229**
A	0.0050**	0.0599**	−0.2244**	−0.0135	−0.0235**
BAA	0.0153**	0.0885**	−0.3368**	0.0108	−0.0200
BA	0.0185**	0.1059**	−0.2580**	0.1336*	−0.0363**
GBP					
AAA	0.0096**	−0.0151	0.0939	−0.0448	−0.0222*
AA	0.0122**	−0.0313	0.0980*	−0.0479*	−0.0173*
A	0.0214**	−0.0472	0.1217	−0.0338	−0.0304*
BAA	0.0355**	−0.0643**	0.1698**	−0.0372	−0.0183

[a] See Table 5.10 for definitions.

short horizons for any of the currency portfolios except for the German mark. The Swiss and French franc portfolios show a significant positive relationship at the medium and long horizons while the US dollar portfolios show a significant negative relationship at the medium and long horizons. The rest of the portfolios show few significant relationships at any of the horizons.

The weak relationship in general is not unexpected given that the currency of issue does not have to coincide with the country in which the firm is domiciled. A US company issuing a Swiss franc-denominated bond may be more affected by movements in the US stock market than by movements in the Swiss market. Additionally, if world markets are integrated, the larger stock markets should have a disproportionate effect on asset returns through comprising a larger share of the world market capitalization. Our results show a significant negative relationship of US dollar credit returns with stock market returns at the longer horizons. The lack of significance at various horizons may suggest that country of origin is not an important issue in determining the relationship between credit returns and excess stock market returns.

The previous discussion has looked at the non-exchange rate factors which affect credit returns. After taking account of these factors, we investigate whether there is any residual relationship between exchange rates and credit returns. The results for the short-horizon portfolios show no evidence of a relationship between credit returns and the exchange rate factor. The lack of any relationship is evident across all currency portfolios. Only three of the fifty portfolios[13] show a significant relationship of exchange rate changes with the short-horizon credit returns. Given the number of regressions performed, a few significant coefficients are expected.

Similar to the short-horizon results, the medium-horizon portfolios show little evidence of a significant relationship between credit returns and exchange rates. Fourteen of the fifty portfolios have significant coefficients but the signs differ depending on currency and horizon. For example, the six-month horizon shows a positive relationship for three of the German mark portfolios and two of the Swiss franc portfolios while showing a negative relationship for two US dollar portfolios. The three-month results show a negative relationship for two US dollar and two British pound portfolios.

The strongest evidence for exchange rates affecting credit returns is in the long-horizon returns. Of the twenty-five portfolios in this group, thirteen have significant coefficients on the exchange rate factor. A positive relationship is found in three Canadian dollar, three Swiss franc, two French franc, and three German mark portfolios. The results for the previous horizon show no relationship in the Canadian dollar or French franc portfolios. The lack of consistent relationship across horizons leads us to explore the robustness of these results.

To examine further whether the above results are robust, we look at alternative definitions for the exchange rate factor. The previous results used a trade-weighted exchange rate factor with the weights coming from the proportion of economic activity

---

[13] There are twenty-five portfolios per holding period.

conducted between countries. This definition need not represent the true proportions of a country's exchange rate exposure. To check the sensitivity of our result, we look at the alternative measures of exchange rate risk mentioned previously.

The first measure is an average of the exchange rate returns on two of the major exchange rates. The exchange rates utilized for each currency are given in Table 5.2. For the US dollar portfolios, we equal-weight the exchange rates of the British pound and German mark. The other measure is to use the two exchange rates separately as the independent variable. Defining the exchange rate factor this way will isolate the effect of changes in specific exchange rates on credit returns.

The results for the equal-weighted index are similar to the results for the trade-weighted index. With the equal-weighted measure we find no significant exchange rate exposure at the short and medium horizons. The long-horizon results are similar, with eleven portfolios having significant coefficients as compared to the thirteen for the trade-weighted index. This result is not unexpected because the two major exchange rates account for over 50 per cent of the weight in the trade-weighted index.

The results for our second measure of exchange rate exposure are also similar to the previous results. We find little significance except at the short and medium horizons. At the one-year horizon, we find a positive relationship between credit returns and exchange rates except for the French franc and British pound portfolios.

The conclusion we draw from these data is that exchange rates are not related to credit returns for the short and medium horizons. This result is consistent across the currency portfolios, time-horizons, and exchange rate measures. We can infer that exchange rate risk would not be priced given that the factor loadings are not significantly different from zero. At the longest horizon, one year, we find some evidence of exchange rate changes being related to credit returns. To determine whether this is priced risk would be a difficult task given that the one-year-horizon portfolios have only 186 weekly observations, all of which are overlapping.

One possible explanation is that our credit returns are a noisy estimate of the true process owing to the inherent poor quality of individual corporate bond data. However, by forming portfolios, we have attempted to diversify any random errors (owing to stale quotations, bid–ask effects, etc.) inherent in the raw bond price data.

6. Conclusion

This chapter looks at the risk exposures of credit returns in the international corporate bond market. Corporate bond returns are affected by riskless interest rate and default factors. We define the credit return as the return on a corporate bond less the return on an equivalent default-free bond. The credit return is interpreted as compensation for bearing default risk.

One potential factor affecting credit returns is exchange rates, both in their potential effects on companies' cash flows and in the market required rate of return. This factor gains importance in light of the European Monetary Union process, since monetary union would eliminate exchange rate risk. If a risk premium does exist for exchange rate risk, than a benefit of monetary union would be the potential elimination of the associated risk premium in companies' borrowing costs.

We examine whether credit returns are related to foreign exchange changes after controlling for other sources of systematic risk. The relationship between credit returns and the different risk factors is explored at different holding-period horizons. We first examine the systematic factors which affect credit returns. The factors we choose are related to interest rates, stock market returns, and exchange rates. We assume a linear pricing relation between credit returns and the above factors. Regressions are performed to determine which factors are significantly related to credit returns. The resulting factor loadings are inputs to an unconditional multivariate asset pricing model.

The results show a significant negative relationship between credit returns and the term spread. The slope of the term structure is found to be significant at the longest horizon while the excess stock market factor is weakly significant across currencies and horizons. The results show that credit returns are affected by interest rates and to a lesser extent by excess stock returns.

We find that credit returns of corporate bonds are not related to exchange rates at short to medium horizons. This result is consistent across currencies. The results for the longest horizon, one year, show evidence of a significant relationship between exchange rates and credit returns. We check to see whether this result is robust to the definition of the exchange rate factor. We analyse two alternative exchange rate factors and find similar results to the trade-weighted index factor.

The conclusion we draw is that there is a negligible relationship between credit returns and exchange rates for short or medium horizons. Only at the longest horizon studied is there some evidence of exchange rates affecting credit returns. Although whether this risk is priced remains an open question, given their small exposure, the impact of currency union on the borrowing costs of companies will most likely be small.

References

Campbell, John Y. (1987), 'Stock Returns and the Term Structure', *Journal of Financial Economics*, 18: 373–99.

Chang, Eric C. and Roger D. Huang (1990), 'Time Varying Return and Risk in the Corporate Bond Market', *Journal of Financial and Quantitative Analysis*, 25: 322–40.

Chow, Edward H., Wayne Y. Lee and Michael E. Solt (1997), 'The Exchange-Rate Risk Exposure of Asset Returns', *Journal of Business*, 70: 105–23.

Coleman, T. S., L. Fisher and R. G. Ibbotson (1992), 'Estimating the Term Structure of Interest Rates from Data that Includes the Prices of Coupon Bonds', *Journal of Fixed Income*, 2: 85–116.

Connor, G. and R. A. Koraczyk (1989), 'Risk and Return in an Equilibrium APT', *Journal of Financial Economics*, 21: 255–89.

Fama, Eugene F. and K. R. French (1989), 'Business Conditions and Expected Returns on Stocks and Bonds', *Journal of Financial Economics*, 25: 23–49.

Grinblatt, M. (1995), 'An Analytical Solution for Interest Rate Swap Spreads', working paper, UCLA.

Hansen, Lars P. (1982), 'Large Sample Properties of Generalized Method of Moment Estimators', *Econometrica*, 50: 1029–54.

International Monetary Fund (1995), *Directory of Trade Yearbook*.

Jorion, Philippe (1991), 'The Pricing of Exchange Rate Risk in the Stock Market', *Journal of Financial and Quantitative Analysis*, 26: 363–76.

Litterman, R. and T. Iben (1991), 'Corporate Bond Valuation and the Term Structure of Credit Spreads', *Journal of Portfolio Management*, 52–64.

Litterman, R. and J. Scheinkman (1991), 'Common Factors Affecting Bond Returns', *Journal of Fixed Income*, 1: 54–61.

Merton, Robert C. (1973), 'Theory of Rational Option Pricing', *Bell Journal of Economics and Management Science*, 4: 141–83.

Newey, Whitney K. and K. D. West (1987), 'A Simple Positive Semi-Definite, Heteroskedasticity and Autocorrelation Consistent Covariance Matrix', *Econometrica*, 55, 703–8.

Saá-Requejo, Jesus and P. Santa-Clara (1997), 'Bond Pricing with Default Risk', working paper, UCLA.

Sarig, Oded and Arthur Warga (1989), 'Some Empirical Estimates of the Risk Structure of Interest Rates', *Journal of Finance*, 44: 1351–9.

Sarig, Oded and Arthur Warga (1991), 'Bond Price Data and Bond Market Liquidity', *Journal of Finance*, 28: 933–55.

Weinstein, M. (1981), 'The Systematic Risk of Corporate Bonds', *Journal of Financial and Quantitative Analysis*, 16: 257–78.

White, Albert (1980), 'A Heteroskedasticity-Consistent Covariance Matrix Estimator and a Direct Test of Heteroskedasticity', *Econometrica*, 48: 817–38.

6

European Futures and Options Markets in a Single Currency Environment

ALFRED STEINHERR

---

1. Introduction

Financial derivatives traded on the exchanges are a recent phenomenon. Section 2 provides an overview of the development of this market to establish a starting point for the subsequent analysis. Section 3 then asks a fundamental question: what makes a successful contract? Answering this question is important for the assessment of the future configuration of European financial futures and options markets.

This future configuration is influenced by three already observable forces that are not easily disentangled. The first, analysed in Section 4, is a world-wide consolidation of the activity, driven by the underlying economies of scale benefiting exchange-based trades and by pressure on costs owing to fierce competition among the exchanges and with OTC markets.

The second is the choice of trading technology. For a long time the view was generally accepted that, for contracts with large trading volume, open outcry was the dominant trading organization and screen-trading a useful complement for off-hours trading or trading of less important contracts. With advances in technology, this view has become challenged in the marketplace. Totally different viable market configurations have now become possible and these are discussed in Section 5.

The third force is European Monetary Union (EMU), the ultimate concern of this chapter. As other chapters in this volume argue, EMU is bound to create an integrated capital market in the European Union with a single price for a given financial product (see the discussions in Chapters 1, 2, and 4). The exchanges, generally, will be affected by this integration process. The desirability of maximum liquidity is expected to produce migration of trading activity to those exchanges that already dispose of a liquidity and environmental advantage. This process will also affect the exchanges for financial derivatives, arguably even more strongly. But the integration forces are very likely unequal across market segments. Section 6, therefore, investigates the major market

Opinions expressed in this chapter are those of the author only.

segments separately: corporate stocks; foreign exchange; futures and options of interest rate and bond contracts along the yield curve; and swaps, in which the exchanges see increasing scope for future activity.

The strongest argument for concentration of trading in a single, or more likely, a few exchanges, can be made for interest rate contracts. The concentration argument for shares is much weaker. This has obvious implications for the reallocation, cooperative agreements and, in certain cases, the survival of some exchanges.

This chapter emphasizes the ultimate shape of EMU and notes only in passing special features of the transition to complete membership.

2. Evolution of Exchange-Traded Financial Derivatives

This section provides perspective by analysing the past development of exchange-traded financial derivatives. As futures are the most important products on the exchanges in terms of turnover, they receive particular attention in the discussion.

The Chicago commodity futures exchanges in their drive to diversify had, by the late 1960s, developed their interest in new kinds of contracts, building on their accumulated expertise in commodities. In view of higher currency volatility after the demise of the Bretton Woods fixed exchange rate system, the idea of foreign exchange contracts was particularly attractive and contract design was seen as exceptionally easy since foreign exchange is a perfectly standardized commodity.

The International Money Market (IMM) was inaugurated in 1972 as an offshoot of the Chicago Mercantile Exchange (CME)[1] and the era of financial futures trading began,[2] although few people at that time appreciated the historic significance (see Miller, 1991: 11–12). The expectation that a futures contract could substantially lower the costs of managing foreign currency exposure proved to be justified by events. Thanks to the post-Bretton Woods floating exchange rates, the price volatility and hedging demand shot up, so that the IMM attracted a substantial volume of trading virtually from its inception. Overall, trading activity on US futures and options exchanges experienced phenomenal growth: from 1972 to 1994 the number of contracts traded increased nearly fifty-fold.

It is obvious enough with hindsight that the same conditions that opened the niche for foreign currency futures were also present in bond markets. In 1975 the Chicago Board of Trade (CBOT) introduced GNMA (Government National Mortgage Associ-

---

[1] See Appendix for full names of the exchanges.

[2] The Chicago Board of Trade (CBOT) had actually proposed exchange trading of options on common stocks as early as 1969. Such options, however, fell under the jurisdiction of the US Securities and Exchange Commission, which, at that time, was reluctant to grant approval. Setting to rest the SEC's professed concerns about speculation and insider trading in options delayed the opening of the Chicago Board Options Exchange for more than five years. In fact, already in the 1920s there was trading of options at CBOT. They were options on commodity futures, however, not stocks, and they were banned by Congress in the late 1930s.

ation) futures—a contract that some regard as the first true *financial* futures in the strict sense of the term. Shortly after the GNMA, CME introduced Treasury bill futures,[3] a contract still very successful, unlike the GNMA contract.

From short-term T-bills, it was a logical step to long-term Treasury bonds (although the practical step was far from trivial because of the greater difficulty of standardizing instruments with different coupons and maturities and with less regularity in the infusion of new supplies). Long-term T-bonds have become one of the leading financial futures contracts in terms of daily trading volume, only recently surpassed by three-month Eurodollar futures. From Chicago, government bond futures trading has spread to foreign money centres, where its impact in lowering transaction costs was even greater than it was in the United States, given lower volumes and the more heavily cartelized trading structures there. In fact, financial futures must surely be given some of the credit for the wave of deregulation and decartelization that subsequently swept through the European and Asian money and capital markets.

The most important markets outside the United States are the London International Financial Futures Exchange (LIFFE) (see Table 6.1), which was started in September 1982, some ten years after their debut in Chicago; Brazil's BM&F (Bolsa de Mercardorias & Futuros); the French financial futures market, MATIF (Marché à Terme International de France), established in 1986; and Frankfurt's Deutsche Terminbörse (DTB) with its electronic trading system. As with other financial innovations, Europe and Japan trailed the United States by a considerable margin. On all markets trading futures and options ranging from interest rates, foreign exchange and equities to exotic products, the greatest volumes materialize in interest rates futures.

Table 6.2 summarizes turnover by contract category on the world's derivatives exchanges. Between 1986 and 1996, annual turnover grew about four times, from 315 million contracts to 1,162 million contracts, with a peak in 1994. Whilst in 1986 over 90 per cent of trade was carried out on US exchanges, in 1996 the rest of the world had caught up to trade more than 60 per cent. The lion's share of non-US trading takes place on European exchanges. Interest rates futures (nearly 60 per cent of total trade in 1994 and more than 50 per cent in 1996) have known the most rapid growth, increasing sevenfold since 1986.

Impressive as it is, the growth of exchange-traded derivatives does not render full justice to their real importance. Major banks and securities firms that serve as market-makers for securities and OTC derivatives need exchange-traded derivatives to balance their risk positions. They work on the assumption that markets for exchange-traded derivatives will provide sufficient liquidity to offset their risk exposures, even during episodes of major price swings when other markets may become relatively illiquid. During periods of exceptional market volatility the volume of activity on derivatives exchanges can rise dramatically, for certain days up to ten times the average daily turnover. As stated by the Bank for International Settlements (1997: 1), 'When markets

---

[3] The initial impetus was provided by some special features of US tax law that gave substantial unintended tax benefits (since removed) to futures trading in T-bills.

Table 6.1. Top derivatives exchanges

Position	Exchange[a]	Jan.–Sept. 1997	Jan.–Sept. 1996	% Change
1 (1)	CBOT	177,820,673	170,487,642	+4
2 (4)	LIFFE	156,048,813	122,431,974	+27
3 (2)	CME	147,873,750	138,403,877	+7
4 (3)	CBOE	135,769,141	132,421,375	+3
5 (5)	BM&F	98,410,598	104,777,367	−6
6 (6)	DTB	82,511,737	56,205,093	+47
7 (9)	AMEX	66,157,086	44,665,311	+48
8 (7)	MATIF	52,523,377	51,362,500	+2
9(10)	NYMEX	47,294,238	42,066,821	+12
10(11)	LME	42,215,184	34,807,087	+21
11(19)	AEX	37,474,153	20,020,995	+87
12(15)	PE	33,204,884	24,688,494	+34
13(14)	OM	28,713,362	26,084,117	+10
14(12)	SOFFEX	26,403,560	31,983,871	−17
15(17)	TOCOM	22,433,966	22,282,602	+1
16(18)	TGE	22,130,302	21,034,533	+5
17(23)	PHLX	21,943,040	15,742,749	+39
18(20)	SFE	21,425,602	19,333,404	+11
19(22)	MEFF RF	21,317,809	17,290,091	+23
20(16)	TIFFE	18,639,704	23,479,177	−21
21(21)	SIMEX	17,472,349	17,511,071	0
22(24)	COMEX	14,779,528	15,274,818	−3
23(25)	TSE	12,871,845	13,049,419	−1
24(26)	IPE	10,764,082	11,771,334	−9
25(—)	OSE	10,301,625	9,577,010	+8

[a] See Appendix for full names of the exchanges.

Source: Futures and Options Week, 10 November 1997.

are already under stress, the loss of an exchange's market liquidity or a delay in the completion of exchange-related payments or deliveries could well lead to systemic disturbances, the liquidity of other financial markets could be seriously impaired, and payments systems and other settlement systems could be disrupted.' For example, the largest ever daily settlement in relation to the average daily settlement in 1995 reached a factor of fifteen on the MATIF (21 December 1994), a factor of eight on the Tokyo International Financial Futures Exchange (TIFFE) (17 August 1995), a factor of sixteen on the Swiss Options and Financial Futures Exchange (SOFFEX) (18 August 1995), and a factor of nine on the Board of Trade Clearing Corporation (BoTCC) and on CME (October 1987) (BIS, 1997: 116).

Before the range of futures could be significantly extended in the 1970s, two innovations proved necessary: cash settlement and index contracts.

Cash settlement. 'Cash settlement' in lieu of physical delivery was another quantum leap to futures markets. The first contract with cash settlement was a Eurodollar

Table 6.2. Annual turnover in derivative financial instruments traded on organized exchanges world-wide (millions of contracts traded)

	1986	1988	1990	1991	1992	1993	1994	1995	1996
Interest rate futures	91.0	156.3	219.1	230.9	330.1	427.1	627.8	561.0	612.2
Futures on short-term interest rate instruments	16.4	33.7	76.0	84.8	130.8	161.0	282.4	266.5	283.6
3-month Eurodollar[a]	12.4	25.2	39.4	41.7	66.9	70.2	113.6	104.2	97.1
3-month Euro-yen[b]	—	—	15.2	16.2	17.4	26.9	44.2	42.9	37.7
3-month Euro-DM[c]	—	—	3.1	4.8	12.2	21.4	29.5	25.7	36.2
Futures on long-term interest rate instruments	74.6	122.6	143.1	146.1	199.3	266.1	346.1	294.5	328.6
US Treasury bond[d]	54.6	73.8	78.2	69.9	71.7	80.7	101.5	87.8	86.0
Notional French govt. bond[e]	1.1	12.4	16.0	21.1	31.1	36.8	50.2	33.6	35.3
10-year Japanese govt. bond[f]	9.4	18.9	16.4	12.9	12.1	15.6	14.1	15.2	13.6
German govt. bond[g]	—	0.3	9.6	12.4	18.9	27.7	51.5	44.8	56.3
Interest rate options[h]	22.3	30.5	52.0	50.8	64.8	82.9	114.5	225.5	151.1
Currency futures	19.9	22.5	29.7	30.0	31.3	39.0	69.7	98.3	73.7
Currency options[h]	13.0	18.2	18.9	22.9	23.4	23.8	21.3	23.2	26.3
Stock market index futures	28.4	29.6	39.4	54.6	52.0	71.2	109.0	114.8	119.9
Stock market index options[h]	140.4	79.1	119.1	121.4	133.9	144.1	197.9	187.3	178.7
Total	315.0	336.2	478.3	510.5	635.6	788.0	1,142.2	1,210.1	1,161.9
USA	288.7	252.2	312.7	302.7	341.4	387.3	513.5	455.0	428.2
Europe	10.3	40.7	83.0	110.5	185.0	263.5	397.3	353.3	425.8
Asia-Pacific	14.4	34.4	79.18	85.8	82.8	98.4	131.9	126.5	115.2
Other	1.6	8.9	3.9	11.6	26.3	43.7	99.4	275.4	192.7

[a] Traded on CME–IMM, SIMEX, LIFFE, TIFFE and SFE.
[b] Traded on TIFFE and SIMEX.
[c] Traded on LIFFE and since 14 Jan. 1997 on DTB.
[d] Traded on CBOT, LIFFE, MIDAM, NYFE and TSE.
[e] Traded on MATIF.
[f] Traded on TSE, LIFFE and CBOT.
[g] Traded on LIFFE and DTB.
[h] Calls plus puts.

Note: See Appendix for full names of the exchanges.

Sources: Bank for International Settlements, IMF (1996).

contract, now the most successful contract globally. The typical commodity futures contract gives the holder the right to demand delivery of the commodity at the agreed-upon price and the times, places and quality grades specified in the contract. In practice, relatively little physical delivery actually takes place. Between 98 and 99 per cent of long (short) contracts are liquidated by offset—that is, selling (buying) in the market an equivalent contract.[4]

Index contracts. In terms of current volume of trading, the most important innovation was a futures contract in a whole portfolio of individual stocks. Since the settlement for the portfolio of stocks was to be in cash rather than by physical delivery, it was natural to focus on those portfolios most relevant for possible hedging purposes for institutional investors: the major market indexes (and later also industry subindexes) of the kind already widely used in performance evaluation, such as the Dow Jones, S&P 100, S&P 500, etc.

The next step in financial evolution was to use indexes that were closer to being measures of abstract concepts (for example, the inflation index) than to deliverable bundles of commodities.

Options. Like futures, tailor-made options have been around for a long time. But in view of the specific needs for which they were used, they could not be traded. In 1973 the Chicago Board of Options Exchange (CBOE) introduced standardized options with the aim of creating a liquid secondary market. CBOE was immediately successful and by 1984 it had become the second largest securities market in the world, second only to the New York Stock Exchange.

Initially the options traded on exchanges were all options on individual stocks. In the early 1980s options on other instruments were introduced. The first was an options contract on CBOT Treasury bond futures started in October 1982. Subsequently options on other debt instruments were initiated, including options on specific Treasury bonds, notes and bills. In December 1982 the Philadelphia Stock Exchange introduced currency options and was followed in this by a number of other exchanges. Options on indexes began in March 1983, when the CBOE offered an option on the S&P 100 index. This and other index options have proved very popular and are widely used.

The top individual contracts in 1997, futures and options, are listed in Table 6.3. Among the most successful contracts traded on European exchanges are LIFFE's Euromark contract, MATIF's ten-year notional contract, DTB's Dax option and BOBL (five-year) contract, MEFF's ten-year notional contract, and LIFFE's sterling long gilt, BTP, and Eurolira contracts.

---

[4] But some physical delivery does take place, creating problems. Not only must the physical costs of supporting the delivery system be incurred, but the right to demand delivery at contract expiration can confront unwary traders with delivery squeezes when the time for contract close-out comes. Maintaining a regulatory apparatus to deal with such close-out problems is one of the costs of futures trading (see Miller, 1991: 14).

Table 6.3. Top contracts

Position	Contract	Exchange[a]	Jan.–Sept. 1997	Jan.–Sept. 1996	% Change
1 (1)	Eurodollar	CME	73,828,187	71,503,606	+3
2 (3)	US T-bond	CBOT	72,644,098	63,946,651	+14
3 (9)	Bund	LIFFE	34,970,000	29,753,178	+18
4 (8)	US $/Real	BM&F	34,299,625	33,663,196	+2
5(10)	Euromark	LIFFE	30,429,520	27,457,296	+11
6 (7)	1d Int rate	BM&F	29,043,750	40,152,303	−28
7 (5)	S&P 100 (o)	CBOE	28,632,923	43,641,609	−34
8(11)	10-yr Notional	MATIF	26,423,116	26,115,170	+1
9(18)	Dax (o)	DTB	24,674,553	18,386,113	+34
10(16)	US T-bond (o)	CBOT	22,422,182	19,533,940	+15
11(—)	Bund	DTB	22,162,651	11,844,872	+87
12(21)	Eurodollar (o)	CME	20,248,173	16,712,169	+21
13(17)	S&P 500 (o)	CBOE	18,930,660	19,043,332	−1
14(19)	Crude oil	NYMEX	18,579,972	18,142,304	+2
15(14)	Euroyen	TIFFE	18,217,600	23,030,583	−21
16(20)	10-yr T-note	CBOT	17,551,328	16,829,294	+4
17(25)	BOBL	DTB	17,198,812	13,579,237	+26
18(26)	10-yr Notional	MEFF RF	16,817,009	13,111,201	+28
19(—)	Aluminium	LME	16,136,798	10,440,592	+55
20(—)	Sterling	LIFFE	15,071,309	11,380,001	+32
21(23)	S&P 500	CME	14,750,581	15,061,484	−2
22(—)	Long Gilt	LIFFE	14,677,319	10,732,836	+37
23(22)	Corn	CBOT	12,662,370	15,623,436	−19
24(—)	BTP	LIFFE	12,120,546	8,944,187	+36
25(—)	Bovespa	BM&F	11,955,635	11,871,190	+1
26(—)	Pibor	MATIF	11,266,868	11,014,539	+2
27(24)	Copper	LME	11,231,037	13,881,850	−19
28(—)	Corn	TGE	11,020,565	12,495,056	−12
29(—)	Soybean	CBOT	11,016,718	10,597,989	+4
30(—)	Eurolira	LIFFE	10,776,757	4,762,925	+126

[a] See Appendix for full names of the exchanges.

Source: Futures and Options Week, 10 November 1997.

3. What Makes a Successful Exchange–Traded Contract?

This section focuses on futures because they pose more complex problems for product design than options. Options are simply created on liquid cash markets (foreign exchange, corporate stocks) or on successful futures. If the underlying cash product is liquid and has enough volatility then the options contract is successful. The only major innovations for stock options have been index options and longer-dated options.

The number of successful futures contracts is limited by three economic factors: the underlying risk, the need for a homogeneous product definition and the necessary liquidity. Beyond these basic features there are five broad characteristics of importance: those specific to the underlying instrument; those of the contract itself; complementarity with other dimensions of exchange activity; the competitive aspects of the introduction of a new contract on an exchange; and the regulatory restrictions. No single criterion by itself will assure the success of a contract.

3.1. The underlying instrument

A *deep and liquid cash market* for the commodity or instrument underlying the potential futures contract is of key importance, given the tight connections of cash and futures markets. Related to the 'deep and liquid' cash market is the notion that the underlying commodity or instrument ought to be a *homogeneous good*.[5] A homogeneous good facilitates low-cost transactions and parties to a trade do not have to negotiate its qualities with each trade. In other words, it must be sufficiently standardized so that trades can be completed without inspection or extensive oral or written documentation, so that market participants focus on the price not the quantity or quality. For example, one major reason for the failure of various attempts to trade real estate futures is the difficulty of standardization of 'real estate'. In addition, the greater the standardization, the greater the deliverable supply (or the easier the definition of the 'deliverable' in cash-settled contracts). A large deliverable supply means that manipulation is less likely to occur.

One of the major reasons for the existence of a futures market is the efficient allocation of price risk. Thus, a successful contract is aided by *high price volatility in the cash market*. With low price volatility, potential hedgers may find that the cost of hedging outweighs the benefits.

3.2. Product design

Delivery characteristics are among the critical design elements of a futures contract. They determine the convergence between the cash and futures prices as the futures contract approaches expiration. The ability to arbitrage and hedge is based in large part on the delivery specifications. For commodities, it is important to structure the delivery system so that the relation between the quality and location of the various deliverable units conforms to commercial practices. Many financial futures contracts specify the delivery of cash-based contracts on a final settlement price and the procedure for arriving at the settlement price is therefore crucial.

Alternatively, the delivery system for non-perfectly homogeneous financial products must be designed to allow different units to be delivered at 'adjusted' prices. For example, the US Treasury bond contract permits many bonds to be delivered. Similarly on the MATIF, the 'notional contract' is a theoretical bond issued by the French

---

[5] A homogeneous good need not mean that all units of the good are identical, but that, if not identical, they can be made equivalent. Thus, many agricultural commodities have grading guidelines or general criteria which permit delivery of slightly different units. For financial instruments the equivalence may be based on certain maturities being considered deliverable supply and on properly arranged conversion factors.

government, with a maturity between seven and ten years,[6] a coupon of 10 per cent, payable 'in fine'. Deliverable are all fixed-rate French government bonds in French francs with a residual maturity between seven and ten years and issued amounts in excess of FRF 5 billion. The value of each bond to be delivered, its invoice price, is determined by multiplying the final futures price by a 'conversion factor'. The conversion factor is meant to make every bond look as if it had a coupon of 10 per cent and a maturity between seven and ten years.[7] Because the seller of the futures contract decides which Treasury bond to deliver, and will therefore deliver the cheapest one available, the futures contract 'tracks' the cheapest-to-deliver bond. This means that the delivery system does not necessarily have to make every unit equivalent as long as there is a consistent relation between the units that market participants can understand.

Another aspect of contract design that is important is that the *pricing of the contract be easily understood*. Successful contracts attract both hedgers and speculators. If hedgers have exposures as both buyers and sellers of the underlying instrument, one basic role of speculators, namely the one of creating counterparties to allow a futures market to function, is less essential.

3.3. Complementarity with other contracts

When contemplating the design of a futures contract, an exchange needs to examine the *currently available cross-hedges*.[8] Hedgers may be unwilling to switch to a new contract unless the precision of the hedge is enhanced enough so as to offset the lower transaction costs (higher liquidity) of the existing cross-hedge. Usually the product used to cross-hedge has enough liquidity so that the bid–ask spread is small. However, the cross-hedge may not provide very precise offsetting price movements to those for the underlying commodity or instrument. That is, there is a low correlation between the prices of the future contract and of the hedger's instrument so that the basis risk is high. The hedger will be willing to move to the new contract if the basis risk is low enough to offset the higher transaction cost of a new contract. For example, before the EMS crisis of 1992, the DM–dollar contracts were used as a cross-hedge for other EMS currencies. Since the crisis new contracts have been created because the market realized that the cross-hedge had become unsatisfactory for trading.

3.4. Competitive aspects

At times exchanges do attempt to invade another exchange's product line by trading a similar, but not strictly identical, contract. If the contract specifications of the new

---

[6] Until expiration in September 1997. Starting with the December 1997 contract, the bond is defined with a maturity between eight-and-a-half and ten-and-a-half years, a coupon of 5.5%.

[7] The set of conversion factors does not quite make all bonds equivalent owing to 'convexity', a nonlinear relation between price and yield of fixed-income instruments, thereby giving rise to a 'cheapest-to-deliver' bond.

[8] Inclusion of an additional contract at any rate benefits from cost savings in margining cross-product positions.

contract better meet the needs of potential users, the new contract may win volume from the older, more mature contract, or may establish another liquid market. In general, however, contract reapplications fail most often because they lack a sufficient, distinct advantage to compensate for being second.[9]

An interesting case is the German government bond contract, traded on LIFFE and DTB. It is LIFFE's most successful contract (followed by the three-month Euro-Deutsche Mark contract), trading in recent years more than double the volume of the long gilt contract. LIFFE was first to launch the contract and when DTB created its own in 1990, volume on LIFFE was already close to 10 million contracts a year. DTB only started to surpass that level in 1994, trading at that time about one-third of the volume on LIFFE. In 1997, the market shares of both exchanges were converging, DTB reaching 43 per cent of total in July and August, and 51 per cent in September. Contract differentiation is insignificant. What differentiates the two contracts is the underlying trading technology: pit-trading on LIFFE, electronic trading on DTB. This example has rightly become famous because it provides two important practical lessons. First, any national market has a certain natural attraction for trading local products. Despite being late, DTB could capture a slowly increasing share of the market. Secondly, the national exchange is not the inevitable market leader. LIFFE has dominated the contract solidly for nearly a decade. And this is perhaps the most unexpected practical result. Being first with the right trading environment seems more important than being located in the currency zone of the contract.

3.5. Regulation of new contracts

An attractive feature of the exchanges is their self-regulation. Some competition can, therefore, be of a regulatory nature: weaker regulations may attract traders but subject them and other traders to higher risk. There is no conclusive research to show that toughly regulated exchanges enjoy a competitive disadvantage.

Exchanges are, however, not free of external regulatory influences. For example, in the United States the Commodity Futures Trading Commission (CFTC) must approve all contracts prior to their listing. For details on the more diffuse European regulatory scene, see Moody's Investor Service (1995).

3.6. New product developments on the exchanges

The exchanges are under constant competitive pressure from OTC markets and other exchanges to innovate. The most successful contracts are copied (and slightly differentiated) by other exchanges around the world. Innovations are concentrated on new products, new management and dealing systems and wider distribution of established contracts through mergers of exchanges and cooperative agreements.

[9] A well-known failure is the replication on LIFFE in 1991 of the successful ten-year ECU contract on MATIF, launched in 1990. In 1991, 54,000 contracts were traded on LIFFE and 7,000 in 1992 (the contract was suspended in 1993), compared to 546,000 in 1991 and 1,354,000 in 1992 on MATIF.

Strategies of new product development can be seen in three dimensions: new products in areas where some products exist already; more flexible product designs; and products for new applications. The first job is to identify demand for a new product. Very often this demand is perceived from cross-hedges, that is, hedges with a basis risk. New products are created for shorter or longer maturities along the treasury yield curve or for different credit classes (Euro-contracts, commercial paper contracts, mortgage-backed securities). A successful contract may then be replicated in another currency (e.g. bunds on LIFFE). The next step is to create options on the cash instrument or on futures. In currency markets the first futures and options were on dollar–DM or dollar–yen rates; the next step was to expand the set of dollar rates and the final step was to create cross-rate contracts (e.g. DM–yen).

A particularly interesting new product, volatility futures or VOLX, was launched in 1996 by OMLX in London. These futures are based on the price volatility of the reference market (stock market indexes). Since the price reflects current and expected volatility, such contracts create a 'volatility term structure'. They serve to hedge vega and gamma exposures, difficult to hedge otherwise, and long-dated options positions.

A second dimension consists in making the standard design more flexible, either in terms of expiration dates (LEAPS are long-dated options on corporate shares first launched in Amsterdam) or in terms of major contract specifications (flex-options). This is one way of competing head-on with the flexibility of OTC products.

A third dimension is to explore entirely new areas where risk is prevalent but not appropriately packaged yet. *Basis trading* and exchange for physicals are common methods of trading by OTC players. These allow the simultaneous purchase or sale of a bond, for example, in the cash market and offsetting purchase or sale in the futures market. More recently the principle of basis trading has been adopted by the exchanges. LIFFE in London set up its Basis Trading Facility (BTF) to enable traders to cross trades in the bund futures and cash markets[10] In Germany, DTB launched a similar scheme for its bund and BOBL (*bundesobligation*) futures.

Among the most interesting recent contracts for entirely new purposes are insurance derivatives, with an impressive potential for future development.

4. The Need for Consolidation in a Global Market

Alliances between the world's exchanges have become increasingly fashionable, as exchanges step up efforts to distribute products more widely to gain from the underlying economies of scale. The trend has been highlighted by a number of recent developments. One is the creation of global electronic trading systems, such as Globex (set up by CME with Reuters and co-owned with CBOT for a few years, later joined by MATIF

---

[10] On the same day as the launch of BTF, LIFFE also introduced Flex options on the FTSE 100 stock index. This, too, was designed to meet the requirements of the more demanding institutional investors.

and SIMEX), or Project A (after CBOT withdrew from Globex), with overnight sessions to cover other time-zones (CBOT and Bloomberg).[11] Another development is co-operative agreements among the exchanges. Two deals in 1995 have connected LIFFE to markets in other time-zones. In late 1995 LIFFE concluded an agreement with TIFFE allowing it to trade TIFFE's three-month Euroyen contract in London when trading closes for the day in Tokyo. In early 1995 LIFFE and CBOT announced an agreement allowing LIFFE traders to deal in CBOT's Treasury bond contracts in the London morning. In turn, Chicago traders deal in LIFFE's bond contracts after the London close. Since then many more product-exchange agreements have been con-cluded.

Separately, the electronic link-up agreed in the autumn of 1994 and abandoned in 1996 (before a new agreement was reached in 1997) between France's MATIF and Germany's DTB highlights the use of new computer-based trading technologies and the difficulties encountered in cooperation. The exchanges planned to trade a select number of products over a common electronic network and were examining the expansion of the agreement to cash equity markets.

There has been a plethora of other connections. European and US exchanges have made a number of initiatives to link up with smaller but rapidly growing Asian ex-changes, and a number of the world's commodity derivatives exchanges are seeking connections with the bigger financial markets.[12] In 1992 the London International Financial Futures Exchange merged with the London Traded Options Market to be-come the London International Financial Futures and Options Exchange, still called LIFFE. In 1996 LIFFE merged with the London Commodity Exchange (LCE), which had discussed merger with the New York Coffee, Sugar and Cocoa Exchange and the International Petroleum Exchange.

These link-ups are happening for a variety of reasons. The world's largest invest-ment banks and securities houses—which own and control a number of exchanges—are tending to exert greater influence and demanding much greater cooperation between the markets. These banks are increasingly offering *integrated global services* to their customers, ranging from trading to settlement and clearing activities. With banks and investors taking an integrated approach to financial markets, the traditional lines dividing different kinds of commodity exchange and financial markets are seen as increasingly artificial.

At the same time, with trading volumes stagnating since 1994 and costs rising, dealers are becoming conscious of the need to cut costs. The major players have all the infrastructure in place but are not operating at full capacity and want to reduce costs. Of interest in this regard is the agreement between CBOT and CME to establish a com-mon *banking facility* to provide joint clearing and delivery of contracts. Independently

---

[11] The decision to develop Globex was taken in 1987. Efforts to convince CBOT to drop a rival project, Aurora, delayed opening to 25 June 1992. In 1994 CBOT left after governance issues with the CME.

[12] As well as its link with CBOT and TIFFE, LIFFE also has links with SIMEX, the Singapore exchange, which is already tied to CME in one of the most successful exchange link-ups.

of cooperative agreements among the exchanges, economies of scale suggest that the fewer clearing-houses there are, the lower the costs. For historical reasons, many exchanges have their associated clearing-house. The new trend is to share clearing-house facilities to save costs. A model in this respect is the London Clearing-House, clearing four exchanges: LME, LIFFE, IPE and the electronic stock exchange, Tradepoint.

The move towards alliances also reflects the maturity of the domestic markets for financial derivatives, such as bond futures and options. Over the past twenty years, sales of the world's biggest financial contracts have grown at rates which cannot continue and some market participants even think that, unlike for stock options, the great period of contract development of financial futures may be over.

The costs of marketing and researching new products are rising and the exchanges are faced with an increasingly expensive burden of regulation, which is inhibiting their ability or willingness to devote scarce resources to product development. The immediate product range has been exhausted so product-sharing arrangements are in the ascendant. There could be a dearth of big-selling new products at least in established product ranges until the markets of China and Russia and Eastern Europe come on stream.

As a result, exchanges are eager to examine channels through which they can sell more of their existing products or earn a commission by selling products listed by other exchanges.

One channel in emerging markets is to set up exchanges with local investors (prominent examples are Brazil, Mexico and Taiwan) for the commercialization of local products and home products. Chicago-based exchanges have a clear competitive advantage for reasons of expertise and cost, but also because their dollar-based products are demanded world-wide and they can market to their own market, the largest financial community in the world, products from their emerging-market subsidiary (joint venture). This advantage will decline when the integrated European capital market takes shape and the euro becomes a serious competitor to the US dollar.

5. Trading Technology

A much-debated problem in this global and intra-European competitive struggle is the technology of futures trading. Is Chicago's, London's or Paris's colourful open outcry of futures trading a future winner or just a relic of the past? The traditional view is that it is an efficient way of supplying the service of 'immediacy' in those inventory-propelled or arbitrage-driven futures markets, where the demand for speedy executions of trades is high. Opinions are divided, as more and more exchanges around the world opt for electronic trading.

For the plethora of corporate stock options and for more abstract products, such as indexes, there is not much demand for immediacy—not enough, at least, to justify a bunch of traders standing around all day in the pit waiting to handle urgent incoming orders. For financial futures in these abstract products to succeed, electronic trading must replace pit-trading, which has its comparative advantage at higher ends of the volume and urgency scale. Trading of low-urgency contracts poses problems in terms of efficiency, and over time competition will cast its verdict. As there is less room for 'market-makers' on the futures exchanges (given the high liquidity without which the contract would not exist in the first place), the 'order-matching' of electronic trading is perfectly suited for the immediacy of order execution, transparency, and instantaneous recording.

The industry is still far from unanimous about the relative merits of the two basic trading systems. DTB firmly believes in electronic trading, whilst the Chicago exchanges, LIFFE and MATIF still bet on pit-trading. For that (and other) reason(s), the planned cooperation between DTB and MATIF floundered in 1996. Some exchanges combine open outcry and electronic trading by offering the latter once the pits are closed.

Moreover, the distinction between pit-trading and electronic trading is increasingly losing its sharp edge. The New York Stock Exchange already collects 80 per cent of its customer orders via computer. The two Chicago exchanges have a joint project, TOPS, to deliver orders electronically to the floor clerk. LIFFE is also investing heavily in electronic support of pit-trading. Computer screens can be installed in the trading pits themselves, dispensing with clerks entirely. But for the time being, the order is first transmitted to an exchange member, who phones his floor clerk. Depending on the contract, the floor clerk uses his hands to signal the order to the trader or asks another clerk to deliver the order. The results are often chaotic, especially on a busy day, delaying execution of customer orders. Paperwork also creates mistakes. In 1993, 8 per cent of CME's trades did not match with customer orders; this was reduced to 4 per cent in 1995. Electronic transmission or order execution have the advantage of speedier execution and of less-frequent mistakes.

Except for Brazil's BM&F and MATIF, all new derivatives exchanges built since 1986 are fully automated. However, less successful so far have been efforts to exploit the cooperative potential of electronic trading to span the globe. For example, Globex in 1995 accounted for only 1 per cent of Merc's total volume, although it accounted for 8.7 per cent of MATIF's volume, a clear sign of encouragement.

One of the leading experts, who virtually grew up in the pits but was also the champion of Globex, CME's honorary chairman, Leo Melamed, has a very decided vision of electronic trading:

The low level of screen-based transaction volume on after-hour exchange systems gives testimony to a lack of understanding by many futures exchanges that—like it or not—a screen-based transaction process is in their members' future. While it is comforting to know that the mass of futures liquidity is still on the trading floor today, it represents a false security blanket. Foreign exchange, a market institutionalised by futures exchanges, offers a stark and sobering comparison between electronic-driven volume and open outcry . . . the turnover figures for major Forex centers in cash markets between 1992 and 1995 shows whopping increases of between 30 and 60 per cent. However, CME foreign exchange contracts did not benefit from their growth . . . Whilst admittedly some of this OTC volume can be attributed to exotics not traded on the exchange, one must accept the fact that OTC screen-based technology is an extremely attractive medium for FX market transactions. . . .

While I do not advocate turning off the lights on existing trading floors—that could be unforgivably stupid—it is equally suicidal not to seriously prepare for a technological tomorrow. . .

In almost every critical area of advanced technological competence, exchanges with trading floors have fallen behind. For instance, LIFFE is the only exchange with real-time clearing capabilities. Futures exchanges are far behind securities exchanges in automatic order routing . . .'
(Melamed, 1996: 450)

Electronic trading has a number of particularities, beyond the obvious advantage of integrating fully by design order matching, order execution, recording, settling and risk-management—without delay, mishandling or misunderstanding. For one, the precise location of the exchange loses in importance. For instance, the fact that DTB is located in Frankfurt is irrelevant for most traders, who, equipped with a terminal, can be anywhere in the world. Whilst during the first years most traders were, indeed, located in Frankfurt, DTB is making efforts to win traders located all over Europe and even overseas. It has already located terminals in six other European countries and more are planned. In March 1996 CFTC granted permission to open terminals in the United States. In August 1997, out of its 171 members 51 were remote, trading directly from abroad.

DTB claims that it has a strong cost advantage from the electronic system.[13] This claim has to be taken seriously, and is supported by two observations. The first is the steadily increasing share of the DTB in the total trading of the German government ten-year-bond future contract, first launched at LIFFE. The other observation is LIFFE's decision in September 1997 to review the link-up with its two Chicago-based counterparts. CME and CBOT in Chicago have similar debates over the future of open outcry and its costs.

6. EMU and the Single European Capital Market

One of the greatest events in financial history will occur early next century: the emergence of a unified European capital market. Today there is only one efficient, liquid and relatively complete financial market in the world and that is the US market. European countries on their own are simply too small. In addition domestic regulations have stifled the development of capital markets, so that national markets—even in Germany, the largest European economy—are illiquid and offer only a limited menu of financial products.

The European Union has already taken the necessary steps to create a single passport for banks and securities firms under a common regulatory framework. What still segments national markets are national currencies. When in 1999 the euro is launched, a

---

[13] The basis fee for a bund futures transaction on the DTB is DM 0.5 (US$0.90); LIFFE charges about three times as much for the same deal.

fully integrated Euromarket[14] will develop, over time spreading all over Europe. The weight of the European economy, Germany's insistence on conservative monetary policy and UK financial expertise will combine to create the second largest capital market, as liquid and as complete as the dollar market.

In 1998 there is a derivatives exchange in virtually every European country (a new futures exchange was opened in Portugal in 1996), twenty-three in total. All of them are faced with an uncertain future (in August 1996 the Irish Futures and Options Exchange closed down). The only business they are likely to retain is equity derivatives (at least some of them), as long as stock exchanges are surviving in each country; interest and exchange contracts will vanish with the disappearance of national currencies, and the new Euro-contracts will be traded on only a few exchanges.

6.1. The market for stock options

In terms of contracts traded and outstanding open positions, the largest stock options exchanges in Europe are the Amsterdam Exchanges (AEX)–Optiebeurs, SOFFEX, OM, DTB, MONEP and LIFFE (see Table 6.4(*a*)). The merger of DTB and SOFFEX will consolidate their leading position in Europe. Compared to volumes traded in the United States, European exchanges are dwarfs, reflecting the much smaller number of liquid stocks and the lower capitalization of the underlying cash market.

Table 6.4(*b*) ranks the major index futures and options. The Dax option contract ranks second, after the S&P 100, followed by SOFFEX's SMI option, Amsterdam's AEX option, and LIFFE's FTSE option (ranking, respectively, sixth, seventh and eighth in the world league).

A major boost to the development of the European cash market for stocks can be expected from EMU, although all effects are only indirect. For example, the already discernible trends in favour of attaching greater importance to 'shareholder value', privatization of state-owned concerns, and the expected growth of institutional investors, in particular pension funds, are the consequences of globalization, of which EMU is part. EMU will promote the stock market by increasing the home base, free of currency risk with a likely quotation of the largest companies in the national stock exchange *and* the leading exchanges in Europe.

A further positive factor is the likely convergence of trading rules, of corporate governance structures, of fee structures and custody rules.

The expanding cash market in EMU is one major factor for a growing options market, but not the only one. Another is the expected strong growth of institutional investors, who are the major users of options and futures both for position-taking and hedging.

In one area the European exchanges have taken the lead over the US exchanges: in

---

[14] Here is a problem of terminology. What used to be called the Eurodollar market is now called the Euromarket. This needs to be renamed (suggestion: Xenomarket) to distinguish it from the market of instruments in euro.

Table 6.4(a). Stock options volumes, currency futures and options volumes

Exchange[a]	Sept. vol.	Av. day vol. for month	Open int. month end	%OI month of vol.	YTD vol.	Year on year change
CBOE	9,603,276	457,299	12,147,400	126	83,465,220	+28
AMEX	7,099,688	338,080	9,268,851	131	63,022,283	+54
PE	3,938,579	187,551	5,938,790	151	33,164,312	+34
AEX	2,604,290	118,377	7,658,864	294	28,036,002	+115
PHLX	2,432,500	115,833	3,976,257	163	17,908,357	+59
SOFFEX	1,754,077	79,731	2,178,652	124	17,549,942	−26
OM	1,896,436	86,202	1,236,066	65	14,769,987	+63
DTB	632,327	28,742	518,095	82	7,895,244	+1
ASXD	822491	37,386	1,179,390	143	6,926,766	−16
MONEP	444,542	20,206	647,718	146	3,712,245	+26
LIFFE	436,395	19,836	615,887	141	3,442,340	+2
IDEM	239,732	10,897	69,918	29	2,129,348	+705
TORONTO	250,624	11,934	501,338	200	2,101,084	+37
SOM	238,501	10,841	103,500	43	1,468,047	+121
SEHK	184,626	8,792	123,597	67	1,210,342	+25
MEFF RV	166,926	7,949	78,697	47	1,190,581	+78
ÖTOB	101,526	4,615	72,932	72	1,125,687	+18
PN	99,150	4,507	47,900	48	876,875	+54
MONTREAL	101,925	4,854	162,479	159	777,949	+58
BELFOX	30,344	1,379	51,052	168	326,402	+6
PSE	46,701	2,335	16,443	35	144,232	—
NZFOE	14,417	643	24,511	173	94,280	−24
FUTOP	514	23	343	67	32,620	−4
SAFEX	14,460	689	9,060	63	14,460	—

[a] See Appendix for full names of the exchanges.

Source: Futures and Options Week, 20 October 1997.

long-term options (LTOs). First launched in October 1986 at EOE in Amsterdam, they were subsequently introduced in the United States, Switzerland, France and Germany. At present, maturities up to five years are offered. Whereas in the United States LTOs in 1996 accounted for 4.2 per cent of total options open interest, they accounted for 8.5 per cent of Dutch total stock options, 5.5 per cent of Swiss total stock options (and 10 per cent of the Switzerland-index), and 18 per cent of the total number of open contracts in the Dax options. LTOs have expiry dates beyond 1 January 1999, the planned date for the beginning of EMU. On 1 January 1999 the exchanges will change all stock options contracts to a euro denomination.

Unlike interest rate and bond contracts, the number of contracts is expected to increase strongly, rather than contract. This is one reason to expect activities to be retained on existing exchanges. Some migrations will undoubtedly occur, as is the case in the cash markets, but without necessarily putting the activity of individual exchanges at risk.

In addition, as European financial markets integrate effectively, it can be expected

Table 6.4(b). Index futures and options volumes

Contract	Exchange[a]	Sept. vol.	Av. day vol. for month	Open int. month end	%OI month of vol.	YTD vol.	Year on year change
S&P 100 (o)	CBOE	2,647,941	117,521	304,561	12	28,632,923	-34
Dax (o)	DTB	2,148,423	97,656	1,395,502	65	24,674,553	+34
S&P 500 (o)	CBOE	2,249,870	107,137	1,613,180	72	18,930,660	-1
S&P 500	CME	1,778,167	84,675	188,294	11	14,750,581	-2
Bovespa	BM&F	1,156,926	55,092	77,969	7	11,955,635	+1
SMI (o)	SOFFEX	496,984	22,590	823,132	166	7,006,161	+16
AEX	AEX	651,124	29,597	675,311	104	6,325,580	+50
FTSE 100 (o)	LIFFE	432,123	19,642	411,441	95	5,878,669	+25
Nikkei 225	OSE	670,689	33,534	202,812	30	5,512,687	+5
Dax	DTB	677,514	30,796	67,874	10	5,121,306	+27
Cac 40	MATIF	585,184	26,599	78,745	13	4,730,740	+6
Hang Seng	HKFE	676,966	32,236	51,155	8	4,477,311	+29
Ibex 35 plus	MEFF RV	574,023	27,334	65,286	11	4,029,805	—
Nikkei 225	SIMEX	466,596	21,209	95,437	20	3,555,750	-3
Nikkei 225 (o)	OSE	356,416	17,821	67,568	19	3,490,276	+25
S&P 500 (o)	CME	312,979	14,904	155,573	50	3,466,451	-3
JSE All share(o)	SAFEX	315,186	15,009	544,712	173	3,312,076	+13
Mib 30	IDEM	462,325	21,015	25,987	6	3,302,433	+75
FTSE 100	LIFFE	381,161	17,326	69,176	18	2,895,059	+10
OMX (o)	OM	256,203	11,646	36,752	14	2,830,405	-32
Topix	TSE	344,838	17,242	108,254	31	2,261,832	+4
All ordinaries	SFE	339,644	15,438	222,956	66	2,239,455	+10
Cac 40 short (o)	MONEP	212,678	9,667	97,512	46	2,049,481	+16
AEX	AEX	201,513	9,160	35,578	18	1,822,875	+74
Kospi 200	KSE	332,612	14,461	10,918	3	1,790,228	+361
JSE All share	SAFEX	250,984	11,952	81,919	33	1,788,953	+30

[a] See Appendix for full names of the exchanges.

Source: Futures and Options Week, 3 November 1997.

that national stock indexes will lose in importance and sectoral indexes (a Europe-wide index for industrial corporations, financial firms or, in even greater detail, utilities, telecoms, pharmaceuticals, automotive products, etc.) will gain in importance.

The electronic trading used for options makes the precise location of lesser importance and offers the possibility of cooperative agreements among the exchanges.

6.2. Foreign exchange futures and options

The exchange market presents a rather easy case. All contracts involving one or two European currencies which are part of EMU will disappear and the only futures contracts will be dollar–euro and yen–euro, plus, until they become members, European currencies, such as pound sterling against the euro. Their trading volume is, however, likely to match or exceed the sum of the existing contracts. Where these contracts will be traded is to be seen: in all likelihood on CME, although a European electronic exchange may have a chance in bidding for a market share. In any case, most exchange deals are done over the counter so that the impact for the exchanges is relatively marginal.

Table 6.5 lists the major contracts and shows that European exchanges play a very marginal role. Amsterdam's guilder option, DTB's dollar option and BELFOX's dollar option represent together only a small fraction of currency trading on CME.

6.3. Interest rate and bond contracts

Different degrees of interest rate convergence suggest a distinction between money market and capital market instruments along the yield curve. Ranging from overnight rates, influenced by the repo operations of the ECB and its participation in defining overnight rates, to interbank-offered rates of maturities from one week to two years, full convergence can be expected and hence a single reference money market yield curve. Depending on the future ECB policy with regard to reserve requirements, only an onshore, or an offshore, or both types of reference rates are possible.

Present Euromark contracts have been amended to settle to a EURO LIBOR rate, based on the current benchmark BBA London fixings. The alternative solution would be a EURIBOR rate. Which rate will prevail depends on two factors: participation in the TARGET system and the possible imposition of minimum reserve requirements by the ECB. If institutions of countries not participating in EMU do not have full access to TARGET, this would favour greater acceptance of EURIBOR. By contrast, minimum reserve requirements would diminish the relevance of EURIBOR. Bundesbank minimum reserve requirements have effectively killed the FIBOR fixing as an international reference rate, encouraging the flow of business to London.

Table 6.6 gives derivative transactions in money market instruments for the major currencies. Summing the transactions in German marks, French francs and Italian lire (leaving aside the UK pound, as the UK will not participate in EMU from the beginning) shows that European trading volumes in 1997 were far below dollar volumes, but

Table 6.5. Currency futures and options volumes

Contract	Exchange[a]	Sept. vol.	Av. day vol. for month	Open int. month end	%OI month of vol.	YTD vol.	Year on year change
US$/Real	BM&F	3,910,068	186,194	289,816	7	34,299,625	+2
US$/Real (o)	BM&F	1,075,428	51,211	651,363	61	6,437,620	+48
DM	CME	729,318	34,729	61,020	8	5,455,638	+19
Yen	CME	611,843	29,135	77,580	13	4,420,164	+12
Swiss franc	CME	394,103	18,767	37,371	9	3,221,404	+13
Flex currency(o)	BM&F	159,806	7,610	1,314,967	823	2,297,276	−65
Sterling	CME	234,092	11,147	28,040	12	2,026,815	−12
Canadian $	CME	262,260	12,489	49,379	19	1,819,368	+38
Mexican peso	CME	162,353	7,731	36,279	22	1,295,080	+156
DM (o)	CME	112,717	5,367	92,899	82	1,176,440	−17
Yen (o)	CME	146,320	6,968	90,438	62	1,164,078	−14
Sterling (o)	CME	30,767	1,465	50,108	163	908,201	−66
Guilder (o)	AEX	38,570	1,753	85,594	222	587,763	+43
Swiss franc (o)	CME	30,723	1,463	31,929	104	497,450	−7
Cust. currency(o)	PHLX	37,058	1,765	123,166	332	483,098	−40
Australian $	CME	79,041	3,764	19,606	25	469,305	+44
DM (o)	PHLX	47,579	2,266	41,065	86	424,512	−20
Swiss franc (o)	PHLX	40,727	1,939	36,419	89	332,499	+29
Sterling (o)	PHLX	20,837	992	49,565	238	292,723	+31
Rolling forex	HKFE	5,527	263	6,285	114	235,413	+60
US$/DM (o)	DTB	15,479	704	16,555	107	227,189	—
Yen (o)	PHLX	22,961	1,093	25,796	112	219,357	−25
Canadian $ (o)	CME	17,819	849	13,995	79	181,290	+51
Mexican peso(o)	CME	31,526	1,501	25,217	80	129,138	+3,780
US$/Bfr (o)	BELFOX	9,466	430	6,831	72	98,975	+5

a See Appendix for full names of the exchanges.

Source: Futures and Options Week, 13 October 1997.

Table 6.6. Short-term interest rate futures and options

Contract	Exchange[a]	Sept. vol.	Av. day vol. for month	Open int. month end	%OI month of vol.	YTD vol.	Year on year change
Eurodollar	CME	7,634,681	363,556	2,710,764	36	73,828,187	+3
Euromark	LIFFE	4,468,933	203,133	1,630,314	36	30,429,520	+11
1d Int rate	BM&F	3,788,588	180,409	625,424	27	29,043,750	−28
Eurodollar (o)	CME	1,955,727	93,130	2,329,661	119	20,248,173	+21
Euroyen	TIFFE	1,850,611	92,531	1,584,572	86	18,217,600	−21
Sterling	LIFFE	2,355,090	107,050	628,216	27	15,071,309	+32
Pibor	MATIF	1,144,153	52,007	222,592	19	11,266,868	+2
Eurolira	LIFFE	1,907,034	86,683	419,962	22	10,776,757	+126
Euroyen	SIMEX	809,875	36,813	538,186	66	7,150,370	+15
Eurodollar	SIMEX	481,061	21,866	81,854	17	5,282,820	−20
90d Bank bills	SFE	561,947	25,543	272,180	48	4,434,196	+20
EuroSwiss	LIFFE	448,754	20,398	155,747	35	3,447,401	+44
Euromark (o)	LIFFE	494,000	22,455	534,175	108	2,948,445	−19
Bankers accept	MSE	359,163	17,103	168,075	47	2,880,145	+66
Pibor (o)	MATIF	204,785	9,308	200,239	98	2,339,510	−7
Sterling (o)	LIFFE	308,585	14,027	404,860	131	2,073,292	+25
Mibor plus	MEFF RF	313,070	14,908	90,621	29	1,843,848	+95
Eurolira (o)	LIFFE	294,082	13,367	235,901	80	1,564,915	+180
Libor	CME	135,281	6,442	72,757	54	1,086,444	+15
90d Bank bills	SFE	90,011	4,091	281,086	312	816,093	+23
Bank bills	NZFOE	88,166	4,008	39,267	45	746,852	+54
30d Int rates	CBOT	70,637	3,364	30,548	43	708,093	+39
ECU	LIFFE	40,974	1,862	35,693	87	409,640	−12
Euroyen (o)	TIFFE	48,070	2,404	137,870	287	368,775	−8
Euroyen (o)	SIMEX	43,568	1,980	120,359	276	337,657	+156

[a] See Appendix for full names of the exchanges.

Source: Futures and Options Week, 27 October 1997.

exceeded yen volumes. It is to be expected that futures in euro money market instruments will be much more liquid than present Deutsche Mark contracts and closer to the liquidity available in US dollar contracts.

This is, of course, a static picture neglecting the expected wave of securitization, that is, the development of repos, commercial paper, and CD markets. As was seen in Section 3, successful new contracts are attracted to markets where cross-hedges are already carried out. The most successful short-term contracts are LIFFE's three-month Euromark, sterling and Eurolira contracts, followed by MATIF's Pibor contract. MATIF also remains a contender for money market contracts on the basis of the liquidity of the French monetary market, in particular repos.

Table 6.7 ranks bond futures and options. In 1997, the combined trading volume of bunds, the French and Spanish ten-year notionals, BOBL, long gilt and BTB matches the volume of US T-bonds. For options Europe lags far behind.

In EMU, for longer-dated contracts, convergence of interest rates across government issuers is limited by credit risk differentials. An operational criterion of an integrated bond market is a single benchmark yield curve for all maturities, with futures contracts along that curve. One question of importance is which issuer, or class of issuers, will provide this benchmark. There are two choices. One is the emergence of a single government debt as the benchmark. The main contenders are the debts of the French and German governments. The liquidity and large size of individual issues and the pre-announced issuance calendar speak in favour of the French Treasury's role. The greater size and turnover in existing bund futures would favour Germany's role.

The other possibility is a set of notional contracts where bonds of several governments are deliverable. Already at present convergence of French, German and Dutch long-term interest rates is such that there is no discernible credit risk spread. Bonds of these governments would form a homogeneous class for delivery.

This is not a far-fetched idea. Concrete precursors are the ECU bond contracts launched at LIFFE and MATIF in 1990. The LIFFE contract permitted the bonds of any European Union issuer, as well as several supranationals, to be delivered into the contract. This turned out to be a problem, as the Italian government bonds were consistently the cheapest to deliver. As a result, the LIFFE contract became flawed as it reflected not only the variation of ECU long-term interests, but also the volatility of the credit spread between single-A-rated Italian debt and triple-A-rated French government debt. The MATIF contract proved much more successful as it limited the deliverable bonds to issues of the French and British governments and triple-A-rated supranationals. In a recent report, MATIF (1996) examined two scenarios: one in which the current long-term contract on French government securities in French francs would become a contract on euro-denominated French government securities, and another scenario in which it would become a contract on euro-denominated bonds of several EU governments.

It is unlikely that futures contracts will be limited to benchmark debt. For example, suppose that Italian debt is not part of the deliverables of the benchmark contracts; hedgers will then have a basis risk when hedging Italian debt exposure with benchmark

Table 6.7. Bond futures and options volumes

Contract	Exchange[a]	Sept. vol.	Av. day vol. for month	Open int. month end	%OI month of vol.	YTD vol.	Year on year change
US T-bond	CBOT	8,356,153	397,912	657,490	8	72,644,098	+14
Bund	LIFFE	3,665,567	166,617	298,067	8	34,970,000	+18
10-yr Notional	MATIF	2,756,218	125,283	136,230	5	26,423,116	+1
US T-bond (o)	CBOT	2,416,299	115,062	856,491	35	22,422,182	+15
Bund	DTB	3,079,345	139,970	233,587	8	22,162,651	+87
10-yr T-note	CBOT	2,062,548	98,217	382,836	19	17,551,328	+4
BOBL	DTB	2,481,727	112,806	277,758	11	17,108,812	+26
10-yr Notional	MEFF RF	2,039,124	97,101	83,649	4	16,817,009	+28
Long Gilt	LIFFE	1,844,839	83,856	174,341	9	14,677,319	+37
BTP	LIFFE	1,339,850	60,902	120,594	9	12,120,546	+36
5-yr T-note	CBOT	1,243,720	59,225	228,806	18	9,923,842	+10
Int rate swap	BM&F	1,118,406	53,257	5,020353	449	9,152,574	+123
10-yr JGB	TSE	1,100,551	55,028	195,205	18	9,063,216	−2
3-yr T-bond	SFE	981,364	44,607	170,449	17	7,890,168	+13
Bund (o)	LIFFE	710,100	32,277	313,704	44	7,407,390	+14
10-yr Notional(o)	MATIF	441,655	20,075	139,281	32	6,770,440	+4
90d Deposit	OM	611,741	27,806	281,734	46	6,019,144	0
ED Midcurve (o)	CME	621,616	29,602	333,402	54	5,845,548	—
10-yr T-bond	SFE	599,683	27,258	98,801	16	4,353,090	+8
10-yr T-note (o)	CBOT	542,689	25,842	352,182	65	4,335,665	−31
Int rate/fx swap	BM&F	484,850	23,088	1,827,674	377	2,549,508	+61
10-yr Notional	MIF	260,214	11,828	12,227	5	2,279,653	+46
10-yr Notional(o)	MEFF RF	284,319	13,539	85,039	30	2,264,133	−14
BTP (o)	LIFFE	171,995	7,818	152,017	88	1,973,326	+18
5-yr T-note (o)	CBOT	157,504	7,500	74,132	47	1,576,767	−28

[a] See Appendix for full names of the exchanges.

Source: Futures and Options Week, 3 November 1997.

Table 6.8. Effect of EMU on central government debt ratings

	Moody's			Standard & Poor's			IBCA		
	FX	DOM	EMU	FX	DOM	EMU	FX	DOM	EMU
Austria	Aaa	n.r.	Aaa	AAA	AAA	AAA	AAA	AAA	AAA
France	Aaa	Aaa	Aaa	AAA	AAA	AAA	AAA	AAA	AAA
Germany	Aaa	Aaa	Aaa	AAA	AAA	AAA	AAA	AAA	AAA
Luxembourg	Aaa	n.r.	Aaa	AAA	AAA	AAA	AAA	AAA	AAA
Netherlands	Aaa	Aaa	Aaa	AAA	AAA	AAA	AAA	AAA	AAA
UK	Aaa	Aaa	Aaa	AAA	AAA	AAA	AAA	AAA	amb.
Belgium	Aa1	Aa1	Aa1	AA+	AAA	AA+	AA+	AAA	pos.
Denmark	Aa1	Aa1	Aa1	AA+	AAAA	AA+	AA+	AAA	pos.
Finland	Aa1	Aaa	Aaa	AA	AAA	AA	AAA	AAA	amb.
Greece	Baa1	A2	A2	BBB–	n.r.	BBB–	BBB–	n.r.	amb.
Ireland	Aa1	Aaa	Aaa	AA	AAA	AA	AA+	AAA	amb.
Italy	Aa3	Aa3	Aa3	AA	AAA	AA	AA–	AAA	pos.
Portugal	Aa3	Aa2	Aa2	AA–	AAA	AA–	AA–	AAA	amb.
Spain	Aa2	Aa2	Aa2	AA	AAA	AA	AA	AAA	pos.
Sweden	Aa3	n.r.	n.r.	AA+	AAA	AA+	AA–	AAA	amb.

Note: For each rating agency, FX indicates the current foreign currency rating, DOM the current domestic debt rating and EMU the prospective unified rating under the hypothesis of participation in the single money; n.r. denotes no rating; for IBCA , amb. denotes an ambiguous effect and pos. denotes a positive effect.

Source: Reproduced from McCauley and White (1997).

futures. Given the large size of Italian debt, a separate futures on Italian debt could become profitable if basis volatility is sufficiently high.

If demand for Italian hedges were not sufficient because the size of the Italian market turned out to be too small, then another scenario could be imagined. This would be contracts along the yield curve of various homogeneous risk classes, with government debt of several countries as deliverables—for example, a benchmark for triple-A debt, for double-A debt, or finer subclasses. This would, of course, be an innovation unknown so far because the euro will be the currency of several otherwise sovereign countries. In the United States, for example, no state or municipality with a credit rating different from that of the Federal government has a large enough outstanding debt to generate sufficient liquidity for a futures contract.

Table 6.8 reproduces the current ratings of European governments' debt. Traditionally, ratings differ for debt denominated in domestic currency and foreign currency, as domestic currency debt, unlike foreign currency debt, could always be repaid by printing money. In EMU, member countries lose control over the printing press so that this distinction becomes blurred. Ratings of Moody's and Standard & Poor's for government debt after the beginning of EMU differ because Moody's considers euro debt of member countries as domestic currency debt, whereas Standard & Poor's assimilates it with foreign currency debt. According to Moody's classification for EMU, eight member countries receive triple-A rating, compared to six countries according to Standard & Poor's. Except for Greece, all other countries fall into categories of the double-A class. Over time, as countries satisfy the fiscal convergence criteria, there will be upgrades so that most countries will be triple-A and double-A+. This would then suggest a liquid government debt market for at least two risk classes and a possible basis for futures contracts along the yield curves of these two risk classes.

Actual derivative transactions in government securities are weak indicators of future trading volume. Table 6.7 showed that the combined trades in futures of European government securities have already achieved the volumes of US treasuries. The future euro volume will undoubtedly be much higher, with a chance of surpassing the trading volumes of derivatives on US government debt.

Several facts lead me to this conclusion. First, the outstanding government debts (in the narrow sense of debt of the central government) of the United States and of the EU are of the same order of magnitude. The combined long-term central government debts of France, Germany and Italy (the three largest debtors in the EU) alone represent about 60 per cent of outstanding long-term US treasuries. Secondly, by moving from national currencies to the euro there is no substitution loss for hedging needs— quite the contrary. Inexistent or illiquid markets in some currencies make hedging with derivatives in these currencies impossible, or unattractive, whilst the basis risk diminishes demand for cross-hedging. The net demand for euro derivatives can, therefore, safely be expected to be substantially higher. Thirdly, the rapid development of institutional investors will further increase this demand, as will a greater role of European debt instruments denominated in euros used by international investors or borrowers. Finally, with greater liquidity and trading volume contract costs fall, stimulating demand further. A concentration of activity on a small number of exchanges diminishes margin requirements, thus lowering costs and contributing to this virtuous circle of greater demand, lower costs, hence greater demand, and so on.

Existing contracts, except for the benchmark contracts, are bound to disappear, including products to hedge basis risk among government debt issues. But the net effect is an overall gain in trading volume.

In addition to the benchmark issues there will be contracts for different financial instruments (such as the recent launch of the *Pfandbrief* futures) as securitization in the integrated European market will catch up with the United States and institutional investors will play a similar role.

6.4. The battle of the exchanges

Exchanges all over the world are under pressure to cut costs and generate additional revenues. In Europe there are twenty-three derivatives exchanges and most of them are too small to be profitable. EMU will further aggravate this situation. Exchanges are reacting in two ways. One is integration with the local stock exchanges/clearing-houses or mergers with other derivatives exchanges in the home country. The second is international mergers or cooperation.

On 1 January 1997 the Amsterdam Stock Exchange, the European Options Exchange and the Agricultural Futures Market Amsterdam merged to form the Amsterdam Exchanges. The new organization has integrated settlement and custody. Amsterdam Exchanges trades options of the Eurotop FTSE 100 and 300 indexes, which cover Europe's most actively traded companies. Futures on these indexes will be traded on another exchange—an invitation to cooperation. It has concluded cooperation agreements with the stock exchanges of Brussels and Luxembourg and is in discussion with BELFOX, the Belgian derivatives exchange. Together with Deutsche Börse, Société de Bourses Françaises and the Brussels Stock Exchange, it participates in Euro NM, the European market for young companies.

Since 1993 Deutsche Börse AG has been running both the Frankfurt Stock Exchange and DTB and has owned Deutsche Börse Clearing and Deutsche Börse Systems, thus effectively integrating the cash and derivatives markets, clearing and settlement, and systems development. In Switzerland SOFFEX is part of the Swiss Stock Exchange; in Austria the futures market and the stock exchange are to be merged before end-1997. Even LIFFE is examining links with the London Stock Exchange, and in Paris the stock exchange (SBF), the options exchange (MONEP) and the futures exchange (MATIF) are intensifying their cooperation for ultimate merger. Similar efforts are underway in Italy, retarded by previous privatization of the exchanges.

The other dominant approach is international cooperation/merger of derivatives exchanges. Scandinavian exchanges are much less threatened by EMU as Norway is not an EU member, while Denmark and Sweden opted out of joining initially. The Swedish and Danish futures exchanges, OM Sweden and FUTOP, which is part of the Copenhagen Stock Exchange, plan to merge in 1998. This is intended as the first step towards the eventual goal of creating a unified Nordic marketplace for stocks and bonds and derivatives on them. Once the technical difficulties are resolved, Norway and Finland will be invited to join.

The major event in transnational cooperation so far has been the formation of EUREX as a result of a merger between SOFFEX of Switzerland and DTB, joined with only little delay by SBF, together with MATIF and MONEP. EUREX has been facilitated by an electronic system used by DTB and initially developed by SOFFEX. Whilst EUREX is a nearly complete integration of SOFFEX and DTB, cooperation with the French bourses is, at least in the initial stage, more targeted. The alliance of the French bourses with EUREX is based on shared management of operations in euro-denominated interest rate derivatives and introduction of a unified market system centred on four axes:

1. A single offering of fixed-income products denominated in FRF and DEM, subsequently in EUR, under joint management. Plans to build a single, unified market linking Paris and Frankfurt call for a wide range of products (the agreement also covers equities and equity derivatives on all three markets). New euro-denominated contracts are to be created jointly. Existing EUREX products will continue to be traded on the EUREX system, while MATIF products will be traded by open outcry. By mid-1998,

MATIF will adopt a new electronic system (NSCVF, which has also been adopted by CME and MONEP; the Paris Bourse has a version of the same for equities) so that both open outcry and electronic trading will be used, with all EUREX and French products accessible to EUREX and MATIF members on screen. Thus, for ten-year maturities, a contract based on French government debt or on German government debt or a joint cocktail of debt instruments from several sovereign issues will become available. At the middle of the yield curve there is the BOBL contract in Frankfurt and the MATIF five-year contract launched on 10 September 1997. Finally, at the short end of the yield curve, there are Frankfurt's Euromark contracts and MATIF's five-month Pibor contract, which ensures a smooth transition to EURIBOR. So the two possible alternatives for the EMU monetary rates discussed above are covered.

2. The EUREX and NSCVF electronic trading systems will be linked by shared front-end technology, with a single log-in. Thus, members will be able to access the entire range of contracts offered by EUREX and MATIF on the same screen.

3. A system of cross-membership will be adopted, with harmonization of rules and regulations.

4. Starting in mid-1998 links between the clearing systems at EUREX and MATIF will ensure cross-margining, thereby reducing members' margin requirements (MATIF has decided to adopt Clearing 21, already used by CME and NYMEX).

This agreement, spanning three major countries, is a first, but certainly not the last, strategic response to a fierce battle for survival and supremacy in tomorrow's Euromarket. Until recently the battle for supremacy involved the three largest exchanges in Europe, namely LIFFE, the uncontested leader, followed by DTB and MATIF. LIFFE has already reacted by launching the idea of a loose collaboration with MEFF, AEX and OM.

To better understand the EUREX–MATIF agreement, it is useful to look at the recent strategic battle between LIFFE, DTB and MATIF in more detail. All three exchanges have done extremely well in recent years, as was shown in Table 6.1. During 1997 LIFFE for the first time in its history overtook CME to become the second-largest futures and options exchange in the world after CBOT. Together MATIF and DTB have about the trading volume of LIFFE. MATIF and LIFFE derive most of their business from a narrow range of contracts. Half of LIFFE's trading depends on three products: the German government bond contract, the German money market contract and the British money market contract. If MATIF were to lose its French government contract, its trading volume would halve (as options are traded on MONEP). DTB is better diversified and relies more heavily on German equity contracts, which are less challenged.

Because MATIF is so dependent on its French government contracts, it has made great efforts to position itself for the euro-bond contract. Its hopes stem from France's central role in the EMU process, whereas Britain is on stand-by. The French Treasury has been helpful in declaring early that it will convert all of its existing debt into euro bonds from the first day of monetary union—but other governments, such as the German government, have followed suit. LIFFE relies on the importance of London as a global financial centre and on its establishment of intercontinental trading links with exchanges in Chicago and Tokyo. DTB banks on the benchmark quality of German government debt and its status as the biggest electronic trading exchange in Europe, with a clear cost advantage.[15]

All three major European exchanges created new contracts along the FRF or DEM yield curves to gain market share before European Monetary Union. LIFFE and DTB have launched a one-month futures contract and DTB a contract based on a thirty-year German government bond. DTB in 1997 intensified the battle for market share by launching a series of equity options and stock market index products based on Europe's leading company stocks; a contract based on a basket of other European government bonds (already mentioned above) and one based on the volatility levels on the Frankfurt stock exchange. LIFFE is catching up by offering similar products. For example, on 18 September 1997 it launched its own version of the five-year German government bond future—the BOBL.[16]

Significantly, of the one-month contracts traded at LIFFE and DTB in May 1997, 2,524 contracts were traded on LIFFE and 6,800 contracts on DTB. It is, of course, very difficult to predict to what extent trading will concentrate on one exchange or on more than one. In the United States CME leads for derivatives on monetary instruments and CBOT for those on bonds. A similar configuration may emerge in Europe. LIFFE, already dominant in the three-month Deutsche Mark, sterling, lira and ECU contracts, could hold the money market instruments, particularly if the ECB imposes minimum reserve requirements, and EUREX/MATIF the bond instruments. Alternatively, Frankfurt, backed by the presence of the European Central Bank, might lead at the short end of the yield curve (if the ECB forgoes minimum reserve requirements and if TARGET favours participants) and London at the long end. As, at least for the initial years, the United Kingdom will not participate in EMU, it is even imaginable that the Continent will contest London's leadership at the longer end.

Smaller exchanges have a vital interest in cooperation,[17] as they are confronted with the loss of their products on debt in national currency with only remote possibilities of participating in the euro benchmark contracts, except through electronic link-ups with the leading exchanges. This then raises the question whether their business in national stocks is sufficient to cover costs. For many exchanges a question of survival will be whether they can create new contracts, in euros, or securities other than the

---

[15] DTB's strategic move to join up with SOFFEX was in large measure motivated by shared technology and the fact that the Swiss exchange is one of the biggest stock options markets. Together with DTB's strong stock options trading, EUREX is establishing a stronghold for equities. EUREX was the first pooling of electronic trading and clearing among two exchanges in different countries to create a single market. Members of one market will be able to trade in the other market free of charge on the same computer screen and with harmonized rules and clearing. EUREX could well be the nucleus for a European exchange, offering an open door to other exchanges.

[16] All three exchanges also engaged in a fierce price competition by offering 'fee holidays' for certain products and limited periods.

[17] Until recently MATIF was a serious contender for a major role in EMU. This is no longer the case, making some sort of cooperation venture even more attractive or even essential.

benchmark products. The US experience provides grounds for optimism. Differently defined stock exchange indexes are traded on different exchanges, some of which are quite small. With a more complete European capital market there are opportunities to be grabbed by innovative exchanges.

6.5. Attracting OTC business to the exchanges

As argued in Steinherr (1997), a large part of the derivatives deals in OTC markets are plain vanilla (estimated at 60–75 per cent of the total market) that could be traded on the exchanges or cleared through clearing-houses. Lower costs owing to regulatory discrimination have so far favoured OTC markets, but concern over the risks in OTC markets has led international regulators to review the existing framework.

Several European exchanges or clearing-houses are about to clear interest rate swaps and FRAs traded on interbank markets. The driving force is the competitive pricing of plain vanilla products, leaving little room for money-making spreads. Banks have, however, an interest in freeing up capital charges on credit exposure and in shedding the administrative cost of managing collaterals, for which clearing-houses are better equipped.

The London Clearing-House (LCH) announced in August 1997 that it would begin clearing of interest swaps and FRAs in the first half of 1999.[18] LCH estimates that it will be able to reduce the net present value of counterparty exposure of individual clients by 70 per cent owing to more widespread netting across all clients. Collateral at LCH can be used for both OTC and futures positions at a single execution point. Stockholm's OM has had a similar project for some time and MEFF, Spain's options and futures exchange, has been ready since 1995 to launch a clearing facility for peseta-denominated interest rate swaps.[19]

While LCH has a clear advantage in the Euromarket, smaller exchanges/clearing-houses have a potential for capturing a specialized part of the clearing, management, or trading of the huge OTC market.

7. Conclusion

After a phenomenal growth since the early 1970s, activity on futures exchanges has stalled during the last two years, whereas growth of the OTC market has continued unabated. A notable exception to this global picture is represented by the European exchanges in the aggregate, with some deviations. EMU and the growth of European

---

[18] CME is working on a project to collateralize OTC credit exposure through a central management system. Luxembourg's CEDEL already has in place its Global Credit Support Service to do much the same. But, unlike LCH, it does not offer full clearing for swaps.

[19] The next step is augured by the recent proposal of NYMEX to offer an exchange-for-swaps facility.

institutional investors, to be sustained for the years to come as they are catching up with their US counterparts, promise a bright future for exchange-based derivative activity in Europe. Euro benchmarks, a deeper European market for stocks, deeper money and bond markets and new products completing the market will drive volumes far above the present total level of contracts in several European currencies.

More-liquid cash markets, the spread of the euro to markets that have, for lack of efficiency and liquidity, not played a significant role, and declining costs, thanks to the economies of scale related to exchange-based transactions, all support such a positive view.

In individual market segments, the impact of EMU is very different. Currency futures and options at present contribute insignificantly to the turnover of European exchanges. Therefore, at worst, little activity is lost. At best, euro–dollar or dollar–yen contracts will be established on the major European exchanges. For stock options EMU produces significant, but only indirect, effects. A unified capital market will put pressure on the existing configuration of stock and hence options markets. Index products will evolve from national to sectoral indexes. Overall volume can safely be expected to increase substantially with a transformation of European ownership structure that moves closer to the American model. Institutional investors, the main users of derivatives, will also gain in importance.

However, the main direct effect of EMU will be on monetary and bond markets. A single currency implies a single money market. Bond markets will still be differentiated by credit risk spreads. As a result there may emerge a single government benchmark or a benchmark per credit risk class. The government debt market in euros has good chances of reaching the size and liquidity of US markets quickly. Non-government securities—such as asset-backed securities or corporate bonds—will require much more time to catch up, and so will the associated derivatives products. All of this promises a future of very rapid growth of exchange-traded derivatives in Europe.

What concerns the existing exchanges most is, of course, the question of how this growing activity will be distributed among themselves. The major exchanges have the best prospects, but in principle there is room for most. A definitive scenario is difficult at this stage as too many important factors interact and as there are several strategic options. Electronic exchanges make cooperation particularly easy and the leading electronic exchange, DTB, has announced an open-door policy. If EUREX and MATIF were to establish cooperation with other Continental electronic exchanges on a level, then with LIFFE this integrated exchange could become Europe's leading one and assure the continued activity of participating exchanges. The other key question concerns the evolution of cash markets in stocks. If there is a major migration of the leading national stocks to the dominating European exchanges, then some national exchanges could suffer to the point of survival as independent organizations. The same is true for an important potential for future clearing-house activity: clearing of stand-ardized OTC contracts, which will be attracted to large exchanges/clearing-houses. It would take great innovative efforts to attract a share of this future market to the smaller exchanges.

Appendix: Abbreviations of Exchange Names

AEX	Amsterdam Exchanges
AMEX	American Stock Exchange
ASXD	Australian Stock Exchange Derivatives
BELFOX	Belgian Futures and Options Exchange
BM&F	Bolsa de Mercardorias & Futuros
BoTCC	Board of Trade Clearing Corporation
CBOE	Chicago Board Options Exchange
CBOT	Chicago Board of Trade
CME	Chicago Mercantile Exchange
COMEX	The Commodity Exchange
CRCE	Chicago Rice and Cotton Exchange
CSCE	Coffee, Sugar and Cocoa Exchange
DTB	Deutsche Terminbörse
FINEX	Financial Instrument Exchange
FUTOP	Copenhagen Stock Exchange and Clearing Centre
HKFE	Hong Kong Futures Exchange
IDEM	Italian Derivatives Market
IPE	International Petroleum Exchange
KANEX	Kansai Agricultural Commodities Exchange
KCBT	Kansas City Board of Trade
KSE	Korea Stock Exchange
LCE	London Commodity Exchange
LIFFE	London International Financial Futures Exchange
LME	London Metal Exchange
MATIF	Marché à Terme International de France
ME	Montreal Exchange
MEFF RF	Meff Renta Fija
MEFF RV	Meff Renta Variable
MGE	Minneapolis Grain Exchange
MIDAM	MidAmerica Commodity Exchange
MIF	Mercato Italiano Futures
MONEP	Marché des Options Négociables de Paris
MONTREAL	Montreal Stock Exchange
NYCE	New York Cotton Exchange
NYFE	New York Future Exchange
NYMEX	New York Mercantile Exchange
NZFOE	New Zealand Futures and Options Exchange
OB	Oslo Stock Exchange
OM	Stockholm Options Market
OMLX	London Securities and Derivatives Exchange
OSE	Osaka Securities Exchange
ÖTOB	Austrian Futures and Options Exchange
PE	Pacific Exchange

PHLX	Philadelphia Stock Exchange
SAFEX	South African Futures Exchange
SEHK	The Stock Exchange of Hong Kong
SFE	Sydney Futures Exchange
SIMEX	Singapore International Monetary Exchange
SOFFEX	Swiss Options and Financial Futures Exchange
SOM	Finnish Options Market
TGE	Tokyo Grain Exchange
TIFFE	Tokyo International Financial Futures Exchange
TOCOM	Tokyo Commodity Exchange
TORONTO	Toronto Stock Exchange
TSE	Tokyo Stock Exchange
WCE	Winnipeg Commodity Exchange

References

Bank for International Settlements (BIS) (1997), *International Banking and Financial Market Developments*, Basle (February, May).

IMF (1996), *International Capital Markets*, Washington, DC.

McCauley, R. N. and R. N. White (1997), 'The Euro and European Financial Markets', BIS Working Papers no. 41 (May).

MATIF (1996), *Report* of the Working Committee on the Changeover to the Euro (December).

Melamed, L. (1996), *Escape to the Futures*, New York: Wiley.

Miller, M. H. (1991), *Financial Innovations and Market Volatility*, Cambridge, MA: Basil Blackwell.

Moody's Investor Service (1995), *Credit Risks of Clearing-Houses at Futures and Options Exchanges*, New York (June).

Steinherr, A. (1997), *Derivatives: The Wild Beast of Finance*, London: Wiley.

Part III

The Equity Markets

7

The European Single Currency and World Equity Markets

GIORGIO DE SANTIS, BRUNO GERARD AND PIERRE HILLION

The 1991 Treaty on European Union (Maastricht Treaty) set 1 January 1999 as the starting date for the final stage in the creation of the European Monetary Union (EMU). As of 1 January 1999, the exchange rates between EMU participants will be irrevocably fixed to start the transition towards a unique currency, the euro, which is expected to become the legal tender for EMU participants by the year 2002.

Most advocates of EMU describe the introduction of the euro not as a major currency reform, but rather as a currency changeover which will simplify international transactions and increase market liquidity by eliminating conversion costs and exchange rate risk. This, in turn, should provide a boost to international investments and to the overall level of economic activity.

Although the arguments in favour of a unique European currency are intuitively appealing, a more thorough analysis of the concept of currency risk may be useful to better appreciate the relevance of EMU to investors. In general, it is well known that the existence of uncertainty in financial markets is not necessarily bad. First, because it is often possible to hedge against it, at least in part. Secondly, because efficient financial markets reward investors for their exposure to systematic risk. In addition, despite the elimination of currency fluctuations within the EMU, European consumers will still be exposed to exchange rate uncertainty towards non-EMU currencies such as the US dollar, the Japanese yen and the British pound.[1] The price sensitivity of their consumption baskets with respect to such currencies is also an important factor in determining the effects of adopting the euro. Surprisingly, very limited empirical evidence is available on these issues.

The main objective of this study is to analyse the impact on world financial markets of the adoption of a single European currency and the subsequent elimination of intra-European currency risk. We estimate the EMU and non-EMU components of aggreg-

We thank the Bank for International Settlements in Basle for graciously providing some of the Eurocurrency deposit data and CIBEAR–USC for research support.

[1] We treat the British pound as a non-EMU source of currency risk because the United Kingdom (and Denmark) have decided to keep their option to join EMU open through an opt-in clause.

ate currency risk using a conditional version of the international CAPM of Adler and Dumas (1983). Our results indicate that investors are rewarded for their exposure to both sources of exchange risk. The premium for EMU risk is mostly positive, but has decreased over the years. The non-EMU risk is consistently negative and is much larger, in absolute value, than its EMU counterpart. This suggests that the adoption of a single currency is likely to have a limited impact. European financial markets will still be exposed to the large and dominant impact of the non-EMU currency risk.

In addition, the adoption of a single currency is likely to have a significant impact also on European equity markets and, in particular, on their correlation structure. For example, it is often argued that the convergence of economic structures and policies, the existence of a unique currency and identical interest rates will increase correlations and, as a consequence, reduce the benefits of portfolio diversification (see, among others, Frankel, 1995). Although our chapter does not address these issues directly, it yields interesting insights on the way European investors are likely to adjust their portfolio holdings under EMU and on the home bias phenomenon.

The rest of the chapter is organized as follows. In Section 1 we briefly review some basic concepts in the theory of portfolio choice and then in Section 2 we present a model of international asset pricing which includes both market and currency risk. In Section 3 we describe the data-set. In Section 4 we present the empirical evidence. In Section 5 we discuss our results and present concluding remarks.

1. Portfolio Choice and Currency Risk

Modern portfolio theory suggests that investors should hold internationally diversified portfolios to improve the reward-to-risk ratio of their asset holdings. The attractiveness of international diversification is mostly due to the low level of correlation among national markets, which has been documented in a large number of studies (see, for example, Levy and Sarnat, 1970; Solnik, 1974*a, b*, 1995; French and Poterba, 1991; Elton and Gruber, 1992).

It is often argued, however, that standard mean–variance analysis does not necessarily apply when investors can allocate their wealth across assets traded in different national markets. In addition to market risk, one can think of a variety of sources of uncertainty that may be of concern to investors who are internationally diversified. For example, political turmoil in foreign countries may lead to restrictions on the repatriation of capital. Other deterrents may be differences in accounting procedures and, more generally, the costs involved in acquiring information in foreign markets. Typically, however, currency (or exchange rate) risk is the factor most commonly used to explain investors' resistance to international diversification.

The return on any foreign stock fluctuates not only because of asset-specific risk, but also because of unpredictable fluctuations in the exchange rate. Loosely speaking, the latter effect is often referred to as currency risk. Although apparently obvious, this

Table 7.1. Volatility decomposition for monthly asset returns in DM

Asset	(a) $\text{var}(R_i^{DM})$	(b) $\text{var}(R_i^l)$	(c) $\text{var}(v_i^{DM})$	(d) $\text{cov}(R_i^l, v_l^{DM})$	(e) (b)/(a)%	(f) (c)/(a)%	(g) 2(d)/(a)%
(a) Entire sample (1974:1–1997:4)							
USA	31.18	19.40	11.39	0.19	62.2	36.5	1.2
Japan	40.74	28.09	8.96	1.84	69.0	22.0	9.1
France	40.98	37.91	1.67	0.62	92.5	4.1	3.0
Nl.	22.94	22.82	0.24	−0.05	99.5	1.1	−0.5
UK	50.79	40.34	7.04	1.71	79.4	13.9	6.7
EurFr	1.60	0.16	1.67	−0.12	9.9	104.5	−14.5
EurNl	0.34	0.05	0.24	0.02	15.5	72.9	11.6
Eur£	7.16	0.10	7.04	0.02	1.3	98.2	0.4
Eur$	11.68	0.09	11.39	0.10	0.8	97.5	1.7
Eur¥	9.12	0.07	8.96	0.05	0.8	98.2	1.0
(b) First half of the sample (1974:1–1985:8)							
USA	27.83	20.41	10.95	−1.76	73.3	39.3	−12.7
Japan	27.52	15.23	9.88	1.21	55.3	35.9	8.8
France	45.67	39.96	2.82	1.28	87.5	6.2	5.6
Nl.	25.13	25.16	0.45	−0.22	100.1	1.8	−1.7
UK	66.80	54.52	8.33	1.98	81.6	12.5	5.9
EurFr	2.70	0.18	2.82	−0.15	6.8	104.3	−11.1
EurNl	0.59	0.06	0.45	0.04	10.9	76.0	13.1
Eur£	8.63	0.08	8.33	0.11	0.9	96.5	2.6
Eur$	11.41	0.10	10.95	0.18	0.9	95.9	3.2
Eur¥	10.07	0.07	9.88	0.06	0.7	98.1	1.1
(c) Second half of the sample (1985:9–1997:4)							
USA	34.74	18.42	11.85	2.24	53.0	34.1	12.9
Japan	54.00	40.94	8.10	2.48	75.8	15.0	9.2
France	36.53	36.13	0.48	−0.04	98.9	1.3	−0.2
Nl.	20.91	20.64	0.04	0.11	98.7	0.2	1.1
UK	35.11	26.40	5.79	1.46	75.2	16.5	8.3
EurFr	0.50	0.05	0.48	−0.02	9.6	97.6	−7.2
EurNl	0.08	0.03	0.04	0.00	39.8	51.5	8.6
Eur£	5.74	0.08	5.79	−0.07	1.4	101.0	−2.4
Eur$	11.78	0.03	11.85	−0.05	0.2	100.5	−0.8
Eur¥	8.20	0.04	8.10	0.03	0.5	98.7	0.8

Notes and sources: Monthly Deutsche Mark returns on the equity indexes of five countries (the USA, Japan, France, the Netherlands and the UK) are from MSCI. The Eurocurrency one-month deposit rates for the French franc, German mark, Dutch guilder, British pound, US dollar and Japanese yen are from DRI Inc. and BIS. All returns are continuously compounded. The sample covers the period January 1974–April 1997 (280 observations). R_i^{DM} is the DM return on asset i, R_i^l is the return on asset i measured in local currency, v_l^{DM} is the relative change in the exchange rate between the DM and the local currency.

interpretation may lead one to largely overstate the relevance of currency risk for several reasons.[2]

First, the sources of total return volatility differ among asset classes. For example, in panel (*a*) of Table 7.1 we decompose the monthly return volatility of some national stock indexes as well as Eurocurrency deposits, taking the perspective of a German investor. For the stock markets in our sample the data show that at most 36.5 per cent of the total volatility is due to exchange rate fluctuations. For the European equity markets that we consider this value is even lower, at 14 per cent. Panels (*b*) and (*c*) confirm this result over subsamples. Therefore, in the case of stock returns, total volatility is mostly due to fluctuations of the domestic stock market rather than to exchange rate volatility. On the other hand, the same volatility decomposition for returns on Eurocurrency deposits shows that most of the volatility is due to exchange rate fluctuations.

Secondly, for most developed markets, a large part of currency risk can be hedged by using derivative securities or, even more simply, by trading on foreign bond markets.[3] Obviously, hedging involves a cost; but as long as exposure to currency risk can be eliminated (or significantly reduced) at a cost that is lower than the expected benefits of international diversification, investors should include foreign assets in their optimal portfolios.

Thirdly, and most importantly, the practical relevance of currency risk can be appropriately measured only within the context of an international asset pricing model. For example, in the domestic CAPM we know that asset-specific volatility is not a proper measure of risk, since a possibly significant part of it can be diversified when the asset is included in a portfolio. In that framework, the appropriate measure of risk —usually referred to as systematic risk—is given by the covariance of each asset return with the return on the market portfolio. In equilibrium, investors should be rewarded for their exposure to systematic risk with a premium in excess of the risk-free rate. Intuition suggests that a similar idea should apply when investors can purchase assets traded in different national markets. The volatility of the return on a foreign asset (or market index) contains a country-specific component and a currency component. However, neither component should be interpreted as a measure of risk, since they can be diversified, at least in part, by including the asset in an internationally diversified portfolio. In the next section we build on this intuition to discuss an international version of the traditional CAPM which is carefully derived in Adler and Dumas (1983).

2. The Model

The traditional version of the CAPM of Sharpe (1964) and Lintner (1965) can be rescued in an international framework only by introducing two strong assumptions:

---

[2] See Solnik (1996) for a thorough discussion of these issues.

[3] It is well known, from interest rate parity relations, that the pay-off of a forward contract in a foreign currency can be replicated by purchasing the domestic bill and shorting the foreign bill.

investors from different countries consume the same basket of goods, and relative purchasing power parity (PPP) holds exactly at any point in time.[4] Examples of this literature are Grauer *et al.* (1976) and Hodrick (1981). Collecting empirical evidence on the first assumption can be rather difficult, although some work on this issue is discussed in Adler and Dumas (1983). The evidence on the second assumption, on the other hand, is rather compelling. Even if there is still an ongoing debate on whether PPP holds in the long run, the consensus is that the parity condition is violated in the short run, even in its relative form. As a consequence, investors from different countries have a different perception of the real return from the same asset and, because of this heterogeneity, the domestic CAPM does not hold in an international framework. Fortunately, the tools of standard mean–variance analysis can still be applied on a country-by-country basis and the results used to derive implications for optimal portfolio allocation and asset pricing restrictions in equilibrium.

Assume that, in each country, investors maximize the expected utility of future real consumption and that domestic inflation in non-stochastic.[5] The ICAPM predicts that, in equilibrium, all investors hold a combination of two risky portfolios, in addition to the risk-free asset. The first one, usually referred to as the *universal logarithmic portfolio*, is the world portfolio of all assets, partially hedged against currency risk.[6] As indicated by its definition, this portfolio is common to investors from all countries. The second portfolio, referred to as the *personalized hedge portfolio*, is country-specific, and only includes the bill denominated in the home currency.[7] The relative allocation across assets determines the optimal hedge ratio, which does not have to be equal to 1 since it is not necessarily optimal for investors to fully hedge their exposure to currency risk.

In addition to providing optimal portfolio weights, the model also yields pricing restrictions for all assets. These restrictions need to be expressed in a common currency but, as shown by Sercu (1980), the results are invariant with the choice of the reference currency. In equilibrium, the expected return on any asset is equal to the return on the risk-free asset, denominated in the reference currency, plus a premium for exposure to market and currency risk. The size of market risk is given by the covariance of the asset return with the return on the world-wide portfolio of all traded assets, whereas

[4] Absolute PPP states that, given two countries, the ratio of their price indexes must be equal to the exchange rate. The relative form of PPP requires instead that the change in the exchange rate be equal to the inflation differential between the two countries.

[5] The model can be solved without the assumption that inflation is non-stochastic. In this case, however, it is hard to disentangle inflation and currency risk. Since the evidence suggests that the volatility of inflation in most developed markets is negligible compared to exchange rate volatility, we proceed with this assumption. This allows us to focus on the empirical relevance of currency risk alone.

[6] The hedging portion of this portfolio derives from the fact that it contains bills denominated in the currencies of the various national markets. As mentioned earlier, combinations of local and foreign bills can be used to replicate the pay-offs of forward contracts and, therefore, as hedging instruments against currency risk.

[7] The model thus predicts that a significant fraction of an investor's assets will be invested in domestic securities, through the hedge portfolio, and therefore generates 'home bias'. However, the model does not necessarily justify the extent of equity home bias documented in practice (see Tesar and Werner, 1995).

exchange rate risk, with respect to a given currency, is measured by the covariance of the asset return with the relative change in the corresponding exchange rate. Formally, if the Deutsche Mark (DM) is used as the reference currency, the model imposes the following pricing restrictions:

$$E\left(R_i^{DM}\right) - R_f^{DM} = \gamma \operatorname{cov}\left(R_i^{DM}, R_M^{DM}\right) + \sum_{j=1}^{n} \delta_j \operatorname{cov}\left(R_i^{DM}, v_j^{DM}\right) \qquad \forall i, \tag{1}$$

where R_i^{DM} is the DM-denominated return on asset i, R_f^{DM} is the return on the DM-denominated bill, R_M^{DM} is the DM-denominated return on the world-wide market portfolio and v_j^{DM} is the relative change in the DM price of currency j. The coefficient γ measures the trade-off between the expected return on the asset and its market risk and, for this reason, can be interpreted as the shadow price of market risk. Using the same argument, each coefficient δ_j in equation (1) is usually referred to as the price of exchange rate risk for currency j.

To better understand the nature of currency risk in this model, consider the following example. Assume there exist only two countries, the USA and Germany, and that investors hold well-diversified portfolios (e.g. country funds) for both countries. Take the point of view of a German investor and use the DM as the measurement currency. The model predicts that the expected DM return on the US fund, in excess of the return on the DM-denominated bill, should be proportional to the covariance of the return on the fund with the return on the world portfolio (i.e. market risk), and to the covariance of the fund with the relative change in the exchange rate between the DM and the US dollar (i.e. currency risk). If R_{US}^{DM} is the DM-denominated return on the US fund and $v_\$^{DM}$ the relative change in the DM–dollar exchange rate, then equation (1) can be written as follows:[8]

$$E\left(R_{US}^{DM}\right) - R_f^{DM} = \gamma \operatorname{cov}\left(R_{US}^{DM}, R_M^{DM}\right) + \delta \operatorname{cov}\left(R_{US}^{DM}, v_\$^{DM}\right). \tag{2}$$

The US fund is held by both US and German investors. Obviously, US investors are not concerned with currency risk for a fund that contains US assets; therefore, the currency risk component in equation (2) is justified by the fact that a fraction of the fund is held by German investors. If returns are continuously compounded, the return on the US fund, measured in DM, is equal to the return on the fund measured in US dollars plus the relative change in the DM–dollar exchange rate. As a consequence, the covariance between the DM return on the US fund and the relative change in the exchange rate is equal to the sum of the covariance between the dollar return on the US fund and the change in the exchange rate and the variance of the change in the exchange rate:

$$\operatorname{cov}\left(R_{US}^{DM}, v_\$^{DM}\right) = \operatorname{cov}\left(R_{US}^\$, v_\$^{DM}\right) + \operatorname{var}\left(v_\$^{DM}\right). \tag{3}$$

---

[8] Similarly, the expected return on the German fund will be proportional to its market and currency risk exposures. Here, we focus on the US fund to interpret its currency risk component.

This shows that, in this model, exchange rate volatility alone is not an appropriate measure of currency risk. Consider, for example, a scenario in which the covariance between $R^\$_{US}$ and $v^{DM}_\$$ is negative. This implies that when the DM gains value *vis-à-vis* the US dollar $v^{DM}_\$$ is negative), the dollar-denominated return on the US fund is positive. Therefore, the German investor who holds the US fund loses from the devaluation of the dollar, but profits from the capital gain on the fund. In this sense, the US fund itself is, at least in part, a hedge against exchange rate fluctuations. As a consequence, the appropriate measure of currency risk exposure for the US fund is lower than the volatility of the DM–dollar exchange rate.

Two specific cases are of interest. First, in the unlikely case in which cov $(R^\$_{US}, v^{DM}_\$)$ is negative but equal, in absolute value, to var $(v^{DM}_\$)$, then the US fund has no DM currency risk exposure. Secondly, if the covariance is negative and larger, in absolute value, than the variance, then the currency risk associated with the US fund becomes negative, since the fund is more than a hedge against fluctuations of the DM–dollar exchange rate.[9] Obviously, equation (3) also implies that currency risk is larger than the volatility in the exchange rate changes if the dollar-denominated return on the US fund is positively correlated with $v^{DM}_\$$ (i.e. the dollar return on the fund is positive when the DM depreciates *vis-à-vis* the US dollar). Finally, exchange rate volatility is the appropriate measure of an asset's exposure to currency risk only when the return on the asset, denominated in the domestic currency, is uncorrelated with exchange rate changes.

In a multi-currency world, the expected return on any asset is affected by multiple premia for exposure to currency risk. For instance, if Japan is added to the USA and Germany in the previous example, the appropriate measure for currency risk for the US fund would include the covariance between the DM return on the fund and the relative change in the DM–dollar exchange rate as well as the covariance between the DM return on the fund and the relative change in the DM–yen exchange rate.

The preceding discussion implies that, ultimately, the relevance of currency risk in international financial markets is an empirical issue. Unfortunately, many authors have tried to approach this question in the past with inconclusive results. Examples are contained in Solnik (1974a), Stehle (1977), Eun and Resnick (1988) and Korajczyck and Viallet (1989). Arguably, the reason why the evidence has been inconsistent across studies is that most authors have used an unconditional approach for different sampling periods.[10] As pointed out by De Santis and Gerard (1998), this type of analysis can be very misleading if the conditional distribution of asset returns changes over time. For example, they find that although currency risk is priced and economically relevant, both its size and sign change significantly over the 1973–94 period. Interestingly, they estimate that the average premium for currency risk is close to zero for most markets,

---

[9] Implicit in this discussion is the assumption that the German investor consumes goods denominated in DM.

[10] In practice, this amounts to assuming that the distribution of asset returns does not change with changing economic conditions, and thus that exposures to market and currency risks and their premia are invariant with market conditions and institutional changes.

when looking at the overall sample. Over subperiods, however, its size and persistence are often non-trivial. Since unconditional analysis essentially amounts to averaging the conditional premia, one may learn very little from applying it to long sampling periods. On the other hand, an analysis based on a short sample, as in Eun and Resnick (1988), can be misleading if the period being investigated displays unusual characteristics.

In light of these issues, we focus on the conditional version of the model. When new information becomes available, investors may update their beliefs with respect to both expected returns and volatility in equity and currency markets. In addition, they may change their attitude towards risk.[11] In practice, choosing a conditional specification of the model amounts to specifying how the moments of the asset return distribution change over time. To accommodate these dynamics into the model, we modify the notation in equation (1) as follows. Let $R_{i,t}^{DM}$ be the DM-denominated return on asset i between time $t-1$ and time t; also let $E_{t-1}(\cdot)$ and $\text{cov}_{t-1}(\cdot)$ denote the expectation and covariance operators, respectively, conditional on the information available at the end of time $t-1$. Equation (1) in its conditional form can be written as

$$E_{t-1}\left(R_{i,t}^{DM}\right) - R_{f,t}^{DM} = \gamma_{t-1}\,\text{cov}_{t-1}\left(R_{i,t}^{DM}, R_{M,t}^{DM}\right) + \sum_{j=1}^{n} \delta_{j,t-1}\,\text{cov}_{t-1}\left(R_{i,t}^{DM}, v_{j,t}^{DM}\right). \tag{4}$$

It is obvious from the equation that the choice of the dynamics for the first and second moments is not independent. Because the asset pricing model postulates a relation between expected returns and covariances among returns, one can freely parameterize only the first or the second moments. Here, we follow the approach of De Santis and Gerard (1997, 1998), who use a parsimonious generalized autoregressive conditionally heteroscedastic (GARCH) specification for the dynamics of the second moments.[12] We also assume that the price of market risk (γ_{t-1}) as well as all the prices of currency risk ($\delta_{j,t-1}$) can change over time. We estimate the model using the quasi-maximum likelihood (QML) methodology discussed in Bollerslev and Wooldridge (1992). A detailed discussion of the empirical methods can be found in De Santis and Gerard (1997, 1998) and De Santis *et al.* (1997).

3. Data

We use monthly returns on stock indexes for five countries (the USA, France, Germany, Netherlands and the UK) plus a value-weighted world index. All the indexes are obtained from Morgan Stanley Capital International (MSCI) and the sampling period covers 280 observations from January 1974 until April 1997. The geographical composition of our sample is the result of a compromise between two objectives: first, we

---

[11] For example, an asset which provides only a limited hedge against exchange rate risk may become much more attractive when investors expect an increase in exchange rate uncertainty.

[12] See Bollerslev *et al.* (1992) for an overview of the GARCH literature.

want to cover a non-negligible portion of the international equity markets, both within and outside the EMU; secondly, we want to limit the size of the system to keep the estimation feasible. All MSCI indexes are available with and without dividends reinvested so that we can compute returns that include both capital gains and dividend yields. The monthly dividend yield is equal to one-twelfth of the ratio between the previous year dividend and the index at the end of each month.

To estimate the currency risk component of the model, we use Eurocurrency rates offered in the interbank market in London for one-month deposits in US dollars, Japanese yen, French francs, Dutch guilder and British pounds. The Eurocurrency rates are from Data Resources Incorporated (DRI) and the Bank for International Settlements (BIS) in Basle.

Returns on both equity and Eurodeposits are measured in Deutsche Marks, based on the closing European interbank currency rates from MSCI. We compute the monthly excess returns by subtracting the conditionally risk-free rate from the monthly return on each security. Given the choice of the measurement currency, an obvious candidate for the conditionally riskless asset is the one-month Eurocurrency deposit denominated in Deutsche Marks and quoted in London on the last day of the month.

The summary statistics reported in Table 7.2 reveal a number of interesting facts. The excess returns on the stock indexes have higher means, but also higher volatility than the excess returns on the Eurodeposits. In most cases the index of kurtosis and the Bera–Jarque test statistic strongly reject the hypothesis of normally distributed returns, which supports our decision to use QML to estimate and test the model. Panel (*b*) in the table contains the unconditional correlations among markets. The values are

Table 7.2. Summary statistics of asset excess returns

(*a*) *Summary statistics*

	Mean	Std. Dev.	Skewness	Kurtosis[a]	B–J[b]	Q_{12}[c]	Weights[d]
USA	0.370	5.59	−0.77**	3.40**	156**	0.815	0.35
Japan	0.311	6.40	−0.13	1.15**	15.2**	0.690	0.31
France	0.363	6.42	−0.30*	1.68**	35.2**	0.459	0.03
Germany	0.407	5.12	−0.82**	3.65**	180**	0.365	0.04
Nl.	0.752	4.81	−0.53**	4.13**	203**	0.127	0.02
UK	0.518	7.14	0.02	5.58**	348**	0.162	0.11
EurFr	0.141	1.25	−0.68**	4.38**	235**	0.043	
EurNl	0.030	0.54	−0.22	3.77**	160**	0.003	
Eur£	0.385	6.08	0.12	0.99**	11.2**	0.522	
Eur$	0.001	3.41	0.18	0.68*	6.49*	0.436	
Eur¥	0.076	3.02	0.31*	0.34	5.48	0.191	
World	0.332	4.61	−0.84**	3.41**	162**	0.211	1

[a] Equal to zero for the normal distribution.
[b] Bera–Jarque test statistic for normality.
[c] P-values for Ljung–Box test statistic of order 12.
[d] As of 31 December 1990.

Table 7.2. (*cont.*)

(*b*) *Unconditional correlations of* r_{it}

	Japan	France	Ger.	Nl.	UK	EurFr	EurNl	Eur£	Eur$	Eur¥	World
USA	.321	.473	.374	.667	.564	.178	.064	.568	.609	.240	.884
Japan	1	.337	.255	.372	.346	.113	.066	.141	.214	.566	.664
France		1	.508	.549	.529	.287	.040	.087	.126	.146	.591
Ger.			1	.606	.391	−.046	−.067	.083	.099	.019	.480
Nl.				1	.661	.077	.055	.231	.282	.148	.747
UK					1	.257	.168	.082	.250	.202	.696
EurFr						1	.348	.183	.275	.282	.188
EurNl							1	.026	.120	.081	.094
Eur£								1	.917	.358	.416
Eur$									1	.442	.506
Eur¥										1	.386

(*c*) *Autocorrelations of* r_{it}

Lag:	1	2	3	4	5	6	12
USA	0.045	0.039	−0.001	−0.004	0.061	−0.112	0.044
Japan	0.053	−0.002	0.081	0.079	0.041	0.014	−0.060
France	0.099	−0.055	0.084	0.025	0.014	−0.015	−0.074
Germany	0.077	−0.045	0.079	0.050	−0.103	−0.054	−0.028
Nl.	0.085	−0.021	0.032	−0.093	0.017	−0.052	0.074
UK	0.114	−0.100	0.038	−0.024	−0.145*	−0.024	−0.042
EurFr	0.036	0.038	0.022	−0.099	−0.094	−0.063	−0.029
EurNl	0.139*	0.057	−0.045	−0.094	−0.140*	−0.121*	0.024
Eur£	0.016	0.068	−0.008	−0.013	0.040	−0.111	−0.015
Eur$	0.018	0.105	0.021	−0.013	0.027	−0.081	0.014
Eur¥	0.073	0.091	0.071	0.050	0.076	−0.107	−0.051
World	0.122*	0.038	0.021	0.008	0.069	−0.065	−0.004

(*d*) *Autocorrelations of* r_{it}^2

Lage:	1	2	3	4	5	6	12
USA	0.149*	0.009	0.052	−0.003	−0.044	0.007	0.005
Japan	0.087	0.159*	0.045	0.046	0.063	0.094	−0.038
France	0.026	−0.008	0.033	0.231**	0.019	0.056	−0.041
Germany	0.282**	−0.018	0.063	0.163*	0.086	−0.003	−0.045
Nl.	0.129*	−0.053	−0.028	0.055	0.035	−0.020	−0.032
UK	0.112	0.182**	0.080	0.031	0.141*	−0.008	−0.040
EurFR	0.354**	0.330**	0.294**	0.291**	0.199**	0.177**	0.049
EurNl	0.145*	0.192**	0.120*	0.189**	0.152*	0.101	0.189**
Eur£	0.158*	−0.030	−0.035	0.052	0.011	−0.045	−0.016
Eur$	0.174**	−0.006	−0.021	−0.034	−0.029	−0.030	−0.034
Eur¥	0.038	0.037	0.043	0.137*	−0.032	0.047	0.007
World	0.055	−0.031	0.047	−0.001	−0.012	−0.037	−0.047

Table 7.2. (*cont.*)

(*e*) Cross-correlations of r_{it}^2: world and asset j

Lag	USA	France	Ger.	Nl.	UK	EurFr	EurNl	Eur£	Eur$	Eur¥
−6	.036	−.073	.002	.022	.010	−.038	−.010	.017	.025	−.028
−5	−.027	.037	.028	.039	.059	−.046	−.042	−.028	−.069	−.075
−4	−.015	.218**	.184**	−.000	.078	−.012	−.036	−.028	−.051	−.085
−3	.034	.050	.039	−.027	.003	−.009	−.012	.036	.019	−.063
−2	.007	−.030	−.018	−.015	.035	−.006	−.006	.032	.023	.107
−1	.144*	−.002	.234**	.102	.020	.019	−.014	.148*	.146*	−.031
0	.888**	.588**	.672**	.789**	.551**	.031	−.011	.185**	.239**	.068
1	.045	.073	.062	.073	.016	.039	−.027	−.040	−.011	−.070
2	−.032	−.055	−.048	−.040	−.035	.061	−.003	−.040	−.049	−.035
3	.059	−.001	.059	.013	.009	−.004	−.056	−.033	−.040	−.036
4	.006	.140*	.001	.027	−.032	.011	−.041	−.054	−.041	.016
5	−.059	−.032	.052	−.034	−.008	.012	−.011	−.050	−.057	−.000
6	.003	−.024	−.014	−.031	−.023	.028	−.005	−.050	−.032	.032

Number of significant cross-correlations of order (−2, −1, 1, 2): 23 out of 264

* and ** denote statistical significance at the 5% and 1% levels, respectively.

Notes and sources: Monthly Deutsche Mark returns on the equity indexes of six countries and the value-weighted world index are from MSCI. The Eurocurrency one-month deposit rates for the French franc, Dutch guilder, German mark, Japanese yen, British pound and US dollar are from DRI Inc. and BIS. Excess returns are obtained by subtracting the EuroDM one-month rate. All returns are continuously compounded and expressed in percentage per month. The sample covers the period January 1974–April 1997 (280 observations).

relatively low, especially if compared to the average correlation among sectors of the US market.[13] Interestingly, the correlation between the returns on Eurodollar and Europound deposits is very high, thus implying a potentially high correlation between US dollar and British pound risk.

Panel (c) in the table reports autocorrelations for the excess returns and panel (*d*) autocorrelations for the excess returns squared. The predominant lack of autocorrelation in the returns series reveals that, in our analysis, we do not need to correct for the possibility of autocorrelation in the market indexes. On the other hand, autocorrelation is detected, at short lags, in the squared returns, thus suggesting that a GARCH specification for the second moments might be appropriate, at least for the stock return series.

Finally, for the squared returns, panel (*e*) in the table contains the cross-correlations, at different leads and lags, between the world index and the other assets. We report these statistics to determine whether we should use a GARCH parameterization which can

---

[13] For example, Elton and Gruber (1992) document that during the 1980–8 period, the correlation between the value-weighted index of the 1,000 largest stocks traded in the USA and the value-weighted index of the next 2,000 largest stocks is 0.92.

accommodate cross-market dependence in volatility. With few exceptions, only the contemporaneous correlations are statistically significant. Although this is only a sub-sample of all the relevant cross-correlations, when we analyse the cross-correlations with at most two leads and two lags, only 23 out of 264 are statistically significant at the 5 per cent level. In this sense, the diagonal GARCH parameterization that we use is not too restrictive.

In choosing the instruments that describe the investor's information set, we are guided by previous research (Ferson and Harvey, 1993; Dumas and Solnik, 1995; De Santis and Gerard, 1998) and by economic intuition. The instruments include a constant, the dividend yield on the world equity index in excess of the one-month Euromark rate, the change in the one-month Eurodollar deposit rate and the US default premium, measured by the yield difference between Moody's Baa- and Aaa-rated bonds. In addition to these common variables, we also use one country-specific variable to predict changes in currency risk premia. We hypothesize that the relative attractiveness of each currency and the reward required to bear its associated risk are affected by the difference between the real return on the local short-term deposit and the real return on the short-term deposit in the reference currency, which we refer to as the real risk-free rate differential. Real returns are computed by deflating local nominal one-month Eurocurrency rates by the change in the local CPI index. Inflation data are from the International Financial Statistics (IFS) database. All variables are used with a one-month lag, relative to the excess return series. The summary statistics in Table 7.3 show that the correlations among the instruments are low, which indicates that our proxy of the information set does not contain redundant variables.

4. Empirical Evidence

The ICAPM described in Section 2 offers a number of testable implications which are of primary interest in our study. First, we can determine whether world-wide market risk and currency risk are priced factors in international financial markets. Secondly, we can separately identify and test the relevance of EMU-specific currency risk. However, some additional considerations are necessary before we proceed to analyse the empirical evidence. As mentioned earlier, we assume that all prices of risk are time-varying. The parameterization that we choose is inspired by previous work (see, in particular, De Santis and Gerard, 1998). For each price, we assume that the dynamics can be described by a set of instrumental variables. Moreover, in each case we have to choose both the set of relevant instruments and the functional form.[14] For the price of market risk the vector of instruments $z_{M,t-1}$ includes a constant, the dividend yield on the world equity index in excess of the one-month Euromark rate ($XDPR$), the change

---

[14] Unfortunately, in the absence of a general equilibrium model, the choice of relevant instruments is inevitably *ad hoc*. In general, there is no reason to assume that the same set of instruments should be used for all prices of risk.

Table 7.3. Summary statistics of the information variables

	Mean	Median	Std. Dev.	Min.	Max.
XDPR	−0.245	−0.205	0.217	−1.017	0.206
ΔEuro$	−0.002	−0.005	0.112	−0.544	0.553
USDP	1.177	1.010	0.473	0.560	2.690
FrRRD	0.115	0.118	0.407	−1.098	2.324
NlRRD	0.015	0.041	0.495	−1.477	2.051
£RRD	0.026	0.120	0.631	−2.995	2.642
$RRD	−0.016	−0.025	0.372	−1.089	0.975
¥RRD	−0.077	−0.046	0.656	−3.362	1.481

(*a*) *Autocorrelations*

Lag:	1	2	3	4	5	6	12
XDPR	0.901	0.869	0.868	0.825	0.797	0.772	0.578
ΔEuro$	−0.232	−0.078	0.200	−0.316	0.048	0.001	0.090
USDP	0.958	0.902	0.859	0.829	0.797	0.750	0.539
FrRRD	0.310	0.139	0.068	−0.018	0.028	0.055	0.080
NlRRD	0.232	−0.060	−0.281	−0.152	0.112	0.282	0.567
£RRD	0.256	0.027	−0.004	0.036	0.132	0.236	0.474
$RRD	0.384	0.254	0.182	0.060	0.164	0.106	0.327
¥RRD	0.128	−0.155	−0.101	−0.109	0.130	0.219	0.437

(*b*) *Correlations*

	XDPR	ΔEuro$	USDP	FrRRD	NlRRD	£RRD	$RRD	¥RRD
ΔEuro$	0.183	1						
USDP	−0.020	−0.127	1					
FrRRD	−0.048	−0.118	0.074	1				
NlRRD	0.002	0.015	−0.021	0.438	1			
£RRD	−0.001	0.003	−0.007	0.388	0.362	1		
$RRD	0.164	0.033	0.340	0.481	0.401	0.218	1	
¥RRD	0.126	−0.027	0.179	0.350	0.437	0.349	0.348	1

Notes and sources: The information set includes the world dividend yield in excess of the one-month EuroDM rate (*XDPR*), the change in the one-month Eurodollar deposit rate (*ΔEuro$*), the US default premium (*USDP*), and the difference between the local currency one-month Eurodeposits real return and the real return on the Deutsche Mark one-month Eurodeposit (*FrRRD, NlRRD, £RRD, $RRD, ¥RRD*). The world dividend yield is the DM-denominated dividend yield on the MSCI world index. The US default premium is the yield difference between Moody's Baa- and Aaa-rated bonds. The real return on one-month Eurodeposits is equal to the difference between the quoted nominal deposit rate and the previous month's change in the consumer price index. Inflation rates are obtained from the IFS database. The sample covers the period January 1974–April 1997 (280 observations).

in the one-month Eurodollar rate ($\Delta Euro\$$) and the US default premium ($USDP$), measured by the yield difference between Moody's Baa- and Aaa-rated bonds. In choosing the functional form for γ_{t-1} we take into consideration the implications of the theoretical model. The price of market risk is a weighted average of the coefficients of risk-aversion of all national investors;[15] therefore, under the assumption that all investors are risk-averse, γ_{t-1} must be always positive. To guarantee that this restriction is satisfied, we assume that γ_{t-1} is an exponential function of the instruments in $z_{M,t-1}$

$$\gamma_{t-1} = \exp(\kappa_M' z_{M,t-1}).$$

On the other hand, the theory does not impose any restriction on the sign of the prices of currency risk. For this reason, we adopt a linear specification for each $\delta_{j,t-1}$ in the model:

$$\delta_{j,t-1} = k_j' z_{j,t-1}.$$

The vector $z_{j,t-1}$ includes a constant, two variables which are common to all prices ($\Delta Euro\$$ and $USDP$, as defined above) and a currency-specific variable measured by the difference between the real interest rate of country j and the real Euromark rate.[16]

4.1. The statistical relevance of currency risk

Table 7.4 contains parameter estimates and a number of diagnostic tests for the model. In panel (*a*) we report point estimates and QML standard errors for the individual parameters of the model, whereas in panel (*b*) we use robust Wald-test statistics to evaluate joint hypotheses. All the statistics in panel (*b*) support the ICAPM discussed earlier. In particular, the price of world-wide market risk γ_{t-1} is statistically significant and time-varying, since the null hypothesis that all the k_M coefficients are equal to zero is strongly rejected. Even more interesting for our purposes is the result that currency risk is also a priced factor. In fact, the null hypothesis that the k_j coefficients for all currencies are equal to zero is rejected at any standard level.

Having established the empirical relevance of currency risk, it is useful to disaggregate it into EMU and non-EMU components. Obviously, since the Deutsche Mark is used as the measurement currency, the two sources of currency risk which are bound to disappear with the inception of EMU are French franc and Dutch guilder risk. On the other hand, currency risk associated with the US dollar, the Japanese yen and the British pound is not going to be eliminated by the adoption of the unique currency. For this reason, in panel (*b*) of Table 7.4 we include two additional tests on the relevance of currency risk. Under the null hypothesis that EMU (non-EMU) currency risk is not priced, all the κ_j coefficients for the relevant currencies must be equal to zero. The results for these tests show that both EMU and non-EMU currency risk are priced, at least at the 5 per cent level.

---

[15] See Adler and Dumas (1983).
[16] We use the term country j to indicate the country whose goods are denominated in currency j.

Table 7.4. Quasi-maximum likelihood estimates of the conditional international CAPM with time-varying prices of risk

(*a*) *Parameter estimates*

	Const.		XDPR		ΔEuro$		USDP	
κ_m	−4.74	(1.26)	2.75	(2.23)	−3.40	(1.43)	1.29	(.756)

	Const.		ΔEuro$		USDP		Loc RRD	
κ_{FFr}	.163	(.220)	.484	(.497)	−.078	(.203)	.019	(.245)
κ_{Nl}	.443	(.307)	−.631	(.959)	−.324	(.229)	.394	(.188)
$\kappa_{£}$	.123	(.076)	.330	(.206)	−.098	(.061)	−.017	(.036)
$\kappa_{¥}$	−.109	(.062)	.210	(.167)	.066	(.052)	.050	(.056)
$\kappa_{\$}$	−.068	(.072)	−.014	(.102)	.057	(.061)	.069	(.032)

	France	Ger.	Nl.	UK	USA	EurFr	EurNl	Eur£	Eur$	Eur¥	World
a_i	.104	.287	.169	.252	.200	.377	.208	.112	.233	.226	.151
	(.029)	(.061)	(.036)	(.025)	(.024)	(.075)	(.024)	(.039)	(.044)	(.047)	(.019)
b_i	.989	.300	.939	.945	.921	.867	.976	.991	.702	.822	.975
	(.009)	(.220)	(.020)	(.014)	(.026)	(.066)	(.005)	(.015)	(.084)	(.056)	(.004)

(*b*) *Specification tests*

Null hypothesis	χ^2	d.f.	p-value
Is the price of market risk constant?			
$\quad$ H$_0$: $\kappa_{m,k}=0$ $\quad$ $\forall k>1$	18.812	3	0.000
Are the prices of currency risk equal to zero?			
$\quad$ H$_0$: $\kappa_{c,k}=0$ $\quad$ $\forall c,k$	62.742	20	0.000
Are the prices of currency risk constant?			
$\quad$ H$_0$: $\kappa_{c,k}=0$ $\quad$ $\forall c,k>1$	50.178	15	0.000
Are the prices of currency risk of EMU countries equal to zero?			
$\quad$ H$_0$: $\kappa_{c,k}=0$ $\quad$ $\forall k,c=1,2$	15.150	8	0.056
Are the prices of currency risk of non-EMU countries equal to zero?			
$\quad$ H$_0$: $\kappa_{c,k}=0$ $\quad$ $\forall k,c=3,4,5$	24.013	12	0.020

Table 7.4. (cont.)

(c) Summary statistics and diagnostics for the residuals

	France	Ger.	Nl.	UK	USA	EurFr	EurNl	Eur£	Eur$	Eur¥	World
Avg. ExRet	0.36	0.41	0.75	0.52	0.37	0.14	0.03	0.13	0.00	0.23	0.15
Avg. PrErr.	−0.23	0.15	0.37	−0.18	−0.03	0.04	0.02	0.05	0.05	0.05	−0.11
RMSE	6.41	5.11	4.75	7.12	5.51	1.23	0.53	2.64	3.37	2.98	4.50
R^2_m [a]	0.59	0.47	2.37	1.63	2.64	0.13	−0.69	−0.92	−0.04	0.88	3.74
R^2_{m+c} [b]	0.30	0.45	2.54	0.53	2.79	2.17	4.24	2.49	2.31	2.81	4.43
Kurt.[c]	1.77*	3.46*	4.34*	3.89*	4.30*	4.32*	1.84*	1.77*	0.93*	0.22	4.43*
B–J[d]	40.7*	157*	226*	185*	241*	300*	42.3*	38.7*	10.3*	4.15	256*
$Q_{12}(z)$ [e]	0.57	0.36	0.20	0.74	0.80	0.28	0.42	0.19	0.52	0.41	0.40
$Q_{12}(z^2)$ [e]	0.15	0.02	0.94	0.84	0.99	0.80	0.28	0.91	0.88	0.64	0.99
EN–LM[f]	0.73	0.51	0.83	0.62	0.21	0.05	0.08	0.43	0.46	0.23	0.75

Likelihood function: −6964.184

[a] Pseudo-R^2 when market risk is the only pricing factor.
[b] Pseudo-R^2 when both market and currency risk are pricing factors.
[c] equal to zero for the normal distribution.
[d] Bera–Jarque test statistic for normality.
[e] p-values for Ljung–Box test statistic of order 12.
[f] p-values for Engle–Ng test on the predictability of conditional second moments using the instruments.
* denotes statistical significance at the 1% level.

Notes and sources: Estimates are based on monthly DM-denominated continuously compounded returns from January 1974 to April 1997. Data for the country equity indexes and the world portfolio are from MSCI. One-month Eurocurrency deposit rates are from DRI Inc. and BIS. Each mean equation relates the asset excess return r_{it} to its world covariance risk $\text{cov}_{t-1}(r_{it}, r_{mt})$ and its currency risk $\text{cov}_{t-1}(r_{it}, r_{5+c,t})$. The prices of risk are functions of a number of instruments, z_{t-1}, included in the investors' information set. The instruments include a constant, the world index dividend yield in excess of the one-month Euromark rate (*XDPR*), the change in the one-month Eurodollar rate ($\Delta Euro\$$), and the US default premium (*USDP*) as well as the difference between the one-month real rates for the local currency Eurodeposits and the DM Eurodeposits (*Loc RRD*):

$$r_{it} = \delta_{m,t-1}\,\text{cov}_{t-1}(r_{it}, r_{mt}) + \sum_{c=1}^{5}\delta_{c,t-1}\,\text{cov}_{t-1}(r_{it}, r_{5+c,t}) + \varepsilon_{it},$$

where $\delta_{m,t-1} = \exp(\kappa'_m\, z_{t-1})$, $\delta_{c,t-1} = \kappa'_c\, z_{t-1}$ and $\varepsilon_t\, \Im_{t-1} \sim N(0, H_t)$. The conditional covariance matrix H_t is parameterized as follows:

$$H_t = H_0 * (\iota\iota' - aa' - bb') + aa' * \varepsilon_{t-1}\varepsilon'_{t-1} + bb' * H_{t-1},$$

where * denotes the Hadamard matrix product, **a** and **b** are 11×1 vectors of constants and ι is an 11×1 unit vector. QML standard errors are reported in parentheses.

Finally, the statistics in the table also show that the GARCH parameterization that we propose adequately describes the dynamics of the conditional second moments. However, since this is not the main focus of the study, we do not expand this part of the analysis here.

4.2. The economic relevance of currency risk

The fact that currency risk is a priced factor, both in its EMU and non-EMU components, has interesting implications. In fact, as long as exposure to exchange rate fluctuations is rewarded by the market in the form of a risk premium, it may not be optimal to eliminate multiple currencies, since this would only eliminate potentially attractive assets from the menu of choices available to investors. A more educated assessment of this issue requires an explicit measure of the premium associated with each source of risk, which can be easily done using our approach. Specifically, the premium for market risk for asset i is simply computed as the product of the price of market risk γ_{t-1} and the conditional covariance $\text{cov}_{t-1}(R_{i,t}^{DM}, R_{M,t}^{DM})$. Since both quantities are explicitly parameterized in the model, the premium for market risk can be computed for any asset included in the system of equations (4). For the same asset, the aggregate measure of currency risk, as well as its components, can be obtained from the expression $\sum_{j=1}^{n} \delta_{j,t-1} \text{cov}_{t-1}(R_{i,t}^{DM}, v_{j,t}^{DM})$. In Table 7.5 and Figures 7.1–6, we report information on the estimated premia, using the following definitions

- Market premium: $MP = \gamma_{t-1} \text{cov}_{t-1}(R_{i,t}^{DM}, R_{M,t}^{DM})$,
- Aggregate currency premium: $ACP = \sum_{j=1}^{n} \delta_{j,t-1} \text{cov}_{t-1}(R_{i,t}^{DM}, v_{j,t}^{DM})$,
  - EMU currency premium: $ECP = \sum_{j=1}^{n_1} \delta_{j,t-1} \text{cov}_{t-1}(R_{i,t}^{DM}, v_{j,t}^{DM})$,
  - Non-EMU currency premium: $NECP = \sum_{j=n_1+1}^{n} \delta_{j,t-1} \text{cov}_{t-1}(R_{i,t}^{DM}, v_{j,t}^{DM})$, and
- Total premium: $TP = MP + ACP$,

where we assume that of the n sources of currency risk in the model, the first n_1 are EMU-specific.

We focus on the equity markets. The data in Table 7.5 show that for both the US and the world equity index, the average premium for currency risk is negative and, in absolute terms, represents a non-negligible fraction of the total premium. For example, the average market premium for holding US equities over the 1974–97 period is equal to 8.17 per cent on an annual basis. Yet, since the average aggregate currency premium over the same period is equal to −3.32 per cent, the total premium is reduced to 4.85 per cent. The evidence is qualitatively similar for the world equity index. For the remaining equity markets in our sample, the statistics in the table should be interpreted more carefully. In most instances, the average market premium is the dominant component of the average total premium. However, using this evidence to conclude that currency risk is economically negligible in most markets could be misleading, for at least two reasons. First, as argued earlier, the average premium can be close to zero when

Table 7.5. Decomposition and structural changes of the total premia for equity markets

| | Overall | | $RP_t = b_0 + b_1 D_{(t > 6/90)} + v_t$ | | | |
	Avg.	s.e.	b_0	s.e.	b_1	s.e.
US equity						
TP	4.85	1.38	8.66	1.47	−13.00	1.64
MP	8.17	1.02	10.53	1.22	−8.05	1.25
ACP	−3.32	0.52	−1.87	0.52	−4.95	0.78
ECP	1.26	0.23	1.18	0.31	0.28	0.35
NECP	−4.58	0.63	−3.05	0.70	−5.23	0.90
French equity						
TP	7.18	0.78	9.26	0.85	−7.11	0.95
MP	6.27	0.79	7.99	0.96	−5.87	0.98
ACP	0.91	0.25	1.28	0.31	−1.24	0.43
ECP	2.11	0.28	1.91	0.39	0.70	0.43
NECP	−1.20	0.23	−0.63	0.25	−1.94	0.37
German equity						
TP	3.07	0.59	4.48	0.68	−4.82	0.75
MP	4.05	0.50	5.16	0.60	−3.79	0.62
ACP	−0.97	0.14	−0.67	0.15	−1.03	0.25
ECP	−0.38	0.09	−0.28	0.12	−0.37	0.14
NECP	−0.59	0.08	−0.40	0.07	−0.66	0.19
Dutch equity						
TP	4.62	0.79	6.66	0.88	−6.96	0.98
MP	5.90	0.75	7.58	0.90	−5.73	0.92
ACP	−1.28	0.19	−0.92	0.21	−1.23	0.36
ECP	0.42	0.13	0.31	0.17	0.38	0.20
NECP	−1.70	0.20	−1.23	0.20	−1.61	0.34
UK Equity						
TP	8.41	0.95	10.75	1.05	−8.02	1.28
MP	8.67	1.22	11.26	1.51	−8.84	1.53
ACP	−0.27	0.84	−0.51	1.16	0.82	1.34
ECP	1.86	0.57	1.64	0.79	0.73	0.83
NECP	−2.12	0.42	−2.15	0.55	0.09	0.77
World index						
TP	5.26	1.13	8.31	1.23	−10.42	1.38
MP	7.40	0.92	9.43	1.11	−6.95	1.14
ACP	−2.14	0.40	−1.12	0.40	−3.47	0.63
ECP	1.09	0.20	1.01	0.28	0.27	0.31
NECP	−3.23	0.47	−2.13	0.52	−3.75	0.70

Notes: The table contains the overall means and standard errors of the risk premia estimated from the model with time-varying risk as well as the parameter estimates from the regressions of these estimated premia on a constant and a dummy variable for the post-June 1990 period ($D_t = 1$, if $t > $ June 1990). The total risk premium (*TP*) is measured as the sum of the market risk premium (*MP*) and the aggregate currency premium (*ACP*). The currency premium is the sum of the premium associated with the currencies to be included in the EMU

Table 7.5. (*cont.*)

(*ECP*), i.e. French franc and Dutch guilder, and the premium associated with the currencies not included in the EMU (*NECP*), i.e. the British pound, the US dollar and the Japanese yen. The premia for asset i are measured by

$$MP_{it} = \delta_{m,t-1} \operatorname{cov}_{t-1}(r_{it}, r_{mt}) \quad \text{and} \quad ACP_{it} = \sum_{c=1}^{5} \delta_{c,t-1} \operatorname{cov}_{t-1}(r_{it}, r_{5+c,t})$$

$$ECP_{it} = \sum_{c=1}^{2} \delta_{c,t-1} \operatorname{cov}_{t-1}(r_{it}, r_{5+c,t}) \quad \text{and} \quad NECP_{it} = \sum_{c=3}^{5} \delta_{c,t-1} \operatorname{cov}_{t-1}(r_{it}, r_{5+c,t})$$

Standard errors are computed using the Newey–West heteroscedasticity and autocorrelation robust procedure. All estimates are reported in percentages per year.

computed over the entire sample, while oscillating between positive and negative values for relatively long subperiods. Secondly, the cross-sectional aggregation over different sources of currency risk may fail to reflect currency-specific premia of different sign which are economically significant.

The (*a*)-labelled parts of Figures 7.1–6 can be used to address the first issue. For France, Germany and the Netherlands, the graphs indicate that the aggregate currency premium fluctuates around zero within a rather narrow band. On the other hand, for the UK the same premium is often large in absolute value and persistent in sign during the first half of the sample. In Figure 7.7(*a*) we provide an alternative way of summarizing our findings by plotting the average aggregate currency premia and the corresponding confidence intervals, obtained using Newey–West (NW) standard errors.[17] The average premia for the US and the world portfolios are clearly large and negative and more than two standard deviations away from zero. The average currency premia are much smaller for the other four equity markets in our sample.

The decomposition of the aggregate currency premium into the EMU and non-EMU components reveals some interesting regularities. Visual inspection of the (*b*)-labelled parts Figures 7.1–6 suggests two main things. First, the premium for exposure to EMU currency risk is mostly positive whereas the premium for non-EMU risk is negative. Secondly, the premium for non-EMU risk is considerably larger in absolute value. These findings are confirmed by the average disaggregated premia reported in Table 7.5 and by the confidence intervals plotted in Figures 7.7(*b*) and 7.7(*c*). The numbers in the table indicate that, in most cases, the non-EMU component of the currency premium attains rather large values. For example, the average non-EMU premium is equal –4.58 per cent per year for the US equity market, –3.22 per cent for the world index, and four times as large as the EMU premium for the Dutch market. In the German case, both components are small, owing to the fact that the Deutsche Mark is the reference currency. Finally, the French market is the only case in which the

[17] See Newey and West (1987).

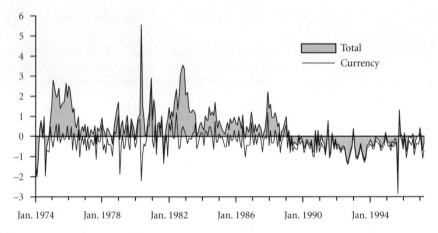

Figure 7.1(a). Risk premia: US equity

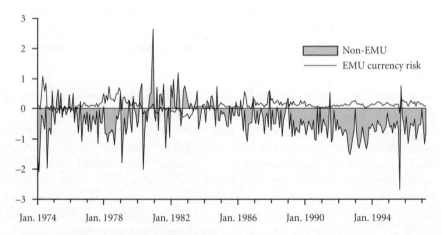

Figure 7.1(b). Currency premium decomposition: US equity

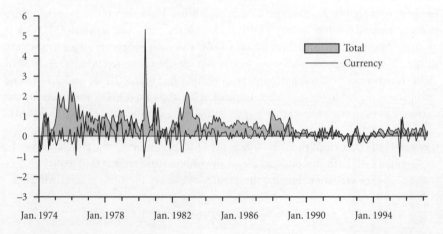

Figure 7.2(a). Risk premia: French equity

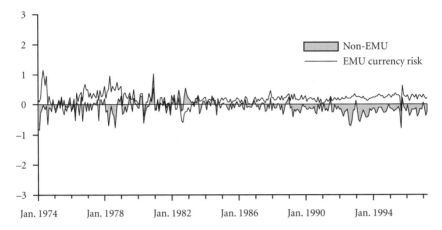

Figure 7.2(b). Currency premium decomposition: French equity

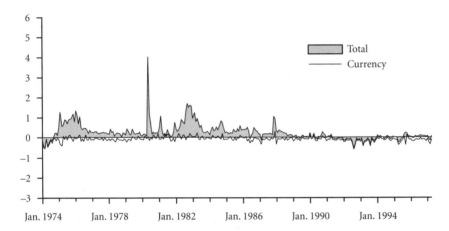

Figure 7.3(a). Risk premia: German equity

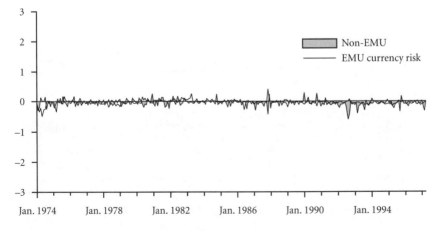

Figure 7.3(b). Currency premium decomposition: German equity

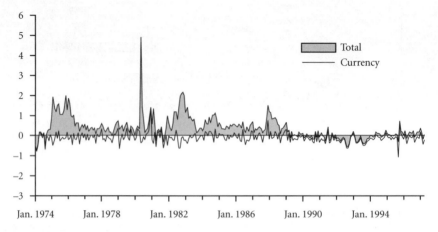

Figure 7.4(a). Risk premia: Dutch equity

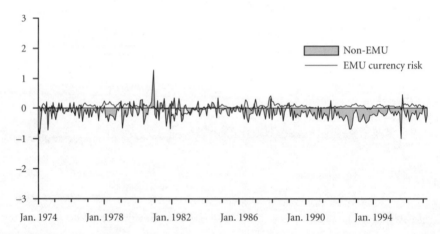

Figure 7.4(b). Currency premium decomposition: Dutch equity

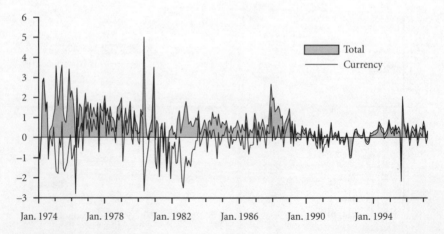

Figure 7.5(a). Risk premia: UK equity

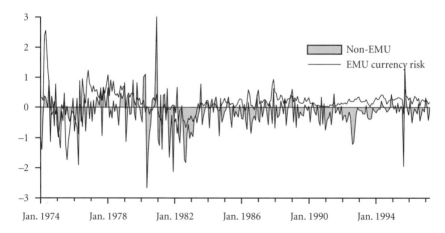

Figure 7.5(b). Currency premium decomposition: UK equity

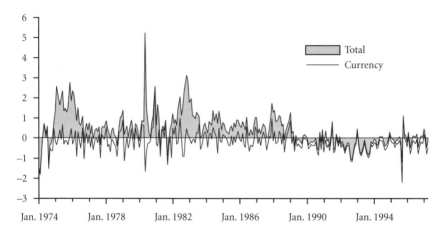

Figure 7.6(a). Risk premia: World equity

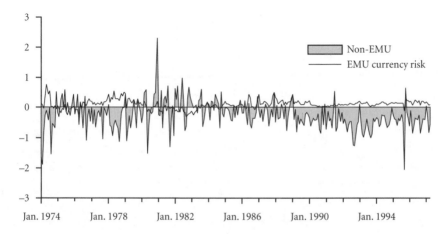

Figure 7.6(b). Currency premium decomposition: World equity

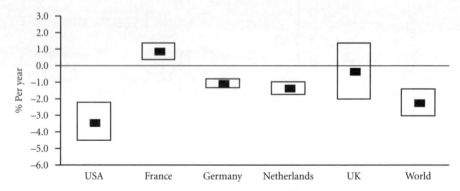

Figure 7.7(a). Average aggregate currency premia with 2 std. dev. bounds

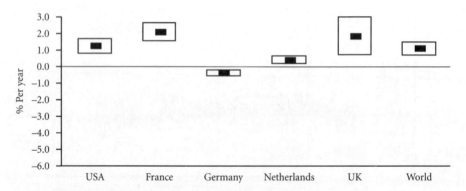

Figure 7.7(b). Average EMU currency premia with 2 std. dev. bounds

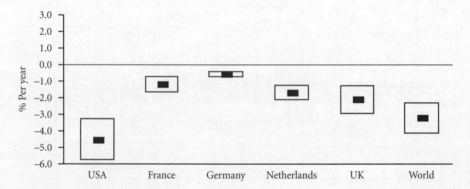

Figure 7.7(c). Average non-EMU currency premia with 2 std. dev. bounds

Table 7.6. Summary statistics and structural changes of the prices of risk

Prices of	Overall		$\delta_t = b_0 + b_1 D_{(t > 6/90)} + v_t$			
	Avg.	s.e.	b_0	s.e.	b_1	s.e.
Market risk	3.13	0.40	4.00	0.49	−2.98	0.50
French franc risk	7.22	0.61	5.94	0.73	4.37	0.90
Dutch guilder risk	6.88	2.50	1.57	2.99	18.15	3.55
British pound risk	0.71	0.70	−0.79	0.83	5.13	1.04
US dollar risk	−3.28	0.53	−1.95	0.59	−4.56	0.68
Japanese yen risk	−0.68	0.52	0.30	0.64	−3.35	0.78

Notes: The table contains the overall means and standard errors of the prices of risk estimated from the model with time-varying risk as well as the parameter estimates from the regressions of these estimated prices on a constant and a dummy variable for the post-June 1990 period ($D_t = 1$, if $t >$ June 1990). The price of market risk, δ_m, is estimated as an exponential function of a constant, the world index dividend yield in excess of the one-month Euromark rate, the change in one-month Eurodollar rate and the US default premium. The prices of currency risk (δ_c, $c = 1, \ldots, 5$) are estimated as a linear function of the change in the one-month Eurodollar rate, the US default premium and the difference between the one-month real rates for the local currency Eurodeposits and the DM Euro-deposit. Standard errors are computed using the Newey–West heteroscedasticity and autocorrelation robust procedure.

average premium for EMU risk (2 per cent) is larger, in absolute value, than the non-EMU premium (−1.20 per cent).

Although not displayed here, the results for the five Eurocurrency markets show that, not surprisingly in this case, the total risk premium is mostly driven by reward for exposure to currency risk.

The large negative premium for non-EMU currency risk is an interesting finding which requires an explanation. The definitions of risk premia introduced earlier in this chapter imply that each premium is affected by two components: covariance risk and the corresponding shadow price. In Table 7.6 we report summary statistics for the estimated prices of risk. For the three non-EMU currencies it is obvious that the most relevant risk factor is the US dollar, since its price is more than four times the price of either British pound or Japanese yen risk. In addition, the average price of dollar risk is statistically significant and negative. As a consequence, the negative premium for non-EMU currency risk stems from positive average covariance risk and negative average shadow prices. This suggests that investors are willing to forgo part of the market premium to hold assets whose DM-denominated return is positively correlated with the relative change of the DM–US dollar exchange rate.[18] In other words, investors are willing to pay a premium to hold assets which provide a good hedge against fluctuations of the US dollar. This is possibly due to the fact that most investors include (directly or indirectly) dollar-denominated goods in their consumption basket.

---

[18] We omit the British pound and the Japanese yen from this discussion owing to their smaller relevance (see Table 7.6).

4.3. European liberalization and currency premia

One potentially interesting date to study in our sample is 1 July 1990. The European Community set that date as the deadline for its country-members to complete the process of financial liberalization.[19] It would be difficult to implement a direct test of structural change within the ICAPM that we estimate; therefore, in Table 7.5 and Figure 7.8 we propose a simple, albeit not as general, test for the hypothesis that financial liberalization has affected the average premia for currency risk. For each asset, we test the null hypothesis of a structural change in the average currency premium (aggregate, EMU-specific and non-EMU) and we choose July 1990 as the shifting point. The results can be summarized as follows. The change in the average aggregate currency premium is statistically significant in five out of six cases. All significant changes are rather large in size and negative. In the most extreme cases, the average currency premium for the US equity market reaches a value lower than –6 per cent per year after July 1990. The disaggregation between EMU and non-EMU currency premia is equally interesting. The average EMU premium is positive, but mostly rather low and in four out of six cases it is not statistically different after July 1990, relative to the earlier period. On the other hand, the non-EMU component of the premium is negative and significantly larger in the last part of the sample for five of the six equity indexes.

These findings are better understood after looking at the evidence on the changes in the prices of currency risk reported in Table 7.6. The prices of both US dollar and Japanese yen risk are significantly more negative in the post-1990 period, whereas the prices of risk for the two EMU currencies and the British pound are significantly more positive. In absolute terms, the combined change in price for the French franc and Dutch guilder is considerably larger than the change for the three remaining currencies. Yet our results show that the change in premium associated with the EMU currencies is relatively smaller and statistically insignificant. Given the definition of currency risk that we use, this suggests that risk exposure to the EMU currencies has declined in the last part of the sample.

To summarize, also from this perspective, the elimination of EMU-specific currency risk appears to be of relatively little relevance to investors.

5. Discussion and Concluding Remarks

In this study, we analyse the impact of European Monetary Union and, more specifically, of a single European currency on European and world equity markets. This requires an in-depth examination of currency risk and of its EMU and non-EMU components. We use the approach of De Santis and Gerard (1998) to investigate the economic and statistical relevance of currency risk for both European and non-

---

[19] See Carrieri (1997) for a study of the effects of European liberalization on the price of currency risk.

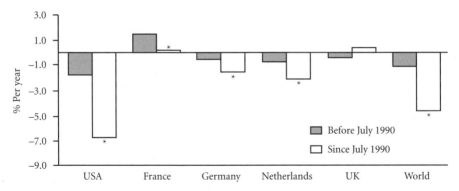

Figure 7.8(a). Structural changes in aggregate currency premia

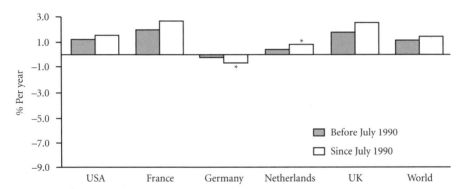

Figure 7.8(b). Structural changes in EMU currency premia

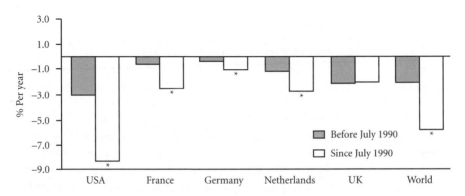

Figure 7.8(c). Structural changes in non-EMU currency premia

European equity markets, an issue that, surprisingly, has received little attention thus far.

It is clear that, in addition to the liquidity and transaction costs benefits, the adoption of the single currency will reduce the risk exposure of international investors. It is usually taken for granted that a decline in risk is always a desirable outcome. In fact, the issue of whether a decrease in risk is beneficial is complex. It depends on whether the risk that will be eliminated is fully diversifiable and, to the extent this risk is not diversifiable, on the reward investors receive for bearing it (i.e. the reward-to-risk ratio). The elimination of a source of risk, as will be the case under a single European currency, could have no impact, a positive impact or even, more surprisingly, a negative impact on investors' risk–return trade-offs. For example, if EMU currency risk is fully diversifiable, then the adoption of a single currency will have limited benefits for international portfolio investors. On the other hand, if EMU currency risk is not diversifiable but commands a premium, the adoption of a single currency will reduce the menu of assets available to investors and affect the expected returns of international portfolios.

In the context of EMU, the relevant issues are: how important is the EMU currency risk in both absolute and relative terms compared to its non-EMU counterpart, and by how much have international investors been rewarded for their exposure to EMU currency risk? These questions can only be addressed by looking at past evidence. We examine both equity and Eurodeposit markets over the last twenty-three years. Three main results emerge from our investigation:

1. Currency fluctuations induce a systematic source of risk in returns. However, the EMU component is small relative to the non-EMU component (dollar, yen and pound). The most relevant currency risk factor is linked to the US dollar.
2. Currency risk is priced. The EMU currency risk commands a positive but small risk premium. The non-EMU currency risk premium is negative, which suggests that investors are willing to forgo part of their expected returns to hold assets that provide a hedge against currency risk.
3. Currency risk and its impact on returns vary over time as a function of changes in economic conditions and the institutional environment. In particular, the risk exposure of international equity markets to the EMU currencies has declined significantly since 1990.

What do these findings imply for the transition to a single currency? First, to the extent that exposure to EMU currency risk is systematic, asset return volatility is likely to decrease, both for European and non-European equity markets. Secondly, since investors are rewarded with a positive premium for being exposed to the EMU currency risk, its elimination will also reduce expected returns on international equities. However, it will still be the case that all markets will be subject to the large and dominant impact of the non-EMU currency risk. When combined with the recent decline in the EMU component of exchange risk, these results suggest that the adoption of a single currency will have a limited impact on international asset prices, risk and expected returns.

Our findings also yield interesting insights about the 'home bias' phenomenon. Common wisdom and academic research suggest that European unification is likely to increase investments by EU residents in stocks from non-EU countries and decrease the 'home bias'. The existence of a single currency, the emergence of European pension funds, the reduction of informational and agency costs, and the computerization and interconnection of trading centres are often quoted as the key drivers of such a change (see, for example, Biais, 1997). The results of our study challenge this view. Given its relative small size and the positive premium it commands, the EMU currency risk is unlikely to be responsible for the 'home bias' observed in the past.

In addition, our findings suggest that if the home bias will indeed decrease in the future, European investors are more likely to diversify into non-European equities, for at least two reasons. First, as documented by Heston and Rouwenhorst (1994), the low correlations of European equity markets observed in the past can be explained by country-specific rather than industrial structure. This is because macroeconomic disturbances are shared by all firms within a country, but not across countries. In Europe, the country-specific components include local monetary and fiscal policies, differences in institutional and legal regimes, and regional economic shocks. Under EMU, this heterogeneity is likely to disappear. Though the issue is not directly addressed here, one would expect to observe an increase in the correlation of European equity markets and hence lower diversification benefits, forcing European investors to look at non-EMU equity markets to diversify risk.

The second reason is related to the currency risk associated with the consumption of foreign goods. A natural hedge for this risk is provided by an investment in foreign assets. The empirical evidence in this chapter suggests that assets are used as a hedge for consumption-induced currency risk. For example, we document that investors are willing to forgo part of their expected returns, in the form a negative risk premium, to hold assets that provide a hedge against fluctuations of the US dollar. This presumably stems from the fact that dollar-denominated goods constitute a significant fraction of their consumption basket. With the adoption of the euro, the currency risk related to the EMU component of the consumption basket will disappear for European consumers. They will be left with the currency risk arising from the consumption of non-European goods only. Unless European consumers modify substantially their consumption basket (towards more European goods), this could reduce their incentives to hold European equities as a hedge and increase their incentives to hold non-EMU equities.

Overall, the investigation leads us to believe that, beyond the benefits of enhanced liquidity, lower transactions costs and improved transparency in cross-country investments, the adoption of the single currency will have limited impact on international asset prices, risk and expected returns. Further it is likely to increase the flow of investments towards markets outside the EMU.

References

Adler, Michael and Bernard Dumas (1983), 'International Portfolio Selection and Corporation Finance: A Synthesis', *Journal of Finance*, 46: 925–84.

Biais, Bruno (1997), 'European Stock Markets and European Unification', unpublished manuscript, University of Toulouse.

Bollerslev, Tim and Jeffrey M. Wooldridge (1992), 'Quasi-Maximum Likelihood Estimation and Inference in Dynamic Models with Time-Varying Covariances', *Econometric Reviews*, 11: 143–72.

Bollerslev, Tim, Ray T. Chou and Kenneth F. Kroner (1992), 'ARCH Modeling in Finance', *Journal of Econometrics*, 52: 5–59.

Carrieri, Francesca (1997), 'Integration, Liberalization and Currency Risk in the European Economic Community', unpublished manuscript, Dept. of Economics, University of Southern California.

De Santis, Giorgio and Bruno Gerard (1997), 'International Asset Pricing and Portfolio Diversification with Time-Varying Risk', *Journal of Finance*, 52: 1881–912 (forthcoming).

De Santis, Giorgio and Bruno Gerard (1998), 'How Big is the Premium for Currency Risk?' *Journal of Financial Economics*, 49 (forthcoming).

De Santis, Giorgio, Bruno Gerard and Pierre Hillion (1997), 'The Relevance of Currency Risk in the EMU', unpublished manuscript, Marshall School of Business, University of Southern California.

Dumas, Bernard and Bruno Solnik (1995), 'The World Price of Foreign Exchange Risk', *Journal of Finance*, 50: 445–79.

Elton, Edwin J. and Martin J. Gruber (1992), 'International Diversification', in Summer N. Levine (ed.), *Global Investing*, New York: Harper Business.

Eun, Cheol S. and Bruce G. Resnick (1988), 'Exchange Rate Uncertainty, Forward Contracts, and International Portfolio Selection', *Journal of Finance*, 43: 197–215.

Ferson, Wayne E. and Campbell R. Harvey (1993), 'The Risk and Predictability of International Equity Returns', *Review of Financial Studies*, 6: 527–67.

Frankel, Jeffrey (1995), 'Exchange Rates and the Single Currency', in B. Steil (ed.), *The European Equity Markets*, London: Royal Institute of International Affairs.

French, Kenneth R. and James M. Poterba (1991), 'Investor Diversification and International Equity Markets', *American Economic Review*, 81: 222–6.

Grauer, Frederick L. A., Robert H. Litzenberger and Richard E. Stehle (1976), 'Sharing Rules and Equilibrium in an International Market under Uncertainty', *Journal of Financial Economics*, 3: 233–56.

Heston, Steven L. and K. Geert Rouwenhorst (1994), 'Does Industrial Structure Explain the Benefits of International Diversification?' *Journal of Financial Economics*, 36: 3–27.

Hodrick, Robert J. (1981), 'International Asset Pricing with Time-Varying Risk Premia', *Journal of International Economics*, 11: 573–88.

Korajczyk, Robert A. and Claude J. Viallet (1989), 'An Empirical Investigation of International Asset Pricing', *Review of Financial Studies*, 2: 553–85.

Levy, Haim and Marshall Sarnat (1970), 'International Diversification of Investment Portfolios', *American Economic Review*, 60: 668–75.

Lintner, John (1965), 'The Valuation of Risk Assets and the Selection of Risky Investments in Stock Portfolios and Capital Budgets', *Review of Economics and Statistics*, 47: 13–37.

Newey, Whitney and Kenneth West (1987), 'A Simple Positive Semi-Definite, Heteroskedasticity and Autocorrelation Consistent Covariance Matrix', *Econometrica*, 55: 703–8.

Sercu, Piet (1980), 'A Generalization of the International Asset Pricing Model', *Revue de l'Association Française de Finance*, 1: 91–135.

Sharpe, William (1964), 'Capital Asset Prices: A Theory of Market Equilibrium under Conditions of Risk', *Journal of Finance*, 19: 425–42.

Solnik, Bruno (1974a), 'The International Pricing of Risk: An Empirical Investigation of the World Capital Market Structure', *Journal of Finance*, 29: 365–78.

Solnik, Bruno (1974b), 'Why not Diversify Internationally?' *Financial Analysts Journal*, 30: 48–54.

Solnik, Bruno (1995), 'Why not Diversify Internationally rather than Domestically?' *Financial Analysts Journal*, 51: 89–94.

Solnik, Bruno (1996), *International Investments*, 3rd. edn., Addison Wesley.

Stehle, R. (1977), 'An Empirical Test of the Alternative Hypotheses of National and International Pricing of Risky Assets', *Journal of Finance*, 32: 493–502.

Tesar, Linda L. and Ingrid M. Werner (1995), 'Home Bias and High Turnover', *Journal of International Money and Finance*, 14: 467–92.

8
European Stock Markets
and European Unification

BRUNO BIAIS

The goal of this chapter is to assess the current situation and the possible evolution of the European stock markets. What is and what could become their role in the European economy? How integrated are they currently and are they likely to be in the future? How do firms, investors, financial intermediaries and regulators intervene in the marketplace, and how are their respective roles likely to change?

In conducting this analysis we focus on the interaction between those issues and the European unification process. The latter includes European Monetary Union as well as the unification of regulation at the European level, or the interplay of political forces leading to or hindering European integration. We also try to build on recent theoretical, empirical and experimental work analysing the microstructure of markets, privatizations, corporate finance and investments, and rely on the insights it delivers, while omitting the technical aspects of these analyses.

The first section surveys the current situation of the European stock markets. The relative underdevelopment of Continental stock markets is documented and related to the financing and governance patterns of Continental European firms: the limitations of the financing and of the governance of firms by their outside shareholders are emphasized. It is also argued that the privatization wave as well as the reforms and improvements in the microstructure of the markets which have taken place over the last fifteen years have somewhat reduced the underdevelopment of European stock markets. Finally, empirical results documenting the significant home-country bias affecting the portfolio choices of European investors are reported. It is argued that this pattern is likely to be related to (1) regulatory constraints on portfolio choices, and (2) asymmetric information and agency costs related to investment in foreign shares.

The second section briefly investigates the likely short-term evolutions of European stock markets, in relation to European Monetary Union. It is argued that no radical alterations should be expected in the short term as regards such structural factors as corporate governance patterns or the asymmetric information costs associated with investments in foreign stocks. Yet regulatory restrictions on investments in foreign stocks could be alleviated (in particular if they were challenged at the European Court of Justice), since the argument for 'investors' protection' (against foreign exchange risk) would no longer apply.

The third section offers some conjectures on the medium- to long-term evolution of the European stock markets. We first mention some structural trends, such as the growing importance of technology in the workings of markets, and the necessity for households to save and invest more in stocks, given the changes in the pension system. We argue that in this context large Europe-wide pension funds are likely to emerge. We also argue that restrictions on investments in stocks of foreign countries should be lifted within Europe, to improve the allocation of capital. Such a lift is possible, in part thanks to the enhanced coordination on regulatory policies that the European unification could bring about.

Secondly, we discuss how these evolutions should affect the behaviour of investors, firms, brokers and dealers, markets and regulators. As regards investors, we argue that because of (1) the likely reduction in regulatory restrictions on investments in foreign stocks, (2) the enhanced dissemination of financial information owing to the computerization of markets, and (3) the European scope of large pension funds, the home bias could be reduced within Europe. As regards firms, we discuss how the behaviour of these large funds will be crucial for the evolution of corporate governance and stock markets in Europe, and as a result for the financing of corporations. As regards markets, we argue that while it is possible that trading in European stocks could become concentrated on one single marketplace, there is no compelling reason to believe that this will indeed be the case. It is quite possible, on the contrary, that a few market centres might coexist, competing for the supply of efficient market information, order routing, order execution and settlement and delivery systems. We also argue that, in this context, it is crucial that transparency and priority rules be enforced by regulation at the European level. In the absence of such a regulation, market organizers would face a prisoner's dilemma. Although it would be socially optimal to enforce transparency and priority, each market might have incentives to allow some opacity and to violate execution priority established on other markets.

The last section offers some concluding comments.

1. The Current Situation

1.1. Stock markets are less developed in Continental Europe than in the UK and the USA

As can be seen in Table 8.1, the size of Continental European stock markets, both in terms of capitalization and in terms of numbers of households owning shares, is much smaller than that of their Anglo-American counterparts.

This contrast between Continental Europe and the UK and the USA is related to the contrast between the Continental European 'bank-based' system and the Anglo-American 'market-based' system. In the former, banks collect funds from households and allocate them to firms in the form of loans. In the latter, households invest their savings in securities, traded on markets, and firms raise their fundings on these

Table 8.1. Size of stock markets in the USA, the UK, Germany and France

	Stock market capitalization/ GDP, 1995	% Change/1986	% Households owning shares, 1997
France	43.5	1.22	0.11
Germany	36.2	0.40	0.07
UK	1.71	1.04	0.18
USA	1.14	1.29	0.28

Sources: 1995 data on stock market capitalization and GDP are from *L'Ex-pansion*, 15 May 1997; data on 1986 market capitalization and GDP are from Rajan and Zingales (1995); data on households' shareholdings are from the *Wall Street Journal Europe*, 12 May 1997.

markets. Although this picture is quite stereotypical, and not entirely adequate, it is true that the relative roles of banks and markets are quite different in Continental Europe and in the UK or the USA.

Note that, in the context of a bank-based system, it may be quite difficult for a firm to move towards market financing. Indeed, a crucial agent in this move would be the firm's banker, who has superior information about the performance of the firm and its prospects. Yet it is possible that the firm's banker has few incentives to favour this move. If the firm switches from bank financing to market financing he loses a customer, and hence a source of compensation. Indeed, even if the same bank stays in charge of engineering the IPO or the securities issues of the firm, this task (and the associated compensation) will be given to a different service in the bank, and the banker who previously managed the loans to this firm will lose this business.

Franks and Mayer (1997) present interesting new empirical evidence enabling one to better understand the difference between bank-based and market-based systems, from the point of view of corporate control. They show that, while the ownership of large US or UK corporations is widely dispersed among a large number of institutions and individuals, in France and in Germany corporations are to a very large extent held by other companies. Table 8.2 presents empirical evidence from their paper.

Now, it is likely that this cross-holdings system is not very conducive to the development of large stock markets. Once control of one company is in the hands of a close group of corporations (the managers of which have incentives to cooperate in the long term to maintain their collective position), it is not very attractive to purchase shares of this company. Indeed the management of that company is not likely to be driven by the consideration of minority shareholders. In this context, it is quite difficult for companies to raise funds through equity issues. On the one hand, potential in-vestors are not willing to purchase shares unless managers give up the system of cross-ownership and the associated interlocking of control. On the other hand, managers are not willing to give up this system because they want to keep the private benefits of control.

Table 8.2. Share stakes in excess of 25% in German and French companies, 1991[a]

Shareholder	% Of firms for which one shareholder of this type held 25% of the shares	
	Germany	France
Bank	5.8	6.4
Other company	37.2	56.6
Family	20.5	7.5

[a] The sample consists of 171 German and 155 French industrial and commercial quoted companies.

Source: Franks and Mayer (1997).

1.2. But privatizations have led to an increase in the size of stock markets

The privatization wave that has taken place in the last fifteen years has contributed to an increase in the size of the European stock markets. The increase in the size of the French market between 1986 and 1995 illustrates this trend.

In the UK the privatization wave mainly took place between 1977 and 1991. Between 1979 and 1991, the net proceeds of privatizations in the UK amounted to £36,851 million (see Perrotti and Guney, 1993). Table 8.3 (which reproduces data given in Perrotti and Guney, 1993) documents the pattern of privatization proceeds in the UK between 1979 and 1991.

In France there were two waves of privatizations, one in 1986–8 (when J. Chirac

Table 8.3. Privatization proceeds in the UK (£m.)

	Proceeds
1979	290
1981	373
1982	611
1983	862
1984	4,655
1985	1,602
1986	6,963
1987	3,541
1988	2,500
1989	5,239
1990	5,181
1991	5,034

Source: Perrotti and Guney (1993).

Table 8.4. Number of shareholders in France

	No. (millions)	% Of total population
1982	1.7	2.98
1987	6.2	10.87
1992	4.5	7.89
1994	7.0	12.28
1997	6.27	11.0

Source: Rapports Commission des Opérations de la Bourse.

became Prime Minister), the other in 1993–5 (when E. Balladur became Prime Minister). The total proceeds from the first wave amounted to 80 billion French francs. During the second wave, in 1994 the proceeds from the privatizations of Elf, UAP and Renault amounted to 27.5 billion French francs.

These privatization waves both in the UK and in France resulted in a large increase in the number of shareholders. As shown in the Table 8.4 the number of shareholders in France rose from 1.7 million in 1982 (a little less than 3 per cent of the population) to 6.27 million in 1997 (around 11 per cent of the population). Table 8.4 suggests that, although the effect of each of the two privatization waves is partly transient, it also has a permanent component.

1.3. And structural reforms have contributed to increasing the role and efficiency of stock markets in Europe

1.3.1. *The reform of the London market*

The first step in the modernization of European stock markets was taken by the London Stock Exchange in 1986. The traditional division of labour between brokers and jobbers was repealed. Access to the market-making business was considerably liberalized, and in particular the entry of foreign institutions was allowed. Brokerage commissions became negotiable. The stamp duty was halved for British equity and suppressed for foreign equity. A screen-based system was adopted, inspired by the American NASDAQ. In this new trading system the trading floor was replaced by computerized quotations and telephone negotiations. These reforms considerably increased the efficiency of the London market, and attracted a large fraction of the order flow from Continental exchanges to the International SEAQ.

1.3.2. *The response of the Continental European markets*

Continental European exchanges reacted to this competitive threat:[1]

---

[1] Excellent bird's-eye views of recent developments in European financial markets are offered by Benos and Crouhy (1996) and Pagano (1997).

- The Paris Bourse moved to continuous and computerized trading. Stockbrokers became incorporated and banks and financial institutions were allowed to own shares in the equity capital of the stockbrokers. These new, incorporated broker-age houses were allowed to act as agents (transmitting the orders of their customers) and as principals (engaging in proprietary trading). The stamp duty was repealed for foreign investors. The strong priority and transparency system prevailing on the Bourse was somewhat alleviated for block trades. Based on original data collected directly from brokers, the empirical analysis of Gresse and Jacquillat (1995) is consistent with the hypothesis that, as a result of these reforms, the migration of the order flow to London was stopped and even somewhat reversed.
- In 1989, the Bolsa de Valores in Madrid moved to computerized trading, opened the capital of the brokers to domestic and foreign financial institutions, and allowed them to act as principals and as agents. Also, commissions were deregulated.
- The same year, the Bourse de Bruxelles moved to an electronic limit order market. Among other reforms, in 1990 off-exchange trades were allowed, provided they did not deviate from the previous central market trade by more than 2.5 per cent.
- In Germany, a continuous screen-based system called IBIS was launched in 1991. The German stock exchanges were united in a single corporation: Deutsche Börse A.G. Yet trading remained somewhat fragmented among the regional exchanges. As discussed below (in Section 3) trading in Germany is becoming more and more centralized, however.

1.3.3. *The microstructure of European stock markets*

While London still plays a major role and is an active trading centre for many stocks of Continental Europe firms, the Continental European exchanges have been quite successful at reversing the migration of the order flow.

Competition between financial centres has led to improvements in market architectures and efforts to trim down costs. The competitive threat represented by the London stock market has had very positive consequences for the efficiency of the European stock markets in general.

Competition between trading systems has also led to some convergence between the different types of market structures. On the one hand, centralized Continental European exchanges, such as the Paris Bourse, the Bourse de Bruxelles and the Bolsa de Valores in Madrid, have introduced block trading facilities. Thus they have given investors some flexibility to trade large amounts outside the centralized market. On the other hand, the limit order market model is now recognized as extremely efficient in serving the needs of investors. Since October 1997, the shares of the 100 largest British companies have been traded on the London Stock Exchanges within an electronic order book (the 'Stock Exchange Electronic System'), which is very similar to the French limit order market created in 1986. Table 8.5 offers a comparison of the features of the French limit order market (CAC) and its English counterpart (SETS). The table shows that although both trading systems are order-driven, they exhibit some differences. In

Table 8.5. Comparison between the Paris and London computerized limit order books

Paris Bourse (CAC)	London Stock Exchange (SETS)
Pre-opening: 08:30 to 10:00; indicative prices	Pre-opening: 08:00 to 08:30; no indicative prices
Trading: 10:00 to 17:00	Trading: 08:30 to 16:30
Five best limits are observable in the book	Only the best limit is observable
Retail trades, as other trades, placed and executed in the limit order book	The largest brokers execute retail orders off the limit order book at prices within the best quotes

particular, the limit order book in Paris is more transparent than its London counterpart. First, during the pre-opening period, indicative prices can be observed in the Paris Bourse but not in the London market.[2] Secondly, while the five best limits are observable in continuous time in the CAC system, in SETS only the best limit is displayed.

These evolutions have paralleled the growth in institutional trading in European stocks. Clearly, institutions strongly demanded that brokerage commissions be negotiable, and also insisted on being given facilities to trade blocks. Also, the connections of large institutional traders to the major European financial centres enabled them to arbitrage between the different European stock markets. Further, the move to a limit order market in London was spurred by the demands of large foreign institutions.

Another important driving force was the European Directive on Investments, which allowed members of all European stock exchanges to become members of other exchanges and conduct trades, without having to set up local subsidiaries. This facilitated interventions by brokers and hence investors outside their home market.

1.4. European investors, however, still tend to favour home-country stocks in their portfolio choices

As documented for example in Cooper and Kaplanis (1995), investors bias their portfolio holdings in favour of their home market. Hence they benefit much less from international diversification than they could. Table 8.6 (which reproduces data presented in Cooper and Kaplanis, 1995) shows the significance of this phenomenon.

By investing 92 per cent of their equity portfolio in French shares, French investors forgo very large diversification benefits. Even UK investors, who are relatively the most prone to international diversification, invest much less in foreign stocks than prima-facie evidence on international diversification would suggest they should. What are the

---

[2] Biais *et al.* (1997) show that the indicative prices during the pre-opening period in the Paris Bourse have significant informational content.

Table 8.6. The home bias in the equity portfolios of institutional investors, 1993

	Market capitalization as % of OECD	% Portfolio in domestic stocks
France	4	92
Germany	3	78
UK	10	69
USA	42	95

Source: Cooper and Kaplanis (1995).

causes of this home bias? Financial economists have identified a number of potential causes.

Adler and Dumas (1983) show that, to the extent that there are deviations from Purchasing Power Parity, investors in different countries consuming different bundles of goods are exposed to different risks and therefore should hold different portfolios. Hence the domestic CAPM result that all investors should hold the market portfolio does not extend to the international context. Could that explain the home bias? Cooper and Kaplanis (1995) show that the observed magnitude of the home bias exceeds the differences in portfolios across countries which would be predicted by this model for reasonable parameter values.

Another potential explanation is that investing abroad could lead to large transactions costs, which would more than offset any diversification benefits. If this was the explanation, however, then in order to save on those costs, portfolio managers would be expected to choose a much lower turnover for their international holdings. Yet, quite to the contrary, Tesar and Werner (1995) have shown empirically that the turnover on internationally invested portfolios is larger than that on domestic portfolios.

Yet another candidate explanation is that investors would be deterred from investing abroad because they would be unwilling to bear foreign exchange risk. This cannot be the explanation, however, since exchange rate risk is relatively easy to hedge, for example by using currency futures. Further, Smith and Sofianos (1997) find that trading and investment in foreign stocks increases after they become listed on the NYSE, while such listing obviously cannot generate a decrease in the exchange rate risk.

Regulations can impose barriers to foreign stock holdings. For example in 1993 Germany foreign investments were limited to 5 per cent of the value of the portfolios of insurance companies and pension funds (see Folkerts-Landau and Goldstein, 1994). Another example is the case of France, where the 'Plans d'Epargne en Actions' offer fiscal support to investment in French shares, but not foreign shares. Also there are some regulatory constraints on the investments of French mutual funds (OPCVM) in foreign stocks. Overall, it is likely that regulatory constraints on foreign investments are one of the causes of the home bias.

It may also be the case that foreign investors are less well informed than local investors about the prospects of the local firms and economy. This may be due to less casual exposure to everyday news, to more difficult access to sources of private information (owing to less good connections with insiders), or to lesser ability to interpret data about the country.[3] Gehrig (1993), Kang and Stulz (1994), and Brennan and Cao (1996) analyse theoretically the consequences of such information asymmetries on international portfolio choices. They show that in this context there is indeed a home bias: investors tilt their portfolios in favour of their home-country stocks, on which they have superior information. The intuition is that less-informed foreign investors suffer from a winner's curse: their buy orders tend to get filled when the market goes down, while their sell orders tend to be executed when the market goes up. This reduces the profitability of investments in foreign shares and therefore deters international diversification.

Yet if informational disadvantages to local investors and traders caused institutions to forgo very valuable international diversification benefits, one would expect that they could design ways of alleviating these informational problems. One way to do so would be to hire local traders, based abroad, who could monitor foreign markets, analyse their evolutions and conduct portfolio allocations. This could be done by setting up a local branch or by delegating investments to local brokers. This strategy can certainly mitigate partially the above-mentioned information problems. It has some drawbacks, however. First it is rather costly to set up a local branch. Secondly, and maybe more importantly, agency problems can arise once portfolios decisions are delegated to brokers or traders located abroad and having access to information that the central organization does not have. On the one hand, the local agent may have little incentive to follow appropriate strategies since the informational disadvantage of the central organization makes monitoring difficult.[4] On the other hand, the local agent might be tempted to collude with local investors and traders, at the expense of the foreign-based investor, which would enhance the above-mentioned winner's curse problem. To the extent that these agency problems are significant (which seems plausible) they can go a long way towards providing an explanation for the home bias.

2. The Near Future

2.1. Short-term consequences of EMU for investment and trading in stocks

By definition, monetary union will eliminate foreign exchange risk within the countries adopting the single currency. Note, however, that a significant fraction of European countries will not join EMU immediately. For those countries, exchange rates with the euro may remain quite volatile. Also, the use of only one currency will facilitate accounting and the measurement of value.

---

[3] Consistent with this view, Shiller *et al.* (1996) present empirical evidence of differences in expectations between investors from different countries.

[4] The Barings crisis may be viewed as an example of the difficulties of such monitoring.

These two facts, along with other steps taken towards European integration (such as competition policy), could contribute to some alignment in the economic fundamentals of the countries adopting the single currency. The decrease in the transactions costs associated with foreign currency exchange could also lead to an increase in intra-European trade and facilitate mergers and financial integration of Europe-wide industrial or services groups.

2.2. Possible short-term effects in Europe

As discussed in Section 1, it is likely that the home bias is not due to foreign exchange rate risk. Rather it is likely to stem from regulatory and institutional constraints on investment in foreign markets and from asymmetric information and agency problems arising when investing abroad.

To the extent that it cannot immediately lead to a significant decrease in informational asymmetries, European Monetary Union should not be expected to lead directly to much greater European diversification of equity portfolios. It is only in the long run that European unification will alleviate such problems. We analyse the prospects for this evolution in the next section.

Regulatory restrictions on investments in foreign assets (bearing on mutual funds or pension funds) used to be motivated by the need to protect investors from foreign exchange risk. Even with volatile European exchange rates, this type of argument is rather questionable, since investors desiring to avoid exchange rate risk are always left the choice to invest in domestic funds. Anyhow, within the context of European Monetary Union, this 'investor's protection' argument cannot be used any more. Hence, it can be expected that regulatory restrictions on foreign investments will be lifted, especially if they are challenged at the European Court of Justice. The economics of these restrictions and the long-term prospects regarding their evolution are examined in the next section

Yet, to the extent that trading in a single currency facilitates accounting and reduces the administrative complexity of investing in foreign equities, European Monetary Union might lead to an increase in foreign investment between countries adopting the single currency.

Further, investors from countries outside Europe, such as US pension funds, might also find attractive the enhanced simplicity obtained by the switch from multiple currencies to a single European currency.

These benefits, however, will only accrue to the extent that operationally the stock exchanges and market participants are able to switch from trading and values denominated in national currencies and euros. This involves significant restructuring of clearing, settlement and delivery, and back-office operations.[5] Market centres and financial institutions unable to cope efficiently with this switch are likely to be in an

---

[5] For example, the Paris Bourse has already engaged significant investments in computer systems to be able to quote, trade and clear stocks in euros in 1999.

uncomfortable situation, and might oppose or to try to slow down the European Monetary Union process. On the other hand, those institutions and market centres well prepared to accommodate the shift from an operational point of view should enjoy relatively strong competitive positions. This suggests that technology issues are a significant aspect of the consequences of European Monetary Union for equity markets.

3. The Medium- and Long-Term Prospects

The prospects of long-term evolutions presented below are not necessarily directly related to *monetary* unification only. Rather we try to take a look at the global picture, taking into account some other important factors in the evolution of securities markets, such as the political and technological context.

3.1. Changes in investment and trading strategies

3.1.1. *Stock markets are likely to rely more and more on computerized networks*

The technology used in the marketplace has experienced very significant changes during the last ten years and is likely to experience further major evolutions. It is likely that markets will increasingly operate on the basis of computerized networks. Maybe floors will disappear. Indeed computerized networks are less costly to maintain than trading floors or pits. Also they are likely to generate more efficient facilities in terms of transmission and processing of the information, as well as in terms of connection of (1) different marketplaces or clearing systems and (2) the trading side with the clearing and settlement side.

3.1.2. *Structural changes in the European pension systems will make it more necessary for households to save and invest in stocks*

European state pensions systems are for the most part 'pay-as-you-go' systems whereby, at a given point in time, the pensions of the current retirees are paid by the

Table 8.7. Unfunded pension liabilities as a percentage of GDP

	Unfunded pension liability
Belgium	153
France	102
Germany	62
Italy	60
UK	24
USA	23

Source: *The Wall Street Journal Europe*, 12 May 1997: 8.

current workers. Now, owing to changes in the demographic structure, the number of workers per retiree is due to decline sharply. This will make it difficult to maintain state pensions at their current level. Statistics reported in the *Wall Street Journal Europe* and presented in Table 8.7 show that in Continental Europe unfunded pension liabilities are ominously large.

In this context, it is reasonable to expect that households will need to engage more and more in savings and investments to finance their future retirement pensions. This is likely to translate into a larger demand for stocks, either through direct investments from individuals or through funds.

3.1.3. *Regulatory and institutional constraints on foreign investment within the EU should and could be lifted*

As mentioned above there are currently a number or regulatory restrictions on investment in foreign stocks, in particular for funds. One official justification for these restrictions is that such foreign investments are deemed to be too risky. Although it is already possible to hedge foreign exchange risk (for example using currency futures), under European Monetary Union it will become even more obvious that foreign exchange risk cannot be a good reason not to invest in stocks from other members of the Union. Hence, regulatory restrictions on these investments will become even more difficult to justify.

In fact there are a number of reasons why restrictions on investments in foreign stocks should be lifted. First, very much in the spirit of the European Common Market, it is important not to hinder the allocation of scarce resources (here capital) across Europe where they are the most valuable. Hence it is important to let the market freely play its allocative role. Secondly, by hindering international diversification, restrictions on investment in foreign stocks increase the risk investors have to bear. Hence it increases the risk premium they require, which in turn raises the cost of capital. Consequently, restrictions on investment in foreign stocks reduce investment in the real economy and hence growth.

Does this mean that restrictions on investment in foreign stocks will be repealed once EMU is achieved? To analyse this issue one needs to investigate further what the motivations underlying restrictions on investment in foreign stocks could be.

A first possible motivation for regulatory restrictions on investment in foreign stocks is that, as discussed in the previous section, investing in foreign securities generates exposure to asymmetric information and agency costs. Note, however, that if those costs are such that investment in foreign stocks is not profitable, then rational investors will simply choose to invest only in domestic stocks, and the regulatory constraints will be useless. Hence, to justify regulatory constraints on investment in foreign stocks, one would need to appeal to some form of irrationality on the part of the investors, who would be unable to assess the costs of these investments. This does not seem very convincing.

An alternative motivation for regulatory restrictions on investment in foreign stocks is the following. Suppose that, owing to lobbying by corporations, governments decide on whether or not to enforce these regulations with a view to minimizing the cost of capital for domestic firms (and do not take into account the welfare of investors who would benefit from international diversification nor the impact of their decisions on foreign countries). Now, it is arguable that corporations in a given country prefer that their own country imposes such restrictions than not. Indeed, making it difficult and costly for investors in one country to buy stocks from other countries creates a captive clientele for domestic stocks in this country.

One can analyse this situation in a simple game-theoretic framework. For simplicity consider the case with two countries, denoted A and B.[6] Consider the simultaneous-move game whereby each country chooses whether or not to impose restrictions on investment in foreign shares. Suppose that the costs of capital for the firms in the two countries are as follows:

- If country A imposes restrictions on investments by its citizens in stocks of country B:
  - If country B also imposes restrictions on investments by its citizens in stocks of country A, then investors cannot benefit from the international diversification of risks, hence they end up bearing high risks, hence they demand a high risk premium, hence the cost of capital in the two countries is high, say 15 per cent.
  - Now consider the case where country B does not impose restrictions on investments by its citizens in country A. In this case the demand for the stocks of country A is large. Indeed, domestic investors in country A can only invest in home-country stocks. In addition, investors from country B are eager to invest in stocks of country A to reap the gains from international diversification. As a result of this large demand for stocks of country A, the cost of capital in this country will be low, say 10 per cent. Now, in country B, by contrast, the demand for stocks is rather low, since investors from country A cannot purchase stocks from country B, while investors from country B will allocate part of their savings to stocks from country A. Consequently the cost of capital for investors in country B will be high, say 16 per cent.
- If country A imposes no restrictions on the investments of its citizens in stocks of country B:
  - If country B does impose restrictions on investments by its citizens in stocks of country A, by symmetry with the case just above, the cost of capital in country A is large (16 per cent) while in country B it is low (10 per cent).
  - If country B does not impose restrictions on investments by its citizens in country A, investors from both countries can diversify internationally. This leads to a decrease in their risk exposure and hence in the risk premia they demand. As a result the cost of capital is low in the two countries. For example, suppose it is equal to 12 per cent.

The normal form of the game is represented in Table 8.8. This is in fact a prisoner's

---

[6] Similar results would obtain with n countries.

Table 8.8. The simple game where two countries (*A* and *B*) decide whether to impose constraints on investments in stocks of the other country

	A imposes restrictions	*A* does not impose restrictions
B imposes restrictions	*cost of capital in* country *A*: 15% country *B*: 15%	*cost of capital in* country *A*: 16% country *B*: 10%
B does not impose restrictions	*cost of capital in* country *A*: 10% country *B*: 16%	*cost of capital in* country *A*: 12% country *B*: 12%

dilemma. Assume the social optimum is when no country imposes restrictions on investment in foreign stocks. In this case the average cost of capital is minimized (and is equal to 12 per cent). Yet, for each country it is a dominant strategy to impose restrictions on investment in foreign stocks.

Consider the case of country *A*. If country *B* imposes such restrictions then country *A* prefers to impose constraints also (and obtain a cost of capital of 15 per cent) than not to impose them (and obtain a higher cost of capital of 16 per cent). On the other hand, if country *B* does not impose constraints, then country *A* prefers to impose constraints (and obtain a cost of capital of 10 per cent) rather than not to impose them (and obtain a cost of capital of 12 per cent). The average cost of capital in this dominant-strategy equilibrium is quite high (15 per cent). This is detrimental to social welfare. And to this social cost, one must add the welfare loss due to the inability of investors to diversify internationally.

This simple example illustrates why, while restrictions on investment in foreign stocks are detrimental to social welfare, they can still be chosen by rational governments seeking to minimize the cost of capital for their domestic firms.

How could European Monetary Union, and maybe more generally the European unification process, alter this bad equilibrium and enable the switch to the social optimum where there are no restrictions, the cost of capital is minimized and investors can diversify internationally?

First, the European Union could rule that these restrictions are illegal because they go against fair trade practices. After all they are a form of protectionism.

Secondly, European financial institutions with Europe-wide networks of bank branches, working with international institutional investors, and connected with Europe-wide networks of brokers may have incentives to lobby for the repeal of constraints on cross-border investments.

Thirdly, note that while the situation with no restrictions on investments in foreign stocks is socially optimal (as in the above example), it is a coordination failure between the two governments that prevents it from being attained. It is to be expected that supranational institutions, such as the European Union, would be able to cope with such coordination failure and could help governments coordinate on the social optimum. Suppose for example that the European Union proposed a regulation banning restrictions on investment in foreign stocks in all countries in the EU. Suppose further that this proposal stated that this regulation would be enforced only if all EU nations voted in favour of it. In the simple example above, the two governments would find it optimal from their point of view to vote in favour of the regulation. Consider for example the case of country A. If A votes in favour of the regulation, either B also votes in favour of it and the cost of capital for A's firms is 12 per cent, or B does not vote in favour of the regulation and the cost of capital is 15 per cent. On the other hand if A votes against the ban on restrictions over investment in foreign stocks, then the cost of capital is at least 15 per cent. Clearly it is preferable for A to vote in favour of the ban. For the same reason B also votes in favour of the ban. Hence the social optimum can be attained.

For these three reasons, one can hope that regulatory constraints on investments in foreign stocks will be lifted as the European unification process is carried further.

3.2. Consequences for stock markets and stock markets participants

3.2.1. *Consequences for investors*

As mentioned above, owing to the structural changes in pensions systems, households will need to save and invest more in securities. This will make it all the more important for them to benefit from international diversification. Also, it is likely that a large proportion of these investments will take place through funds. Hence the role of institutional investors is likely to go on increasing.

The following question arises in this context: will the European unification process be paralleled by a decrease in the home bias, and an increase in investments in stocks of other European countries?

We argued in Section 1 that the main causes of the home bias are likely to be (1) regulatory restrictions on investments in foreign stocks and (2) asymmetric information and agency issues arising when investing abroad.

We discussed above the benefits and likelihood of lifting the regulatory restrictions on investments in foreign stocks, and how this evolution is linked to the European unification process. In this respect, European unification is likely to be paralleled by a decrease in the home bias and an increase in investments by European investors in stocks from other European countries.

As far as the asymmetric information and agency costs of investing abroad are concerned, the following remarks can be made.

First, note that the cost of acquiring and processing information about companies in different countries is a fixed cost (it does not depend on the number of shares of each company that are bought). So is, to a large extent, the cost of monitoring the trading of stocks in a foreign country. Indeed such monitoring may require setting up local subsidiaries and communication networks. Now, it is likely that the pension funds that will emerge as a consequence of the restructuring of the European pensions systems will be rather large. Hence, for those institutions the fixed costs that must be incurred to be able to invest profitably in foreign stocks could be relatively negligible. Consequently, one can expect these large pension funds to be able to engage significantly in diversification across stocks from different European countries (provided there are no regulatory constraints preventing them from doing so).

Secondly, note that, as mentioned above, the markets are likely to become ever more computerized. This will facilitate the transmission of information about prices, trades and market conditions. This will make it easier for investors (and in particular institutional investors such as large pension funds) to monitor the quality of the execution of their orders. One can imagine that sophisticated institutional investors will be able to monitor the evolution of market liquidity and pricing on all major European equity markets, and compare this information on market condition with the execution price reported to them by their brokers. This is likely to reduce the informational and agency costs mentioned in Section 1 as a plausible cause of the home bias.

Consequently one can expect to observe in the medium term a reduction in the home-country bias within Europe. It is plausible that (in particular through pension funds) citizens from one European country will increasingly invest in the stocks of other European countries.

Of course, as the European unification process goes on, the economies of the different European countries are likely to become increasingly integrated. This will somewhat reduce the diversification benefits of spreading one's investments across these countries. But we do not expect that this effect will offset the above-mentioned likely trend towards more diversified European portfolios.

3.2.2. *Consequences for firms*

International diversification throughout Europe should enable the firms with the best investment projects to obtain better, larger, and cheaper financing. Note, however, that for this potential source of financing to be used in fact significant changes in the governance of Continental European firms will be needed. Indeed, as discussed above, within the current system of governance, investors may be reluctant to purchase shares of Continental European firms, while the managers of these firms are reluctant to accept the loss of private benefits of control which would ensue from a reform of this corporate governance system.

Yet, Europe-wide, pension funds, in charge of the investment of very large amounts of capital, might contribute to changing this system. They might indeed play the role of outside monitors, disciplining managers, and making sure that the maximization of the value of the shares is the objective of the firm. This is reminiscent of the role played by large funds in the USA. If this course of action was followed, then the Continental European financial system would become significantly closer to the Anglo-American market-based system. It is arguable that in this new system, investment in positive NPV firms' projects would be increased somewhat.

Note, however, that it is not clear whether European pension funds will actually play this role. Another model is indeed possible whereby the conduct of these funds would be very similar to the current behaviour of German banks. In this case, funds would not intervene in monitoring the management of companies, maybe in exchange for long-term cooperation on other dimensions. For example, one could imagine that to the extent that the managers of one company have some influence on which fund will be allocated the savings of their employees, they would favour those funds which commit not to follow an active monitoring policy.

One can fear that this latter evolution would be quite detrimental to the development of stock markets in Europe, as well as to investment and social welfare.

Finally, as mentioned in Section 1, European unification, and in particular EMU, is likely to facilitate the operations of European firms at the European level, either through trade or through some form of integration of ownership. Such European firms, with customers and suppliers throughout Europe, would be in a good position to raise capital at the European level. When customers or suppliers (in particular suppliers of financial services) in a given country have a good knowledge of the business and prospects of a firm, they are more likely to be willing to purchase shares issued by this firm. Indeed this knowledge reduces adverse selection about the value of the firm.

This likely trend towards industrial and services firms operating and raising funds at the European level should contribute to the reduction of the home bias in Europe. Shares issued by these companies would indeed reflect some averaging of the different national risks of the European countries.

3.2.3. *Consequences for brokers and market-makers*

The likely increase in the computerization of markets should facilitate the dissemination of information and the monitoring of the quality of the execution of trades. This should enhance the competition between market-makers and brokers, both within one exchange and across marketplaces.

Also, the likely development of large funds and institutional investors will shift the balance of power more in favour of these investors. Consequently they will be in a position to be more demanding with regard to the handling of their trades. Further, these large funds might increasingly demand improved facilities for the trading of medium-sized trades or large blocks. In addition these institutional investors might engage in some vertical integration and take stakes in brokers or securities houses.

Finally, since, as mentioned above, firms will have a tendency to operate more at the European level, and consequently also to raise capital at the European level, brokers will need to adapt and extend their own scope of operations. This could be achieved through the formation of Europe-wide brokerage houses able to match supply and demand of funds and of liquidity throughout Europe. Note that such Europe-wide brokerage houses should be less exposed to the asymmetric information and agency costs related to investment in foreign securities (as discussed in Section 1). This is another factor which should contribute to decreasing the home bias within Europe.

3.2.4. *Consequences for markets*

As the European unification process goes on, how will the European stock markets evolve? One major issue is the following: will there be one single large European stock market where trading and listing will be concentrated, or will different market centres coexist and compete?

Historical evidence. In the past, there has been a historical trend towards the concentration of trading in dominant market centres.[7] For example, while there were twenty-two stock exchanges in the USA in 1935, there are only ten left nowadays, among which the NYSE represents 95 per cent of the trading volume (see Smith, 1991). Similarly in France trading has migrated from the provincial bourses, such as Lille, Marseilles or Lyons, towards the Paris Bourse. Further evidence is provided by the case of Switzerland. The number of Swiss stock exchanges had decreased from eight to three in 1995. In 1996 these three exchanges (Zurich, Geneva and Basle) were integrated within the new single Electronic Exchange BES (Bourse Electronique Suisse). The German markets have been following the same trend. There were twenty-one stock exchanges in Germany during the Weimar republic. There are only eight today, among which Frankfurt plays a very dominant role.[8] As a final step towards the centralization of the German stock market, in 1996 the Deutsche Börse decided to switch to a centralized electronic market: XETRA. It replaced IBIS in 1997, and the different open-outcry markets in 1998.

Theoretical foundations. Why is there such a trend towards the concentration of trades? The theoretical analysis of Pagano (1989) offers useful insights regarding this issue. The intuition of his analysis is the following. Consider trading in one security. Suppose trading in that security can take place in two markets, *A* and *B*, with identical microstructures. First note that liquidity is a positive externality: if one agent desires to buy for liquidity reasons, this increases the liquidity of the market for the traders who desire to sell. Consequently, when one has the choice between two markets for the same security with identical microstructures, it is preferable to trade on the market where the majority of other investors have chosen to trade, since this market is the most liquid. In other words, liquidity attracts liquidity. The next step of this analysis is to study the Nash equilibrium of the game whereby traders choose to direct their trades to one or other of the two markets. Because of the above-discussed complementarity, if each trader expects that all the others will direct their trades to market *A*, then each trader strictly prefers to trade on this market. Hence there is a Nash equilibrium whereby all trading takes place on market *A*. By symmetry there also exists an equilibrium where all trading is on the other market, *B*. Finally, there exists a third equilibrium where half of the trading is on one market and the other half is on the other market. This third equilibrium is unstable, however. Indeed in that equilibrium each trader is indifferent between the two locations. Hence traders who in equilibrium are deemed to trade on market *A* might costlessly deviate to the other market (this contrasts with

---

[7] An insightful discussion of this pattern in offered in Gehrig *et al.* (1995).
[8] See Gerke and Rasch (1993).

the equilibrium where all trading is on market A, in which case traders *strictly* prefer to direct their orders to this market). Yet, if one trader was to deviate from market A to market B, then each of the other traders would then prefer to direct their orders to market B. Thus the equilibrium where trading is split equally between the two markets can be destabilized. The conclusion of this intuitive description of the theoretical analysis of Pagano (1989) is that, because liquidity attracts liquidity, it is natural to expect all trading in one security to be concentrated in one location, rather than split across markets.

Some prospective remarks. Does this analysis suggest that all trading in European stocks is likely to become concentrated in one single marketplace, such as London? There are a number of reasons why this conclusion might be premature:

1. Pagano (1989) analyses the case of one security. What would be the equilibrium outcome in an extension of this analysis to the case of many securities? For simplicity consider the case of two securities X and Y.

To study this case one needs to question whether there are spill-over effects from the liquidity of one security to the other. Suppose the share of a small, relatively unknown company trades on the same market as General Electrics? Does the liquidity of General Electrics spill over to that small stock? There is no obvious answer to this question. Maybe the broker in charge of routing orders for General Electrics could advise his clients to also place orders to buy or sell shares of that small company. On the other hand it could also be that the broker would be too busy dealing with orders for GE to worry about the small stock. To take a neutral stance on this issue we therefore assume that there is no negative or positive externality of the liquidity of one stock on the other.

In that case, the analysis of the venue for trades is separable for the different securities. There are four stable equilibria of the game where the traders independently and simultaneously choose where to route their orders in the two securities. In one equilibrium all orders are concentrated on market A; in the second all orders are concentrated on market B; in the third all orders for Y are on A while all the orders for Y are on B; in the last equilibrium all orders for Y are on B, while all orders for Y are on A.

This analysis suggests that while concentration of the trading of all European securities in one market is a possibility, another possible equilibrium entails concentration of the trading in one set of securities on one exchange and concentration of the trading in another set of securities on another exchange.

2. The above analysis focuses on a relatively direct trading situation, where the order of one investor is directly confronted with the order of another investor. In practice, however, brokers and sometimes dealers intermediate the order flow. How could this intermediation affect the location of the order flow? Delegating the management of one's order to a broker creates an agency problem. Such problems can be mitigated by appropriate incentive contracts. Yet when the asymmetric information between the principal and the agent is severe, the power of contracting may be limited. In this case, building relationships can help to alleviate agency problems. For example, if the

investor and the broker are engaged in a long-term relationship, involving a number of different services (order placement, block trading, placement of shares on the occasion of an IPO or a seasoned issue, etc.), then the principal can hold up the threat to terminate the relationship in order to induce the agent to perform. Further, after the principal and the agents have engaged in repeated interactions, the agent has had the opportunity to build a good reputation with the principal. Hence it is to be expected that the principal and the agent will continue to work with one another (except of course if the principal finds out that the agent is inefficient). Consequently there is a form of hysteresis or path-dependence, and investors are likely to continue routing their orders to the brokers they have been using in the past.[9] Now, a broker is likely to be from the same country as the investor. Hence, to the extent that the broker himself has a tendency to trade on his home market (maybe again because of relationships established in the past with the other participants in this market) the investor will also tend to execute his orders on the domestic market.

This analysis suggests that agency, reputation-building and relationship considerations may prevent to some extent the migration of the order flow from different countries to one single market.[10]

3. The above remarks do not take into account the differences which may exist between markets, both in terms of microstructure and in terms of technology. It may be that certain market architectures, such as relatively opaque dealer markets, serve better the needs of block traders, while other market structures, such as rather transparent computerized limit order markets, could better serve the needs of investors seeking to execute medium-size trades or to conduct programme trading. Still it is conceivable that one market centres could offer different trading facilities for different types of investors. This is the case for example on the NYSE, where the upstairs market and the floor coexist to serve the needs of different types of customers. It is also conceivable, however, that different market centres with different physical locations could specialize in offering different trading facilities. The reason why this latter outcome could emerge is that different trading facilities require different types of skills and capital, which may not be available simultaneously at the same marketplace. The efficient workings of a dealer market require the formation of the human capital and skill of efficient market-makers as well as the financial capital enabling them to bear large risky positions. On the other hand, the efficient workings of a computerized limit order book require mastering computer technology, investing in the associated physical capital, and the ability to open the system to other computerized trading devices, such as those required for programme trading for instance.[11]

---

[9] Note that this might work against the above-mentioned trend towards increased competition, at the European level, between brokers, possibly from different countries.

[10] Note, however, that the creation of Europe-wide brokerage houses should alleviate the above-discussed phenomenon.

[11] Note, however, that, as analysed by Davydoff (1997) one can observe a trend towards homogenization of microstructures of the European stock markets. For example, the London Stock Exchange is introducing a limit order trading facility. Symmetrically, the Paris Bourse has been developing block trading facilities.

To sum up the above remarks, while it is possible that trading in European stocks could become concentrated on one single marketplace, there is no compelling reason to believe that this will indeed be the case. It is quite possible, on the contrary, that a few market centres might coexist, competing for the supply of efficient market information, order routing, order execution and settlement and delivery systems.

What is the optimal system? This being said, what is the optimal system? Should trading be centralized or is it desirable that the order flow be split between a few exchanges?

One advantage to keeping competing markets is that it reduces the inefficiencies and rents associated with monopoly situations. It is likely for example that the modernization of the microstructure of the Paris Bourse that has taken place over the last ten years has been spurred by the competition of the London market. It might be the case on the other hand that the current move of London towards introducing limit order trading facilities is linked to the experience of the Paris Bourse.

There are some drawbacks to the fragmentation of the order flow, however. First, as shown theoretically by Pagano and Röell (1996) fragmentation can reduce the informational efficiency of prices. Secondly, if ex ante transparency between the different market centres is limited, fragmentation can lead to certain orders being executed outside the best available quotes on the market, and thus to an increase in transactions costs.[12] Thirdly, if priority rules are not enforced across market centres then the incentive to provide liquidity are reduced.[13] We discuss this issue further in the next subsection.

Still the move towards increased computerization should make it technologically possible to interconnect markets. In such a computerized network of markets, it would be possible to ensure that information would flow efficiently, and that priority rules would be enforced. Thus, informational efficiency can be restored, as well as transparency.

It must be noted, however, that the interconnection between markets is not only a matter of technology. It also depends on the strategy of the market organizers, who can decide whether or not to take the steps needed to interconnect the markets. Now, in certain circumstances, the organizers of the markets do not have incentives to do so. Consider for example the case of the regional exchanges in the USA. One way for them to prevent the order flow from migrating to the NYSE is to follow a policy of matching the best quote posted on that market. This clearly violates time priority, and as a consequence reduces the incentives of traders to place limit orders and hence decreases liquidity. Yet, the regional exchanges have no incentive to modify this approach, since it would reduce their market share.[14]

---

[12] Ex ante transparency refers to the ability to observe the current best offered and demanded price in the market. Ex post transparency refers to the ability to observe the previous trades.

[13] This problem is encountered in the USA where time priority is not enforced between the competing regional exchanges and the NYSE.

[14] Still, technology plays a role. It would be difficult in practice to enforce priority rules between the different markets in the USA. Since these markets are not interconnected in a computerized network it is impossible to enforce computerized trade-execution algorithms making sure that priority rules would be obeyed.

Hence the European stock markets will be connected, efficient information about market conditions will be provided, and priority rules will be followed only if there exists a centralized European regulatory body designing and enforcing these rules. We discuss this issue below.

3.2.5. *Consequences for regulators*

Transparency. Transparency can enhance the efficiency of securities markets. Ex ante transparency ensures that trades are routed to the best available quotes in the market, which minimizes transactions costs. Ex post transparency ensures that the informational content of trades is impounded in the following quotes and transactions prices, which enhances the informational efficiency of the market. In a recent experimental study Flood *et al.* (1997) show that transparency significantly enhances the price discovery process.

Yet, while all traders and market centres wish their competitors to display transparently their quotes and trades, they also have incentives to keep their own doings somewhat hidden.

- Individual traders may see it as being in their own interest to reduce ex post transparency regarding their own transactions. Consider a dealer purchasing a block of shares from a fund. This dealer has incentives to keep his purchase hidden, to avoid being taken advantage of by his competitors. Indeed on observing that he has a long position, which he needs to unwind, his competitors could be tempted to post rather low bid quotes.
- Market organizers may have incentives to reduce the ex ante transparency of their own market. One of the central tasks of stock exchanges is the discovery of the equilibrium valuation of shares. This involves a difficult process of *tâtonnement* and confrontation of offers and demands. This process is not only difficult, it is also costly: (1) the exchange must offer the technical facilities for the confrontation of supply and demand in the form of a trading floor or a computerized marketplace; (2) traders, brokers, market-makers and specialists must spend time and effort thinking through the order flow and inferring from it the information needed to value the security, as well as contributing to this order flow by the placement of offers to buy or sell. Now, once one market centre has incurred these costs and found the equilibrium value of the stock, other trading centres might be tempted to free-ride on this information.

It is possible that this free-rider problem between exchanges arises in the case of the NYSE and the US regional stock exchanges. Once price discovery has been achieved on the NYSE, other exchanges can use the publicly displayed transaction prices and best offers from this market to conduct their own trades.[15]

---

[15] In private conversation, an NYSE official told us that the main reason the NYSE did not have a formalized pre-opening procedure such as that used in the Paris Bourse was the fear that other market centres would free-ride on the price information thus generated.

It may also be the case that a similar problem arises in the coexistence of a relatively transparent market centre like the Paris Bourse and a somewhat more opaque market like the International SEAQ. For example, Pagano and Röell (1990) show that, before Paris opens (and hence before price discovery has been conducted on the Paris Bourse), dealer spreads are very large in London and very little trading takes place.

In the early 1990s the imposition of tight post-trade transparency standards at the European Union level was debated with regard to the drafting of the Investment Services Directive.[16] Around the same time, in the UK, the Office of Fair Trading argued in favour of post-trade transparency, and against long delays before trades are published. The basis of this position was that there is a risk that delays in publication could be anti-competitive.

This regulatory debate has not led to very strong policy moves, however. As regards European regulation, the transparency standards set in 1992 are rather minimal. In the UK, as a result of the action of the Office of Fair Trading it was decided that smaller transactions (of up to six times the median trade size) were to be reported immediately, while the larger trades could be reported with some delay (60 minutes except for the very largest trades). In fact, the impact of this regulation is weakened by the practice of 'protected trading' (see Franks and Schaefer, 1995). Suppose a dealer receives a rather large order to buy say 100,000 shares of stock *XYZ*. One possibility is for the dealer to sell to the customer on his own account, and to report the trade immediately. The problem from the perspective of the dealer is that once the others know he has a short position, they may quote him relatively large prices. Alternatively, the dealer can work the order through the market, by conducting on behalf of the customer a sequences of purchases, adding up to 100,000. Only when this sequence of purchases has been achieved is the deal with the customer finalized, and the trade reported. Thus, the trade is not reported before the dealer has, in effect, unwound his position. In addition, in such 'protected trades', the dealer sets a cap on the maximum price the customer might have to pay. The cost for the dealer of extending this option is offset by the benefits of not having to report the trade immediately. Although such protected trades are advantageous from the individual perspective of the dealer and his customer, they can be detrimental to the transparency and hence to the overall quality of the market. Board and Suttcliffe (1995) show empirically that 'protected trades' are very frequent in London. The practice of protected trades thus shows that even if the regulatory framework seeks to enhance transparency, there may exist ways for the players of the trading game to circumvent the regulatory constraints.

Another rationale for regulations favouring transparency is that even if the market as a whole benefits from transparency, it may be detrimental for some market participants. For example, Flood *et al.* (1997) find experimentally that while uninformed traders gain from an increase in transparency, this comes at a cost to the informed traders. This implies that traders with superior information might favour less transparent market regimes.

---

[16] Flood *et al.* (1997) provide a very insightful discussion of these issues.

As conclusion of this discussion one can note that there is a tension between the optimal regulation which should be implemented to ensure the efficiency and development of the European stock markets and the actual regulation which is likely to emerge:

- One the one hand, it is important that the regulator intervene, at the European level, to ensure that transparency is preserved. In the absence of such an intervention, there is a danger that a perverse equilibrium would prevail, whereby each market centre would find it individually optimal not to disseminate information about the prices and trades it generates, and that as a result a very low overall level of transparency would be achieved.
- On the other hand, it is not clear that such a regulatory framework will be effectively implemented. Indeed, as shown by the above discussion, there are two impediments to this. First, it is possible that regulation does not reflect only what is socially optimal, but also what benefits influential interests groups. The latter might include players of the trading game whose interest is not to enhance transparency. Secondly, even if regulation favours transparency, certain traders could be able to design clever schemes to circumvent the regulatory constraints.

Priority rules. The posting of limit orders and bid and ask quotes is essential for the liquidity of the market. Yet posting these offers is a risky activity. If the market rapidly moves away from its current level, before the traders have time to revise their offers, then they obtain unfavourable execution. Further, traders with superior information or insight about the market could assess whether these quotes deviate from the true value of the stock. In this case also, the quotes would obtain unfavourable execution. To be compensated for these risks, the traders posting limit orders or bid or ask prices demand a premium, which generates the bid–ask spread.

First consider a single marketplace. Consider a trader willing to supply liquidity when it is safe, and thus earn the spread, but not to bear the risk associated with this activity. Such a strategy can be implemented (to some extent) by monitoring the market, and announcing oneself to be ready to provide liquidity only when observing the arrival of orders demanding liquidity while the market pricing is not very volatile. Now, suppose there is no time priority. In this case, such 'opportunistic' traders can participate in these safe and profitable trades nearly as actively as traders who have taken the risk of previously posting firm quotes or limit orders. This reduces the profitability of limit orders and reduces the incentives to offer liquidity by posting these quotes. On the other hand, if there is time priority, then these 'opportunistic' traders must queue up after the traders who have placed limit orders or quotes previously. This improves somewhat the profitability of limit orders, and reduces that of opportunistic trading strategies. Consequently this increases the incentives to place limit orders or bid and ask quotes and thus improves the liquidity of the market. Hence, within a single market centre, it is important to enforce time priority, to give traders the appropriate incentives to supply liquidity.

Now consider the case where a number of trading centres are competing for the order flow. If there is no regulatory obligation to enforce time priority between trading centres, it is optimal for each marketplace to violate the time priority of the others, to increase its own market share. Similarly to the case of transparency, regulation is needed here to prevent the emergence of a bad equilibrium.

4. Conclusion

Prospective views offered by adepts of the dismal science have unfortunately often been quite far off the mark. There is no reason why the present chapter should be an exception to this rule. It might consequently be quite entertaining in a few years to compare the actual evolutions of the European stock markets to the conjectures offered in this work. These conjectures are summarized below.

European Monetary Union might have some long-term impact on stock markets but its direct and immediate impact is likely to be more limited. Its long-term indirect impact will be related to the more general process of European Unification, which will intertwine political, regulatory and economic aspects with the monetary process.

Two important driving forces for the unification and integration of the markets are likely to be the emergence of large Europe-wide pension funds and the computerization and interconnection of market centres.

Two important elements will be at the back of the evolution of the stock markets:

1. Technology will matter for the ability of markets (1) to benefit from the enhanced simplicity generated by a single currency and (2) to interconnect their price dissemination, order matching and settlement and delivery systems.
2. Political considerations (and their underpinnings in terms of lobbying) will interact with economic efficiency arguments when decisions are taken as to whether (1) regulatory constraints on investment in foreign stocks should be lifted and (2) Europe-wide regulation should be applied on such issues as transparency or priority rules for stock markets.

Two open issues are the following:

1. It is possible, but should not be taken for granted, that the emergence of large European pension funds will lead to a change in the pattern of corporate governance in Continental Europe.
2. Will the European stock markets integrate into one single market centre, or will a few markets coexist and compete? It is quite possible that a few market centres will coexist and compete for the supply of efficient market information, order routing, order execution and settlement and delivery systems.

The present chapter has also underscored the two following policy implications:

1. Regulatory constraints on investments in foreign shares should be lifted to facilitate and improve the efficiency of the allocation of capital within Europe.

2. European regulation should enforce transparency and priority rules so as to create the appropriate incentives for price discovery and liquidity supply.

There are of course many other dimensions of European unification and competitiveness than the monetary and financial aspects. Yet we believe that the efficiency with which European stock markets will play their role will matter for Europe's chances to remain a major player in the next century.

Finally, we would like to emphasize that the different aspects of financial markets are intertwined:

- Liquid stock markets reduce transactions costs and attract investors, which in turn reduces the cost of capital for corporations, and thus spurs investment.
- Active stock markets, where efficient block trading facilities exist, make it easier for large shareholders to play their monitoring role, which enhances the performance of corporations.[17]
- Transparent stock markets are less prone to the asymmetric information and agency costs deterring investments in foreign stocks and thus preventing investors from reaping the gains of international diversification.

References

Adler, M. and B. Dumas (1983), 'International Portfolio Choice and Corporation Finance: A Synthesis', *Journal of Finance*, 38: 925–84.

Benos, A. and M. Crouhy (1996), 'Changes in the Structure and Dynamics of European Securities Markets', *Financial Analysts Journal*, 52: 37–50.

Biais, B., P. Hillion and C. Spatt (1997), 'Price Discovery and Learning during the Preopening Period in the Paris Bourse', working paper, Institut d'Economie Industrielle, Toulouse.

Board, J. and C. Suttcliffe (1995), 'The Effects of Trade Transparency in the London Stock Exchange: A Summary', LSE Financial Markets Group Special Paper no. 67.

Bonte-Friedheim (1997), 'Little Bulls', *Wall Street Journal Europe*, 15(68) May 12: pp. 1 and 8.

Brennan, M. and H. Cao (1996), 'International Portfolio Investment Flows', working paper, UCLA.

Cooper, I. and E. Kaplanis (1995), 'Home Bias in Equity Portfolios and the Cost of Capital for Multinational Firms', *Journal of Applied Corporate Finance*, 8: 95–102.

Davydoff, D. (1997), 'Global Equity Issuance and Trading', communication at the 1997 NYSE conference in Cancun.

Flood, M., R. Huisman, K. Koedijk, R. Mahieu and A. Röell (1997), 'Post Trade Transparency in Multiple Dealers Financial Markets', working paper, Limburg Institute of Financial Economics.

Folkerts-Landau, D. and M. Goldstein (1994), 'International Capital Markets: Development, Prospects and Policy Issues', Washington, DC: IMF.

Foucault, T. and F. Palomino (1997), 'Large Shareholders', mimeo, Carnegie Mellon University.

---

[17] Foucault and Palomino (1997) offer an interesting theoretical analysis of this point.

Frankel, J. (1997), 'Exchange Rates and the Single Currency', in B. Steil (ed.), *The European Equity Markets*, London: Royal Institute of International Affairs.

Franks, J., and C. Mayer (1997), 'Corporate Ownership and Control in the UK, Germany and France', *Journal of Applied Corporate Finance*, 10: 30–45.

Franks, J., and S. Schaefer (1995), 'Equity Market Transparency on the London Stock Exchange', *Journal of Applied Corporate Finance*, 8: 70–7.

Gehrig, T. (1993), 'An Information Based Explanation of the Domestic Bias in International Equity Investment', *Scandinavian Journal of Economics*, 97–109.

Gehrig, T., K. Stahl and X. Vives (1995), 'Competing Exchanges', working paper, Institut d'Analisi Economica, Barcelona.

Gemmill, G. (1996), 'Transparency and Liquidity: A Study of Block Trades in the London Stock Market', *Journal of Finance*, 51: 1765–90.

Gerke, W. and S. Rasch (1993), 'Europas Wertpapierbörsen im Umbruch', *ZEW Wirtschaftsanalysen*, 1: 306–36.

Gresse, C. and B. Jacquillat (1995), 'The Divergence of the Order Flow From the CAC Market to London: Myth or Reality', working paper, Université Paris Dauphine.

Kang, J. K. and R. Stulz (1994), 'Why Is there a Home Bias? An Analysis of Foreign Portfolio Equity Ownership in Japan', working paper, Ohio State University.

Nash, R. C., J. Netter and W. Megginson (1997), 'The Long Term Return to Investors in Share Issue Privatizations', mimeo, Terry College of Business, University of Georgia.

Pagano, M. (1989), 'Trading Volume and Asset Liquidity', *Quarterly Journal of Economics*, 255–74.

Pagano, M. (1997), 'The Cost of Trading in European Equity Markets', working paper, Università degli Studi di Napoli Federico II.

Pagano, M. and A. Röell (1990), 'Trading Systems in European Stock Exchanges', *Economic Policy*, 10: 63–115.

Pagano, M. and A. Röell (1996), 'Transparency and Liquidity: A Comparison of Auction and Dealer Markets with Informed Trading', *Journal of Finance*, 51: 553–611.

Perrotti, E. and S. Guney (1993), 'The Structure of Privatization Plans', *Financial Management*, 22: 84–98.

Rajan, R. and L. Zingales (1995), 'What Do We Know about Capital Structure? Some Evidence from International Data', *Journal of Finance*, 50: 1421–60.

Shiller, R., F. Kon-Ya and Y. Tsutui (1996), 'Why Did the Nikkei Crash? Expanding the Scope of Expectations Data Collection', *Review of Economics and Statistics*, 78: 156–64.

Smith, C. (1991), 'Globalization of Financial Markets', in A. Meltzer and C. Plosser (eds.), *Carnegie-Rochester Series on Public Policy*, 77–96.

Smith, K. and G. Sofianos (1997), 'The Impact of an NYSE Listing on the Global Trading of non-US Stocks', NYSE Working Paper 97-02.

Tesar, L. L. and I. Werner (1995), 'Home Bias and High Turnover', *Journal of International Money and Finance*, 14: 467–92.

Part IV

Strategic Industry Implications

9
The Asset Management Industry in Europe: Competitive Structure and Performance under EMU

INGO WALTER

The institutional asset management industry is likely to be one of the largest and most dynamic parts of the global financial services sector in the years ahead. As of 1996, the global total of assets under management was estimated at close to US$30 trillion, comprising some US$8.2 trillion in pension fund assets, about US$5.3 trillion in mutual fund assets, US$6.4 trillion in fiduciary assets controlled by insurance companies, and perhaps US$7.5 trillion in offshore private client assets.[1] Not only will this already massive industry experience an extraordinary rate of growth in comparison with other segments of the financial services sector, but cross-border volume—both regional and global—is likely to take an increasing share of that activity. Much of the action will be centred in Europe, which remains well behind the United States in institutional asset management and where many of the global pension problems reside, even as the rapid growth of performance- oriented managed funds alters the European financial landscape under EMU—including traditional approaches to corporate control.

Within this high-growth context, asset management attracts competitors from an extraordinarily broad range of strategic groups—commercial and universal banks, investment banks, trust companies, insurance companies, private banks, captive and independent pension fund managers, mutual fund companies, and various types of specialist firms. This rich array of contenders, coming at the market from several very different starting points, competitive resources and strategic objectives, is likely to render the market for institutional asset management a highly competitive one even under conditions of large size and rapid growth.

The underlying drivers of the market for institutional asset management are well understood. They include the following:

- A continued broad-based trend towards professional management of discretionary household assets in the form of mutual funds or unit trusts and other types of collective investment vehicles, a development that has perhaps run much of its course in some national financial systems but has only begun in others.

---

[1] *Source*: 'Global Fund Management', *Financial Times*, 24 April 1997, and Chase Manhattan Bank.

- The growing recognition that most government-sponsored pension systems, many of which were created wholly or partially on a pay-as-you-go (PAYG) basis, have become fundamentally untenable under demographic projections that appear virtually certain to materialize, and must be progressively replaced by asset pools that will throw off the kinds of returns necessary to meet the needs of growing numbers of longer-living retirees.
- Partial displacement of traditional defined-benefit public and private sector pension programmes backed by assets contributed by employers and working individuals—under the pressure of the evolving demographics, rising administrative costs, and shifts in risk allocation by a variety of defined-contribution schemes.
- Reallocation of portfolios that have—for regulatory, tax or institutional reasons—been overweighted to domestic financial instruments (notably fixed-income securities) towards a greater role for equities and non-domestic asset classes, which not only promise higher returns but also may reduce the beneficiaries' exposure to risk owing to portfolio diversification across both asset classes and economic and financial environments that are less than perfectly correlated in terms of total investment returns.

The growth implied by the first three of these factors, combined with the asset-allocation shifts implied by the fourth factor, will tend to drive the dynamics and competitive structure of the global institutional asset management industry in the years ahead.

EMU is likely to have a number of important implications for the global asset management industry. It will have an impact on total asset returns and the potential for international portfolio diversification, for example, by eliminating national currencies, interest rate differentials and divergent monetary policies within the region covered by a common currency. It will give rise to a whole new class of government securities denominated in euros that will be broadly equivalent to municipals in the US context. These securities will be rated, priced and distributed to increasingly dominant, performance-driven institutional asset managers, and will have to compete with an expanding array of euro-denominated corporate bonds, asset-backed securities, equities and other investment alternatives available to institutional investors in a single capital market that will eventually rival that of the United States in both size and competitive structure. This, in turn, will enhance market liquidity, transparency, performance-orientation, and benchmarking standards by which both asset managers and issuers are assessed. And it will shift competitive relationships among universal banks, full-service investment banks, specialist and generalist fund management companies, insurance companies and other players in the fund management business, including highly experienced non-domestic competitors in various national markets that were previously sheltered from foreign competition.

This chapter assesses in some detail the three principal sectors of the asset management industry—mutual funds, pension funds, and private clients, as well as foundations, endowments, central bank reserves and other large financial pools requiring

institutional asset management services. In each case, the European experience is compared with that of the United States as well as, where appropriate, those of Japan and certain emerging-market countries. This is followed by a discussion of the competitive structure, conduct and performance of the asset management industry. Finally, the European dimensions of the issue considered in each section are brought together in an impact assessment with respect to the evolution of the European capital market, including the implications of a single currency.

1. Asset Management in a Financial Intermediation Framework

The asset management services that are the focus of this chapter are depicted in Figure 9.1, as follows:

- First, retail clients have the option of placing funds directly with financial institutions such as banks or of purchasing securities from retail sales forces of broker–dealers, possibly with the help of fee-based financial advisers. Alternatively, retail investors can have their funds professionally managed by buying shares in mutual funds or unit trusts (again possibly with the help of advisers), which in turn buy securities from the institutional sales desks of broker–dealers (and from time to time maintain balances with banks).

- Secondly, private clients are broken out as a separate segment of the asset management market in Figure 9.1, and are usually serviced by private bankers who bundle asset management with various other services—such as tax planning, estates and trusts—placing assets directly into financial instruments, commingled managed asset pools, or sometimes publicly available mutual funds and unit trusts.

- Thirdly, foundations, endowments, and financial reserves held by non-financial companies, institutions and governments can rely on in-house investment expertise to purchase securities directly from the institutional sales desks of banks or securities broker–dealers, use financial advisers to help them build efficient portfolios, or place funds with open-end or closed-end mutual funds.

- Fourthly, pension funds take two principal forms, those guaranteeing a level of benefits and those aimed at building beneficiary assets from which a pension will be drawn (see below). Defined-benefit pension funds can buy securities directly in the market or place funds with banks, trust companies or other types of asset managers, often aided by fund consultants who advise pension trustees on performance and asset-allocation styles. Defined-contribution pension programmes may operate in a similar way if they are managed in-house, creating proprietary asset pools, and in addition (or alternatively) provide participants with the option to purchase shares in publicly available mutual funds.

The structure of the asset management industry encompasses significant overlaps between the three types of asset pools to the point where they are sometimes difficult to distinguish. We have noted the linkage between defined-contribution pension funds

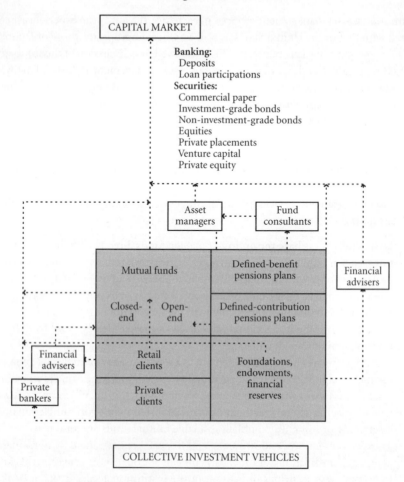

Figure 9.1. Organization of asset management

and the mutual fund industry, and the association of the disproportionate growth in the former with the expansion of mutual fund assets under management. There is a similar but perhaps more limited linkage between private clients' assets and mutual funds, on the one hand, and pension funds, on the other. This is particularly the case for the lower bound of private client business, which is often commingled with mass-marketed mutual funds, and pension benefits awarded high-income executives, which in effect become part of the high-net-worth portfolio.

The following three sections of this chapter will consider the development of mutual funds, pension funds and private banking as the three principal types of asset management institutions dominating the global and European financial environment.

2. Mutual Funds

As it has in the United States, the mutual fund industry in Europe has enjoyed rapid growth during the 1990s, although there are wide differences among national financial markets in the pace of development, in the character of the assets under management, and in the nature of mutual fund marketing and distribution. The pattern of development in Europe has also differed significantly from the United States, where at the end of 1996 there were more than 6,000 mutual funds in total and over 4,500 equity mutual funds available to the public—more than the number of stocks listed on the New York Stock Exchange—with average annual growth in excess of 22 per cent between 1975 and 1996 and almost US$4 trillion of assets under management in all funds at the end of 1997 (about 13 per cent of household net financial wealth, more than life insurance companies and about equal to the total assets of commercial banks). Only a part of mutual fund growth is attributable to new net investments in this sector of the financial system, of course, with the balance of the growth in assets under management attributable to reinvested earnings and capital gains. So the relative importance of equity funds and the performance of national stock markets is directly linked to observed differences in mutual fund growth patterns among countries and regions. Much of the growth is also attributable to the use of mutual funds for retirement savings, capturing roughly 17 per cent of US retirement assets in 1996 (see below).

Figure 9.2 shows the distribution of mutual fund assets in terms of market capitalization at the end of 1996. The United States accounts for slightly over half the assets under management, the EU about 31 per cent and Japan 9 per cent of the total.[2] Within Europe, France had the top position in 1994 with 30 per cent, followed by Germany with 17 per cent, the United Kingdom with 12 per cent and Switzerland with 11 per cent. In Europe, mutual funds and unit trusts are roughly evenly split between money market funds, fixed-income funds and equity funds, but this masks the wide inter-country differences shown in Figure 9.3. The French market has been dominated by money market funds, in part owing to tax advantages, while the British market has virtually been monopolized by equity funds. At the same time, fixed-income funds take a disproportionate share of the market in other European countries, notably in Germany, reflecting both investor preferences and the limited state of development of national equity markets in the countries concerned.

In the United States, on the other hand, mutual funds were traditionally invested mainly in equities—in 1975, over 82 per cent of the fund assets under management were equities and a mere 10 per cent and 8 per cent were in bonds and money market instruments, respectively. By 1985 this picture had changed completely, with the equity component declining to 24 per cent and money market funds capturing 49 per cent,

---

[2] According to the OECD, personal financial assets in Europe grew at an average rate of about 11% in the decade ending 1996, compared to about 8% in the United States and Japan, with an disproportionately high growth rate of over 18% in the case of Italy during this period.

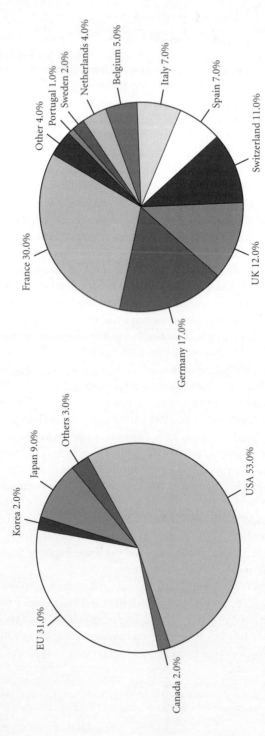

Figure 9.2. Breakdown of global and European mutual fund markets, 1996 (US$5.3 trillion)
Source: FEFSI.

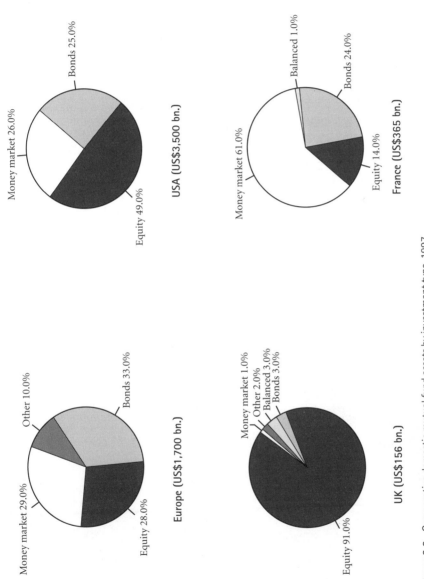

Figure 9.3. Comparative domestic mutual fund assets by investment type, 1997

Sources: EFID; Lipper Analytical Services International; Goldman Sachs.

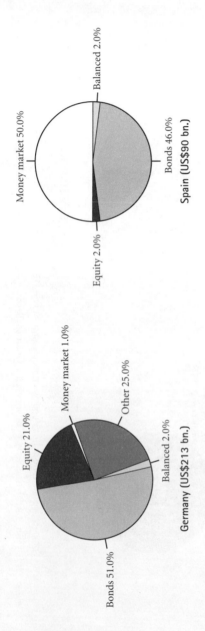

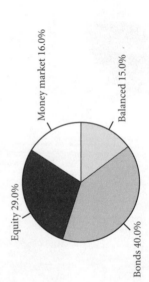

Figure 9.3. _(Cont.)_

owing both to relatively poor stock market performance in the 1970s and early 1980s, and to the substitution of money market mutual funds for bank savings products by households searching for higher yields at a time when banks continued to be limited by interest rate regulation on deposits. By 1995 the US pattern of mutual fund investments had shifted yet again, with equities accounting for 44 per cent of the total, and money market and bond funds 28 per cent each (Investment Company Institute, 1996).

2.1. Mutual fund distribution

There are also wide differences among countries in how mutual funds are distributed, which in turn are linked to comparative mutual fund growth and structure. As shown in Figure 9.4, European mutual fund distribution through bank branches dominates in countries such as Germany (80 per cent), France (70 per cent) and Spain (61 per cent), with UK distribution concentrated among independent advisers and Italian distribution roughly split between bank branches and independent sales forces. The dominance of universal banks, savings banks and cooperative banks as financial intermediaries in most of the Continental European countries explains the high concentration of mutual fund distribution via branch networks.[3] One major exception to bank-based fund distribution was Robeco, a Dutch asset management company, which was highly successful in penetrating the retail market, only to be taken over by Rabobank after a brief joint venture to market each other's products.

In contrast, US mutual fund distribution has been concentrated on full-service broker–dealers which maintain large retail sales forces capable of penetrating the household sector and which are compensated mainly on the basis of commissions earned and assets under management (AUM). In recent years, discount brokers have made substantial inroads into mutual fund distribution, compensating for reduced sales effort and limited investment advice by lower fees and expenses. Insurance agents account for 15 per cent of US mutual fund distribution, focusing on mutual funds with an insurance wrapper such as fixed and variable annuities and guaranteed investment contracts (GICs). Bank branches have played a limited role in the USA owing to the legacy of regulatory constraints—accounting for the relatively small 13 per cent distribution share through bank branches—although deregulation and cross-selling opportunities with retail commercial banking products are likely to boost the share of bank-based mutual fund sales in the future.

A key question is how mutual funds will be distributed in the future European unified financial market. Distribution without advice will clearly be most efficient over

---

[3] For example, German mutual fund distribution is dominated by the major banks, with DWS (Deutsche Bank) controlling a 24% market share, DIT (Dresdner Bank) 14.1%, and ADIG (Commerzbank and the merged Bayerische Hypo and Bayerische Vereinsbank) 21.1%. However, foreign players such as Fidelity of the USA and Bank Julius Baer of Switzerland appear to be making significant inroads even as local competitors strive to improve investment performance, increase the range of products available, and enhance their non-European (particularly US) funds marketed to German investors.

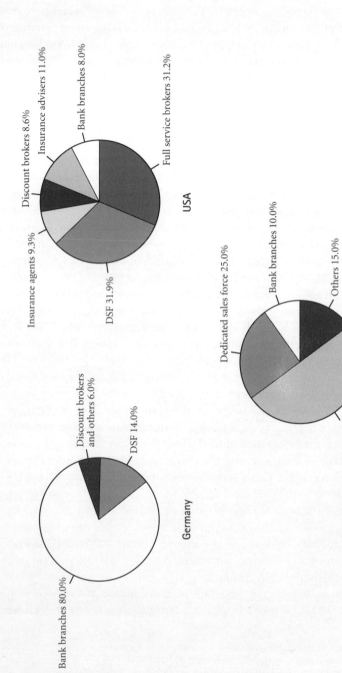

Discount brokers 8.6%

Insurance advisers 11.0%

Bank branches 8.0%

Full service brokers 31.2%

Insurance agents 9.3%

DSF 31.9%

USA

Dedicated sales force 25.0%

Bank branches 10.0%

Others 15.0%

Independent advisers 50.0%

UK

Discount brokers
and others 6.0%

DSF 14.0%

Bank branches 80.0%

Germany

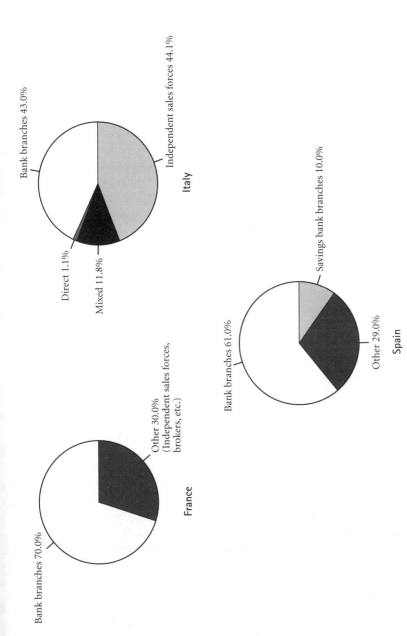

Figure 9.4. Estimated mutual fund market share by distribution channel in major markets, 1996

Note: DSF = dedicated sales forces.

Sources: EFID; Banca Fideuram; Investment Company Institute; Securities Industry Association; Boston Consulting Group.

the Internet or other on-line interfaces with the retail client. This means that *trans-actions services* can be separated from *investment advice*, both functionally and in terms of pricing. Advice can be delivered only in part in disembodied form, with value-added depending partly on interpretative information on investments and partly on personal counselling that the client must be willing to pay for. With this advice increasingly likely to come from independent financial planners in many markets, traditional distributors of mutual funds are encroached upon from both sides and have had to react in order to maintain market share.

It is also probable that the major American mutual fund companies like Fidelity and Vanguard will try to penetrate the European bank-based distribution channels that have traditionally prevailed in most countries, along with US broker–dealers like Merrill Lynch (having acquired the UK's dominant Mercury Asset Management in 1997) and Morgan Stanley Dean Witter Discover, discounters such as Charles Schwab, as well as Citicorp (as the only US bank with a European presence of sufficient mass to use as a platform for mutual fund distribution). UK fund managers and insurance companies will try to do the same thing on the Continent, even as Continental European banks and insurance companies strive to adapt their powerful distribution systems to more effective asset management and mutual fund marketing, and to sharpen up their product range and investment performance.

2.2. Mutual fund competition

Competition among mutual funds can be among the most intense anywhere in the financial system, heightened by the aforementioned analytical services which track performance of funds in terms of risk and return over different holding periods and assign ratings based on fund performance. These fund-rating services are important, because the vast majority of new investments tend to flow into highly rated funds. For example, in the United States during the period 1993–6, about 85 per cent of all new money was allocated to funds rated 4- or 5-star by Morningstar, Inc. These same highly rated funds captured roughly three-quarters of all mutual fund assets at the end of 1996. In addition, widely read business publications publish regular 'scoreboards' among publicly available mutual funds based on such ratings and, together with specialized investment publications and information distributed over the Internet, have made mutual funds one of the most transparent parts of the retail financial services sector. These developments are mirrored to varying degrees in Europe as well, notably in the United Kingdom.

Despite clear warnings that past performance is no assurance of future results, a rise in the performance rankings often brings in a flood of new investments and management company revenues, with the individual asset manager compensated commensurately and sometimes moving on to manage larger and more prestigious funds. Conversely, serious performance slippage causes investors to withdraw funds, taking with them a good part of the manager's bonus and maybe his or her job, given that the mutual fund company's revenues are vitally dependent on new investments and total assets under management. A gradual decline in the average sophistication of the investor in many markets—as mutual funds become increasingly mass-market retail-oriented and interlinked with pension schemes (see below)—performance ratings, name recognition and 'branding' appear to be progressively more important in defining competitive performance in the industry.

Historically, at least in the United States, there has been little evidence of increasing market concentration in the mutual fund industry. There are 25,000 entities that run funds and/or give investment advice, of which some 6,000 have assets under management in excess of US$25 million. The five-firm ratio has been between 32 per cent and 34 per cent, the top-5% ratio between 65 per cent and 68 per cent, and the top-10% ratio between 81 per cent and 82 per cent from 1990 to 1996.

Factors that seem to argue *for* greater industry concentration in the future are economies of scale and brandname concentration among progressively less sophisticated investors in taxable funds and mutual funds that are part of retirement accounts battling for attention among the enormous number of funds vying for their business.[4] Arguments *against* further concentration include shifts in performance track-records and the role of mutual fund supermarkets in distribution, which increase the relative marketing advantage of smaller funds. One factor that may promote continued *fragmentation* of the mutual fund industry is that size itself can lead to significant performance problems.

In addition to promoting their performance, when favourable, mutual fund companies and securities broker–dealers have aggressively added banking-type services such as checking and cash-management accounts, credit cards and overdraft lines. They provide user-friendly, integrated account statements and tax reporting. Client contact is based on easy access by telephone, mail and the Internet. In the United States, commercial bank competitors in the mutual fund business have thus seen their retail competitive advantage increasingly reliant on a fragile combination of high-cost branch networks and deposit insurance. Securities firms have likewise increased their mutual fund activity, presumably with the view that this part of the securities industry is more capable of supporting significant, sustained returns than is wholesale investment banking, such as debt and equity capital markets and corporate advisory services, where competition has become cutthroat, capital-intensive, and subject to a high degree of earnings instability. Insurance companies have also considered the mutual fund business to be a strong candidate for strategic development, especially in the face of competition in their traditional annuities business and the cross-links that have emerged in some countries between the pension fund and mutual fund industries.

There have also been successful examples of direct fund distribution even in heavily bank-dominated European financial systems, such as Direct Anlage in Germany and Virgin Direct in the United Kingdom. Cortal Banque (affiliated with Banque Paribas)

---

[4] A 1996 money management IQ test designed to calibrate basic investing skills was passed by less than 20% of respondents. Another survey indicated that only a small minority of mutual fund investors actually perused the prospectus, or even a summary of the prospectus, before they invested. See Goldstein *et al.* (1997).

in France had a client base of 150,000 and assets under management of US$3 billion in 1995, built entirely though telephone sales and other direct media (Davis International Banking Consultants, 1996). Examples of effective cross-border mutual fund distribution include Fidelity Investments of the United States and Fleming Flagship of the United Kingdom. Such cross-border incursions into idiosyncratic national markets require high levels of product performance, excellence in service quality, and effective distribution techniques that are appropriate to the national environment—either on a stand-alone basis or in joint ventures with local financial firms. This suggests that highly targeted approaches which provide specific client segments with products superior to those available from traditional vendors is probably the only viable way to develop a pan-European approach to retail asset management.

Competition in the mutual funds business thus covers a rich array of players, ranging from commercial banks and securities broker–dealers to specialized mutual fund companies, discount brokerages, insurance companies and non-financial firms. Such interpenetration of strategic groups, each approaching the business from a different direction, tends to make markets hypercompetitive. This is the likely future competitive structure of the mutual fund industry, particularly in large, integrated markets such as the United States and—with currency unification—the European Union.

2.3. Comparative regulation of mutual funds

In the United States, mutual fund regulations require strict, fit-and-proper criteria for management companies of mutual funds sold to the public, as well as extensive disclosure of pertinent information. The National Securities Markets Improvement Act of 1996 makes the Securities and Exchange Commission responsible for overseeing investment advisers with over US$25 million under management, with state regulators alone responsible for investment advisers with smaller amounts under management— advisers who had previously been coregulated together with the SEC. The large investment advisers falling under SEC jurisdiction account for about 95 per cent of US assets under management, although the vast majority of abusive practices and enforcement problems occur among the smaller firms (Siwolop, 1997).

Threat of regulatory action and civil liability lawsuits keep the pressure on US mutual fund boards to take their obligations to investors seriously to ensure that the fund objectives are faithfully carried out. Some fund management companies, however, nominate individuals to serve as directors of numerous—sometimes a very large number of—funds from among those managed by the firm, perhaps raising questions of whether such directors can fulfil all of their responsibilities to their investors. Still, if they are thought not to be doing so, they can expect to be the object of suits brought by lawyers representing the investors as a class. All of this information is in the public domain, accompanied by the aforementioned high degree of transparency with respect to fund performance plus ample media coverage and vigorous competition among funds and fund managers. This means that investors today face a generally fair and efficient market in which to make their asset choices. If they fail to choose wisely, that's their own fault. Overall, the mutual fund business, at least in the more developed markets, is probably a good example of how regulation and competition can come together to serve the retail investor about as well as is possible.

In contrast to the United States, the rules governing the operation and distribution of mutual funds in the EU have traditionally been highly fragmented—fragmentation that will gradually come to an end in the years ahead. As of the mid-1980s, definitions of mutual funds varied from country to country, as did legal status and regulatory provisions. Door-to-door selling was forbidden in Belgium and Luxembourg, for example, and strictly regulated in Germany. In Britain, on the other hand, direct marketing was the norm. Market access to clients varied between the extremes of high levels of impenetrability to virtually complete openness.

The EU directive governing the operation and sale of mutual funds—Undertakings for the Collective Investment of Transferable Securities (UCITS)—came into force on 1 October 1989 after fifteen years of negotiation. It specifies general rules for the kinds of investments that are appropriate for mutual funds, and how they should be sold. The regulatory requirements for fund management and certification are left to the home country of the fund management firm, while specific rules governing the adequacy of disclosure and selling practices are left to the respective host countries.[5]

Consequently, mutual funds duly established and monitored in any EU member country such as Luxembourg—and that are in compliance with UCITS—can be sold without restriction to investors in national financial markets EU-wide, and promoted and advertised through local marketing networks and via direct mail, as long as selling requirements applicable in each country are met. Permissible investment vehicles include conventional equity and fixed-income securities, as well as high-performance 'synthetic' funds based on futures and options not previously permitted in some financial centres such as London. Under UCITS, 90 per cent of mutual fund assets must be invested in publicly traded companies, no more than 5 per cent of the outstanding stock of any company may be owned by a fund, and there are limits on investment funds' borrowing rights. Real estate funds, commodity funds and money market funds are specifically excluded from UCITS.

2.4. European taxation and the mutual fund industry

Unlike funds in the EU, US mutual funds have operated in a comparatively coherent tax environment. There is a uniform federal income tax code, which requires mutual fund companies to report all income and capital gains to the Internal Revenue Service (IRS)—normally there is no withholding at source—and requires individuals to self-report the same information in annual tax returns, with data reconciliation undertaken by the IRS. Taxable fund income is subject to regular federal income tax rates, while capital gains and losses are recorded as they are incurred in mutual fund trading

---

[5] For a discussion, see Story and Walter (1997).

and net gains are attributed to the mutual fund investor and taxed at the federal capital gains rates. Tax fraud, including the use of offshore accounts to evade tax, is a criminal offence. States and sometimes municipalities likewise tend to tax mutual fund income and capital gains (and sometimes assets) at substantially lower rates. Under the US Constitution the states and the federal government cannot tax each other. So there is a broad range of mutual funds that invest in securities issued by state and local governments with income exempt from federal tax as well as (usually) tax on the income from the state's own securities contained in the portfolio. Similarly, the states do not tax income derived from federal government securities. The US tax environment, while complex, provides the mutual fund industry with opportunities for product development such as tax-efficient funds (e.g. investing in municipals and capital-gains-oriented equities) and imposes compliance costs in terms of the required tax reporting both to the IRS and to the investor client.

The European tax environment is far more heterogeneous by comparison, with the power of tax authorities stopping at the national border and—in the presence in many EU countries of very high tax rates on capital income—widespread tax avoidance and evasion on the part of investors. In the light of intra-EU capital mobility, the move towards a single currency and the UCITS initiative, narrowing or eliminating intra-EU differentials in taxation of capital income and assets and the establishment of a coherent tax environment that is considered equitable and resistant to evasion have been of growing interest.

In 1988, Germany announced consideration of a 10 per cent withholding tax on interest and dividend income in what became an embarrassing demonstration that such taxes can provoke immediate and massive capital flight. Overall, Bundesbank estimates showed a total long-term capital outflow of US$42.8 billion during 1988, even though the 10 per cent withholding tax was only being discussed and had not yet been implemented. An estimated US$10.7 billion of German investment funds flowed into the Luxembourg bond market alone following the announcement that the tax was to be effective 1 January 1989. Investor reactions to the German tax bid up the price of Euromark issues and depressed yields to the point where in early 1989 it was cheaper for PepsiCo to borrow DM in Luxembourg than it was for the German federal government to do so in the domestic bund market. Four months later, on 27 April, the German authorities announced that the withholding tax would be abolished on 1 July 1989.

In February 1989, midway through the German tax *débâcle*, the European Commission formally proposed a minimum 15 per cent withholding tax (administered at source) on interest income of investments (bonds and bank deposits) by residents of other EU countries, as well as on Eurobonds. Non-EU residents were to be exempt from the withholding tax, as were savings accounts of young people and small savers who were already exempt from taxation in a number of EU countries. Member states were to be free to impose withholding taxes above the 15 per cent floor. Governments could exempt interest income subject to withholding at source from declaration for tax purposes. Also exempted were countries that already applied equal or higher withholding taxes on interest income. Additional aspects of the proposal concerned cooperation

in enforcement and exchange of information among EU fiscal authorities. Dividends were omitted from the proposals because they were generally less heavily taxed by EU member countries, and because national income tax systems were thought to capture this type of investment income relatively effectively (Levich and Walter, 1990).

Supporters of abolishing capital income tax differences within the EU argued that tax harmonization was essential if financial market integration was not to lead to widespread tax evasion. The effort was led by France, together with Belgium, Italy and Spain. All four countries also argued that the absence of tax harmonization would weaken their currencies in relation to those of other EU members. All four had tax collection systems considered relatively weak in terms of enforcement and widely subject to evasion.

Opponents to the EU tax harmonization initiative, mainly the United Kingdom and Luxembourg as well as the Netherlands, argued that tax harmonization was both unnecessary and harmful to the functioning of efficient financial markets, and that substantial investments would subsequently flow outside the EU, especially to Switzerland and other non-resident tax havens. They argued that the proposal failed to recognize that Europe is part of a global financial market and that EU securities returns might have to be raised to levels providing equivalent after-tax yields in order to prevent capital outflows from becoming a serious problem. The United Kingdom was also concerned about the special role of the Isle of Man and the Channel Islands (which are fiscally 'semi-detached' from the EU) and their treatment in any EU withholding tax initiative.

After two years of intense debate on the issue, the 15 per cent EU withholding tax proposal finally collapsed in mid-1989 as Germany withdrew its support of the Commission's initiative and shifted to the opposition. The idea of harmonizing EU taxes was quietly shelved, with the Finance Ministers agreeing to seek alternative ways of cooperation and more effective measures against money-laundering. Nevertheless, there remained little doubt that greater uniformity in capital income taxation and closer cooperation between EU tax authorities would eventually have to be revived—although harmonization of withholding tax rates and enforcement remained constrained by the possibility of capital flight to low-tax environments outside the EU. At the very least, it was difficult to see how an active EU-wide mutual fund industry could develop under UCITS without a reasonably coherent trade environment.

Meantime, Luxembourg has remained the centre of EU tax attention. Funds registered in the country are exempt from local taxation. Investors pay no withholding tax on dividends, and a 1983 law recognized French-type Sociétés d'Investissements à Capital Variable (SICAVs). In March 1988, Luxembourg became the first EU member state to ratify the UCITS in a successful bid to become the functional centre for marketing mutual funds throughout the EU. By this time Luxembourg had already attracted 132 foreign banks—of which 37 were German and 16 were Scandinavian, as well as 506 mutual funds, up from 76 registered in 1980[6]—and had licensed 245 new

---

[6] 'The Switzerland of the Future', *The Banker*, November 1988.

funds by October 1989.[7] The Luxembourg Prime Minister at the time (and now President of the European Commission), Jacques Santer, pointed out that open competition in Europe's financial space would determine which financial centre won out. But there were no provisions, he suggested, in EU law for cooperation between tax authorities.[8] Evasion and/or avoidance of its EU partners' taxes was thus implicitly conceded as Luxembourg's principal source of competitive advantage in the European asset management industry.

The months leading up to the prospect of uniformity in mutual funds management and distribution via UCITS had already led to moves in a number of high-tax member countries to liberalize constraints imposed on domestic mutual fund asset allocation and to reexamine levels of capital income taxation. For example, mutual funds in France were no longer obliged to hold 30 per cent of their assets in Treasury bonds, and were permitted to focus exclusively on equities.[9] Indeed, the 1989 French Budget encouraged funds to convert into capital-appreciation vehicles which did not distribute interest as current income. Instead, accrued interest was paid in the form of capital gains subject to a 17 per cent rather than a 27 per cent tax, which reduced the incentive to shift assets to Luxembourg.

In the 1990s Germany, by now hard-pressed by the cost of reunification, once again went after interest income with a 30 per cent withholding tax at source, triggering an estimated US$215 billion capital outflow, mostly once again to Luxembourg. Helping their clients to flee taxation became good business for the German banks' Luxembourg affiliates' deposit and fiduciary accounts. This time, however, the German tax authorities reacted much more aggressively, investigating a number of banks and prominent individuals for aiding and abetting or engaging in tax evasion. Unlike their past position, German authorities in the 1990s have repeatedly called for intra-EU tax harmonization to eliminate the suction of the massive fiscal hole in the middle of the EU—in the memorable words of former EU President Jaques Delors, 'We will deal with Luxembourg when the time comes.' There seems little doubt that, in the end, he will be right. A financially integrated Europe can no more afford a haven for tax evaders that the US federal government could afford permitting one of the states declaring itself a domestic version of Luxembourg.

3. Pension Funds

The pension fund market has proven to be one of the most rapidly growing sectors of the global financial system, and promises to be even more dynamic in the years ahead. Consequently, pension assets have been in the forefront of strategic targeting by all

---

[7] *Financial Times*, 2 October 1989.

[8] The Economic and Social Council expressed concern that capital be invested in tax-free bonds (J.O. no. C. 221/29). The European Parliament also regretted that the EU had been unable to reach an agreement on an EC system of taxation on interest (J.O. no. C. 68/145, 19 March 1990). See also *Les Echos*, 19 June 1990.

[9] *Les Echos*, 15 September 1989.

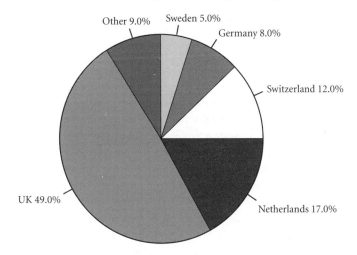

Figure 9.5. European pension fund market, 1994 (US$1,577 bn.)
Source: Intersec.

types of financial institutions, including banks, trust companies, broker–dealers, insurance companies, mutual fund companies, and independent asset management firms. Pension assets in 1995 in countries where consistent and comparable data are available (Australia, Canada, Japan, Switzerland, the United Kingdom and the United States) were estimated to amount to US$8.2 trillion, roughly two-thirds of which covered private sector employees and the balance covered public sector employees. Total Western European pension assets at the end of 1994, depicted in Figure 9.5, had an estimated market value of about US$1.6 trillion, with the United Kingdom accounting for almost half the total and the Netherlands second largest with a 17 per cent share.[10]

The basis for such projected growth is, of course, the demographics of gradually ageing populations colliding with existing structures for retirement support which in many countries carry heavy political baggage. They are politically exceedingly difficult to bring up to the standards required for the future, yet doing so eventually is an inevitability.[11] The global epicentre of this problem will be the European Union, with profound implications for the size and structure of capital markets for the competitive positioning and performance of financial intermediaries in general and asset man-

---

[10] There are a number of dissenting opinions with regard to this high-growth scenario, however, some of which suggest that the growth in pension assets may actually decline from the rates achieved in the 1990s. These forecasts are based on the presumption that Germany's system of defined-benefit plans with limited dedicated external asset pools is basically sound (and carries a high weight in the European total), and that enabling legislation to change PAYG systems like France and Italy will be politically difficult and slow to develop (Davis International Banking Consultants, 1996).

[11] For a more detailed discussion, see Turner and Watanabe (1995).

agers in particular, and for the systems of corporate governance that have existed in the region.[12]

3.1. Demographics of dependency

The demographics of the pension fund problem are very straightforward, since demographic data are among the most reliable. Table 9.1 provides data for the so-called dependency ratio (roughly, those of retirement age as a percentage of those of working age). Unless there are major unforeseen changes in birth rates, death rates or migration rates, for the EU as a whole the dependency ratio will have doubled between 1990 and 2040, with the highest dependency ratios being attained in Italy, Germany and the Netherlands, and the lowest in Ireland. While the demographics underlying these projections may be quite reliable, dependency ratios remain subject to shifts in working-age start and end points. Obviously, the longer people remain out of the active labour force (e.g. for purposes of education), the higher the level of sustained unemployment, and the earlier the average retirement age, the higher will be the dependency ratio. In recent years all three of these factors have contributed to raising the EU's dependency ratio, certainly relative to that in the United States, although there are early signs that this may eventually stabilize or be reversed under pressure of the realities of the pension issue.

Table 9.1. Projected dependency trends in EU countries vs. the USA and Japan[a]

	Old age dependency ratios	
	1990	2040 (est.)
Belgium	21.9	41.5
Denmark	22.2	43.4
France	21.9	39.2
Germany	23.7	47.1
Greece	20.5	41.7
Ireland	18.4	27.2
Italy	20.4	48.4
Luxembourg	20.4	41.2
Netherlands	17.4	48.5
Portugal	16.4	38.9
Spain	17.0	41.7
UK	23.5	39.1
USA	19.0	38.5
Japan	22.7	44.9

[a] Population aged 65 and over as a percentage of population aged 15–64.

Sources: EUROSTAT; World Bank; OECD; EBRI.

---

[12] For a discussion, see Story and Walter (1997).

3.2. Alternative approaches to old–age support

There are basically three ways to provide support for the post-retirement segment of the population:

1. *Pay-as-you-go (PAYG) programmes.* Pension benefits under this approach are committed by the state based on various formulas—number of years worked and income subject to social charges, for example—and funded by current mandatory contributions of those employed (taxes and social charges) that may or may not be specifically earmarked to covering current pension payouts. Under PAYG systems, current pension contributions may exceed or fall short of current disbursements. In the former case a 'trust fund' may be set up which, as in the case of US Social Security, may be invested in government securities. In the latter case, the deficit will tend to be covered out of general tax revenues, government borrowing, or the liquidation of previously accumulated trust fund assets.

2. *Defined-benefit programmes.* Pension benefits under such programmes are committed to public or private sector employees by their employers, based on actuarial benefit formulas that are part of the employment contract. Defined-benefit pension payouts may be linked to the cost of living, adjusted for survivorship, etc., and the funds set aside to support future claims may be contributed solely by the employer or with some level of employee contribution. The pool of assets may be invested in a portfolio of debt and equity securities (possibly including the company's own shares) that are managed in-house or by external fund managers. Depending on the level of contributions and benefit claims, as well as investment performance, defined-benefit plans may be *overfunded* or *underfunded*. They may thus be tapped by the employer from time to time for general corporate purposes, or they may have to be topped up from the employer's own resources. Defined-benefit plans may be insured (e.g. against corporate bankruptcy) either in the private market or by government agencies, and are usually subject to strict regulation—e.g. in the United States under ERISA, which is administered by the Department of Labor.

3. *Defined-contribution programmes.* Pension fund contributions are made by the employer, the employee, or both into a fund that will ultimately form the basis for pension benefits under defined-contribution pension plans. The employee's share in the fund may be managed by the employer or placed with various asset managers under portfolio constraints intended to serve the best interests of the beneficiaries. The employee's responsibility for asset allocation can vary from none at all to virtually full discretion. Employees may, for example, be allowed to select from among a range of approved investment vehicles, notably mutual funds, based on individual risk–return preferences.

Most countries have several types of pension arrangement operating simultaneously—for example a base-level PAYG system supplemented by state-sponsored or privately sponsored defined-benefit plans and defined-contribution plans sponsored by employers or mandated by the state.

As of the end of 1997, fifty-four countries had defined-contribution pension systems of some kind, ranging from nationwide compulsory schemes to funds intended to supplement state-guaranteed pensions. Assets in these funds are expected to grow at a rate of 16 per cent per year outside the United States, compared to a US growth rate of 14 per cent, with the fastest growth (24 per cent annually) expected in Latin America, and European pension pools growing at a rate of 14 per cent.[13] Overall, global pension pools are likely to grow from US$8.5 trillion in 1997 to perhaps US$13.5 trillion in 2002.

The collision of the aforementioned demographics and heavy reliance on the part of many European countries on PAYG approaches is at the heart of the pension problem, and forms the basis for future opportunities in this part of national and global financial systems. In the United States, for example, the PAYG attributes of Social Security and projections as to the future evolution of the trust fund have been highlighted by a number of commissions to study the problem, and the conclusions have invariably pointed to some combination of increased retirement eligibility, increased Social Security taxes, increased taxation of social security benefits, and means-testing of benefits so that those who have saved more for retirement on their own would receive smaller benefits or be taxed at higher rates on the benefits they receive.[14]

While the American pension problem is cause for concern—and is being more or less adequately addressed by government, employers and individuals on their own—it pales by comparison with the problems confronting Europe and to a lesser extent Japan. With a population of some 261 million people at the beginning of 1995, the United States had accumulated pension pools worth US$3.76 trillion. Western Europe, with a population almost twice as large, had accumulated pension assets of only US$1.61 trillion. Japan's population and pension accumulations at that time were 125 million and US$1.12 trillion, respectively.[15] Table 9.2 shows the percentage of the labour force in various countries covered by occupational pension schemes, with countries such as Italy, Belgium and Spain highly dependent on PAYG state-run pension systems and with little asset accumulation and countries such as the Netherlands, Denmark and the UK having long traditions of defined-benefit pension schemes backed by large asset pools. The French system involves a virtually universal state-directed defined-benefit scheme which, given the demographics, is heavily underfunded.

These very different EU systems, in turn, are reflected in pension assets per capita and pension assets as a percentage of GDP, shown in the last two columns of Table 9.2. Among the EU countries only Denmark, the Netherlands and the UK appear to be in reasonably good shape. German companies have traditionally run defined-benefit plans, with pension reserves booked within the balance sheets of the employers themselves as opposed to externally managed asset pools, backstopped by a government-mandated pension fund guarantee scheme (First Consulting, 1997).

---

[13] Data from InterSec Research Corporation, 1997.
[14] For a survey, see Cadette (1997). See also 1994–96 Advisory Council on Social Security (1997).
[15] Data from InterSec Research Corporation and Goldman Sachs & Co.

Table 9.2. European vs. US pension assets and populations, end-1994

	Population (m.)	% Of labour force covered by occupational pension scheme	% Of population over 65	Pension assets (US$ bn.)	Pension assets per capita (US$000)	Pension assets as % of GDP
Belgium	10.1	5	15	17	1.7	8
Denmark	5.2	n.a.	16	105	20.2	72
Finland	5.1	n.a.	14	28	5.5	29
France	58.1	80	15	n.a.	n.a.	n.a.
Germany	81.2	65	15	285	3.5	14
Ireland	3.6	n.a.	11	15	4.2	28
Italy	57.0	5	11	50	0.9	5
Netherlands	15.4	82	13	380	24.7	116
Portugal	9.9	n.a.	13	5	0.5	6
Spain	39.2	3	15	10	0.3	2
Switzerland	7.1	92	15	187	12.3	73
UK	58.3	55	16	775	3.3	76
USA	261.0	55	13	3,760	14.4	56

n.a. = not available.

Sources: William Mercer; EBRI; World Bank; EIU Limited, 1995; InterSec and Euromoney; Davis (1995); World Bank (1994).

Even a number of the Eastern European countries seem to be ahead of their Western European counterparts such as Germany and Italy in designing viable pension systems, most of which follow a defined-contribution model. Hungary and Poland, for example, have drawn on experience of the Chile and other Latin American countries in reforming their PAYG systems. In the case of Hungary, the PAYG system will be phased out gradually and new entrants to the workforce must join one of a number of new private pension schemes. Workers under the age of 47 may choose between the state system and private schemes, while those 47 and older are expected to remain with the state system, thus easing the transition process. This is expected to make a major contribution to future capital market development, as well as creating a permanent constituency for economic reforms.

Today's conventional wisdom is that the pension problems that are centred in Europe will have to be resolved in the foreseeable future, and that there are only a limited number of options in dealing with the issue:

- Raise mandatory social charges on employees and employers to cover increasing pension obligations under PAYG systems. It is unlikely that any degree of uniformity in the EU can be achieved in this regard, given the aforementioned large inter-country differences in pension schemes and their financing. The competitive effects of the required major increases in employer burdens, especially in a unified market with a common currency, are unlikely to make this a feasible alternative. No more palatable is likely to be saddling employees with additional social contributions in what are already some of the most heavily taxed environments in the world.

- Make major reductions in retirement benefits, cutting dramatically into benefit levels. This is unlikely to be any more feasible politically than the first option, especially considering the way many PAYG systems have been positioned—as 'contributions' (not taxes) which would assure a comfortable old age. Taking away something people feel has already been 'paid for' is far more difficult politically than denying them something they never had in the first place. The sensitivity of fiscal reforms to social welfare is illustrated by the fact that just limiting the growth in pension expenditures to the projected rate of economic growth from 2015 onwards would reduce income-replacement rates from 45 per cent to 30 per cent over a period of fifteen years, leaving those among the elderly without adequate personal resources in relative poverty.

- Significant increases in the retirement age at which individuals are eligible for full PAYG-financed pensions, perhaps to age 70 for those not incapacitated by ill health. This is unlikely to be any more palatable than the previous option, especially in many countries where there has been active pressure to go the other way, that is, to reduce the age of eligibility for PAYG retirement benefits to 60 or even 55. This is compounded by a chronically high unemployment rate in Europe, which has been widely used as a justification for earlier retirements.

- Major increases in general taxation levels or government borrowing to top up eroding trust funds or finance PAYG benefits on a continuing basis. Again, this is an unlikely alternative owing to the economic and competitive consequences of further increases in tax rates, major political resistance, and Maastricht-type fiscal constraints that are likely to obtain in the EU. Even if they do not, the fact is that national states maintaining PAYG systems—under a single currency and without the ability to monetize debt—will have to compete for financing in a unified, rated bond market, which will constrain their ability to run large borrowing programmes to something akin to those of the states in the USA.

- Major pension reforms to progressively move away from PAYG systems towards defined-contribution and defined-benefit schemes such as those widely used in the USA, Chile, Singapore, Malaysia, the UK, the Netherlands, Denmark and certain other EU countries. Each of these differs in detail, but all involve the creation of large asset pools that are reasonably actuarially sound. Where such asset pools already exist, more attention will have to be focused on investment performance, with a shift away from government bonds towards higher-yielding assets in order to help maintain benefit levels.

Given the relatively bleak outlook for the first several of these alternatives, it seems inevitable that increasing reliance will be placed on the last of these options. The fact that future generations can no longer count on the 'free ride' of the present value of benefits exceeding the present value of contributions and social charges as the demographics inevitably turn against them—in the presence of clear fiscal constraints facing governments—requires fundamental rethinking of pension arrangements in most OECD countries, notably those of the European Union. Alternatively, the fiscal deficits required by unreformed national PAYG pension schemes in those EU countries that are part of a single-currency zone would imply higher interest rates across the euro zone than would otherwise be the case and/or higher levels of inflation if there is monetization by the European Central Bank of some of the incremental public debt.

3.3. Asset allocation and cross-links with mutual funds

As there are wide differences among countries in their reliance on PAYG pension systems and in the degree of demographic and financial pressure to build actuarially viable asset pools, so there are equally wide differences in how those assets have been allocated.

As shown in Table 9.3, the United States (not including the Social Security Trust Fund) and the United Kingdom have relied quite heavily on domestic equities, 48 per cent and 56 per cent, respectively. The largest fifteen pension fund managers in 1997 had about 50 per cent of equity assets invested in passive funds, versus about 5 per cent in the case of mutual funds. The share of asset allocation to domestic bonds is highest in Germany and Denmark, followed by Portugal, Switzerland and the Netherlands. Foreign equity holdings are proportionately highest in Ireland, the Netherlands and Belgium (each with small domestic stock markets). Foreign bond holdings play a

Table 9.3. Pension fund asset allocation, end-1994 (%)

	Domestic equities	Domestic bonds	Foreign equities	Foreign bonds	Real estate	Cash
Belgium	17	22	33	18	4	6
Denmark	14	70	3	2	9	2
Germany	6	72	3	4	13	2
Ireland	25	19	42	3	6	5
Netherlands	9	49	20	7	13	2
Portugal	3	58	6	7	1	25
Switzerland	8	54	5	5	19	9
UK	56	7	26	5	4	2
USA	48	26	12	2	4	8

Note: Figures for the USA reflect defined-benefit assets only.

Sources: Global Investors; Greenwich Associates.

major role only in the case of Belgium. Equity holdings among the US$1.9 trillion in pension assets (mid-1996) varies widely, ranging from 75 per cent of assets in the UK, to 42 per cent in Belgium, 34 per cent in the Netherlands, 13 per cent in France, and 11 per cent in Spain.

With the euro, regulations that require pension funds to match the currency of their assets with the currency of their liabilities drop away within the single-currency zone, which will greatly broaden the equity opportunities open to fund trustees. In some cases currency-exposure restrictions have forced pension fund equity allocations to be overweight in certain industries (such as petroleum in the Netherlands) owing to the importance of a few companies in national equity market capitalization, in which case the euro will permit significantly improved sectoral asset allocation in pension port-folios. This suggests large increases in cross-border equity flows in Europe, and the creation of pan-European pension fund performance benchmarks to replace existing national benchmarks (Martinson, 1997).

The growing role of defined-contribution plans in the United States has led to strong linkages between pension funds and mutual funds. Numerous mutual funds—notably in the equities sector—are strongly influenced by 401(k) and other pension inflows. At the end of the ten-year period 1986–95, mutual funds controlled almost 40 per cent of such assets. At the end of 1996, over 35 per cent (US$1.2 trillion) of mutual fund assets represented retirement accounts of various types in the United States. Some 15 per cent of total retirement assets were invested in mutual funds, up from about 1 per cent in 1980 (Reid and Crumrine, 1997). This is reflected in the structure of the pension fund management industry in the United States. The top twenty-five defined-benefit asset managers in 1995 were trust departments of commercial banks, with the top ten averaging discretionary assets of about US$150 billion each. There is little evidence of increasing market concentration in the fixed-income part of the trust business, with the top twenty-five firms controlling 62 per cent of assets in both 1990 and 1995. However, the top twenty-five market share in the equities segment (which was roughly twice as large) rose from 29 per cent in 1990 to 35 per cent in 1995, presumably owing to the importance of performance differentials in attracting assets.[16] Among the top twenty-five 401(k) plan fund managers in 1995, three were mutual fund companies, ten were insurance companies, five were banks, one was a broker–dealer, two were diversified financial firms, and four were specialist asset managers.[17]

European pension funds' retention of asset managers has changed significantly over the years. In 1987 banks had a market share of about 95 per cent, while insurance companies and independent fund managers split the rest about evenly. By 1995 independent fund managers had captured over 40 per cent of the market, banks were down to about 55 per cent and insurance companies captured the rest. There is also some evidence of increasing pension fund management concentration, at least in the UK, where in 1995 six pension fund managers accounted for about 70 per cent of the market. Of these, five were actively managed funds and one (Barclays Global Investors) specialized in index funds.

4. Asset Management for Private Clients

One of the largest pools of institutionally managed assets in the world is associated with high-net-worth individuals and families, generally grouped under the heading of 'private banking'. Total funds under management have been variously estimated at up to US$10 trillion[18]—significantly exceeding the size of the global pension asset pool—although the confidentiality aspect of private banking makes such estimates little more than educated guesses. Figure 9.6 provides a rough estimate of sources and destinations of private wealth held outside the home country of the investor.

Private clients' asset management objectives are an amalgam of preferences across a number of variables among which liquidity, yield, security, tax-efficiency, confidentiality, and service level are paramount. Each of these plays a distinctive role.

- *Yield.* The traditional European private banking client was concerned with wealth preservation in the face of antagonistic government policies and fickle asset markets. Clients demanded the utmost in discretion from their private bankers, with whom they maintained lifelong relationships initiated by personal recommendations. Such high-net-worth clients have to some degree given way to more active and sophisticated customers. Aware of opportunity costs and often exposed to high marginal tax rates, they consider net after-tax yield to be far more relevant than the security and focus on capital preservation traditionally sought by high-

---

[16] *Sources*: JP Morgan, US Department of Labor, *Pensions and Investments*, EBRI.
[17] *Source*: *Pensions and Investments*.
[18] *Source*: Chase Manhattan, 1994 estimate.

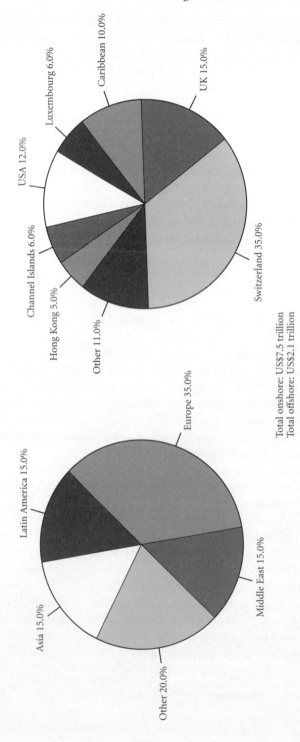

(a) Source

(b) Destination

Total onshore: US$7.5 trillion
Total offshore: US$2.1 trillion

Figure 9.6. Estimated source and destination of offshore private banking wealth
Source: Chase Manhattan Private Bank, 1996.

net-worth clients. They may prefer gains to accrue in the form of capital appreciation rather than interest or dividend income, and tend to have a much more active response to changes in total rate of return.

- *Security*. The environment faced by high-net-worth investors is arguably more stable today than it has been in the past. The probability of revolution, war and expropriation has declined over the years in Europe, North America, the Far East and Latin America. Nevertheless, a large segment of the private banking market remains highly security-conscious. Such clients are generally prepared to trade off yield for stability, safety and capital preservation.
- *Tax-efficiency*. Like everyone else, high-net-worth clients are highly sensitive to taxation, perhaps more so as cash-strapped politicians target 'the rich' in a constant search for fiscal revenues. International financial markets have traditionally provided plenty of tax-avoidance and tax-evasion opportunities ranging from offshore tax havens to private banking services able to sidestep even sophisticated efforts to claim the state's share.
- *Confidentiality*. Secrecy is a major factor in private banking—secrecy required for personal reasons, for business reasons, for tax reasons and for legal or political reasons. Confidentiality, in this sense, is a 'product' that is bought and sold as part of private asset management business through secrecy and blocking statutes on the part of countries and high levels of discretion on the part of financial institutions. The value of this product depends on the probability and consequences of disclosure, and is 'priced' in the form of lower portfolio returns, higher fees, suboptimum asset allocation, or reduced liquidity as compared with portfolios not driven by confidentiality motives (see Walter, 1990).
- *Service level*. While some of the tales of personal services provided for private banking clients are undoubtedly apocryphal, the 'fringe benefits' offered to high-net-worth clients may well influence the choice of and loyalty to a particular financial institution. Such benefits may save time, reduce anxiety, increase efficiency, or make the wealth management process more convenient. Personal service is a way for personal asset managers to show their full commitment to clients accustomed to high levels of personal service in their daily lives.

The essence of private banking is to identify accurately each client's unique objectives, and to have the flexibility and expertise to satisfy these as fully as possible in a highly competitive marketplace. On the assumption that the vast majority of funds managed by private banking vendors have not been accumulated illegally, the demand for financial secrecy in Europe relates mainly to matters of taxation and transfers of funds across borders. EMU will eliminate the latter among the participating countries, something that has long been a concern of virtually all Europeans with assets to preserve. As noted earlier, tax issues will take much longer to address, and will probably always be a major driver of the international private banking industry.

In particular, substantial private assets have traditionally made the one-way journey to Switzerland, Luxembourg, Austria, or other locations where they can be concealed from local fiscal authorities while being prudently managed by trustworthy and reliable bankers or investment managers. This is likely to change. We have already noted that the tax-haven status of Austria and Luxembourg will sooner or later be eliminated under fiscal pressure from partner countries, and EU states will eventually come together on rules regarding personal taxation and disclosure of tax information. Should this happen, the ability to conceal private wealth from tax collectors will diminish within the EU, and with it the 'value' of secrecy as one of the services offered by EU investment managers. Only Switzerland will remain as a European haven for tax evaders (as distinct from those committing tax fraud as defined under Swiss law).[19]

Competition among European and other private banking firms is likely to continue to intensify, and will have to contend as well with a serious effort on the part of American and other non-European asset managers to offer global real-time asset management services to European private banking clients. Others will be offering very sophisticated products, perhaps at lower cost than the European private banks have charged in the past. Some will be offering innovative mutual funds or shares in limited partnerships or other specialized investments. Certainly there will be a profusion of both services and those offering them. And the field of competitive struggle will be in marketing just as much as it is in product development and investment performance. Such competition is bound to lower fees and commissions for private client asset management, and the inherent strength of the European banks' control over their high-net-worth clients will be tested.

5. Competitive Restructuring of the Asset Management Industry

We have noted that various kinds of financial firms have emerged to perform asset management functions—commercial banks, savings banks, postal savings institutions, savings cooperatives, credit unions, securities firms (full-service firms and various kinds of specialists), insurance companies, finance companies, finance subsidiaries of industrial companies, mutual fund companies, financial advisers and various others. Members of each strategic group compete with each other, as well as with members of other strategic groups. There are two questions. First, what determines competitive advantage in operating distribution gateways to the end-investor? Secondly, what determines competitive advantage in the asset management process itself?

---

[19] As long as a decade ago, Dr Marcus Lusser, then President of the Swiss National Bank, conceded the diminishing value of banking secrecy. In his opinion, the strengthening of the EU was bound to weaken Switzerland as a centre for the management of private wealth. He advised bankers in Switzerland to concentrate on the institutional investment management sector in the future ('Good-bye to Complacency', *Financial Times*, 19 December 1988). In conversation, Swiss private bankers appear to agree that upwards of two-thirds of assets under management of OECD-based private clients could disappear if Swiss banks reported assets and income to home-country tax authorities.

One supposition is that distribution of asset management services is both scope-driven and technology-driven. That is, it can be distributed jointly with other types of financial services, and thereby benefit from cost economies of scope as well as demand economies of scope (cross-selling). This would tend to give retail-oriented financial services firms like commercial and universal banks, life insurance companies and savings institutions a competitive advantage in distribution. At the same time, more-specialized firms may establish cost-effective distribution of asset management services using proprietary remote-marketing techniques like the mail, telephone selling or the Internet, or by 'renting' distribution through the established infrastructures of other financial intermediaries like banks, insurance companies or mutual fund supermarkets. They may also gain access through fund management consultants and financial advisers.

Asset management itself depends heavily on portfolio management skills as well as economies of scale, capital investment and technologies involved in back-office functions, some of which can be outsourced. Since fiduciary activities must be kept separate from other financial services operations that involve potential conflicts of interest, either through organizational separation or Chinese walls, there is not much to be gained in the way of economies of scope.

Intersectoral competition, alongside already vigorous intrasectoral competition, is what will make asset management one of the most competitive areas of finance, even in the presence of rapid growth in the size of the market for asset management services. Certainly the dynamics of competition for the growing pools of defined-benefit and defined-contribution pension assets in various parts of the world, and its cross-linkage to the mutual fund business, has led to various strategic initiatives among fund managers. These include mergers, acquisitions and strategic alliances among fund managers as well as between fund managers, commercial and universal banks, securities broker–dealers, and insurance companies. This is reflected in Table 9.4, which presents the volume and number of mergers and acquisitions involving asset managers, both in total and managers of open-end mutual funds only, covering the twelve-and-a-half-year period from 1985 until the first half of 1997. Altogether, there were over a thousand transactions, valued at US$36.5 billion, of which 242 transactions, worth US$15.7 billion, involved mutual funds—note that the average size of mutual fund transactions was much larger than the average size of the overall deal flow. About 70 per cent of the total M&A value involved European targets, and 25 per cent involved US targets. Geographically, British asset managers represented the largest single target group, with 260 transactions, worth US$12.3 billion, during this period, with the predominant buyers representing Continental European institutions, mainly banks and insurance companies. There was roughly the same volume of activity within Continental Europe, with 231 transactions, valued at US$12.5 billion. US acquirers were mostly confined to domestic transactions, and only represented about one-quarter of the volume of intra-European transactions. Note also that in the case of mutual fund acquisitions, the focus of transactions again was within Continental Europe. These data suggest that M&A market action and strategic repositioning substantially reflect

Table 9.4. Merger and acquisitions activity in the asset management industry, 1985–1997 (US$ m. and no. of transactions)

(*a*) *Total*

	Total asset managers	Open-end mutual fund managers
Global target	36,502 (1,038)	15,677 (242)
European target	25,213 (509)	11,808 (135)
US target	9,146 (341)	3,706 (67)
Other target	2,143 (188)	163 (40)

(*b*) *Total asset managers*

	Total	European acquirer	US acquirer
US target	9,146 (341)	2,477 (19)	6,102 (311)
UK target	12,326 (260)	11,434 (227)	289 (35)
Continental European target	12,617 (245)	12,504 (231)	0 (0)

(*c*) *Open-end mutual fund managers*

	Total	European acquirer	US acquirer
US target	3,706 (67)	1,549 (5)	1,661 (64)
UK target	870 (21)	736 (17)	33 (2)
Continental European target	10,991 (119)	10,683 (107)	0 (0)

Note: Data up to June 1997; the figure in parentheses in each case is the number of deals.

Source: Securities Data Corporation; author's calculations.

the economic drivers of the asset management industry's restructuring. The action, with respect to both pension funds and mutual funds, is in Western Europe.

Market valuations of asset management companies have been quite high in comparison with other types of firms in the financial services industry, and this has been reflected in prices paid in M&A transactions. At mid-year 1996 in the United States, when the price to earnings ratio (based on expected 1996 earnings) for the S&P 500 stocks averaged 16.2, the price to earnings ratios of the top ten domestic commercial banks with strong retail banking businesses averaged 10.3, and the top life and casualty insurance companies averaged price to earnings ratios of about 10, the top eight publicly owned investment banks (including JP Morgan and Bankers Trust) only 7.9, while the price to earnings ratios of the top nine asset managers averaged about 14. The average share price to book value ratio for the top ten US commercial banks in 1996 was 1.83; for the top investment banks it was only 1.27, while for the top nine asset managers it was 4.64.

Besides providing access to distribution and fund management expertise, the underlying economics of this deal flow presumably have to do with the realization of economies of scale and economies of scope, making possible both cost reductions and cross-selling of multiple types of funds, banking and/or insurance services, investment advice, high-quality research, etc. in a one-stop-shopping interface for investors— despite a good deal of evidence that investors are quite happy to shop on their own with low-cost fund managers. Empirical evidence of either economies of scale or economies of scope in this sector is lacking, although the plausibility of scale economies exceeds that for scope economies. In any event, there has been little evidence so far that M&A activity in this sector has led to lower fees and charges to retail investors (Gasparino, 1997).

Table 9.5 provides some indication of the relative size of the thirty-six top asset managers. Overall, countries with traditional reliance on funded pension schemes and mutual funds marketed to retail investors—the United States, Japan and the United Kingdom—were home to seventy-two of the top one hundred asset managers and 76 per cent of the assets under management.[20] Continental European countries captured only a quarter of the top spots and 22 per cent of the assets, although this is likely to change as PAYG pension programmes increasingly give way to dedicated asset pools and as financial market integration stimulates a competitive battle among different types of financial institutions for asset management services. Specifically, within Europe, 31 per cent of assets are managed in the United Kingdom, 20.3 per cent in Switzerland, 16.5 per cent in Germany, 15.6 per cent in France, 8.4 per cent in the Netherlands, and the balance in Liechtenstein, Denmark, Spain, Belgium, Sweden and Italy.[21]

6. Institutional Asset Pools and European Capital Market Development

The impact of EMU on European financial markets in the context of a growing role of performance-driven asset managers is likely to run the gamut from the composition of financial assets and the scope available for portfolio diversification to competition among financial centres and corporate governance.

6.1. Composition of financial assets

The role of a burgeoning European asset management industry in promoting disintermediation in an increasingly unified financial market is unlikely to differ very much in

---

[20] 'Watson Wyatt World-500', *Pension Age*, September 1996.
[21] *Institutional Investor*.

Table 9.5. Top global money managers, as of 31 December 1997 (total assets under management US$ m.)

Japan Life Insurance Bureau (Tokyo, Japan)	865,020	Morgan Stanley, Dean Witter & Discover Co. (New York, NY)	234,806
FMR Corp. (Boston, MA)	515,300	Allianz AG (Munich, Germany)	210,000
Groupe AXA (Paris, France)	500,300	J.P. Morgan & Co. (New York, NY)	208,605
Zurich Group (Zurich, Switzerland)	460,000	Equitable Life Assurance Society of the U.S. (New York, NY)	207,999
Merrill Lynch & Co. (incl. MAM) (New York, NY)—merged Nov. 97	450,000	Franklin Resources (San Mateo, CA)	174,954
Union Bank of Switzerland (Zurich, Switzerland)	449,000	Marsh & McLennan Cos. (New York, NY)	173,443
Barclays Bank PLC (London, UK)	385,449	United Asset Management Corp. (Boston, MA)	168,024
Credit Suisse/Winterthur (Zurich, Switzerland)	380,000	American Express Co. (New York, NY)	147,696
Swiss Bank Corporation (Basle, Switzerland)	375,100	Internationale Nederlanden Groep (Amsterdam, The Netherlands)	140,000
The Prudential Corporation (London, UK)	350,000	Travelers Group (New York, NY)	133,337
Nippon Life Insurance Co. (Tokyo, Japan)	342,800	Wellington Management Co. (Boston, MA)	133,162
State Street Boston Corp. (Boston, MA)	300,947	Northern Trust Corp. (Chicago, IL)	130,252
The Prudential Ins. Co. of America (Newark, NJ)	271,700	Chase Manhattan Corp. (New York, NY)	130,095
Capital Group Cos. (Los Angeles, CA)	259,704	Invesco Group Ltd. (London, UK)	126,172
Mellon Bank Corp. (Pittsburgh, PA)	258,923	Nomura Securities Corp. (Tokyo, Japan)	115,000
The Vanguard Group (Valley Forge, PA)	257,800	PNC Bank Corp. (Pittsburgh, PA)	110,396
Deutsche Bank AG (Frankfurt, Germany)	240,000	Pimco Advisors (Newport Beach, CA)	110,022
Bankers Trust Co. (New York, NY)	239,582	T. Rowe Price Associates (Baltimore, MD)	100,390

character from what has occurred in the United States, except that its pacing may be quite different under distinctly European institutional and regulatory conditions.

Europe, with roughly twice the proportion of financial assets on the books of banks and other financial intermediaries of the United States, will go through much the same process of financial disintermediation that characterized the United States in the 1970s and 1980s. A recent study suggests that the aforementioned, gradual shift from banking to securities transactions is likely to be accelerated by EMU because the factors that underlie this development, by reducing transactions and information costs (both heavily driven by technology) and making available new products to end-investors, cannot be fully exploited in a fragmented foreign exchange environment, that is, one characterized by widespread currency-matching rules bearing on issuers and investors. This includes a range of financial instruments that are broadly available in the United States but have been unable to reach the critical mass needed for trading efficiency and liquidity in Europe. 'If EMU has the side-effect of bringing those assets to the market, then the playing-field will tilt a little. If technology shifts the "management expenses" goal posts as well, then we may be in a new ball game' (Bishop, 1997).

The rise to prominence of institutional asset managers in Europe will do a great deal to enhance financial market liquidity. Mutual funds—whether part of defined-contribution pension schemes or mass-marketed as savings vehicles to the general public—and other types of money managers are so-called noise traders who must buy and sell assets whenever there are net fund purchases or redemptions, in addition to discretionary trades to adjust portfolios. They therefore tend to make a disproportionate contribution to capital market liquidity. Mutual funds alone account for the largest share of US equity turnover, for example, with the trades of the largest mutual fund company (Fidelity) estimated to account for 12–15 per cent of daily stock trading and generating some US$200 million annually in dealing commissions.

Overall, it is likely that EMU will favour the asset management industry, both in terms of market share in the financial intermediation process and in terms of growth prospects. Asset managers will be less affected than banks in terms of the cost implications of EMU and will benefit disproportionately from the increased depth and breadth of the European capital market that a single currency implies. At the same time, they will be favoured by the fiscal implications of Maastricht-type criteria, which will place greater pressure on governments to accelerate the transition from PAYG pension schemes to various types of defined-contribution programmes.[22]

6.2. The market for markets and the location of financial activity

Given their size and the performance pressures bearing on them, institutional asset managers try to focus their trading on financial markets that are marked by the following characteristics:

- a high degree of liquidity, notably for block trades, and good after-hours capabilities;
- low transactions costs, notably for commissions and spreads, clearance and settlement services, back-office operations, custody services, telecommunications and other financial infrastructure services;
- high levels of transparency in securities transactions and in the securities themselves, including strong regulatory and enforcement capabilities to ensure honest dealing and a level playing-field;
- a broad product range of underlying securities and derivatives, and strong innovative capabilities;

---

[22] For a discussion of the overall capital market effects of EMU, see JP Morgan (1997).

- a uniform accounting and legal infrastructure that meets global standards; and
- a major equities component of capital markets, of prime interest to both pension funds and mutual funds, running from large-cap global companies to IPOs and private equity, with strong turnover and deep investor participation.

The EU in 1997 still had a highly fragmented system of thirty-two stock exchanges and twenty-three futures and options exchanges, among which only one market, London, came close to meeting the needs of major institutional asset managers and their probable future evolution. In the presence of electronic links and low-cost transactions services to institutional investors this market fragmentation should disappear relatively quickly, especially under pressure of a single currency.

The battle among EU equity markets will perhaps be the one most heavily affected by the behaviour of highly performance-oriented asset managers. Already the Investment Services Directive (ISD) has permitted exchanges to place trading screens in other financial centres. Easdaq has been in the process of creating a pan-European over-the-counter exchange patterned on NASDAQ in the United States to attract new, high-growth companies. National markets in Frankfurt, Paris, Brussels and Amsterdam have been trying to do the same thing and link up in the form of Euro NM to compete with both NASDAQ and Easdaq, even as comparable initiatives are underway among the Nordic countries. The rapid growth of institutional asset management in Europe, however, is likely to promote a fairly rapid shakeout of these competing market initiatives based on how they meet the aforementioned criteria, certainly under conditions of a common currency—with perhaps two or three OTC and organized exchanges accounting for the vast bulk of European trading activity in the medium-term future. The large, integrated US market supports only one major exchange, and one major OTC trading system, alongside a number of specialist exchanges in New York, Philadelphia, Chicago and San Francisco plus continued challenge from electronic exchanges such as the Arizona Stock Exchange (AZX). The US 'equilibrium' market structure may well be an inappropriate indicator for a future integrated European market supporting the rapidly growing needs of institutional asset managers.

Indeed, the US locational pattern as it has evolved over a much greater span of time may also be a reasonable model of what will eventually develop in Europe:

1. a single wholesale market for transactions execution (New York) not necessarily identical to the seat of monetary policy and financial regulation (Washington), with a reasonable argument to be made that a bit of 'distance' between the markets and their regulators can be helpful;
2. dispersed asset management centres (Boston, Chicago, Philadelphia, Stamford, San Francisco), and sometimes no centres at all in a business where the necessary information, interpretation and transactions services can all be delivered electronically and in real time;
3. specialist centres focusing on particular financial instruments (Chicago, Philadelphia) or industries (San Francisco) that have their roots in history or ongoing economic developments.

With respect to the location of asset management activity in Europe *per se*, few comprehensive data are available, although it is likely that Switzerland (Zurich and Geneva) and London will continue to share the top spot, with very different businesses centred on private banking and institutional asset management, respectively. Other Continental European asset management centres are far behind. In the equity sector, London ranks first with over US$1 trillion under management, followed by Zurich, Basle and Geneva combined with US$740 billion, Frankfurt with US$157 billion (excluding intercorporate holdings), Edinburgh with US$138 billion and Stockholm with US$89 billion. None of the other European financial centres rank in the top twenty-five. These numbers compare with US$1.5 trillion managed in Tokyo and US$896 billion in New York.[23] Such rankings in the future are likely to shift as European financial integration continues, especially under a single currency, with greater polarization possible.

6.3. Portfolio diversification and globalization

Professional fund managers attempt to optimize asset allocation in line with modern investment concepts by taking advantage of the potential for domestic and international portfolio diversification inherent across the range of financial instruments being offered, as well as by using the most efficient (friction-free) available securities markets and infrastructure services. Both dimensions are likely to be affected by European financial integration and a common currency.

For EU institutional investors, national currencies will obviously disappear among participating EU countries as a source of portfolio diversification. So will variations in interest rates, with a single rate structure prevailing in the entire region. Investors seeking sources of diversification across less than perfectly correlated exchange rates and interest rates will thus have to look outside the region covered by the euro, while external investors will lose any comparable diversification gains that may have existed within the region. The euro zone becomes a single market risk and sovereign risk 'bucket' from the perspective of portfolio diversification.

EMU is also likely to increase correlations across equity markets covered by the euro, representing a continuation of the gradual increases in inter-market correlations that have already been observed.[24] This will force portfolio managers to focus relatively more heavily on diversification strategies involving non-European markets. The attractiveness of emerging-market equities may therefore increase owing to potentially lower correlations between emerging-market stock returns and the major market in-

---

[23] 'Survey of Global Fund Management', *Financial Times*, 27 April 1997.

[24] See, for example, Longin and Solnik (1995). Portfolio diversification gains tend to be greater across global equity markets than across global bond markets, where they derive solely from less than perfectly correlated interest rate and exchange rate movements. Moreover, unlike the global bond markets, stocks tend to be more highly differentiated and subject to local trading conditions, although listings on foreign stock exchanges through depository receipts have made some foreign equities considerably more accessible to foreign investors.

dexes such as Standard & Poor's 500 index, the French CAC-40 or the German Dax equity averages.

In terms of asset classes, we have already noted that EMU will create a new, generic type of fixed-income security that will be very similar to municipal bonds in the United States. Since the possibility of debt monetization at the national level will disappear among EMU countries, borrowing requirements of national governments will involve rated debt instruments denominated in euros that will be available to institutional investors, with spreads differing among issuing governments based on the market's perceptions of the degree of risk involved. Since currency risk will be eliminated within the EMU region, the focus will be entirely on market risk and credit risk, and such 'Euro-munis' will represent a major asset class in institutional funds pools for both EU and non-EU portfolios such as those managed in the United States and Japan.

Taxation remains a major problem in the creation of efficient pension asset allocations via international portfolio diversification. The reason is that governments often do not provide reciprocal tax exemption for pension assets invested abroad. For example, many countries exempt employee and employer pension contributions and pension fund earnings from tax, and subsequently tax income at prevailing personal income tax rates when it is distributed upon retirement—although some countries tax retirement income at concessionary rates as well. If part of a retirement fund is invested abroad, however, the host country often treats the assets the same as all other financial assets, and levies taxes on interest, dividends and/or capital gains at regular withholding rates. Such differential tax treatment obviously biases asset allocation towards domestic investments, and can significantly affect portfolio optimization. Several proposals have dealt with this issue. The OECD Model Tax Convention would tax dividend income at 15 per cent, interest income at 10 per cent and capital gains at 0 per cent without regard to the distinction between retirement and non-retirement assets. The US Model Income Tax Convention would tax dividend income of foreign assets at 15 per cent and exempt interest income and capital gains, but would also exempt all income on retirement assets as long as at least half of the participants of the fund were residents of the home country. Ideally, of course, there should be reciprocal exemption from tax of all retirement assets invested internationally together with reciprocal acceptance of certification of retirement plan qualifications (Schott Stevens, 1997).

6.4. Asset managers, shareholder value and corporate governance

Assuming that the rapid advance in prominence of institutional asset managers follows along the lines suggested in this chapter, the capital markets will increasingly be the major source of external financing for European corporations in the future—as against the traditional heavy Continental European reliance (compared with American and British companies) on bank finance for debt and bank and corporate long-term shareholdings for equity. Fiduciary asset pools managed against performance benchmarks by mutual funds and pension funds will create increasingly fluid sources of capital for industry, and a fundamental shift in the accountability of management and monitoring of corporate performance in Europe.[25]

In such a system, industrial restructuring will increasingly be triggered by the emergence of a control premium between the existing share price of a corporation and the value that an unaffiliated acquirer (whether an industrial company or an active financial investor) perceives could be unlocked by changes in management strategies or policies.

Based on such a view of corporate underperformance, an investor may purchase a significant block of shares and signal his unhappiness with the company's performance, or perhaps initiate a full takeover bid for the target firm (which is now 'in play'). Institutional asset managers can assume a critical role in such a scenario. They may agree that a control premium does indeed exist and themselves begin purchasing shares, thereby placing still greater pressure on the management of the target company.[26]

Even in the absence of a potential acquirer putting the company in play, major institutional asset managers who, because of their size or portfolio constraints, find it difficult or impossible to dispose of their ownership interest in a company they feel is performing poorly can request a meeting with management about the firm's strategy, financial performance, and realization of shareholder value, and perhaps speak out at annual general meetings. Concerns about unwanted takeover efforts and institutional investor dissatisfaction may in turn prompt management to undertake a self-restructuring, seek an acceptable merger partner ('white knight'), pay out special dividends or initiate share repurchases, or find other ways to enhance shareholder value and efficiency in the use of capital to preclude the emergence of a control premium and hostile action.

Such a transition—from the traditional Continental European corporate governance process with two-tier boards and large, friendly ownership stakes (*noyeux durs*) insulating management from the pressure of external shareholders seeking improved total returns to a more 'contestable' model along Anglo-American lines—is an important possible consequence of the growing role of professionally managed asset pools. The potential benefits of such developments involve reduced cost of capital through higher share prices and improved access to global financial markets and a greater capacity for restructuring the European economy in response to changes in technology, market competition and other fundamentals.

Investor-driven, market-based systems such as this will require much higher levels of transparency in corporate accounting and disclosure than has been the norm in most of Europe, together with greater reliance on public information provided by management and systemic surveillance by research analysts working aggressively on behalf of investors. It implies arm's-length financing on commercially viable terms by banks and financial markets, with financial institutions active in giving strategic and

---

[25] For a full discussion, see Sametz (forthcoming).

[26] For a comparison between traditional market-based and institution-based approaches to corporate control, see Story and Walter (1997).

financial advice and sometimes taking transitional, non-permanent equity positions in (and occasionally control of) corporations in the process of restructuring.

It also assumes that the principal stakeholders in corporations (shareholders, employees, managers and customers) accept that the central claim to legitimacy of free, investor-driven capital markets is that they generally provide the most efficient way of augmenting economic wealth, as against less viable politically driven allocation of capital. This approach assumes that government will not prove a light touch for corporate lobbies seeking to avoid restructurings or takeovers through access to the public purse as a less demanding and less disciplined source of capital. The labour market likewise needs to be supportive, so that workforces can be adapted and reallocated both functionally and geographically with the minimum of friction. Government's major task will be to provide EU-wide macroeconomic stability together with the regulatory and legal structure within which open capital markets may function, and to supply an acceptable and affordable social safety net.

7. Summary and Conclusions

The focus of this chapter has been the structure, conduct and performance of the asset management industry, with special reference to its evolution in the context of European financial integration and creation of an economic zone covered by a common currency. The industry was positioned in a domestic and global flow-of-funds framework as 'collective investment vehicles', with emphasis on its three principal components—mutual funds, pension funds and assets under management for high-net-worth individuals—and their interlinkages. There are six principal conclusions that can be drawn.

First, the asset management industry is likely to grow substantially in the years ahead. Institutionalization and professional management of household discretionary assets through mutual funds has probably run its course for the time being in terms of market share in some countries, such as the United States and the United Kingdom, but has barely begun in many of the Continental European countries that have traditionally been dominated by bank assets. Demographic and structural problems in national pension systems will require strong growth in dedicated financial asset pools as pay-as-you-go systems become increasingly unsupportable fiscally and alternative means of addressing the problem show themselves to be politically difficult or impossible to implement. There are, however, substantial differences of view as to the timing of these developments within national environments, since pension reform is politically difficult to carry out and the political willingness to do so is difficult to predict. In both mutual funds and pension funds, and their linkage through participant-influenced defined-contribution pension schemes, the centre of global growth is likely to be Western Europe.

Proliferation of asset management products, which is already exceedingly high in the United States and the United Kingdom, will no doubt be no less impressive in the remainder of the EU as financial markets become more fully integrated, especially under a common currency. There will be a great deal of jockeying for position and higher levels of concentration, especially in the fast-growing pension fund sector, that will begin to permeate the mutual fund business through defined-contribution plans—given the importance of economies of scale and the role of pension fund consultants. However, as in the United States, the role of fund supermarkets, low-cost distribution via the Internet, as well as the very large contingent of universal banks, insurance companies and non-European fund management companies is likely to prevent market structure from becoming monopolistic to any significant degree. Fund performance will become a commodity, with few differences among the major players and the majority of actively managed funds underperforming the indexes. This implies a competitive playing-field that, as in the United States, will be heavily conditioned by branding, advertising and distribution channels, which in turn are likely to move gradually away from the traditional dominance of banks in some of the EU markets. All of this implies that asset management fees—historically quite high, particularly in Continental Europe—will come under pressure as competition heats up, to the benefit of the individual investors and participants in funded pension plans.

Secondly, despite the prospects for rapid growth, the asset management industry is likely to be highly competitive. In addition to normal commercial rivalry among established players in the European national markets for asset management services, these same markets are being aggressively targeted by foreign suppliers from other EU countries as well from outside the EU, notably Switzerland and the United States. Moreover asset management (including private banking) is being marked for expansion by virtually every strategic group in the financial services sector—commercial and universal banks, private banks, securities firms, insurance companies, mutual fund companies, financial conglomerates, and financial advisers of various types.

Normally, the addition of new vendors in a given market would be expected to reduce market concentration, increase the degree of competition, and lead to an erosion of margins and trigger a more rapid pace of financial innovation. If the new vendors are from the same basic strategic groups as existing players, the expected outcome would be along conventional lines of intensified intra-industry competition. But if, as in this case, expansion-minded players come from very different strategic groups, the outcome may involve a substantially greater increase in the degree of competition. This is because of potential diversification benefits, possibilities for cross-subsidization and staying-power, and incremental horizontal or vertical integration gains that the player from 'foreign' strategic groups may be able to capture. And natural barriers to entry in the asset management industry—which include the need for capital investment in infrastructure (especially in distribution and back-office functions), human resources (especially in portfolio management), technology, and the realization of economies of scale and scope—are not excessively difficult for newcomers to surmount. So the degree of internal, external and intersectoral competition in this industry is likely to promote market efficiency for the benefit of the end-users in managing discretionary household asserts, pension funds, the wealth of high-net-worth individuals, and other types of asset pools in Europe.

Thirdly, the rapid evolution of the European institutional asset management industry will have a major impact on financial markets. The needs of highly performance-oriented institutional investors will accelerate the triage among competing debt and equity markets in favour of those that can best meet their evolving requirements for liquidity, execution efficiency, transparency, and efficient regulation. In turn, this will influence where firms and public entities choose to issue and trade securities in their search for cost-effective financing and execution. At the same time, the growing presence of institutional investors in European capital markets will greatly increase the degree of liquidity owing to their active trading patterns, and create a ready market for new classes of public sector securities that will emerge under EMU. And it will intensify competitive pressure and enhance opportunities for the sales and trading activities of banks and securities firms, and for the role of product development and research in providing useful investment ideas.

Fourthly, cross-border asset allocation will grow disproportionately as a product of institutional investors' search for efficient portfolios through international diversification, although such gains will disappear among those financial markets covered by EMU. However, IPD is inherently a global process, so that the gains will depend on inter-market correlations of interest rates, exchange rates, equity markets and other asset classes world-wide. With the EMU zone as essentially one 'bucket' with respect to currencies and interest rates, IPD options will shift to other asset classes, including emerging-market debt and equities. Arguably, much of this has already occurred as intra-EMS rates have converged in anticipation of EMU. This development will tend to promote the market share of passive funds, and increase the need for portfolio management skills applied to diversification outside the EMU region.

Fifthly, the development of a deeper and broader pan-European capital market spurred by the development of the institutional asset management industry will fundamentally alter the European market for corporate control, into a much more fluid one focused on financial performance and shareholder value. This in turn has the potential of triggering widespread and long-overdue European economic restructuring and creating a much trimmer, more competitive global economic force willing and able to disengage from uncompetitive sectors through the denial of capital, promoting leading-edge industries though venture capital and other forms of start-up financing. Such a transformation will hardly be painless, and will depend critically on political will and public support for a more market-driven growth process.

Finally, developments in institutional asset management will pose strategic challenges for the management of universal banks and other traditional European financial institutions in extracting maximum competitive advantage from this high-growth sector, in structuring and motivating their organizations, and in managing the conflicts of interest and professional conduct problems that can arise in asset management and can easily cause major problems for the value of an institution's competitive franchise. The fact that institutional asset management requires a global perspective, both on the buy side and on the sell side, reinforces the need to achieve a correspondingly global market positioning for many financial institutions, although technology and the changing economics of distribution virtually assure the survival of a healthy cohort of asset management boutiques and specialists.

References

1994–96 Advisory Council on Social Security (1997), *Report of the 1994–96 Advisory Council on Social Security: Findings and Recommendations*, Washington, DC: US Government Printing Office.

Bassi, Mario (1996), *Der Bankunabhängige Vermögensverwalter*, Zurich: Schulthess Polygraphischer Verlag.

Bernstein Research (1996), *The Future of Money Management in America—1997 Edition*, New York: Sanford Bernstein.

Bishop, Graham (1997), *Post Emu: Bank Credit versus Capital Markets*, London: Salomon Brothers, Inc.

Cadette, Walter M. (1997), 'Social Security: Financing the Baby-Boom's Retirement', Jerome Levy Economics Institute Working Paper no. 192 (April).

Chordia, Tarun (1996), 'The Structure of Mutual Fund Charges', *Journal of Financial Economics*, June.

Davis, E. P. (1995), *Pension Funds*, Oxford: Clarendon Press.

Davis International Banking Consultants (1996), *Trends in European Asset Management*, New York: Smith Barney.

Dermine, Jean (1993) (ed.), *European Banking after 1992*, rev. edn., Oxford: Basil Blackwell.

Epstein, Neil and Bruce R. Brewington (1997), *The Investment Management Industry in the United States*, New York: Putnam, Lovell & Thornton.

First Consulting (1997), *European Pensions*, London: AMP Asset Management.

Gasparino, Charles (1997), 'Do Mutual Fund Mergers Hurt Small Investors?' *Wall Street Journal*, 8 July.

Giddy, Ian, Anthony Saunders and Ingo Walter (1996), 'Alternative Models of Clearance and Settlement: The Case of a Single European Capital Market', *Journal of Money, Credit and Banking*, November.

Goldstein, Michael L. *et al.* (1997), *The Future of Money Management in America*, New York: Bernstein Research.

Griffin, Mark (1997), 'The Global Pension Time Bomb and Its Capital Market Impact', New York: Goldman Sachs & Co.

Gruber, Martin J. (1996), 'Another Puzzle: The Growth of Actively Managed Mutual Funds', Presidential Address presented at the American Finance Association, San Francisco, January 1996; *Journal of Finance*, May 1996.

Hale, David (1994), 'The Economic Consequences of America's Mutual Fund Boom', *International Economy*, March/April.

Harrison, Debbie (1995), 'Pension Fund Investment in Europe', London: FT Financial Publishing.

Holzmann, Robert (1996), 'Pension Reform, Financial Market Development and Economic

Growth: Preliminary Evidence from Chile', Working Paper 96/94, Washington, DC: IMF (August).

Hurley, Mark P., Sharon I. Meers, Ben J. Bornstein and Neil R. Strumingher (1995), *The Coming Evolution of the Investment Management Industry: Opportunities and Strategies*, New York: Goldman Sachs & Co.

Investment Company Institute (1996), *Mutual Fund Fact Book*, Washington, DC: Investment Company Institute.

JP Morgan (1997), *EMU: Impacts on Financial Markets*, New York: JP Morgan.

Levich, Richard and Ingo Walter (1990), 'Tax-Driven Regulatory Drag and Competition among European Financial Centers', in Horst Siebert (ed.), *Reforming Capital Income Taxation*, Tübingen: J.C.B. Mohr/Paul Siebeck.

Longin, François and Bruno Solnik (1995), 'Is the Correlation of International Equity Returns Constant?', *Journal of International Money and Finance*, 14(1).

Martinson, Jane (1997), 'Management Revolution', *Financial Times*, 21 November.

Neave, Edwin (1992), *The Economic Organization of a Financial System*, London: Routledge.

Patel, Jayendu, Richard J. Zeckhauser and Darryll Hendricks (1994), 'Investment Fund Performance: Evidence from Mutual Funds, Cross-Border Investments, and New Issues', in Ryuzo Sato, Richard Levich and Rama Ramachandran (eds.), *Japan, Europe and International Financial Markets: Analytical and Empirical Perspectives*, Cambridge: Cambridge University Press.

Reid, Brian and Jean Crumrine (1997), *Retirement Plan Holdings of Mutual Funds, 1996*, Washington, DC: Investment Company Institute.

Remolona, Eli M., Paul Kleiman and Debbie Gruenstein (1997), 'Market Returns and Mutual Fund Flows', *Federal Reserve Bank of New York Economic Policy Review*, July.

Sametz, Arnold (forthcoming), *The Power and Influence of Pension and Mutual Funds*, Amsterdam: Kluwer.

Saunders, Anthony and Ingo Walter (1994), *Universal Banking in the United States*, New York: Oxford University Press.

Saunders, Anthony and Ingo Walter (1995) (eds.), *Universal Banking*, Burr Ridge, IL: Irwin Professional.

Schott Stevens, Paul (1997), 'Selected Issues in International Taxation of Retirement Savings', *Investment Company Institute Perspective*, August.

Sittampalam, Arjuna (1993), *Coming Wars in Investment Management*, Dublin: Lafferty Publications.

Siwolop, Sana (1997), 'Regulating Financial Advisers: Are the States up to it?' *The New York Times*, 29 June.

Smith, Roy C. and Ingo Walter (1997a), *Global Banking*, New York: Oxford University Press.

Smith, Roy C. and Ingo Walter (1997b), *Street Smarts: Linking Professional Conduct and Shareholder Value in the Securities Industry*, Boston, MA: Harvard Business School Press.

Story, Jonathan and Ingo Walter (1997), *Political Economy of Financial Integration in Europe*, Manchester: Manchester University Press/Cambridge, MA: MIT Press.

Turner, John and Noriyasu Watanabe (1995), *Private Pension Policies in Industrialized Countries*, Kalamazoo: W. E. Upjohn Institute for Employment Research.

Walter, Ingo (1985a), *Barriers to Trade in Banking and Financial Services*, London: Trade Policy Research Centre.

Walter, Ingo (1985b) (ed.), *Deregulating Wall Street*, New York: John Wiley & Sons.

Walter, Ingo (1988), *Global Competition in Financial Services*, Cambridge, MA: Ballinger/Harper & Row.

Walter, Ingo (1990), *The Secret Money Market*, New York: HarperCollins.

Walter, Ingo (1993), *High-Performance Financial Systems*, Singapore: Institute for Southeast Asian Studies.

Walter, Ingo and Roy C. Smith (1989), *Investment Banking in Europe: Restructuring for the 1990s*, Oxford: Basil Blackwell.

Warther, Vincent A. (1995), 'Aggregate Mutual Fund Flows and Security Returns', *Journal of Financial Economics*, September.

World Bank (1994), *Averting the Old Age Crisis*, Washington, DC: World Bank.

10
The European Securities Industry under a Single Currency

ROY C. SMITH

This chapter examines the competitive dynamics of the securities industry in Europe and seeks to identify the major sources of competitive advantage for firms participating in the European industry in the future. The future of the European securities industry will be affected not only by the forthcoming conversion to a single currency but also by a variety of developments and powerful forces that have been reshaping the global securities industry over the past fifteen years. Indeed, these developments have already changed the European securities industry more, perhaps, than have any other broad environmental changes throughout its long history.

Accordingly, in order to evaluate the specific impact of Economic and Monetary Union (EMU) on the European securities industry, it is necessary to have a complete review of the development of its global characteristics and involvement and its current exposure to the change-forces of the marketplace.

This chapter compares a variety of developments to date in the European market with those that have occurred in the United States over the past fifteen years to establish a benchmark position. It then attempts to assess what impact on the European securities industry the forthcoming adoption of a single European currency and EMU will have. It restricts its examination, however, to the wholesale finance sector, focusing only on matters that affect markets for debt and equity securities that are issued or traded within Europe or across its borders, and related advisory services of investment banks and securities firms. It does not address retail financial services, including brokerage in stocks, investment trusts or insurance, or retail banking services. Participants in the wholesale finance industry are broadly defined to include European universal banks and securities firms as well as all firms operating in Europe that are owned or controlled by non-Europeans. The aim is to create a composite picture of the European securities industry of the future and what will be required to succeed in it.

I am grateful for useful comments on this chapter from David Backus, Jean Dermine, Ingo Walter and Holger Wolf.

1. Introduction

In the thirty-five years since the first Eurobond issue, the global securities market has changed beyond recognition. But the first issue, a US$15 million bond issued by Autostrade, the Italian state highway system, began an irreversible process of capital market development that has been of great importance to the growth and development of European (and non-European) public and private sector institutions. At the end of 1996, the total market capitalization of all European debt and equity securities exceeded US$11,800 billion, or approximately 28 per cent of the total global value of all outstanding securities. Approximately US$7,600 billion of these outstanding securities were debt issues, and US$4,200 billion were equities. See Table 10.1.

This progress is also reflected in the increasing importance of debt securities issued in Euromarket transactions in several different categories. During 1996, new issues of Eurobonds exceeded US$500 billion, an amount greater than the volume of new issues of corporate debt securities in the United States, a distinction the Euromarket also earned in three of the preceding four years. In addition to Eurobonds, US$380 billion of Euro-medium-term notes (EMTNs) were also issued, as compared to US$250 billion of such notes in the United States.[1] In 1996, the total volume of 'international'

Table 10.1. Capitalization of major securities markets, end-1996 (nominal value outstanding; US$ bn.)

Country of issuance	Bond market		Equity market	Total market capitalization
	Public sector	Private sector		
USA	6,366	3,217	8,484	18,067
Japan	2,246	1,410	3,089	6,745
Germany	839	1,464	671	2,974
Italy	998	276	258	1,532
France	732	312	591	1,635
UK	448	214	1,740	2,402
Canada	313	133	486	932
Netherlands	200	201	379	780
Other European	992	925	550	2,467
Other non-European	200	50	3,911	4,161
Total	13,334	8,202	20,159	41,695
Total European	4,209	3,392	4,189	11,790
European %	32	41	21	28

Sources: Salomon Brothers; *1996 Securities Industry Fact Book*.

[1] Similar to Eurobonds, medium-term notes are unsecured corporate obligations of from one to ten years in maturity which are usually sold off-the-shelf on a 'tap' issue basis using standardized documentation by banks which underwrite their sale.

Table 10.2. Capital market activity, 1991–1996 (US$ bn.)

	1996	1995	1994	1993	1992	1991
US domestic new issues						
US MTNs	255.9	404.9	282.8	260.3	169.4	142.3
Investment-grade debt	511.4	417.3	342.5	389.2	281.1	193.7
Collateralized securities	248.7	154.1	252.5	478.9	428.2	292.6
Junk and convertibles	129.4	30.2	36.4	69.5	53.7	20.9
Municipal debt	151.5	154.9	161.3	287.8	231.7	162.8
Total debt	1,296.9	1,161.4	1,075.5	1,485.7	1,164.1	812.3
Preferred stock	40.5	16.3	15.5	22.4	20.9	20.2
Common stock	115.1	81.7	61.6	101.7	72.4	54.8
Total equity	155.6	98.0	77.0	124.1	93.3	75.0
Total domestic	1,452.5	1,259.4	1,152.5	1,609.8	1,257.4	887.3
International issues						
Euro MTNs	384.3	251.6	257.2	149.8	96.9	38.5
Euro and foreign bonds	546.7	385.1	485.2	482.7	335.9	260.8
International equity	47.7	32.1	32.4	27.7	17.7	12.0
Total international	978.7	668.8	774.8	660.2	450.6	311.4
World-wide total	2,431.2	1,928.2	1,927.3	2,270.0	1,708.0	1,198.6
Global syndicated bank loan and NIFs	1,400.0	1,098.0	785.6	555.4	403.0	727.0

Sources: Securities Data Corporation; *Investment Dealer's Digest*.

capital market new issues (predominantly Euro-issues but including some foreign bond and stock issues) was nearly US$1,000 billion, approximately three times the volume in 1990. See Table 10.2. European governments and corporations accounted for approximately half of the volume of the new Euromarket debt issues, the largest regional sector of the market for such issues (BIS, 1996: Table VIII.5). The Euromarkets were also extremely active in the issuance of Euro-commercial-paper (ECP) and in Eurocurrency syndicated bank loans and associated note-issuance facilities. At the end of 1966, ECP and EMTNs outstanding were approximately US$840 billion, and Eurocurrency loans outstanding were estimated at US$5,000 billion (BIS, 1997: Table VII.1).

Moreover, the European share of the world equity market capitalization had increased by 1996 to approximately 28 per cent, up from 15 per cent in 1980, reflecting a growth in the value of European shares outstanding of nearly 800 per cent. The growth in secondary market trading activity in these shares was even greater. European equity new issues increased fourfold in the 1990s to US$48 billion, the level of new issue activity reached in the United States in 1990. See Tables 10.1 and 10.2.

Also during 1996, European corporations completed a record number of mergers and acquisition transactions valued at approximately US$266 billion, more than the

Table 10.3. Global mergers and acquisitions

	1996	1995	1994	1993	1992	1991	1990	1989	1988	1987	1986	1985
Volume of transactions (US$ bn.)												
US domestic	330.7	218.5	199.8	101.1	119.3	108.5	124.9	250.1	293.2	203.9	200.9	192.3
US cross-border	84.5	106.5	58.4	34.9	33.5	40.5	73.0	85.6	77.9	50.2	39.3	15.9
Intra-European	193.3	151.8	85.6	59.9	91.0	117.2	127.2	130.1	86.4	54.9	20.7	11.5
European cross-border	73.2	72.4	57.1	33.0	43.0	53.8	97.7	74.3	54.6	41.4	35.4	8.8
US–European cross-border	(52.9)	(43.5)	(39.0)	(27.4)	(13.3)	(22.8)	(36.6)	(46.3)	(38.2)	(28.3)	(17.4)	(5.9)
All other	84.9	47.1	34.3	60.2	43.0	54.2	47.8	69.7	37.5	28.2	15.9	10.5
Global total	713.7	552.8	396.2	261.7	316.5	351.4	434.0	563.5	511.4	350.3	294.8	233.1
Percentages												
USA	58.2	58.8	65.2	52.0	48.3	42.4	45.6	59.6	72.6	72.5	81.5	89.3
Europe	37.3	40.6	36.0	35.5	42.3	48.7	51.8	36.3	27.6	27.5	19.0	8.7
US domestic	46.3	39.5	50.4	38.6	37.7	30.9	28.8	44.4	57.3	58.2	68.1	82.5

Roy C. Smith

Table 10.4. World's largest 100 fund managers, end-1992

	Amount managed (US$ bn.)	No. of managers
USA	4,641	39
Japan	3,874	22
UK	1,183	11
France	1,145	8
Switzerland	839	8
Germany	549	6
Netherlands	255	3
Canada	124	2
Australia	62	1
Total	12,672	100
Total European	3,971	36
European %	31	36

Sources: P&I Watson Wyatt, *World 100 Largest Fund Managers*, Sept. 1996.

value of all completed US domestic deals in any year except 1989. The European deals accounted for 37 per cent of the global volume of merger activity in 1996. This continues a trend begun in the late 1980s of aggressive European corporate restructuring through market transactions. See Table 10.3.

And finally, European banks managing funds for institutional investors and government or multinational investment entities have also become extremely important in the global funds management business. This was estimated in 1995 to comprise assets of more than US$22,000 billion—including US$8,200 billion in pension fund assets, US$6,400 billion in insurance companies, and about US$5,300 billion in mutual funds. Of the world's one hundred largest fund managers in 1992, thirty-six were European-owned, and these accounted for approximately 31 per cent of all global assets under management. See Table 10.4. Institutional equity holdings under management represented 34 per cent of the global total in 1995.[2]

These data defy some conventional perceptions of Europe as a capital markets backwater, only just beginning to stir itself to participate in global activity. On the contrary, Europe has made enormous progress in adapting to global capital market developments and opportunities. This is the direct result of widespread deregulation, reforms and improvements associated with the economic revival of the former European Economic Community (hereafter, the European Union, or EU) that began during the 1980s. These developments were based on the idea that open markets and free competition would improve economic performance. Capital markets were

---

[2] Riley (1997), reporting studies by British Invisibles PLC, and Technimetrics, Inc.

significantly affected by banking deregulation, financial market reforms and massive privatization and corporate restructuring programmes throughout Europe. An increasing volume of funds has consequently flowed into the European markets from many sources. This flow was stimulated by the removal of foreign exchange controls, increasingly efficient markets, improved investment opportunities, the growth of new financial institutions such as pension and investment trusts (mutual funds), and by the continuing appeal of the world's least regulated, most innovative financial marketplace, the 'Euromarket'.

1.1. Euromarket characteristics

The Euromarket began long before the current period of reforms. Technically, it is a market for offshore funds; originally an interbank market for collecting and lending offshore deposits in dollars (and a few other currencies). The market does not officially exist, nor is it regulated by any country. Yet it has operated effectively for more than three decades. The market allows money to flow untaxed between countries, and for securities to be owned in bearer form so ownership can be disguised. The market is operated by reputable and competent banking institutions and is very attractive to clients seeking financial safety, security and anonymity. The typical investor has been described as a 'Belgian dentist', but more realistically the market serves tax-shy wealthy families and individuals, both shady and distinguished, from all over the world (Hayes and Hubbard, 1990).

The market has been tolerated by European governments because it did not involve the sale of unregistered securities to retail investors in individual countries, and therefore was outside the jurisdiction of each. Sales could be made, however, to wholesale investors (i.e. large, sophisticated investors) as private placements. As a result securities issued in the Euromarket are not sold to retail investors *except* through the agency of a bank or other qualified representative. The retail market for corporate securities in Europe, however, was never very significant (except in the United Kingdom, which had a more active capital market). The distribution of large privatization issues of stocks in well-known companies has changed this situation somewhat. But for the most part, the securities market in Europe is comprised of institutional investors such as central banks and government agencies, commercial banks (acting for their own accounts and for customers), investment funds, insurance companies and similar fiduciaries. The Euromarket is the principal trading arena for such investors.

The boundaries of the Euromarket are indistinct. Issuers of securities come from North and South America, from Japan and other parts of Asia, as well as from all parts of Europe itself. They include supranationals, governments and agencies, corporations and banks. Their securities are sold within Europe, and in Asia, the Middle East and America under certain, private placement rules. Thus the Euromarket is substantially integrated with important financial markets outside Europe.

Euromarket participants are very sophisticated. They understand investment opportunities around the world, foreign exchange effects, derivative instruments such as warrants and options to purchase or sell securities, and with approximately 500 international banks and investment banks involved in the market, it is very competitive. There are no restrictions as to who can participate, and few rules and regulations affect those who do. Innovation is prized but so is the ability to copy a competitor's idea in record time. All commissions and service fees are negotiable, and competition for new issue mandates is intense and sometimes rough: frequent issuers shop around for the lowest rates, banks will often deliberately take losses on deals in order to show their importance as an underwriter in published 'league' tables, or stuff poorly priced deals into passive customer accounts to get rid of them. But many firms compete on the basis of innovation and bold initiative. As a result, the Euromarket saw the first significant use of the floating-rate note, the zero-coupon bond, the warrant bond, the swapped foreign currency bond, ECU-denominated securities, and other new ideas. It also saw the first use of the 'bought deal', or fully underwritten issue by one bank, the tap issue, and the note-issuance facility. It has also begun to accept some of the more complex and controversial products of the US bond market, such as asset-backed issues, and recently, the first Euro-junk bonds.

1.2. Industry deregulation and reform

The Euromarket was well established by the mid-1980s, when the current wave of EU economic and financial reforms began. These reforms included not only the Bank for International Settlements' (BIS) minimum capital adequacy regulation for banks (1987) and the EU's Second Banking Directive under the Single Market Initiative (1987), but also the various internal market reforms such as 'Big Bang' (UK, 1986) and stock exchange market system upgrades that came to be widely adopted throughout Europe. These also included substantial re-regulation of the financial marketplace in most of the European countries along convergent if not entirely common lines.

The reforms also included the now common practice of 'privatization'—the public sale by governments of shares of state-owned enterprises—which has resulted in over US$200 billion of new European equity securities being issued and traded in the market by individual and institutional investors, both European and non-European. Privatization programmes were adopted by almost all European countries, and in aggregate these contributed enormously to the outstanding supply of securities, especially in countries with restricted public ownership of equities.

With such large volumes of debt and equity securities issuance has come a large supporting infrastructure for the financial services industry. Such infrastructure consists almost entirely of human talent and organizations. It includes not only underwriting, legal and accounting firms trained to accommodate new issues, but also market-makers and brokers and merger and acquisition specialists and firms specializing in securities research, bond ratings, clearance and settlement, information technology, and even recruitment. In the beginning of the Euromarket, this infrastructure was located in London, but since then most major firms have spread their significant operations to Frankfurt, Milan and Paris as well. Many of these firms came to Europe first to assist their own clients, but then to compete for market share with the European banks with long-standing ties to traditional clients. Their success has stirred the larger, long-established European banks to respond, and competition in all financial services sectors has become more intense as a result, much to the benefit of market users. Today, with no impediments to funds crossing borders, and cheap and efficient telecommunications systems that instantly transmit price information all over the globe, the market in Europe is closely linked with those in New York, Tokyo and elsewhere. Any price disparities are quickly removed by arbitrage trading. Indeed, the wholesale finance market has become totally globalized and open to competition.

1.3. Redefining wholesale financial markets

Wholesale financial markets are those in which the issuers and investors benefit, relative to the retail market, from significant volume discounts. Only those with large capacity and reputations for knowledgeable behaviour need apply. Users of wholesale financial markets have had a choice in the past between bank loans and the issuance of securities. As in the United States, in recent years, entities that have full access to the European securities markets have found these markets cheaper than traditional bank financing. Full access generally requires that the issuer obtains investment-grade bond ratings from two rating agencies, but there are exceptions for better-known government and corporate issuers. The securities markets now provide short- (ECP) and medium-term borrowing (EMTNs) for full-access entities at significantly lower net interest cost than do banks. For such companies, banks mainly provide standby and bridging facilities and swaps that are later refunded in capital markets, but today banks also compete to underwrite and distribute the securities. Smaller, more regional or less well-known companies may have insufficient access to the markets to issue securities on the same basis. These companies usually rely on their commercial banking relationships for financing needs. Gradually, however, the wholesale market is reaching out to smaller companies and those with below-investment-grade bond ratings.

As the world's largest securities market is in the United States, and since with market integration US securities firms have been highly active in capital markets in Europe and Asia, the principal firms attracting the leading shares of the market for *global* wholesale financial services have been US firms. See Table 10.5. In the United States, capital market activity has been intensely competitive for at least twenty years. The success of US firms is partly explained by the fact that a large portion of full-access issuers are US entities. But they have also been effective in gaining business from an increasing number of government bodies and corporations from Europe, Japan and other areas outside the United States because of their technical skills and marketing abilities.

Table 10.5. Global wholesale banking and investment banking, 1996 (full credit to bookrunning manager only; US$ bn.)

Firm	Global debt and equity securities underwriting and placement[a]		Global M&A advisory[b]		International loans arranged[c]		Medium-term notes lead managed		Total[d]		% Of industry total
Merrill Lynch	215.74	1	100.06	3	2.97	27	54.82	1	373.58	1	11.94
Chase Manhattan Bank	31.53	15	17.37	18	249.12	1	2.99	24	301.00	2	9.62
JP Morgan	104.34	7	77.95	4	90.43	2	19.77	6	292.49	3	9.35
Goldman Sachs	146.71	2	116.50	2	2.70	28	24.02	4	289.92	4	9.26
Morgan Stanley	125.47	4	116.72	1	—		28.52	3	270.72	5	8.65
CS First Boston	107.33	6	60.88	5	39.44	6	17.06	7	224.71	6	7.18
Salomon Brothers	119.06	5	47.94	7	—		41.46	2	208.46	7	6.66
Lehman Brothers	125.61	3	47.41	8	—		19.89	5	192.91	8	6.16
UBS	34.96	13	46.38	9	38.16	7	9.86	9	129.37	9	4.13
Bear Stearns	57.75	8	18.58	17	—		13.39	8	89.73	10	2.87
Citicorp	—		—		84.51	3	4.89	20	89.40	11	2.86
Deutsche MG	36.87	11	13.51	22	27.85	10	7.40	13	85.64	12	2.74
SBC Warburg	37.58	10	29.41	11	5.47	26	8.99	10	81.44	16	2.60
DLJ	52.93	9	28.07	13	—		—		81.01	13	2.59
NatWest	20.72	20	33.21	10	25.19	12	—		79.12	14	2.53
Nations Bank	22.94	17	—		49.27	5	5.41	18	77.62	15	2.48
ABN/Amro	23.64	16	13.11	23	30.90	8	7.63	12	75.28	17	2.41
Smith Barney	36.02	12	28.36	12	—		5.20	19	69.58	18	2.22
Bank of America	—		—		65.40	4	—		65.40	19	2.09
Lazard Houses	—		51.95	6	—		—		51.95	20	1.66
Total top twenty	1,299.19		847.40		711.41		271.31		3,129.31		
Total industry	1,769.86		684.62[e]		1,093.71		371.73		3,919.92		
Top ten as % of total	61.73		102.10		64.33		63.97		55.89		55.89
Top twenty as % of total	77.77		134.31		79.17		80.48		73.62		73.62

[a] Global rankings, top twenty-five, completed deals only; includes all US private placements; [b] By market value of completed global transactions, full credit to both advisers, top twenty-five advisers; [c] Top arrangers of international syndicated credits by volume; [d] Global MTNs, top twenty-five managers; [e] As a result of double accounting, the total for the top twenty-five firms is higher than the industry total.

Source: Securities Data Corporation.

2. The US Experience

The history of the modern securities industry in the United States begins on 1 May 1975, when major reforms were implemented by the New York Stock Exchange.[3] For some years previously, the large financial institutions had complained that the Exchange's fixed, or minimum, commission rates that applied regardless of transaction size were excessively expensive and restrained trade. Institutions could only buy shares of NYSE-listed companies on the Exchange, but the institutions were not permitted to become members to obtain lower rates. The US Department of Justice became interested in the issue and threatened anti-trust action unless the Exchange voluntarily agreed to negotiate commission rates, which (very reluctantly) it did. Lower commissions were the immediate result, and these greatly stimulated trading and increased competition. There were a number of failures and mergers in Wall Street as a result.

2.1. The declining role of banks

Also developing around this time were the beginnings of the great banking and savings and loan crisis of 1980–95. During this episode banks, savings and loan corporations (S&Ls) and other depository institutions suffered massive losses which ultimately involved taxpayer expense of about US$200 billion, and their competitive positions plummeted. Much of the difficulty, beginning in 1978, was the result of sharply increasing US interest rates which raised the costs of variable-rate, short-term borrowing that many institutions had relied upon to fund large long-term, fixed-rate positions in home mortgages and term loans. The resulting asset–liability mismatches produced enormous write-offs of bank capital. To alleviate the pressure on the S&Ls, Congress allowed them to undertake riskier investments to increase lending spreads, but many of these loans failed. More than a thousand savings and loan institutions were closed or taken over by the Federal Savings and Loan Insurance Corporation as a result.

Also during this period, financial deterioration visited American commercial banks, many of which had been overly aggressive lenders during the 1970s to Third World countries and ailing American corporations and failed. Others suffered forced reorganization or severe lending constraints.[4] The banks' credit ratings were drastically lowered, opening the door to competition from capital markets and foreign lenders. Money market mutual funds, paying investors interest rates significantly higher than bank deposits, siphoned funds out of the banks and into commercial paper and other fixed-income securities. Indeed, the assets of money market funds grew from US$9.5 billion in 1978 to US$327 billion in 1988. Meanwhile, the banks were also absorbed by

---

[3] A day called 'Mayday' by journalists, signifying both the magnitude and the irony of the changes: Mayday is also an international radio call for distressed ships and aircraft, and the national day of the Russian Communist Party.

[4] Over US$150 billion of this expense was incurred by failed savings and loan institutions, the rest by the failure of banks with assets of US$264 billion (data from the Federal Deposit Insurance Corp., 1996).

the Third World debt crisis, which would cost billions and cause further management upheavals and heightened regulatory requirements (White, 1991: 76–123).

Partly because of these difficulties, most banks experienced a loss of wholesale business to the capital markets, where commercial paper, corporate bonds and new asset-backed securities could be put together at lower rates than the banks could provide. This disintermediation was countered by efforts on the part of banks to increase holdings of assets of lesser (below-investment-grade) credits; however, competition for these assets drove lending spreads downward to unsatisfactory levels.

US banks were restricted by the Glass-Steagall provisions of the Banking Act of 1933 from entering the securities business, so they were unable to diversify away from the banking business when they might have wanted to do so. However, most banks were not sufficiently healthy to make much progress in the securities industry, even if they had been permitted to do so at the time.[5] During this period, however, capital market activity increased sharply. In 1975, the value of shares traded on the NYSE was US$127 billion; by 1985 it had grown to US$970 billion and by 1996, US$4,100 billion. Total corporate underwriting in 1975 was US$47 billion; by 1985 it had reached nearly US$140 billion, and by 1996 US$1,452 billion.[6] The burst of capital market growth that began in the 1970s ignited an explosion of activity that continued for over twenty years.

During the latter part of the 1980s new laws were passed that tightened banking regulation. Most banks went through a painful ordeal of loss recognition, downgrading and lowered stock prices. Management changes and downsizing were common throughout the industry. The banks were forced to focus on what they could do well, and substantially reduce operating costs and investments in non-core businesses. Many banks chose during this time to emphasize their consumer and small company lending businesses, and to take advantage of opportunities to expand their businesses into other states and regions. Most banks reduced their emphasis on wholesale financing, leaving this territory to investment banks. Some continued to act in the wholesale markets through regular and specialized lending activities supplemented by modest securities businesses. In 1989 the Federal Reserve and other bank regulators allowed banks to apply for securities underwriting powers under Section 20 of the Glass-Steagall provisions which, permitted limited activities in prohibited areas. As of December 1996, fewer than twenty-five domestic US commercial banks had applied for and obtained permission for securities businesses (along with about the same number of non-US banks), even though by this time the regulators had increased the size of permitted securities activities to 25 per cent of the bank's assets and revenues.

2.2. The rise of trading

As the 1970s came to an end, the US fiscal and trade deficits were at all-time highs, but during the next decade these would increase approximately fourfold, requiring the

---

[5] This period in American banking has been well documented by Saunders and Walter (1996) and Smith (1993).

[6] New York Stock Exchange, *1996 Fact Book*.

issuance and sale of trillions of dollars of US government and agency securities. A significant portion of these securities would be placed with foreign central banks and other non-US investors. At different periods, the Saudi Arabian Monetary Authority, the World Bank, Japanese financial institutions and investment companies, and the monetary authorities of Kuwait, Taiwan, South Korea, and Singapore have been extremely important investors in these securities.

US commercial and investment banks in the business of trading and selling US government securities (Glass-Steagall did not restrict banks from the government or municipal bond businesses) found the sudden and huge increase in the volume, and the increasingly competitive and globally diverse markets for government bonds, to have profound effects on their businesses. In the space of only a few years, the capital, position-risk exposures and the aggregate size and skills required of securities firms increased substantially. Government securities are the base against which all fixed-income securities activities are measured. Skills learned in trading government bonds could be used to trade other instruments, corporate bonds and bonds issued by foreign governments and corporations.

Increasing competition in fixed-income securities threatened to narrow the margins, but volatility, calculated risk-taking, and innovation (especially in forms of proprietary, or technical trading) made it possible for some operators to earn very large profits. These were increased further by securitization, especially of mortgage-backed securities, and by the introduction in the early 1980s of interest rate derivatives, such as futures and options contracts and interest rate swaps. Firms soon recognized the profit potential of intensive trading activity, and began to look for new instruments to trade—such as foreign exchange, commodities, and other forms of corporate securities. For many of the larger US investment banks, trading (in its various forms) would soon comprise more than 50 per cent of the firm's non-interest revenues, and even more of its profits.

The emphasis on trading, however, changed the nature of the investment banking business. Increased competition and access to the clients of other banks placed a great premium on tight pricing and lower dealing spreads. As a result, banks often thought more about their dealing profits than whether their quotes best served their clients. For many clients, these developments encouraged shopping around for the best prices and ideas, at the expense of traditional, nearly exclusive banking relationships. The pendulum swung away from a business in which client relationships were the essence of the business, towards a position where the pricing of issues was more important.

2.3. Globalization and market integration

Early in the years of the Reagan Administration, interest rates began a dramatic decline. This was partly in response to inflation-checking monetary policy changes introduced by the Federal Reserve in October 1979, and partly a result of the economic and foreign policies of the new administration. Although real interest rates remained high in light of the continuing fiscal deficit, the nominal rates declined as sharply as inflation did. As a result a bull market in bonds (and in stocks) began in 1982 that, except for a few brief interruptions in 1987 and 1990, has continued until the present time, a factor which greatly underpinned the shift towards trading activities.

The improved US economic performance and confidence in the new President seemed to contribute too to the dollar's strengthening, from 202 yen per dollar in 1980 to 260 in 1985. During this period non-American investors found US securities to be very desirable and advantageous. Some, such as Swiss banks investing client funds, bid for US corporate Eurobonds at interest rates that could not be equalled in the United States. Because the unregulated Eurobond market was so flexible, a large bank seeking US$100 million or so of new bonds for investment could contact a US corporation directly and offer an extremely attractive interest rate with the deal to be agreed on the telephone. The transaction was not subject to underwriting, marketing, due diligence, documentation, or anything else. It had been agreed as a 'bought deal' between the European bank and the issuer, something that was not at the time possible in the United States. Some issues at this time were made at interest rates *below* the US Treasury bond rates, instead of at the premium of 0.50 per cent to 1.00 per cent or so required in the US market.[7] As a result, a wave of US Eurobond issuance occurred, resulting in more investment-grade corporate bonds being sold outside the United States in 1982 and 1983 than domestically. This had never happened before (Smith, 1989: 151–90).

One consequence of the surge in overseas financing was an important change in the regulatory procedures governing new issues of securities in the United States. The change, Securities and Exchange Commission (SEC) Rule 415 (1983), provided for 'shelf-registration' of securities with the SEC. This in effect meant that the issuer could pre-register securities, and draw them 'off the shelf' to be issued on demand. For those companies that qualified to use Rule 415, it meant that no longer would an issuer seeking access to financial markets have to file a registration statement with the SEC and then wait approximately thirty days for permission to proceed to the market. Rule 415 allowed firms to go to the market when they wanted to—without any appreciable wait. Firms that wanted to do so could engage in bought deals inside the United States, and they could shop around among competing underwriters for the lowest interest rate. Experienced by the competitive struggles in the Eurobond market, many US firms decided to compete on European terms in their home market. Soon the whole of the corporate bond market had been brought to accept the Euromarket practices. No longer could a securities firm rely on a long-standing relationship with a client for assurance that when it needed financing the firm would arrange it. No longer could a firm assume that its proposed interest rate would be accepted, or that another firm would not appear with a lower rate. This change alone profoundly affected the nature of the relationships between investment banks and their clients. Exclusive, traditional

---

[7] US Treasuries were not available free of withholding taxes and in bearer form, two important requirements of Swiss Bank money managers, so prime US corporate bonds, which were, became the benchmark for Eurobond pricing.

banking relationships, in which clients and banks showed great loyalty to one another and few banks bothered to call on the clients of others, became a thing of the past. Many stable investment banking products, like debt financing, turned into commodities. Often, a 'winning bid' would cause the firm a loss. Clients wanted winning bids and bankers became wary of them. Many decided there was more money to be made in simply trading with clients, rather than in providing services at uncompetitive rates.

This condition, in which the competitive elements of one market (Eurobonds) were transferred to another, less competitive market (the US bond market), represented a form of involuntarily imported deregulation. It was caused by disequilibrium of competitive conditions in markets that were otherwise closely linked. The disequilibrium was caused by regulation that existed in one market but not the other. When the regulation was changed (Rule 415) the disequilibrium disappeared, and American firms continued to do business with their American clients, but under European competitive conditions. The change was drastic for American banks, but it was also very sudden, occurring less than three years after the revival of interest in the Euromarkets by US companies.

There were several responses to these changed competitive conditions in the United States. One was to strengthen firms' trading and distribution capabilities, especially by reaching out to the global investor pool to a greater extent. Another response was to become more innovative, and to introduce more customized securities tied to derivatives contracts of various types. Yet another was to withdraw from aggressive, money-losing underwriting activities to specialize in trading and non-commodity financings like equities, and new instruments like mortgage-backed securities. Thus, there was a dispersion of competitive energy expended on the bond and related securities markets, creating more niches and areas of highly concentrated specialization. The result was a shift, as in the Euromarket, in the value-added of investment banking from the financial intermediary to the issuers and investors.

Soon the US market and the Eurobond market became very closely integrated. Issuers and investors compared interest rates and issuing costs in both markets. Currency and interest rate swaps permitting floating-rate contracts to be converted to fixed-rate contracts operated across borders and continents. Virtually full globalization of the debt securities markets soon resulted. Debt securities became subject to a global pricing matrix with rating and liquidity (bond quality) on one axis, and maturity (duration) on the other. Pricing aberrations were subject to arbitrage, and soon disappeared.

The US market was subject to a further round of securities deregulation in 1990 with the adoption by the SEC of Rule 144a, which provided for the resale (i.e. trading) of securities that were exempt from registration by virtue of 'private placement' provisions. The effect of this regulatory change was to permit unregistered securities to be issued, sold and traded within a special community of several hundred 'qualified institutional buyers', a community that was indistinguishable from the institutional bond market which accounted for more than 90 per cent of the market for new issues of registered corporate bonds in the United States.

Provided with greatly enhanced liquidity, the private placement market began to offer rates much closer to the rates of fully tradable, registered bonds. One result of this regulatory change was to disengage the SEC from the task of protecting qualified investors from normal disclosure deficiencies, so the SEC could devote itself more appropriately to regulating financial transactions affecting the retail public. Another result was the opening of the US debt and equity markets under Rule 144a to foreign issues unable or unwilling to go through the expense, difficulties and time required for a full SEC filing. Numerous Latin American issuers, for example, have made Rule 144a offerings. Thus, foreign issuers of unregistered securities totalling US$38 billion in 1996 were able to access the US institutional investor market, the world's largest by far, on a very low cost basis. Those issuers preferring to develop access to this market would forgo using the Eurobond market, unless the interest rate or stock price offered was superior to that in the USA.

2.4. Takeover booms

During the 1980s the United States experienced its largest period of takeover activity ever. Beginning in the 1900s, there had already been three previous takeover booms, or waves of mergers and acquisitions, but the one in the 1980s was different in several respects. Although the largest in value terms (it was not the largest in terms of the percentage of GNP represented by the value of the transactions), its main identifiable characteristic was the extent to which hostile transactions and leveraged buyouts were included. Between 1985 and 1990, more than 8,500 mergers and corporate reorganizations valued at more than US$1,250 billion took place in the United States, about 22 per cent of which were initially resisted transactions. Much of this activity has since been attributed to the need to improve the competitive performance of industry in the United States, by challenging corporate control and instituting performance measures that would improve profits and shareholder returns from the relatively low levels to which these had sunk during the gloomy decade of the 1970s.

Much of this restructuring and reorientation to shareholder value has been effective, but the intensity of the effort was so great that it turned to excess, and the boom burned out in 1989–90. However, fundamental economic needs in the American economy for industry reorganization in banking and financial services, technology, defence and other sectors caused the boom to reappear in the early 1990s, and between 1991 and 1996 a further 15,000 transactions valued at more than US$1,070 billion occurred.

These developments affected investment banks in four significant ways.

They provided a bonanza of merger and refinancing fees, opened up the market for below-investment-grade corporate bonds, and gave many firms the opportunity to invest their own money in LBO deals. This produced a considerable increase in profits for those investment banks and commercial banks participating in the activity.

They affected the banks' relations with their clients in significant ways. Takeover targets, of course, disappeared as clients after the deal was completed. Sometimes buyers hired banks to help them launch raids against other clients. And sometimes when clients wished a firm to act for them, the firm was prevented from doing so by a conflict of interest. Clients were annoyed when their banks were not available to them, and also became suspicious of banks they thought might be seeking to 'put them in play', or making them subject to an unwanted offer. The whole effect was to loosen the bonds of trust between the firms and their, or anyone's clients.

They also affected the banks and investment banks because many of the acquisitions that occurred involved firms in their industry. Many leading investment banking firms have been acquired by others in the industry since 1980 (some more than once), including such well-known names as Alex. Brown, Dillon Read, First Boston, Kidder Peabody, Lehman Brothers, Morgan Stanley, Oppenheimer, Robertson Stephens, Salomon Brothers, Smith Barney and Dean Witter. Also, top money-centre banks were being merged into other banks, including Chase Manhattan, Continental Bank, Manufacturers Hanover, Irving Trust, Security Pacific, and First Interstate. Further, significant second- or third-tier US securities firms have been acquired since 1996 by Canadian Imperial Bank of Commerce, SBC Warburg, Bankers Trust, Bank of America, and NationsBank. Mergers and acquisitions, many involuntary, have helped to reshape the commercial banking and investment banking businesses in the United States as much as any other single factor. The result was industry consolidation into a smaller number of powerful players—large, globally diversified firms with greater emphasis on output and profitability and on competitive performance.

Finally, the rising level of merger activity attracted the attention of European corporations, and Europe's first merger boom began, involving many of the same globalizing industries that were being restructured in the United States. Motivated by concerns about competing in the new European single market, having access through the marketplace to control of some corporations, and helped by aggressive American merger know-how, the merger boom spread to Europe. In 1985, the total volume of mergers and acquisitions involving European companies was 8.7 per cent of the world total; by 1996 this share had grown to 37.3 per cent (DeLong *et al.* 1997). See Table 10.3. American (and American-associated) investment banks, establishing merger specialists in their European offices early in the period, became the market leaders in European cross-border transactions. These firms included four of the top five ranked advisers in 1996, and in aggregate accounted for more than half of the total volume of transactions involving the top fifteen ranked firms.[8]

2.5. Sources of competitive advantage

It is clear that the securities industry in the United States has existed in a condition of tumultuous change since the mid-1970s. Many firms failed to adapt to the competitive conditions that came to prevail, and have since disappeared. Many of those that have survived have merged with others, or otherwise increased their size, geographic reach

---

[8] 'Europe's Top Advisors', *Acquisitions Monthly*, February 1997; 'High Noon in Europe, Wall Street Banks Gallop In', *The New York Times*, 13 July 1997.

and business mix several-fold. Management problems have been continuous, and sometimes extremely painful, as those at Salomon Brothers, Lehman Brothers, Kidder Peabody, and Bankers Trust (to name but a few) could testify. New leaders were appointed, mainly young, trading-oriented managers who replaced the older people whose rise had been associated with client relationships. Many different strategic ideas were tried. Some firms specialized in one or two key areas—Lazard Frères and Dillon Read, for example, remain focused on mergers, corporate finance and money management. Others decided to move aggressively into new areas where they believed market leaders had become cautious, such as Kidder Peabody's briefly successful push into mortgaged-backed securities, a business developed by Salomon Brothers, or Bankers Trust's emergence as a leader in derivative securities. Many firms experienced difficulties with regulators and with the courts as the ground rules of acceptable behaviour in modern finance were progressively made clear (Smith and Walter, 1997: ch. 1). The leading American firms today, however, are mainly highly experienced, battle-hardened survivors. They have had to adapt continuously and often suddenly to changing industry trends, often doing so by ruthlessly laying off large numbers of employees, or by moving before they were ready into new areas of opportunity (such as emerging-market securities) so as not to be left behind in case the new area turned into a bonanza. In the middle of this, these firms had to attract, train, compensate and retain top-quality professional employees, and supervise their work all over the world. Among their important achievements has been the development of new, highly flexible, non-hierarchical management systems and unique *ad hoc* arrangements for dealing with urgent matters. In aggregate these factors constitute a very important comparative advantage for the American firms, compared to European or Japanese firms.

Compared to each other, the American firms would probably agree that their most important comparative advantages include the following:

- They are the right size to be global players, while still remaining flexible and re-sponsive. The top five US investment banks are much larger firms than they have ever been in terms of total assets, now averaging about US$200 billion, but they are still comparatively small in comparison to the largest US, European and Japanese banks. Leaving out the large retail sales forces that Merrill Lynch and Dean Witter Morgan Stanley maintain, the wholesale business headcount is in the area of 8,000 to 10,000, which is much larger than the smaller, niche-oriented American firms but also larger than most of their European counterparts.
- They are specialized in several but not necessarily all areas of wholesale finance. They are focused on what they are able to do well, and demand expertise second to none. Bond traders are bond traders, not general managers on rotation through the bank. They will be bond traders for their entire careers, except for the small number pushed up to management positions. Their businesses have been mainly simplified to debt, equity and advisory services. They are market-makers and trading counterparties to everyone in the market, and the importance of indi-vidual clients has diminished with the weakening loyalty of the clients to them.

Being specialized means being able to trade at the best prices possible and to survive and prosper accordingly.

- They recognize that much of what they do has become commoditized, and the trading spreads, commissions and advisory fees have been cut to the bone. To overcome the economic effects of this erosion of margins the firms have increased the volume of trading positions (making themselves more dependent on trading than on anything else). They have also increased efforts to devise innovative new products (that will carry higher spreads at least for a while) and to enter into new markets (Latin America, Eastern Europe) in which opportunities to recreate the sort of businesses they have developed in the USA are just appearing.

- They are constantly experimenting with new strategic initiatives. The firms' business strategies are always under review (if not under attack) by management. There are few sacred cows. As a result widely different long-term business strategies have emerged among the top firms. Morgan Stanley and Dean Witter have merged to create a new competitor to Merrill Lynch. Previous Merrill challengers, Smith Barney and Lehman Brothers, have backed away from the effort to specialize in retail distribution and fixed-income, respectively. Goldman Sachs remains a partnership, devoted to global corporate finance and trading, but with increasing commitments to investing its own capital in private transactions. Salomon Brothers remains a fixed income specialist, though it has recently entered into an imaginative strategic equity securities distribution arrangement with the Fidelity Funds group. Chase Bank remains firmly in second place in the global wholesale rankings by sticking to syndicating bank loans while virtually ignoring the other investment banking activities. Different strategic approaches may constitute distinct comparative advantages in the future, but it is usually difficult to understand which strategy may be better than others while they are being implemented.

- The strategies, however, are mainly meant to be offensive and aggressive, to build market share and profit opportunities. Periodically there is concern that a firm may be overly dependent upon revenues streams from too limited a number of areas, and efforts are made to build another business area to protect the firm's overall profitability. An example of this may be the current rush to acquire money managers to supplement trading and corporate finance revenues streams. But the firms generally do not view their strategies as defensive—to protect their existing market positions and clients, or to enable greater cost reduction and economies of scale.

- Perhaps the one thing all of the firms would agree on is that none of their objectives can be achieved without the highest-quality personnel that it is possible for them to attract. These are top graduates of the best business and law schools, highly competitive persons who have already excelled in the military services, athletics, politics or other businesses. They are team players to a point, but disdain unreasonable authority and are fearless in advancing their own viewpoints. These people have to be recruited, nurtured and developed as strong contributors. They must be paid extremely well, and allowed a great deal of freedom of action. They challenge everything and can be difficult to control and to work with, but they are capable of extraordinary results. They are not traditional organizational men and women: they do not resemble at all those who held high positions in commercial banks in the 1980s, and who occupy similar positions in Europe today. Mastering the difficult art of attracting, managing and retaining such people is certainly a comparative advantage in the securities industry. Much of the success of Goldman Sachs, Merrill Lynch, Morgan Stanley Dean Witter and J.P. Morgan is attributed by their competitors to this capability.

As of September 1997, the US Congress was still considering, for the third time in ten years, a substantial revision to the Banking Act of 1933 that would effectively eliminate all or many of the Glass-Steagall provisions separating banking from the securities and insurance businesses. On this occasion there is no substantial disagreement between the parties on allowing banks to recover powers to conduct securities operations, which *de facto* the Federal Reserve and other regulators have already permitted under the Section 20 exemption. If the Congress does act to repeal all of the restrictions on activities of the banks, it will remove a comparative advantage that some have regarded as important to securities firms—they can participate in whatever businesses they like but the banks cannot. Would repeal mean a widespread movement towards universal banking in the United States? Professors Saunders and Walter (1996) have concluded that universal banking could be conducted safely in the United States, but the potential economies of scale and scope would be few and limited only to exceptionally large banks. So far, evidence from the marketplace seems to suggest that most banks believe they would be better off avoiding the capital-intensive, volatile and difficult-to-manage business. Shareholders investing in banks have indeed been willing on the whole to pay higher prices for banks that are predominately in retail and regional banking, not wholesale banking. Managers and boards of directors have taken this in, and restricted their securities activities accordingly. What acquisitions there have been between banking and securities firms have been of smaller, specialized firms, not large national firms, and even these have been very expensive in terms of price to book value. Further, bank managers and directors do not believe that investors want to see banks retain their stability by transferring profits from successful areas to unsuccessful ones—they would rather see the unsuccessful business improved or sold off. Clients also show little sign of being interested in European-style *Hausbank* relationships, and seem committed to shopping around to gain the lowest financing costs whenever they have business to do.

3. Competitive Dynamics in Europe

The European securities industry has been affected by all of the forces that have changed the American securities industry. Most of the changes came to Europe after they had been tested in the United States—Europe had shared the same conditions that made the United States banking system ripe for change. Certainly for the past several years the European marketplace has been influenced by a gradually declining role of banks, by an increasing usage of global capital markets by corporations and governments, by regulatory reform, by the application of new technology in trading markets, and even by Europe's first takeover boom. An increased volume of financial transactions and competition for them are the result of these changes.

Just as the beginning of events was marked in the United States by 'Mayday' in 1975, it all began in Europe a decade later with the United Kingdom's 'Big Bang', on 27 October 1986.[9] This event was the result of an out-of-court settlement between the Thatcher Government and the London Stock Exchange on charges of restraint of trade by the exchange that were similar to those which the New York Stock Exchange was forced to face. The result was that the London Stock Exchange agreed to open memberships and to allow commission rates to be negotiated. These concessions, however, changed everything, because they changed the economics of the system used by the City for over a hundred years. The reforms led to enormous transformations, among them being the streamlining of markets, a sharp lowering of commissions and increases in volumes of securities traded, new investments in electronic market-making, and efforts to attract institutional investors in securities of other European countries to the more efficient London market. These reforms were thought to so advantage British markets that the other major European countries embarked upon Big Bang-like reforms of their own, and for the first time serious competition between European securities marketplaces began to develop. The improving markets led to the ability to absorb the new, large privatization issues that appeared subsequently, as well as greater investment in European securities by US and Japanese investors.

3.1. The biggest bang

Among the changes caused by Big Bang were major alterations in the competitive structure of the British market and its leading players. The UK market was very old and established, having been at the forefront of global finance throughout the nineteenth century, and earlier. Many brokers, jobbers, banks and merchant banks that could trace roots back to these early days were forced into mergers and alliances, because the firms feared that they could not survive in the securities business without becoming fully capitalized, full-service firms like the Americans. Most of the major market participants in Britain in 1986 endeavoured to do this, either by acquiring capacity they lacked or by building their own.

The results, however, were mixed. The earliest leaders to emerge were Barclays' merchant bank, called Barclays de Zoete Wedd or 'BZW', and S.G. Warburg, both of which had acquired a leading broker and a leading jobber. NatWest Bank made a modest effort to gain prominence in the securities market, but the other British clearing banks

---

[9] 'Big Bang' is the name given by British journalists to the day on which the City of London was to be blown sky-high, and a new financial 'universe' was to be created.

(Lloyds Bank, Midland Bank and Standard Chartered Bank) after initial half-hearted attempts, withdrew. (In 1992, Midland Bank was acquired by Hong Kong & Shanghai Banking Corp., which had earlier acquired British broker James Capel). Many other UK brokers were acquired by foreign banks: Union Bank of Switzerland bought prominent broker Phillips & Drew, and Swiss Bank Corp. bought Savory Milln. Citibank and Chase Manhattan each acquired two brokers, and Security Pacific Bank bought an interest in Hoare Govett, which was later sold to ABN Amro Bank.

Most of the other merchant banks were cautious—Morgan Grenfell entered the trading businesses briefly but withdrew after losing money; it was subsequently acquired in 1989 by Deutsche Bank for its corporate finance and investment management skills. Similarly, Kleinwort Benson acquired a broker but remained on the sidelines after some early unsuccessful attempts at trading, specializing in privatizations and investment management until it was bought in 1995 by Dresdner Bank. Hill Samuel was bought in 1988 by Trustee Savings Bank, after which it subsequently faded into obscurity. Hambros Bank, Robert Fleming, N.M. Rothschild, and Schroders, all family-controlled firms, have remained specialists in corporate finance and investment management. Lazard Brothers, similarly specialized, has strengthened its familial alliance with Lazard Frères of Paris and New York. Rothschild's securities trading subsidiary, Smith Newcourt, was sold to Merrill Lynch in 1995. Barings PLC, also a family-controlled firm, was sold in 1995 to Internationale Nederlanden Groep (ING) after its spectacular failure at the hands of trading rogue Nick Leeson.

The star of the post-Big Bang period, S.G. Warburg, was seen by many to be the only British firm capable of global market leadership in investment banking. However, it stumbled in the difficult trading markets in 1994, and after an aborted effort to be acquired by Morgan Stanley, was sold to Swiss Bank Corp. Swiss Bank immediately integrated it into its investment banking unit, which had been fortified by the acquisition of Chicago-based derivatives specialists O'Connor & Co. Thus in 1997, the two surviving British-owned full-service investment banks were the subsidiaries of the country's two largest commercial banks, National Westminster, ranked fifteenth, and BZW Barclays ranked twenty-first, among the top global wholesale banking firms in 1996. The board of NatWest, however, facing declining profits and a sagging stock price, acted in early 1996 to undo some of its previous commitment to investment banking, by sacking the CEO of its NatWest Markets subsidiary and bringing control of many of its activities back into the banking parent.

Despite these events involving UK firms, an earlier hybrid, British-led, Swiss-owned, and American-styled Credit Suisse First Boston, which ranked sixth in 1996, experienced many years among the top five global finance firms. However, its profitability has not always been satisfactory to its Swiss owners, and the firm has experienced several reorganizations and management changes, though it continues to be a powerful player in the competitive rankings. Out of British origins, however, are now rising three other hybrid market leaders, UBS with Philips & Drew (ninth), and Deutsche Morgan Grenfell and SBC Warburg (ranking twelfth and thirteenth, respectively), and perhaps two other contenders, ABN Amro (seventeenth) and Hong Kong & Shanghai Banking

Corp. (twenty-second). It is possible to say that of the top twenty firms identified as market leaders in Table 10.5, seven are firms that have British origins, though all are now owned by non-British banks.

3.2. Trading markets

Bond markets in EU countries as of 31 December 1996 totalled approximately US$7,400 billion of outstanding issues. Of this amount about US$4,200 billion represented public sector issues, of which US$2,600 billion, or 62 per cent, was issued by government bodies in Germany, Italy and France. Corporate bonds issued by EU countries (companies, banks and savings institutions) amounted to more than US$2,200 billion sold in domestic markets, and US$1,000 billion of international bonds. These bonds are sold within the country of issuance and to other investors in and out of the EU, but they were predominantly bought by institutional investors, both from EU countries and outside them. See Table 10.6.

The bond market is facilitated by the volume of trading in the foreign exchange markets, which during 1995 averaged about US$1,500 billion per day (BIS, 1997: Table V5). Trading is encouraged by arbitrage and proprietary programmes undertaken by investors and large market-makers and financial intermediaries all over the world. Such trading in government bonds is often highly leveraged as well. Further, the availability of currency swaps and other forms of derivative instruments, all of which have increased steadily since their introduction to the market in the mid-1980s, is helpful to traders who can accordingly manufacture 'synthetic' securities by combining a bond and a swap contract, for example, to create a bond with a different financial exposure. Such synthetic securities permit arbitrage against authentic positions. As long as

Table 10.6. European bond market, end-1996 (US$ bn.)

	Total bonds outstanding	Public sector debt	Corporate and other bonds	International bonds
Germany	2,303	839	1,161	304
Italy	1,274	998	188	88
France	1,044	732	153	160
UK	662	447	33	183
Netherlands	401	200	120	81
Belgium	387	223	127	38
Denmark	288	104	175	9
Sweden	253	118	131	4
Spain	234	185	34	15
(ECU)	130	66	—	64
Austria	133	59	61	2
Other EU	252	182	50	20
Total EU	7,361	4,153	2,233	968

Table 10.7. Financial derivative instruments (notional principal outstanding; US$ bn.)

	1996	1995	1994	1993	1992	1991	1990	1989
Exchange-traded instruments	9,884.60	9,188.20	8,862.5	7,771.1	4,634.4	3,519.3	2,290.2	1,766.7
Interest rate futures	5,931.1	5,863.4	5,777.6	4,958.7	2,913.0	2,156.7	1,454.5	1,200.8
Interest rate options[a]	3,277.8	2,741.8	2,622.8	2,362.4	1,385.4	1,072.6	599.5	387.9
Currency futures	50.3	38.3	40.1	34.7	26.5	18.3	16.9	15.9
Currency options[a]	46.5	43.2	55.6	75.6	71.1	62.8	56.5	50.2
Stock market index futures	198.6	172.2	127.3	109.9	79.7	76.0	69.1	41.3
Stock market index options[a]	380.2	329.3	238.3	229.7	158.6	132.8	93.7	70.6
Over-the-counter instruments[b]	24,292.00	17,712.60	11,303.2	8,474.5	5,345.7	4,449.5	3,450.3	1,951.7
Interest rate swaps	n.a.	12,810.70	10,800.0	6,177.3	3,850.8	3,065.1	2,311.5	1,502.6
Currency swaps[c]	n.a.	1,197.40	2,100.0	899.6	860.4	807.2	577.5	449.1
Other swap-related derivative[d]	n.a.	3,704.50	1,500.0	1,397.6	634.5	577.2	561.3	—

[a] Calls and puts.

[b] Data collected by the International Swaps and Derivatives Association (ISDA) only; the two sides of contracts between ISDA members are reported once only.

[c] Adjusted for reporting of both currencies; including cross-currency interest rate swaps.

[d] Caps, collars, floors and swaptions.

Source: BIS (1997: Table VII.5); data from Futures Industry Association, various futures and options exchanges, ISDA and BIS calculations.

profit-making opportunities exist, market operatives will take positions to benefit from them.

Trading in derivatives has grown substantially in Europe, in the over-the-counter markets (mainly for swaps) but also on futures exchanges in London, Paris, Frankfurt and Zurich. See Table 10.7. The availability of such extensive trading in derivatives has also assisted market-makers in taking positions in ECU-denominated bonds, for which markets have existed since the early 1980s. It is likely that this market will be the forerunner of the coming market in bonds denominated in euros. On 1 February 1997 the European Investment Bank issued euro 1 billion (US$1.18 billion) of bonds due in 2004. Payment for the bonds, and payments of interest and principal until January 1999, will be in ECUs, after which time all payments will be made in euros. The issue, known in the market as the first 'euro Eurobond' was three times oversubscribed (Adams, 1997).

Equity markets have also grown in importance and activity. The EU accounted for US$2,200 billion in value of equity market trading, or 16 per cent of all global equity trading, during 1996. (The United States accounted for 52 per cent of the global equity trading total.[10]) However, because of the structure of European ownership of equity securities, the large portion of state-owned enterprises still operating within EU countries and the lower market valuations of many companies, the intensity of European equity market utilization lags well behind that of the United States and Japan. See Table 10.8. It is likely that since the data in Table 10.8 were complied (1993), the European markets have been much more active, and large privatization issues such as the US$13 billion initial public offering of Deutsche Telekom have pushed European utilization higher. The expectation is that this utilization will continue to increase until it approximates the levels of the United States and Japan.

Trading opportunities, however, often depend on market volatility, and this volatility is affected not only by changing domestic market conditions, but also because of global market linkages and changing foreign exchange and interest rates. Many observers (but not all) believe that increasing trading volume in cash markets and derivatives contributes to a dampening of volatility. This may be evident in US dollar

Table 10.8. World equity market utilization, 1993 (US$ bn.)

	No. of domestic listed companies	Market capitalization	GNP	Market capitalization to GNP (%)
USA	7,246	5,136	6,388	80.4
Japan	2,155	3,000	3,927	76.4
EU	4,458	2,830	7,234	39.1

Source: International Finance Corp., 1996.

[10] Securities Industry Association, *1996 Securities Industry Fact Book*.

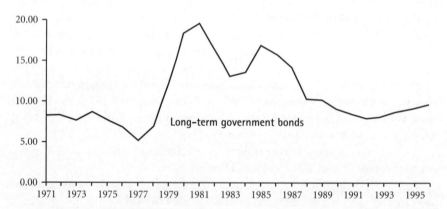

Figure 10.1(a). Volatility of large company stocks and long-term government bonds (annualized monthly standard deviation, three-year average)

bond and stock markets, and in many foreign exchange markets, since the early 1980s. Indeed, volatilities of long-term US government bonds, large US company stocks, the French franc–dollar rate and the DM–dollar rate have fallen to levels about half what they were at their peak in the mid-1980s. Volatility in these instruments was as low in mid-1997 as it had been at any time since 1979–80, though factors others than increased trading volume were involved. See Figure 10.1.

Many market participants have discovered that trading in increasingly efficient markets is not an easy business. Indeed, much money was lost in Europe during 1994, a bear market year for bonds, by traders who had open positions instead of fully hedged ones. The traders discovered that the cost of hedging consumed all their expected profits, so they decided instead to bet on their 'feel' for how the market would develop. Getting the feel wrong may have cost S.G. Warburg its independence.

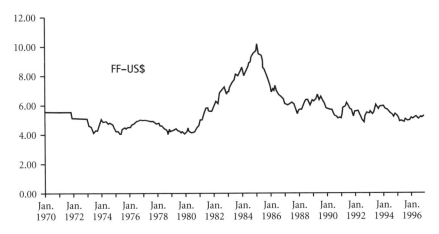

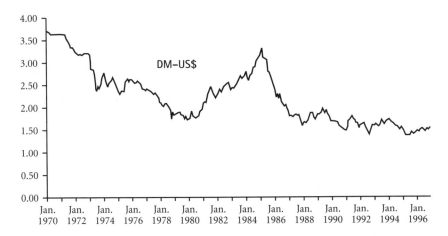

Figure 10.1(b). Volatility of exchange rates (three-month average)

3.3. The emerging power of pension funds

At December 1995, the world's funded pension assets amounted to US$8,000 billion, of which US$4,519 billion were in North America, US$1,963 were in Europe, and US$1,474 were in the Pacific Basin countries. The funded investments in Europe were substantially lodged in the United Kingdom (US$900 billion), the Netherlands (US$327 billion), Switzerland (US$280 billion), and Germany (US$140 billion). A leading American pension fund consultant, InterSec Research Corp., estimates European funded pension funds will grow to about US$3,000 billion by 2000, reflecting a growth rate of about 9 per cent per annum.[11] This growth is in response to popular

[11] InterSec Research Corp., Client Memorandum, 30 June 1996.

demand for greater amounts of pension security, given that in most European countries pensions are on a pay-as-you-go basis that has to be funded each year in the national budget. The US$1,000 billion of growth in pension assets outstanding will provide substantial additional opportunities for money management firms and will add considerably to the support of European equity markets. In the United States and the United Kingdom, between 30 per cent and 50 per cent of new pension fund money has been invested in equity securities.

3.4. European 'restructuring'

Europe of course has experienced other economic and regulatory changes that are unique to itself, the Single Market Act and the Maastricht Treaty perhaps being the most important of these. However, the intense merger and acquisition activity in Europe since 1985, valued at more than US$900 billion in completed transactions, has also been important. This activity has been attributed to the need on the part of corporations to reposition themselves both for the Single Market and for the more closely linked global market for their products and services, and to improve performance and become more competitive (Walter and Smith, 1990: 5–21).

Today, the term 'restructuring' is popular in Europe to describe efforts by major companies to improve profits, returns on investment and market values by shedding subsidiaries, trimming workforces and investing more in new technologies and overseas production.[12] A number of notable restructuring successes have been reported in Germany (Veba, Daimler Benz, and Hoechst), but the effort is generally thought to apply across the continent. A major Wall Street firm pointed to special, self-initiated restructuring success at Zurich Insurance, Unilever and the Rank Group during 1997.[13] Some of the impetus for restructuring has come from aggressive domestic investor groups, partly as a result of observing comparable activity on the part of their US and British fund manager counterparts. Some has come from determined, impatient European managers eager to make headway in the difficult job of remaking companies.

Several hostile transactions have been attempted to achieve restructuring, something not generally associated with European industry. The Krupp–Thyssen takeover effort in early 1997, for example, was resisted by Thyssen, but financed by Deutsche Bank and Dresdner Bank (its *Hausbank*), and included Goldman Sachs as an adviser. The offer was called off in favour of direct negotiations between the companies after protests by the trade unions involved, but the net result was still the consolidation of the two steel works and a significant downsizing of the workforce. A previous successful hostile transaction resulted in the combination of Krupp and Hoechst Steel in 1995.

Similar restructuring efforts have been occurring in Europe for several years, espe-

---

[12] 'Boom and Gloom in Germany', *The Economist*, 5 April 1997.
[13] Goldman, Sachs & Co., 'Passing the Baton on Corporate Restructuring', 9 April 1997.

Table 10.9. German companies going public, as of October 1996

Company	Business	Date of issue
Binder Optik	Opticians	1996/7
Dt. Oberflachenfechnik	Surface treatment plants	1996/7
Deutsche Telekom	Telecommunications	Autumn 1996
DIS	Employment agency	Summer 1997
Dragoso Gerberding & Co.	Perfumes	1996/7
Gardena	Garden equipment	1996/7
Grapel	Mechanical engineering	1996/7
Grammer	Seating	Autumn 1996
Eurobike	Motorcycle accessories	Summer 1996
HLB Bau-Stahl Holding	Steel trading	1997
Homag AG	Mechanical engineering	1998
Integrata Training AG	Training	1996
Klockner & Co.	Trading	After 1 Jan. 1997
Konsortium Stuttgart	Investment company	June 1996
Pro Sleben	Television	Summer 1996
Leicht Kuchen AG	Kitchen furniture	1997
Nordenia	Plastic packaging	1996/7
Remmers	Building, chemicals	1996
Rinol AG	Coating systems	1997
Sanacorp	Pharmaceuticals	Autumn 1996
Stella Musical	Music	1996/7
Tank and Rast	Service	1997
Techem	Heating	1996/7

Source: *Financial Times*, Oct. 1996.

cially in the manufacturing, chemicals, banking and finance, and telecommunications industries. Unfriendly transactions continue to be rare in Europe, where they have averaged 11 per cent of all transactions since 1985 (as compared to an average of 18 per cent in the United States, and 14 per cent in the UK), but they have successfully been completed in all countries (DeLong *et al.* 1997).Even when an unsuccessful takeover attempt is made, there are usually concessions made by the target management that might not have occurred otherwise, so that there may be some restructuring value in even unsuccessful bids. Also, the perceived threat of an unfriendly takeover has shaken many companies out of their complacency and into some form of self-restructuring.

Another development in Europe has been the increasing use of stock markets to affect initial public offerings of privately owned, mid-sized, or *Mittlestand* companies as well as for privatization issues. Creating a public market for a company's stock means that it is subject to reporting requirements, performance measures and investor scrutiny, which tend to contribute to an attitude on the part of management to run the company more profitably and productively. Table 10.9 is a list of several mid-sized German companies that had recently gone public, or were scheduled to go public, in October 1996.

3.5. Changing European players and strategies

Many of the changes affecting European banks during the past decade are the same ones that shaped important changes in American banking. Credit losses, disintermediation, regulatory changes, technology developments and increasing competition from foreigners and from non-banking enterprises have put most European banks under the gun to rethink their long-term strategies. Banks now have to think both offensively and defensively—to ensure access to important new markets in the pan-European context and to protect their existing, mainly domestic, market positions. They have also had to address the changing nature of wholesale banking, which now depends on market activity, and of retail banking, which depends more heavily than ever on improved technology and services. They know that, after centuries of serving mainly as safe places for depositors to put their money, they now have to be competitive as well or they will lose business to those who are. This is a difficult and stressful time for European banks (as the 1980s were for US banks). Several trends have been observed that indicate how many banks are resolving these issues.

The first trend is towards increasing the size of banks, through mergers and consolidations, in order to present a more powerful defence of the domestic franchises. During the twelve years from 1985 to 1996, financial service acquisitions accounted for more than US$2,500 billion, 44 per cent of the global total. Of this amount, US$1,158 billion or 46 per cent, were transactions that occurred outside the United States. Further, non-US domestic and cross-border mergers and acquisitions of banks and other financial service firms during the period involved more than 7,000 transactions valued at US$907 billion (74 per cent of these were domestic transactions). The financial services industry, comprising US$284 billion in transactions for the twelve-year period under study, was the most active of all industries in Europe involved in mergers and acquisitions (as it was in the United States for the same period; DeLong *et al.* 1997). See Table 10.10. Though many of the mergers were the result of failed lending policies during preceding years, they have nevertheless created new banks that are among the largest in Britain, France, Germany, Italy, the Netherlands, Sweden, Norway, Denmark, Belgium, Austria, Spain, and Portugal (as they have also in the United States and in Japan). In many such cases the mergers have resulted in increased competitiveness and the introduction of new products and services, such as insurance, especially at the retail level.

Approximately 87 per cent of all global financial service industry combinations involved intrasectoral transactions (i.e. banks and banks, insurance companies and insurance companies). Few cross-border bank-to-bank acquisitions have occurred, however—though Deutsche Bank's acquisition of Banca d'America e d'Italia (from Bank of America) in 1986, Crédit Lyonnais' acquisition of Bank für Gemeinwirtshaft in 1986, and Hong Kong Shanghai Bank's acquisition of Midland Bank in 1992 are significant exceptions. Also, a few significant intersectoral transactions have occurred, such as Swiss Bank Corporation's acquisition of S.G. Warburg & Co. and Dillon Read & Co., ING's acquisition of Barings PLC, and Dresdner Bank's acquisition of Kleinwort

Table 10.10. Completed global financial services mergers and acquisitions transactions, 1985–1996

	1985				1996				1985–96			
	Value (US$ bn.)	%	Number ('000)	%	Value (US$ bn.)	%	Number ('000)	%	Value (US$ bn.)	%	Number ('000)	%
US Domestic												
All industries	192.5	82.6	0.8	72.7	340.6	45.2	6.9	43.7	2,859.5	49.2	50.9	42.0
All financial services	47.9	82.3	0.7	77.7	114.5	39.8	2.4	42.9	1,172.7	46.6	19.9	45.1
US cross-border												
All industries	15.7	6.7	0.1	9.1	93.4	12.4	1.7	10.8	679.0	11.7	12.6	10.4
All financial services	6.3	10.8	0.1	8.6	15.8	5.5	0.3	5.4	185.9	7.4	2.8	7.4
Non-US												
All industries	24.8	10.6	0.2	18.2	319.2	42.4	7.2	45.6	2,271.4	39.1	57.7	47.6
All financial services	4.0	6.9	0.1	8.6	157.4	54.7	2.9	51.8	1,158.2	46.0	21.7	47.5
Total												
All industries	233.0	100.0	1.1	100.0	753.2	100.0	15.8	100.0	5,809.9	100.0	121.2	100.0
All financial services	58.2	100.0	0.9	100.0	287.7	100.0	5.6	100.0	2,516.8	100.0	44.4	100.0

Source: Securities Data Company.

Benson. The industry's early interest in 'strategic alliances' among banks in different countries appears to have faded. Acquisitions of minority interests in financial service companies accounted for only 15 per cent of global transactions, mainly in emerging-market countries (Smith and Walter, 1996).

Another trend is related to the role of mergers in bringing about changes in corporate control. Corporate governance matters are now the subject of acute interest in Europe, and in the light of the dominant role played by banks in many countries governance issues related to banks have attracted much attention. The most celebrated case was the unsuccessful effort during 1995–6 by Martin Ebner to win control of Union Bank of Switzerland. Ebner, a minority investor in the bank, in essence attempted a proxy fight for control of Switzerland's most prominent financial institution, and lost—but not without gaining months of sympathetic press attention and a number of concessions by management. In the United Kingdom, the board structure and governance procedures of Barclays Bank were much in the press.

Also in France, Germany and Sweden issues have been raised as to the best way for the great power of large universal banking institutions to be governed. In particular, this attention has focused on the industrial holding of banks, and the role of the banks in governing these so-call *Hausbank* companies, especially in the light of very poor results of a number of important (and closely watched) clients of Deutsche Bank, Crédit Lyonnais and Banque Indosuez. In many cases, it is now expected that these and other large universal banks will begin to shed some of their industrial holdings, as they are no longer as important as they were, tie up capital unproductively, and create major headaches for management. Indeed, even Deutsche Bank, through its head of corporate finance Ronaldo Schmitz, has said it had decided that reducing its 28 per cent shareholding in Daimler Benz was appropriate as Germany stood on the brink of 'the most significant industrial reconstruction since the second world war' (Waller, 1993).

A final major trend has been the internal combination within universal banks of their corporate banking operations and their investment banking or securities arms. Originally this was done by Barclays and National Westminster banks in the UK, but later some of the major Swiss, German, Scandinavian and Dutch banks (and US banks such as J.P. Morgan and Bankers Trust) followed suit. This has resulted in a major change in the organizational structure of the European universal bank, from a monolithic, hierarchical, one-board-decides-all structure that emphasized safety and depended on captive clients, to a more streamlined approach that permits autonomy of decision-making within separate sectors of the bank (Walter, 1997).

The new structure assumes that clients will not remain loyal unless they receive the best rates and executions in wholesale finance and that to deliver these the banks have to become more specialized and focused, and free from high-level interference in their competitive activities. These changes have not come without considerable problems, however. The problems mainly concern how much control over overseas activities the head office is to let go, knowing that to be competitive the banks have to delegate considerable autonomy to market specialists—and how much to retain and by whom. Many disputes have arisen between traditional commercial bankers involved with domestic and overseas lending and the new securities people. These disputes cover compensation and matters of 'turf', or who is to be responsible for particular clients and territories. But they also embrace some new areas. Swiss Bank Corp., for example, promoted several of the young, very smart and aggressive American executives from O'Connor to high executive positions in Zurich and London, much to the chagrin of the traditional Swiss officers of the bank who were displaced. Few Swiss were prepared for a system in which they would have to report to a profit-driven American several years younger who was sitting right there at headquarters. Deutsche Bank has struggled with issues of control at Morgan Grenfell, especially after an undisciplined Oxford-educated portfolio manager there cost the bank about US$700 million, and Dresdner has recently let go the popular CEO of its Kleinwort Benson subsidiary over policy disputes about who would control the increasing activities of Dresdner Kleinwort Benson that were not located in London (Fisher, 1997*a*). These cultural and management problems must seem endless to many of the European banks trying to reposition themselves.

3.6. Non-European players in Europe

American firms operating in Europe have, with few exceptions, built their own organizations by hiring talented Europeans and mixing them with American colleagues in on-the-job training. For reasons mentioned earlier, American firms have had certain comparative advantages (including the huge size of their domestic market) that have assisted them in securing leadership in the global market. Nine of the top ten, and fifteen of the top twenty firms in Table 10.5 are American or have American origins. However, even among American banks and investment banks, only a relatively small number (fewer than twenty) continue to compete for global wholesale leadership. Citibank has deliberately given up market share, preferring to concentrate on consumer financial services and services in emerging markets. NationsBank and Bank of America, ranking sixteenth and nineteenth, respectively, generate most of their origination volumes from US domestic business. Bankers Trust failed to make the top thirty wholesale banking firms in 1996 although it has been among the top twenty several times in the past. Nonetheless, J.P. Morgan, now widely recognized as a highly competitive investment bank (no longer a commercial bank) has earned high ranking.

Other Europeans possibly attempting to find places among the top twenty are Schroders and Paribas. Virtually all others (including the Japanese, who a few years before were seen as extremely strong competitors) have decided not to compete for leadership positions in the global wholesale finance market, preferring to concentrate on domestic opportunities of various types. Today these include various other financial services from credit cards, to insurance and funds management.

4. The Securities Markets after the Euro

At this point, one thing should be clear: the securities industry in Europe has been undergoing and is continuing to undergo major changes in its structure and organization regardless of what happens with EMU and the euro. These ongoing changes may be of greater importance to the industry than those related to the change in the European monetary system. However, without doubt, the anticipated changes under EMU will affect the marketplace in which the securities firms operate. To the extent that they increase the overall trading volume in securities, and the premium placed on innovation, trading skills and distribution capacity, and global reach they may also affect the size of firms and their apparent need for consolidation into even larger entities. To the extent that this occurs, the impact of the euro on the securities industry could be very important indeed.

Of course there remain the questions of whether the benefits of establishing the new system will exceed the costs, as is now widely predicted by public officials, and what will happen in 2001 when the opt-out countries are expected to come into EMU. These factors will determine how quickly the euro effect will take hold in the markets.

Those seeking financing in the markets will continue, as they do now, to compete for money, as, for example, when different European governments consider issuing Eurodollar bonds. For the next few years, including probably the period between 1999 and 2001, competition will continue to rely mainly on credit ratings, innovation, tapping particular maturities, and other devices used to achieve lower rates. But in the longer run, it is intended and expected that the effectiveness and transparency of EMU should lead to a further convergence of fiscal policies so no one country within the EU has a significant advantage over other countries. To the extent that this means a movement towards freer and more open markets and away from European mixed-economy social policies and political attitudes, then it may mean a rise in productivity for the entire EU region, but there is no certainty that this will occur.[14] Nor is there certainty to the proposition, made by the EU itself (European Commission, 1995) and many euro advocates, that the changes will increase market integration, lower overall costs of capital, or result in more efficient bond auctions by governments.

But the changes will inevitably affect the markets in a number of ways, and indeed have already begun to do so. The BIS has reported that implied exchange rates calculated out to ten years forward, based on yields on interest rate swaps, indicate that the currencies of a number of European countries are expected to be stable against the DM. It also reported that the volatility of many intra-European exchange rates declined significantly during 1996—the implied volatility in the French franc–DM rate averaged 2 per cent in 1996, compared with 7 per cent in April 1995—and foreign exchange volume diminished somewhat as a result. These factors suggested to the BIS

[14] See also Fisher (1997b). This article refers also to an interesting study by Alexander Schraeder of Bayerische Vereinsbank.

that approximately 10 per cent of the foreign exchange market (based on its 1995 survey of foreign exchange trading in twenty-six countries) could disappear with the advent of the euro (BIS, 1997: 80–1).

A market shrinkage of this proportion could have several effects on market participants. First, foreign exchange trading opportunities, already being squeezed by reduced volatility and electronic trading, would be reduced further, driving some traders and market-makers into new markets in neighbouring countries, thereby perhaps significantly increasing the competition to be faced by smaller market players in individual countries (like Belgium) which had the local market largely to themselves before the introduction of the euro. Secondly, dealers may be driven to expand their business in riskier or higher-margin areas, such as trading derivatives, or the euro against emerging-market currencies. This trend too could be disadvantageous to smaller, national players without experience or an international infrastructure. The BIS estimates that such business may represent over one-third of the volume of the intra-European trading that may disappear with the euro (BIS, 1997: 81–3).

4.1. Money markets

Intra-European trading volume in individual instruments will be replaced, it is assumed, by greater extra-European trading in euro-denominated instruments and in instruments denominated in the currencies of the opt-out countries. The market in euros that will emerge will be larger and more liquid than any single European currency market that it will replace, thus generating perhaps a greater interest by non-Europeans in holding euros. Several portfolio shifts might be expected.

First, non-participating European and non-European central banks will invest a portion of their reserves in euro-denominated investments. Second, major European institutional fund managers will adjust their portfolios to reflect the investment outlook that the euro-denominated instruments present to them. There is already some concern that the euro may be significantly less inflation-proof than the departing DM, and that such a concern may generate higher rates, on one hand, or greater demand for Swiss franc investments, on the other. Many economists, however, believe that the euro may emerge as a better long-term reserve asset than either the Deutsche Mark or the French franc. Accordingly, many investors, including non-European investors (especially from the United States and the Far East) will take up euro positions as a part of their overall portfolio diversification efforts. To them, a larger, more liquid market in euro-denominated securities than the fragmented markets it replaces should be welcome. The latter two portfolio shifts will also be affected by increasing investment in European and Asian pension funds over the next several years, which will direct a substantial flow of new money looking for a variety of liquid and credit-worthy investments into the markets.

Also, the new European Central Bank will presumably absorb all of the reserves of the EMU participating countries (for all EU members, reserves excluding gold totalled US$370 billion at December 1996, far more than those of Japan or the United States).

Even after netting EMU member countries' holding of other members' currencies, this development could lead to a condition of substantial excess reserves. What will be done with the surplus?[15] Unless it can be returned to the countries in the form of a cash distribution, the expectation is that the conservative German-influenced European Central Bank will hang on to the surplus to provide a fund to stabilize the euro against the dollar and the yen. Might this mean a much more active intervention policy on the part of the new central bank, which would push euro rates below their equilibrium level? Such rate levels might become very attractive to issuers of securities. A surge of euro new issues might result, at least for a while. Any interventionist activity would, however, also be of great interest to international foreign exchange speculators, who are inclined to take the opposite side of the market from government operators.

4.2. Bond markets

Despite the many uncertainties associated with EMU, there are some things that nevertheless appear to be fairly predictable.

When the conversion process is complete, it will formalize the existence of the world's second largest bond market after the United States. Initially, about two-thirds of the US$7,600 billion European bond market, and approximately half of the nearly US$4,200 billion government bond market, will be denominated in euros, as the amounts of bonds outstanding in the opt-out countries are relatively small compared to the whole. The new bond market will be segmented into at least three parts:

1. *the euro Eurobond sector* for issues by international institutions such as agencies of the EU and the World Bank, and perhaps some major multinational corporations whose currency composition is European or global (e.g. Nestlé, Unilever, Shell). These will be issued free of withholding taxes and in bearer form as previous Eurobonds were.
2. *the euro-sovereign sector* for issues by the in-governments and major national private corporations. These bonds will replace domestic bonds in the participating countries, and presumably will be issued to retire outstanding domestic currency denominated bonds.
3. *issues in non-euro currencies,* including new bonds issued by the opt-out countries and old bonds still outstanding in non-euro currencies, including Eurodollar bonds, presently the market's largest component.

The first segment of euro-denominated bonds (which is not expected to be a large one because of the limited supply of such supranational issuers) will trade in the market on the basis of the creditworthiness of the issuer and liquidity alone. As there is no benchmark reference for direct EU obligations denominated in euros, the market will have to establish a pricing regime for such issues, perhaps by comparing the offering yields to US Treasury securities on a swapped-in basis.

---

[15] 'The Euro and the Dollar', *The Economist*, 19 October 1997.

Table 10.11. Sovereign debt ratings for EU countries and debt pricing spreads, 10 March 1997

	Standard & Poor's		Moody's		Debt pricing (bp) relative to LIBOR	
	Local currency	Foreign currency	Local currency	Foreign currency	Local currency	Foreign currency
Austria	AAA	AAA	n.r.	Aaa	−18	−8
France	AAA	AAA	Aaa	Aaa	20	−17
Germany	AAA	AAA	Aaa	Aaa	22	−4
Netherlands	AAA	AAA	Aaa	Aaa	−22	n.a.
Luxembourg	AAA	AAA	n.r.	Aaa	n.a.	n.a.
Britain	AAA	AAA	Aaa	Aaa	−6	−11
Belgium	AAA	AAA	n.r.	Aa1	−9	−10
Denmark	AAA	AA+	Aa1	Aa1	−17	−12
Sweden	AAA	AA+	n.r.	Aa3	10	−12
Italy	AAA	AA	Aa1	Aa3	100	55
Greece	AAA	BBB−	n.r.	Baa1	−6	5
Spain	n.r.	AA	Aa2	Aa2	−5	−4
Portugal	AAA	AA−	Aa2	Aa3	n.a.	n.a.
Finland	AAA	AA	Aaa	Aa1	−27	−1
Ireland	AAA	AA	Aaa	Aa1	−8	n.a.

n.r. = non-rated; n.a. = not available.

Source: Deutsche Bank Research, *EMU Watch*, 28, table 4, 10 March 1997.

The second segment, which is expected to be by far the largest, will discriminate between EMU countries and trade at prices reflecting creditworthiness, liquidity and sovereign economic factors. This means the market (like the US municipal bond market) will impose a risk premium relative to a base rate (agencies of the EU itself or possibly German or French sovereign issues) for euro-issues of different sovereign and most corporate credits. The premium will reflect the market's valuation of national fiscal policies and economic results, and the liquidity available in bonds from such issuers. Under such conditions there is as much potential for spread differentials and volatility between issuers as there is in today's market.[16] Indeed, the market makes such distinctions today in choosing between EU member country debt issues (which range in credit ratings from Aaa to Baa1) by applying a yield differential. See Table 10.11. Sophisticated US and Japanese investors may not see much difference in the new system (for either bonds or stocks) from that in which they invested prior to conversion, although the rate differentials will most likely be somewhat different. Also, prior to the euro they could invest in European securities on either a currency-hedged or unhedged

---

[16] Fox (1996). The author acknowledges that the US municipal market is frequently referred to as a good model for the Euromarket. But he notes that the US municipal market is different because the issuers are within a single sovereign state and have operated as a single currency area for a long time, and therefore the Euromarket may operate somewhat differently. Also, most US municipal issues are sold free of US tax liability on income, which means that most investors are individuals not institutions.

basis. Subsequent to the euro, this will still be true but the difference in unhedged returns associated with particular currencies will appear partly in terms of the euro exposure and partly as a result of the intra-EMU sovereign yield differential.

4.3. Equity markets

The euro-denominated stock markets will become the world's third largest, and Europe's largest in terms of market capitalization and trading volume. The market, however, will still be disbursed over a minimum of eight to ten different stock markets that with few exceptions will continue to have a high national concentration. Investors seeking unhedged (against currency risk) investments in different European companies will, as will bond investors, have to accept euro-denominated securities instead, though the prices of the individual stocks should reflect companies' differing exposure to particular national economies. Investors seeking hedged investments may find it easier and less expensive to cover euro risk than the other, preceding currencies, but the substantial majority of investors in European stocks have been willing takers of currency risk. Initially there may be little difference in valuation of stocks from the different countries.

However, as investors become more familiar with the euro, there may be created a fungibility between stocks from different countries that has not yet fully developed. There has been an increase in the correlation in stock market returns between the different European countries in recent years, caused by increasing European cross-border trade, investment and acquisitions, and this correlation may increase further as a result of the market-integrating effects of EMU. See Figure 10.2. The increasing correlation may be seen by some investors seeking diversification under the protocols of modern portfolio theory as a negative development, which would reduce investment activity. On the other hand, to the extent that market liquidity increases as a result of increasing fungibility, institutional activity on the part of large EMU institutions, especially pension funds, also increases and the markets begin to cohere as if under a single trading and regulatory regime, as in the United States. Then there may be substantial advantages to investors in the European market that are absent today. Among these could be substantial increases in block trading activity, investor services and discounts, shareholder activism that promotes improved corporate governance, and anti-fraud enforcement. Such advantages should contribute significantly to improved operating and competitive conditions of the stock markets.

Equally important, however, will be the continuation of (1) privatization programmes in Europe (estimated by one analyst at US$300 billion over the next ten years) that create new supplies of stock to be traded, (2) growing investor activity and sophistication on the part of stock-investing institutions such as pension funds, (3) continued corporate restructuring through mergers and acquisitions, and (4) increased use of capital markets by corporate issuers previously dependent on banks for financing, and on the part of issuers from Eastern Europe and the former Soviet Union. These dynamic factors make big changes in the market environment of the securities industry.

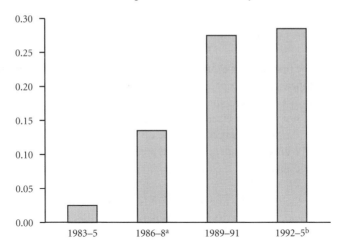

Figure 10.2. Average correlation of EU stock markets with Germany's
 [a] Excluding October 1987.
 [b] February.

5. After the Euro

The totality of the changes anticipated with the introduction of the single currency and EMU are considerable, especially after 2001, when current membership issues will finally be resolved. The prospect of achieving the many goals of European economic and monetary union are exciting to those who are able to look forward to a strengthened, unified and productive European single market, the largest in the world. There are many, however, who are less confident that the benefits of EMU will actually exceed the costs of achieving it. The Deutsche Bank estimated that it alone would spend DM 400 million on conversion of its banking and financial systems to accommodate the euro. Similar costs extended throughout the entire European banking community might well threaten to exceed savings in foreign exchange hedging costs on the sale of goods and services within Europe. Indeed, it is very likely to take several years to recover the initial investments required of the financial services sector in Europe.

On the other hand, EMU makes possible the appearance of a variety of benefits that are not directly related to trading patterns. Among these might be included improved capital market activity, lower financing costs for industry, increased corporate restructuring, more sophisticated pension investment practices, greater global awareness of market opportunities and, in general, a more vigorous and enterprising financial marketplace. But it is unlikely that a single currency and monetary system would have induced such powerful developments in the old European capital marketplace of ten or fifteen years ago. Because of the flood of major changes and competitive pressures that have developed since that time, the markets are now ready to make the most of the next wave of changes. Such changes, by improving market efficiencies further, have the potential to make Europe a contender for world financial leadership in the next century.

But without the first wave of changes—the major reforms and responses to market pressures to compete that have passed over Europe, in many cases after beginning in the United States—it is unlikely that the greatest potential would be realized. Indeed, the first wave has not nearly been completed yet, and much more needs to be done to bring the major European financial houses up to American standards of market-awareness, global reach, competitiveness, and profitability.

However, in the meantime, we can expect to see the following over the next few years:

Market forces, fuelled by the free flow of funds and increasing institutional interest in global diversification, and by the fierce competitive activities of successful American and other firms, will continue to make European capital markets more efficient and attractive to those seeking to raise, or invest, large amounts of funds. These forces will also compel more restructuring of European corporations and institutions, through privatizations, takeover activity, and greater efforts by shareholders to assert their will on entrenched management. They will also induce European banks to make themselves more competitive and to improve the returns to their shareholders.

European banks must cope with these important developments while at the same time realizing that all of their future opportunities may not be contained in the EU. Indeed, the possibilities in Asia, Eastern Europe, Latin America, and the United States do not diminish because of the coming of the common currency. A potentially great danger to European firms in the near term may be to take their eyes off the rest of the world while waiting for things to happen in the EU. Altogether, meeting these various challenges requires formidable management capabilities, and a fair amount of time and capital to spend on getting it all right. Doing this will not be something all banks can expect to achieve, increasing the possibilities that the banking community in Europe in ten or twenty years' time will consist of a much smaller group of highly competitive, indeed Americanized firms. It will be a very interesting time.

References

Adams, Richard (1997), 'Boost for EMU as $1.18 Billion Bond is Sold in Euros', *The Financial Times*, 2 February.

Bank for International Settlements (1996), *66th Annual Report*, 31 March.

Bank for International Settlements (1997), *67th Annual Report*, 31 March.

DeLong, Gayle, Roy C. Smith and Ingo Walter (1997), *Global M&A Tables*, New York: The Salomon Center, New York University.

European Commission (1995), 'Green Paper on the Practical Arrangements for the Introduction of the Single Currency', Brussels, 31 May.

Fisher, Andrew (1997*a*), 'Dresdner to Run Investment Arm from Twin Cities', *The Financial Times*, 14 April.

Fisher, Andrew (1997*b*), 'European Bourses May Get Lift on Back of EMU', *The Financial Times*, 15 April.

Fox, Mark (1996), 'The Shape of the Future Euro Market', Lehman Brothers, 15 August.

Hayes, Samuel L. and Philip H. Hubbard (1990), *Investment Banking: A Tale of Three Cities*, Cambridge, MA: Harvard Business School Press.

Riley, Barry (1997), 'Growth on a Grand Scale', *The Financial Times*, 24 April.

Saunders, Anthony and Ingo Walter (1996), *Universal Banking in the US*, New York: Oxford University Press.

Smith, Roy C. (1989), *The Global Bankers*, New York: E.P. Dutton.

Smith, Roy C. (1993), *Comeback: The Restoration of American Banking Power*, New York: Harvard Business School Press.

Smith, Roy C. and Ingo Walter (1996), 'Global Patterns of Merger and Acquisition Activity in the Financial Services Industry', paper presented at the conference on Financial Institutions Mergers, NYU Salomon Center, 11 October (revised February 1997).

Smith, Roy C. and Ingo Walter (1997), *Street Smarts*, Cambridge, MA: Harvard Business School Press.

Waller, David (1993), 'Deutsche Bank Re-thinks Stake in Daimler Benz', *The Financial Times*, 18 March.

Walter, Ingo (1997), 'Universal Banking: A Shareholder Value Perspective', *European Management Journal*, 15: 344–60.

Walter, Ingo and Roy C. Smith (1990), *Investment Banking in Europe: Restructuring for the 1990s*, London: Basil Blackwell.

White, Lawrence (1991), *The S&L Debacle*, New York: Oxford University Press.

Index

Index